ZIONISM IN TRANSITION

ZIONISM IN TRANSITION

Edited by
Moshe Davis

FOREWORD BY PROFESSOR EPHRAIM KATZIR
Fourth President of the State of Israel

ARNO PRESS
A New York Times Company
New York, 1980

Publications of the Continuing Seminar on World Jewry
under the auspices of the President of Israel

Vol. I   The Yom Kippur War: Israel and the Jewish People

Vol. II   World Jewry and the State of Israel

Vol. III Zionism in Transition

First edition 1980 by Arno Press, A New York Times
Company

Library of Congress Cataloging in Publication Data
Main entry under title: Zionism in Transition

    (Continuing seminar on world Jewry; v. 3)   1.
Zionism—Congresses. 2. Jews—Politics and
government—1948-   —Congresses. I. Davis, Moshe. II.
Series.
DS149.A4Z47   956.94'001   80-23523
ISBN 0-405-13825-3

Manufactured in the United States of America

הישן יתחדש והחדש יתקדש
ויחדיו יהיו לאבוקות אורים על ציון

*The old will become new
and the new will be consecrated
old and new together
will be torches of light
over Zion*

Rabbi Abraham Isaac Hacohen Kook

CONTENTS

- I -

- II -

Diaspora Zionism: Achievements and Problems

Foreword

Ephraim Katzir

The title of this book is *Zionism in Transition*, but the contemporary world as a whole may be said to be in a state of transition. Drastic political and economic change, shifts of power and approach, characterize our time and are reflected in the lives of nations and individuals. Such changes have surely left their mark on Israel since the watershed of the Yom Kippur War in 1973. A national mood of questioning, troubled concern and uncertainty as to goals and directions—that is the background against which we organized World Seminars of Jewish thinkers and leaders in the President's Residence in Jerusalem. Out of these Seminars has grown a Collegium which meets and interacts regularly and is now developing study circles abroad. The third of these continuing meetings in Jerusalem was dedicated to the examination and review of the nature and role of Zionism.

This book derives from that Seminar's proceedings. It is a work of lucid scholarship, an invaluable source book on the growth and present state of Zionism in various countries. It becomes clear that even where—as in a number of Western countries—the general line of development is basically similar, there are important nuances distinguishing particular societies. These are set forth in chapters that follow upon the incisive general survey with which the book opens. In addition, in a number of contributions we find a profoundly philosophic approach, rooted in knowledge and application of the work of the most illustrious of Jewish thinkers in the past.

The stuff of contemporary Jewish life is in these papers, testifying to the validity of the categories proposed by the Chairman of the World Zionist Organization, Mr. Arye Dulzin: distressed, tolerated, emancipated and (in Israel) auto-emancipated Jewish communities. What in all this can give us guidelines for the future—a future very different from that which the early formulators of Zionist theory could have predicted?

Whatever the dimensions of *aliyah*, it is becoming ever clearer that Jews abroad need Israel no less than Israel needs the support of Jews abroad. It is no less than imperative that those abroad cooperate with Israelis towards the realization in contemporary terms of Zionism's original goal—the building of an exemplary society based on modern science and technology, and at the same time suffused with Jewish moral values and tradition, the repository of culture which is our "synthetic gene."

In this twentieth century we have reached the point where scientific technology can make far-reaching changes in human life. It is all the more important, then, that technology be directed by moral values. Here is the new challenge for Zionist planning.

It seems to me that the great intellectual potential of the Diaspora in cooperation with Israel's own capacity can go far towards making Israel a pilot plant for the twenty-first century, a pilot plant created by the combination of science and Jewish values. With such a vision Zionism goes beyond rescue and reconstruction of Jewish life to a role in shaping a better future for mankind as a whole.

Introduction: Renewal of Zionist Thought

In the course of modern Jewish history, Zionism has undergone several transformations, from Messianism to political activism, to virtually complete identification with the goals and strivings of the State of Israel. In each of these transformations, past ideologies were not lost, although their juxtaposition often creates misunderstanding and misinterpretation.

This is not a new phenomenon in history. It has been characteristic of the Jewish People in other epochs, as it is true of Jewish group life in our time. As a People, we have entered the 1980s chronologically; but in the perspective of time, we are living simultaneously in several epochs. What is urgently required is a contemporary reformulation of Zionist ideology and practice which will take into full account the continuing parallelisms within Zionist history as they reveal themselves in the present era of rapidly changing circumstances. This need clearly emerges from the opening summary section on "Ideological Perspectives."

Such a task is a complex one, rendered all the more difficult because in the long history of the Jewish People, there is no analogue to its current physical and spiritual condition. Although the second part of the book focuses on "Zionism in the Diaspora: Its Achievements and Problems," the authors necessarily relate their subjects to the character of Jewish experience in the respective communities, as for example: the pragmatism of American Zionism; the ideological underpinning of German Zionism; the religio-messianic yearnings in Islamic lands. When we review the history of the Zionist Movement in this light and study how it has functioned in the different diasporas, the thought suggests itself that we should perhaps refer to "Zionisms" rather than Zionism.

Moreover, the intertwining of the Zionist Movement and the viability of Jewish communities is illuminated in this comparative context. As regards the present situation, diasporic communities were never so diffuse; nor were they ever so steeped in the cultures of their

surroundings. In most of these communities, the main elements of
Jewish cohesiveness are weakening. We are witness to both a dilution
of Judaism and a steady evaporation of Jewish identity. If we consider
the prevailing demographic, cultural and educational factors of contemporary Jewish existence, the physical and spiritual self-sufficiency
of the diasporic communities becomes seriously questioned as they
are being enveloped by open societies, resulting in loss of will for
indigenous Jewish self-renewal and creativity.

These all-encompassing problems cannot be alien to any contemporary Zionist formulation. For the essence of Zionist ideology is
its worldview, which is the fundamental theme of the third section in
the volume, "Zionism and the State of Israel." Zionism should be
understood not only as the movement for the Return of the Jewish
People to its Homeland in Eretz Israel, but also as that creative historical process which intensifies the content of Jewish life everywhere.
In its pre-State phase, Zionist thought was that stirring power which
served mightily to reinforce the active faith of Jews—religious or secular—in the future of the Jewish People. Our unprecedented period of
Jewish history requires a renewal of Zionist thought, an ideological
basis and polity for institutional and cultural tasks in the immediate
decades ahead.

The fourth section of this volume, "Reformulations," is devoted
precisely to that goal. Representative personalities, writing from the
vantage of Israel as well as the largest Diaspora communities, present
varying conceptions of Zionist ideology. The dominant idea which
weaves through most of these essays calls for a synthesis in our time of
political and cultural Zionism—a combination of the seminal philosophies of Theodor Herzl and Ahad Ha-Am. There seems to be complete agreement that the State of Israel dare not desist from its responsibility to significantly nourish Diaspora culture and education. Inside
Israel, it is suggested that the emphasis on citizenship to the virtual
exclusion of the concept of Jewish Peoplehood is an error. As for Diaspora Jewry, it dare not desist from new initiatives and collective
responsibility in helping Israel become a radiating spiritual center for
the entire Jewish People. It is this mutuality which alone can establish
spiritual links with Diaspora communities and represents the basis for
a unifying formulation.

The evolution of the Continuing Seminar on World Jewry and
the State of Israel, established by Professor Ephraim Katzir during his
presidency, and now under the aegis of President Yitzhak Navon,

symbolizes the kind of spiritual and cultural engagement that can serve as a paradigm towards this unifying formulation.

In the beginning there was the idea; then came the reality. Now it is for reality to recreate the idea.

Lag B'Omer, 5740   Moshe Davis
May, 1980

I

Ideological Perspectives

Ideological Perspectives

Gideon Shimoni

Origins of the Zionist Idea

The fundamental idea of Zionism may be stated thus: return of Jews to Zion and restoration of Zion as a homeland for the Jews. When Herzl wrote his *Judenstaat,* he noted in the preface: "The idea which I have developed in this pamphlet is an ancient one." It was, indeed, an idea inherent in traditional Judaism's interminable grappling with the twin concepts of *galut* (exile) and *ge'ulah* (redemption). A peculiarly compelling relationship with Zion, symbolizing terrestrial Eretz Israel, has always been one of the distinctive marks of Judaism, and Jewish history is punctuated by various ideas of return to Zion and by numerous attempts to actualize them.

What *was* new and revolutionary was the conceptual matrix in which Zionism transformed this idea into a new social force. Whereas the traditional conceptual matrix was essentially eschatological or messianic, the crucial motifs of the Zionist idea were worldly. They concerned the actual problems of Jewish existence, rather than the cosmic dispensation of God; the relationship between Gentiles and Jews, rather than the relationship between God and the Jews; mundane options and means of self-help, such as settlement and political activity, rather than exegetical or mystical explorations into the manifestations of God's will or acts of piety and penitence. These acts, even when leading to the ascent to Zion, remained conditioned by anticipation of God's imminent redemption of His Chosen People. Max Nordau drew the distinction when he stated that the "new Zionism, which is called political, differs from the old, religious messianic variety in that it disavows all mysticism, no longer identifies itself with Messianism, and does not expect the return to Palestine to be brought about by a miracle, but desires to prepare the way by its own efforts."[1] To be

1. Max Nordau, *Zionistische Schriften*, Berlin, 1923, p. 22. On the relationship between Messianism and Zionism see Arthur Hertzberg's incisive introduction to *The Zionist Idea: A Historical Analysis and Reader*, New York, 1959.

sure, this was too sharp a distinction. In considering the historical record, it cannot be said that Zionism dispensed entirely with the eschatological motif. Even so highly secularized a school of Zionism as socialist-Zionism drew heavily on the messianic ideal, in secularized form, while Orthodox-religious Zionism never abandoned the eschatological motif; rather, by exegetical reinterpretation, it rendered that motif compatible with worldly motifs, thereby facilitating full cooperation with the secularized majority of Zionism. Hence it would be apt to describe the conceptual matrix of Zionism as trans-eschatological: that is to say, transcending the messianic motif yet not necessarily dispensing with it.

Although the historian may identify sporadic manifestations akin to this conceptual matrix as early as the seventeenth century,[2] it is not until the middle of the nineteenth century that he confronts a manifestation which has real social consequences.[3] The main figures involved were Rabbi Judah Alkalai, Rabbi Zvi Hirsch Kalischer and Moses Hess. Independently of each other, all three arrived at the same conclusion: let Jews return to Eretz Israel so that it may be restored as a homeland for the Jews. Alkalai, a preacher in a small community near Belgrade, and Kalischer, an Ashkenazi rabbinic scholar born in Poland, were both steeped in the traditional mold of eschatological thought. Thus, on the basis of traditional methods of exegesis, Alkalai argued that collective repentance in the form of a return to Zion was required of the Jews in addition to all forms of individual repentance.[4] Similarly, Kalischer argued that "one should not think that the Almighty, blessed be His Name, will suddenly descend from the heavens to tell His people 'leave.' . . . On the contrary, Redemption will begin by arousing (Jewish) philanthropists and Gentile nations so that they will gather some of the dispersed of Israel into the Holy Land."[5] Yet, notwithstanding their traditionalism, these men were already subject to some of the same stimuli—such as these examples of European nationalisms and the defects of Emancipation—which influenced fully-fledged Zionism. In contrast to the defensive withdrawal of their fellow traditionalists from these stimuli,

2. See Adolf Böhm, Die Zionistische Bewegung, Berlin, 1935, vol. 1, pp. 40–80; Nahum Sokolow, History of Zionism 1600–1918, London, 1919, vol. 1, passim.

3. See Jacob Katz, "Le-Verur ha-Musag 'Mevasrei ha-Zionut,' " Shivat Zion, vol. 1, Jerusalem, 1950, pp. 91–105.

4. See Jacob Katz, "Meshihiyut u-Leumiyut be-Mishnato shel ha-Rav Yehuda Alkalai," Shivat Zion, vol. 4, Jerusalem, 1956, pp. 9–41.

5. Zvi Hirsch Kalischer, Drishat Zion, Israel Klausner, ed., Jerusalem, 1964, p. 88.

they responded to them optimistically, seeking to turn them to positive advantage for the preservation of Judaism in anticipation of the messianic age. Thus, Kalischer perceived the emergence of Jews of great worldly influence, such as Adolphe Crémieux and Sir Moses Montefiore, as an indicator of the impending messianic era. Despite its disruption of traditionalism, the Emancipation thereby assumed the appearance of an early phase in the gradual unfolding of the messianic age.[6]

Much as Alkalai and Kalischer reflected themes which prefigure religious Zionism, so did the thought of Moses Hess prefigure major themes of Zionism among emancipated secularized Jews. Hess' ideas are remarkable for their apparent prescience: he anticipated some of the motifs of socialist-Zionism in asserting that the Jews in exile "cannot devote themselves successfully to productive labor," and that "a common native soil is a precondition for introducing healthier relations between capital and labor among the Jews." The central thesis of the political Zionism of Pinsker and Herzl is also present, though less coherently, in Hess' writing: "The nations of Europe have always regarded the existence of the Jews in their midst as an anomaly. We shall always remain strangers among the nations," he asserted. Similarly, Hess anticipated the core ideas of Ahad Ha-Am's concept of a spiritual center which could inspire and sustain the Jewish Diaspora.[7]

The trans-eschatological conceptual matrix of Zionism is thus clearly evident in the ideas of Alkalai, Kalischer and Hess. By the early 1860s their independent thinking had germinated and converged sufficiently for a small group of people to cohere around these ideas in the *Colonisationsverein für Palästina*, founded by Hayim Lorje. Although somewhat diffusely and ineffectually, they propagated their ideas, communicated with one another, broached their ideas to wealthy Jewish philanthropists, advocated settlement and land purchases in Eretz Israel; indeed, Alkalai himself settled in the Holy Land. If Zionist historiography has not been able to ascribe the origins of Zionism to these men's ideas and actions, it is because their efforts were not at all successful, and because they did not gain a wide or influential following. Evidence is lacking, moreover, of any actual

6. See Jacob Katz, "Dmuto ha-Historit shel ha-Rav Zvi Hirsch Kalischer," *Shivat Zion*, vols. 2, 3, Jerusalem, 1953, pp. 26–41.
7. Moses Hess, *Rome and Jerusalem: A Study in Jewish Nationalism*, Meyer Waxman, tr., New York, 1943, *passim*.

continuity between the actions of Alkalai, Kalisher and Hess and those of the first consequential Zionist groups—the *Hibbat Zion* societies which emerged in the 1880s. Since the relationship between these manifestations appears to have been phenomenological rather than continuous, Alkalai, Kalischer, Hess and their associates have been described as precursors rather than founders.

The idea propounded by those precursors preceded its social utility because the reigning ideological consensus among Jews was incompatible with the Zionist idea. In Eastern Europe, the dominant response was withdrawal from the implications of Emancipation into the protective shell of traditionalism. In the West, and among *maskilim* (adherents of the Enlightenment) of the East, confidence in the successful outcome of the emancipation process was at its peak in the 1860s. This objective absence of social need in the 1860s was, in fact, abundantly reflected in the thought of the precursors themselves. While they already sensed the limitations of Emancipation and offered a response to them, it was a response of complementation rather than of negation. Even they could not escape entirely from the pervasive ideological climate of their time. As traditionalists, Alkalai and Kalischer responded defensively. The innovative aspect of their thinking was in the idea of utilizing the emancipation process to further traditionalist self-preservation. Return to Zion and restoration of Zion to the Jews were the means to that end. As for Hess, he was very far from despairing of the Emancipation. Indeed, he trusted in France, the leading liberal force, to complement its emancipatory role by supporting the creation of a Jewish State in Eretz Israel. Quite explicitly, he stated that Jewish settlement in Eretz Israel did not imply total emigration of the Jews to Eretz Israel: "Even after the establishment of a Jewish State, the majority of the Jews who live at present in the civilized countries of the Occident will undoubtedly remain where they are."[8] It is noteworthy that the physical plight of the Jews, which was to become a crucial motif in political Zionist thought, is not emphasized in the writings of Hess, Alkalai and Kalischer. Thus, unlike Pinsker and Herzl—the first political Zionists—the precursors were proposing a return to Zion, not in order to *supplant* Emancipation as the anticipated condition of Jewry, but rather to *complement* it.

It was the collapse of the ideological consensus, based on Emancipation and Enlightenment, which provided the preconditions

8. *Ibid.*, p. 260.

for the birth of Zionism as a movement.[9] This collapse was precipitated by the wave of pogroms which swept parts of the Pale of Settlement in Russia following the assassination of Czar Alexander II in
1881. Disillusioned by the government's condonation of the pogroms,
and even more by the indifference of the supposedly progressive
forces upon whom they relied for the fulfilment of their hopes, the
maskilim went through a profound ideological reorientation. Many of
them, who had previously advocated assimilation, now reverted to
national identification. Others, like Peretz Smolenskin, who had
already considered national revival, began to doubt that the cultiva-
tion of spiritual and linguistic dimensions in the Diaspora was sufficient. Accordingly, they turned their attention to the idea of a return to
Eretz Israel. Meanwhile, these same events precipitated a vast Jewish
emigration movement, making it possible to direct part of it to Eretz
Israel. In this context, the emergent *Hibbat Zion* groups now began to
articulate an ideology pertaining to the idea of a return to Zion and its
restoration as a homeland for the Jews that not only was trans-eschatological, but also produced extensive social results and a continuous
ideological development.

Common Denominators

From that time on, it has been possible to trace the continuous
development of a highly ramified Zionist ideology within the framework of an organized movement: an ideology in the sense of a system
of ideas which provides those who subscribe to it with a comprehensive cognitive map of their position and purposes and which commands a commitment to action. Underlying this ideology was the common axiom that the Jews are a single, distinctive entity possessing
national, not just religious, attributes. However, the precise definition
or description of that entity varied widely in consonance with the
ideological suppositions of the diverse schools of Zionist thought and
the influence of the political environment in different regions of the
world.

"We are a people—one people," Herzl declared in his *Judenstaat*. In Eastern Europe, where connotations of the term "nation"
were ethnic and cultural rather than political and state-bound, Zionists did not hesitate to describe themselves as a nation possessed,

9. See David Vital, *The Origins of Zionism*, Oxford, 1975, pp. 49-108.

actually or potentially, of the same attributes as, for instance, the Polish nation. In Ber Borochov's Marxist terms the Jews were a nation in
the sense that they were "a community developed in the same conditions of production whose members are united with one another by a
feeling of kinship derived from a common historic past."[10] In Germany, Zionists struggled with uniquely German cultural-national concepts such as *Deutschtum* and *Judentum*, while Sokolow, with his eye
mainly on an English-speaking audience, wrote: "Jews, notwithstanding the spiritual character of their teachings, are, like any other ethnic
group, a species of the genus homo, a distinct people united by their
origin and by their common history."[11] In the United States of America, where the state tended to appropriate the term "nation", "nationality" was sometimes used. Thus Brandeis said: "Let us all recognize
that we Jews are a distinctive nationality of which every Jew, whatever his country, his station, or shade of belief, is necessarily a member."[12] Later, Mordecai Kaplan used the new hybrid term "peoplehood."[13] Orthodox-religious Zionism naturally held that the Jewish
People "is not a people except through its Torah." "The Jews did not
originate as a natural nation like others, for their nationality was not
born of nature, in the sense of race and land, but of the Torah and the
Covenant, and cannot be defined as an ordinary 'natural' nationality,"
wrote Yehiel Michael Pines in objecting to the definition which he
said secular Zionists were attempting to impose.[14]

Notwithstanding such terminological differences, Zionists
shared a sufficiently common understanding of the nature of Jewish
entity to distinguish themselves sharply from those who advocated the
panaceas of Emancipation and religious reform and attempted to deny
the national attributes of the Jewish entity. Further assumptions distinguished Zionist ideology from such other Jewish national ideologies as
that of Simon Dubnow, who advocated a Diaspora-centered nationalism based on national-cultural autonomy. The common denominator
for all the ramifications of these assumptions reflected three dimen-

10. See Ber Borochov, *Nationalism and the Class Struggle: Selected Writings*, New
York, 1937, pp. 135ff.
11. Nahum Sokolow, *op. cit.*, p. xvii.
12. *Brandeis on Zionism*, Solomon Goldman, ed., Washington, 1942, p. 34.
13. See Mordecai Kaplan, *The New Zionism*, New York, 1955.
14. Rabbi Yehiel Michael Pines, *Mivhar Ma'amarav*, G. Kressel, ed., Tel Aviv, 1946,
p. 100.

sions: diagnosis of a given problematic situation, proposal of a solution, and suggested means for attaining that solution. In historical retrospect this common denominator could be formulated thus: *First, the situation of the Jewish entity under conditions of dispersion is critically defective, not just in an eschatological sense, but emphatically in a worldly sense; second, the solution lies in territorial ingathering of Jews in Eretz Israel (or, failing that, transitionally in another territory) under conditions of autonomy at least, and sovereignty at best; third, these purposes should be effected by political diplomacy, settlement activities and the revival of Jewish national morale and culture.* True, these propositions represent an extrapolation rather than any actual formulation articulated by Zionists. But our contention is that all the schools of Zionism in the process of its development can be said to have shared this common denominator.

Within the framework of these propositions, the contours of ideological divergence were very wide. Yet one may discern two rival, integrative conceptions broad enough to encompass most ideological divergencies. One conception emphasized the external dimension of the Jewish situation—the "problem of the Jews," their physical distress and psychological malaise, and their status *vis-à-vis* the peoples of the world. The other stressed the internal dimension of the Jewish situation—the "problem of Judaism," that is, the preservation and regeneration of Jewish cultural individuality. On the basis of the distinction between these two conceptions and the three-fold differentiation of common propositions suggested above—diagnosis, vision and implementation—one may attempt to trace the contours of ideological divergence within Zionism.

Contours of Zionist Diagnosis

The diagnosis which was the begetter of Zionism as a dynamic social and political force was most poignantly formulated by Leo Pinsker, Theodor Herzl and Max Nordau. Its premise was that there was a grave crisis of material and psychological distress in the situation of the Jews within the Gentile societies. This formulation was a departure from the ideas of the precursors, for in contrast, it posed as a radical and comprehensive alternative to the course of Jewish emancipation, rather than as a mere complement to that course. Positing that the Jews are immutably alien in Gentile societies, it argued that neither civic emancipation nor attempts at complete assimilation could alter that fact. "Perhaps we could succeed in vanishing without a trace if they would let us be," Herzl speculated. "But they will not let us be. After brief periods of toleration their hostility erupts again and again." In his *Judenstaat*, Herzl made no qualitative distinction between different parts of the Diaspora: "The Jewish question persists wherever Jews live in appreciable numbers," he asserted. "Wherever it does not exist, it is brought in together with Jewish immigrants." Consequently, the problem of the Jews was a collective problem, not one of individuals; it was a national problem calling for a national solution.[15]

Pinsker, influenced somewhat by notions derived from his medical profession, further diagnosed the cause of the unalterably alien status of the Jew in terms of an almost hereditary Gentile trait, "a psychic aberration," which he called "Judeophobia." Because of the peculiar circumstances of their survival in dispersion the Jews had taken on a ghostlike appearance which the Gentiles feared. This basic psychological cause of hostility was then compounded by objective circumstances: not only were Jews aliens everywhere and hosts nowhere, but they were also economic rivals of their hosts. Out of a despairing pessimism with regard to the attitude of the Gentiles, Pinsker called for "auto-emancipation," or self-liberation, of the Jews. Pinsker's diagnosis also looked inward at the Jews' self-esteem. He argued passionately that centuries of suffering had damaged their national dignity and self-respect. Their national morale had to be restored, in preparation for a renewed and "independent national existence."[16]

Herzl was more perceptive of the varied sociological causes of Jew-hatred, or anti-Semitism, as it had already come to be called, but also more optimistic about the chance of gaining the cooperation of anti-Semites on behalf of a Zionist solution. He was convinced that the Gentiles would support Zionism out of enlightened self-interest: "The world needs the Jewish state, therefore it will arise," he wrote. Just as Alkalai and Kalischer had responded to emancipation and modernism by seeking to use them for a new stage of traditionalism, so Herzl sought to utilize anti-Semitism to the advantage of the alternative to emancipation—Zionism. Max Nordau supplemented Herzl's diagnosis with an incisively drawn distinction between the material distress of the East-European Jew and the "spiritual misery" of the emanci-

15. Theodor Herzl, *The Jewish State*, Harry Zohn, tr., New York, 1970, p. 33.
16. Leo Pinsker, *Auto-Emancipation*, D.S. Blondheim, tr., New York, 1906.

pated Jew in Western Europe, who "has abandoned his specifically Jewish character, yet the nations do not accept him as part of their national communities."[17]

The rudiments of this description of the Jewish situation were accepted also by Zionists who sought a synthesis between the Jewish national revival and socialism. But their own diagnosis was informed by the Marxist terms of discourse which permeated, to a lesser or greater degree, all schools of socialist thought. This demanded identification of the materialist core of the Jewish situation, of its social reflection in class differences, and of the inevitable historical processes which determined both. The influence of this ideological background on early socialist-Zionist thought was ubiquitous. It colored the terminology, if not the substance, of the early ideas of Nahman Syrkin, who became the mentor of an ethical, voluntary socialist-Zionism, and it dominated the early ideas of Ber Borochov, who professed to be an authentic interpreter of Marx's historical determinism.

Thus, in conformity with Marxist axioms concerning the process of class polarization which was inevitably depressing the desperate, lower-middle class into the ranks of the proletariat, Syrkin diagnosed anti-Semitism as "a product of the class structure" which reached "its highest peak in declining classes: in the middle class, which is in the process of being destroyed by capitalists, and within the decaying peasant class, which is being strangled by the landowners." Moreover, he predicted that as the inevitable stage of proletarian revolution drew nearer, "the more the various classes of society are disrupted . . . the higher the wave of anti-Semitism will rise." Although ultimately the final victory of classless socialist society will solve the Jewish problem, this would only happen in the remote future because "the economic structure of the Jewish People, its lack of political rights and its peculiar position in society, combine to place it in a singular situation which cannot be improved, at present, through the socialist struggle."[18]

Far more rigidly Marxist were the diagnostic tools of Ber Borochov, the founding father of one variety of *Po'alei Zion* ideology. He devoted his intellectual energies to developing a materialist theory to justify a proletarian-led Jewish nationalism. The center-pin of this theory was the notion of "conditions of production," which he added

17. Max Nordau, *op. cit.*, p. 50.
18. Marie Syrkin, *Nahman Syrkin–Socialist Zionist: A Bibliographical Memoir, Selected Essays*, New York, 1961, pp. 265, 267.

to the seminal Marxist concepts "forces of production" and "relations of production." The source of the Jewish problem was the lack of national territory in which "common conditions of production" prevailed and which could serve as a "strategic base" for a "normal" class struggle. Under conditions of dispersion, the Jews could never find a normal place for themselves in the economic processes of the territorial majority. Sooner or later, the majority would become competitive with the Jews and would react by barring the way to the sources of its "conditions of production." The Jews would thus be compelled to seek occupations that depended on the resources created by man rather than those provided by nature. They would be driven from the land and from nature and left "hovering in the air." Yet, under this superstructure of materialist theory—to invert a Marxist metaphor—Ber Borochov's diagnosis of the Jewish problem had much in common with that of Pinsker and Herzl. Indeed, in denying the anti-Zionist contention of Jewish socialists that the class struggle and new socioeconomic conditions would eliminate anti-Semitism, Borochov was admitting that there was a deeper, non-materialist, cultural or psychological source of anti-Semitism, much as Pinsker had claimed.[19] Conversely, Herzl, too, had emphasized the role of the frustrated Gentile middle classes as fomenters of anti-Semitism. In sum, both Syrkin and Borochov bequeathed to socialist-Zionism a diagnosis of the Jewish problem which rested, like Herzl's, on the material distress of the Jews.

In sharp contrast to this was the focus on internal regeneration of the Jewish entity. The formative exponent of this approach was Ahad Ha-Am (Asher Ginsberg). It was his premise that Jewish religion was a function of Jewish national culture rather than vice versa. In the galut, before the Emancipation, religion had been the major instrumental expression of the national will-to-live. But this was no longer a viable basis for Jewish survival. Ahad Ha-Am thus identified the critical defect of the Jewish condition as disintegration of Jewish cultural identity under the combined impact of emancipation from the ghetto and secular enlightenment. Irrespective of whether emancipation was abortive, counterproductive or successful, it was bound to undermine Jewish cultural survival. On the one hand, the influence of antiquated Orthodox Judaism was in irreversible decline, while on the other,

---

19. See, for example, Ber Borochov, Ktavim, L. Levite and D. Ben-Nahum, eds., Vol. 1, Tel Aviv, 1955, p. 14.

assimilation and attendant attempts at reform of Judaism were simply a new form of self-abnegation, of "slavery in freedom." "The Jews cannot survive as a scattered people now that our spiritual isolation is ended," wrote Ahad Ha-Am, "because we have no longer any defense against the ocean of foreign culture, which threatens to obliterate our national characteristics and tradition."[20] Hence the problem which Zionism was called upon to solve was less the physical distress of the Jews than the survival of Judaism as a culture.

Ahad Ha-Am's diagnosis was macrocosmic in approach: it was concerned with the survival of the collective culture of the Jewish People. Another version of this diagnosis had a microcosmic approach: emphasis was placed on the regeneration of the individual Jew as a precondition for the national renascence of the Jewish People. Those who held the latter view traced the critical fault of the Jewish condition in *galut* to the deformity it had wrought in the character of the individual Jew. Wide differences of opinion existed, however, as to the nature of this deformity. Thus Micah Joseph Berdichevsky and Joseph Hayyim Brenner saw its cause as the stultifying domination of ossified religious tradition. The former called for a Nietzschean radical "transvaluation of all values": the transformation of the individual Jew in a new earthy national mold which would abrogate the stilted spiritualized mold spawned by the *galut* condition. Similarly, Brenner, railing against the unproductive "parasitism" and pusillanimity of the *galut* Jew, called for his regeneration through productive labor on his own soil.[21]

Less emotively disparaging of the *galut* condition, but equally emphatic on the need for personal regeneration, was Aharon David Gordon. He, too, found the basic defect of the *galut* condition not in "the Jewish plight" or the "problem of Judaism," but rather in the constriction of the individual Jewish personality. Gordon argued that "there is a cosmic element in nationality which is its basic ingredient," and consists of "the blending of the natural landscape of the Homeland with the spirit of the people inhabiting it." He saw the core of the Jewish problem in the loss of this "cosmic element of national identity" as a result of the Jewish dispersion. This deprivation was reflected in the stunted occupational structure of the Jews, in their abstention

20. *Ahad Ha-Am: Essays, Letters* and *Memoirs*, Leon Simon, ed. & tr., Oxford, 1946, p. 213.
21. See Matti Megged, "The Nationalist Thought of Joseph Hayyim Brenner," *Sources of Contemporary Jewish Thought*, Jerusalem, 1972, pp. 81–135.

from manual labor, and consequently, in "the personality of every individual member" of the Jewish People. Therefore, Gordon sought the regeneration of the individual Jew by renewed coalescence with the cosmic element through return to a life of physical labor on the soil of Eretz Israel. He differed from Ahad Ha-Am, however, in defining the "culture" to be revived. He did not share Ahad Ha-Am's concern for the abstract spiritual essence of Judaism. "Culture is whatever life creates for living purposes," Gordon wrote. "Farming, building and road-making, any productive activity is the stuff of culture. Whatever people feel and think both at work and at leisure and the relations arising from these situations, combined with the natural surroundings." The problem was that the Diaspora Jew participated only in the "butter of culture," that is, in the elite expressions of culture: science, the arts and the intellectual pursuits. But, "can a man make butter by using his neighbor's milk and still call the butter all his own?" asked A.D. Gordon.[22]

Another variation of the personalized diagnosis of the Jewish situation is reflected in the thought of Martin Buber. Buber focused his attention on the crisis in the cultural identity of the post-assimilationist Western Jew. Unlike Theodor Herzl and Max Nordau, who confronted the question of identity on the psychological level of offended self-respect, Buber perceived it on the cultural level: a search for the significance of Judaism for the individual Jew. The existential situation of the Western Jew was a function of dual influence—the non-Jewish cultural environment on the one hand, and his own inherent Jewish substance on the other. The Jewish question was, therefore, the personal question of every Jew: self-abnegation or self-affirmation. Buber's philosophy of Judaism, which sought to interpret the social significance of the Jewish cultural ethos, found it in the values of dialogic relations and community which he expounded. His formulation summoned the Jew to self-affirmation by merging into the endeavor to establish a "Hebrew-humanist" society, a "sacred community," which would embody those values. That was the mission of Judaism for mankind. The Bible was the record of attempts to fulfil that mission. As Buber explained in his famous letter to Gandhi:

> At that time we did not carry out that which was imposed upon us; we went into exile with our task unperformed; but the command remained

---

22. *A.D. Gordon: Selected Essays*, Frances Burnce, tr., New York, 1938, pp. 54, 55.

with us and it has become more urgent than ever. We need our own soil to fulfil it; we need the freedom to order our own life. No attempt can be made on foreign soil and under foreign statute.[23]

Orthodox-religious Zionism occupies a distinctive position of its own within the spectrum of Zionist ideologies. In its intrinsic concern with the internal dimension of Jewish life, it was closer to Ahad Ha-Am's diagnosis of the Jewish situation than to Herzl's. Yet its underlying religious premises were diametrically opposed to the secular approach of Ahad Ha-Am. In fact, it was the clash between advocates of a secular Jewish culture and Orthodox Zionists which led to the formation of *Mizrachi* as an Orthodox-religious party within Zionism in 1902. On the other hand, the position of political Zionists like Herzl and his successor as President of the World Zionist Organization, David Wolffsohn, was one of careful neutrality on the cultural question. This facilitated cooperation between the Orthodox and the political Zionist leadership. Indeed, from the outset, Orthodox Zionism accepted, with sober realism, the validity of Herzl's diagnosis of Jewish distress. The severe exigencies of the Jewish plight were perceived by Rabbi Mohilever, one of the earliest leaders of Orthodox Zionism, as a great peril which justified cooperation with the secular Zionists. "They are coming to assist us in an extreme emergency and must be considered in that light," he wrote in his greeting to the first Zionist Congress of 1897.[24]

Over and above its concern with the physical plight of the Jews, the *Mizrachi* religious-Zionist party considered that the critical flaw of the Diaspora condition was the threat to Orthodox Jewish observance and faith resulting from emancipation and secularization: "As exile lingered on and darkened, the Torah's hold, too, began to weaken and no solution remained but a return to Eretz Israel," wrote Rabbi Itzhak Nissenbaum.[25] The decline of Orthodox Jewry's position could be arrested only by altering the circumstances which caused it. Optimal conditions of autonomous life in the rebuilt homeland would remove the barriers to its revival. Another motif in the Orthodox-religious diagnosis of the Diaspora situation was that both in principle and in practice full observance of Judaism was impossible in *galut*. The

23. Martin Buber and Judah Magnes, *Two Letters to Gandhi*, Jerusalem, 1939.
24. *Exponents and Philosophy of Religious Zionism*, Abraham Bick, ed., New York, 1942, p. 21.
25. Cited in *Religious Zionism: An Anthology*, Yosef Tirosh, ed., Jerusalem, 1975, p. 14.

galut stifled and imposed limitations on the fulfilment of many ritual
and socio-political precepts of Judaism. This was a severe spiritual
ailment of galut existence, which could be cured only in the national
homeland. In the ideology of Torah Va'Avodah which synthesized the
objectives of the Labor Zionist movement with those of the Mizrachi,
the meaning of Torah was further broadened to include not only
observance of all mitzvot by individuals, or by the community as an
aggregate of individuals, but "life permeated by Torah and Torah per-
meating life." This, it was contended, could never be realized except
as a nation in one's own land.

Variants of Zionist Vision

The solution which Herzl's political Zionism proposed for the
Jewish problem was unequivocally maximalist: nothing less than the
territorial ingathering of the bulk of the Jewish People and the creation of a sovereign Jewish State. In their initial formulations of this
solution, both Pinsker and Herzl entertained the acceptability of a territory other than Eretz Israel. As late as 1903, with all efforts to obtain
Eretz Israel frustrated, Herzl was willing to consider favorably, as a
Nachtasyl (night-shelter), a strip of territory in colonial East Africa
tentatively offered by Britain. Even so, the primordial attachment of
the Jewish masses to Eretz Israel did communicate itself to Herzl, and
that Land had been the scene for his vision of the ultimate solution
described in Altneuland.

The state he envisaged was a distillation of the best in Western
European technology and society—liberal, non-coercive, tolerant and
socially progressive. Culturally, it was somewhat inchoate: secular,
cosmopolitan and pluralist, rather than Jewish. Even the role of the
Hebrew language was limited to prayer and other traditional functions, Yiddish was spoken in the rural areas, but German seemed to
predominate as the language of commerce and culture. It was a state
for the Jews rather than a Jewish State.[26] This state was envisaged by
Herzl as a total solution to the Jewish problem. All Jews who needed a
place of refuge, or who wished to remain Jews, would gravitate to it.
Those who chose to remain outside "would be able to assimilate in
peace because present-day anti-Semitism would have been stopped
for all time."

26. See Theodor Herzl, Old-New Land (Altneuland), Lotta Levensohn, tr., New York,
1960.

The vision of formative thinkers of socialist-Zionism also involved a maximalist geo-political reordering of the Jewish situation. It, too, postulated a total solution in the form of collective conformity to the pattern of other nations and assumed that the unique individuality of the Jews would find expression in the superlative qualities of the Jewish State. The difference lay in the definition of those qualities. Socialist-Zionists envisaged an egalitarian, classless society, free of exploitation and enjoying an harmonious international relationship with states elsewhere in the world. Yet, notwithstanding the tendency of socialist-Zionism to draw its values from sources extraneous to Judaism, a firm strain of secularized Jewish Messsianism is detectable. In the peroration of his first major formulation of socialist-Zionist ideology, Syrkin waxed eloquent on "the unique historic mission" of the Jews, who were to be the first to realize the socialist vision:

> Israel is to be compared to a sleeping giant, arising from the slough of despair and darkness and straightening up to his infinite height. . . . He knows his task, to do justice and proclaim truth. His tragic history has resulted in a lofty mission. He will redeem the world which crucified him. Israel will once again become the chosen of the nations![27]

This secularized messianism pervaded the thinking of Labor Zionism well into the post-State period. It was epitomized, above all, by Ben Gurion, who repeatedly invoked Israel's prophetic role—to be "a light unto the nations."[28]

The antithesis to Herzl's political Zionist vision was the cultural Zionist vision of Ahad Ha-Am. In contrast to Herzl, the solution proposed by Ahad Ha-Am was the creation of a "spiritual center" in Eretz Israel, where the Jewish cultural heritage would find free expression, be receptive to the best currents of enlightened modernity yet faithful to its own individuality. There, Judaism would "develop in all its respects to the highest degree of perfection of which it is capable. From this center the spirit of Judaism would radiate to the great circumference, to all the communities of the Diaspora, to inspire them with new life and to preserve the overall unity of our people."[29]

Ahad Ha-Am proffered this idea as a realistic alternative to the

27. Marie Syrkin, op. cit., p. 285.
28. See Avraham Avi-hai, Ben Gurion, State-Builder, Jerusalem, 1974, pp. 46-49.
29. Nationalism and the Jewish Ethic: Basic Writings of Ahad Ha-Am, Hans Kohn, ed., New York, 1962, p. 78.

unrealistic illusion that the entire Jewish People could be concentrated in a Jewish State or that such a state could solve the "problem of the Jews." He claimed that his plan, unlike Herzl's, had the realistic virtue of being minimalist in its expectations from the Gentile powers but maximalist in its expectations from the Jewish People, whose will-to-live would, with wise guidance, propel the process of cultural regeneration. For this purpose, Ahad Ha-Am argued, Judaism did "not need an independent state, but only the creation in its native land of conditions favorable to its development: a good-sized settlement of Jews working without hindrance in every branch of civilization from agriculture and handicrafts to science and literature." The important desideratum was that it provide conditions for "a complete national life" which, as he defined it, involved at least two things:

> First, full play for the creative faculties of the nation in a specific national culture of its own and, second, a system of education whereby the individual members of the nation will be thoroughly imbued with that culture, and so molded by it that its imprint will be recognizable in all their ways of life and thought, individual and social.[30]

It cannot be said that Ahad Ha-Am adequately set down the socio-economic basis upon which this superlative cultural creativity would flourish. Still less explicit was the manner in which the cultural creativity of the center would communicate itself to the Diaspora. Considerable inference is required to grasp the meaning of his intimations. While he did make reference to a dimension of "spiritual influence" which today would be called psychological, such as the statement that the center would "restore self-respect" to Diaspora Jews, "strengthen their morale," and "increase their sense of unity," it is unlikely that he valued this as the primary influence radiating from the center. Indeed, he wrote disparagingly of those for whom Zionism provided nothing more than a means to keep their heads erect and "an opportunity for communal work and political excitement."[31]

This psychological dimension of influence was not, in the first instance, what Ahad Ha-Am had in mind when he postulated the lofty idea of a spiritual center. He sought a profound cultural influence, revivified language, creative literature, exemplary mores and modernized thought, which would "'provide a suitable content for their

30. *Ahad Ha-Am, op. cit.*, p. 217.
31. See Leon Simon, *Ahad Ha-Am: A Biography*, London, 1960, p. 293 and cf. Hans Kohn, ed., *op. cit.*, p. 75.

life as Jews." He nowhere attempted to explain how such a transfer of cultural attributes could take place from the wholly Jewish national life of the center to the flawed life of the Diaspora. It is, however, in the reciprocal relationship between his Zionist idea and the Diaspora cultural autonomism of his friend Simon Dubnow, who was his ideological opponent, that the answer may lie.

As both Ahad Ha-Am and Dubnow themselves avowed, their premises concerning the national-cultural identity of the Jews were highly convergent. Indeed, in certain respects, these two thinkers were much closer in outlook than Ahad Ha-Am was to Herzl.[32] Ahad Ha-Am did not agree with Dubnow that national autonomy in the Diaspora could ever provide a satisfactory solution for the problem of national-cultural survival. He insisted that a spiritual center in the Jewish homeland was an absolute prerequisite for maintaining a meaningful cultural life in the Diaspora. But he did not, by any means, discount the prospect of attaining a considerable measure of autonomy "within the bounds of possibility" under Diaspora conditions. Like Dubnow, he refused to accept the contemporary political Zionist negation of the Diaspora, and he, too, insisted that "our national life in the Diaspora, must be strengthened." It was the dual situation of Diaspora Jewry, enjoying a considerable level of cultural autonomy, and a "spiritual center" with flourishing autonomy, which Ahad Ha-Am envisaged when he assumed there could be a meaningful transfer of cultural attributes. But, only in Eastern Europe were there realistic prospects for such a relationship. It is quite evident that Ahad Ha-Am had no such expectations from the Diaspora of Western Europe and the New World. As he wrote to Dubnow from England in 1907:

> What shall I write to you about Jewish life here? . . . Judaism (in our sense) is much more in *galut* here than it is in Russia . . . you feel at once that the whole thing is only an exotic plant which has been brought from abroad and artificially stuck in the ground, without any deep roots.[33]

Unlike Ahad Ha-Am, those who started from the premise that Zionism called for the regeneration of the individual Jew could not assume that it was possible to transfer something that was created in Eretz Israel to those who remained in the Diaspora. The situation they

32. See S. Dubnow, *Nationalism and History*, Koppel S. Pinson, ed., 1958, pp. 53-57; also Ahad Ha-Am's letters to Dubnow, in *Ahad Ha-Am, op. cit.*, pp. 263ff.
33. *Ahad Ha-Am, op. cit.*, pp. 308, 309.

envisaged was more polarized by far: only in Eretz Israel did the prerequisite conditions exist for the renascence of the Jewish entity
through the regeneration of the individuals there. In the final analysis,
therefore, the Diaspora was doomed to atrophy: the solution lay in the
Jewish homeland alone. Hence, for them the main thrust of Ahad Ha-
Am's idea of a spiritual center lost its significance. While they could
agree on the primacy of cultural and practical activity, as well as on
the need for qualitative *aliyah* and the upbuilding of Eretz Israel, they
did not necessarily accept Ahad Ha-Am's political minimalism. Radical literary personalities like Berdichevsky and Brenner would be
satisfied with nothing less than a metamorphosis of the Jew. The restoration of Jewish life to its historic homeland would create a new type
of Jew rooted in his own soil, devoted to a life of labor and freed from
the shackles of a religious tradition which had stultified and distorted
his character. The logical extension of this premise led to severance
not only from Judaism as it manifested itself in *galut*, but also from the
Jew who remained in *galut*. These writers envisaged a complete
dichotomy of the Jewish People—moral and physical disintegration in
galut and regeneration in Eretz Israel. They objected to Ahad Ha-
Am's attempt to substitute a normative secular Judaism for the former
Orthodox-religious mode. What they sought was a society and polity of
Jews free from any normative "spiritual" modes or "missions" whatsoever. They were anarchists in regard to the specific cultural attributes of the new entity which they sought to create in Eretz Israel. As
Brenner wrote: "There is no Judaism outside our own selves and our
own lives. There are no beliefs we regard as obligatory. . . . We are
Jews in our very lives, in our hearts and feelings. We need no rational
definitions, no absolute truths and no written obligations. . . ."[34]

Martin Buber, on the other hand, though personally antinomi-
an in his attitude to observance of the traditional precepts of Judaism,
was closer to Ahad Ha-Am's attempt to posit cultural norms. His conception attempted to bridge the gap between individual and collective
regeneration of the Jews. Moreover, Buber's conception, like Ahad
Ha-Am's, was not dependent for its fulfilment on political maximal-
ism and a sovereign political state. But, more specifically than Ahad
Ha-Am, he underlined the social implications of that regeneration. He
envisaged the ultimate product of Zionism in Eretz Israel as a community, or composite of community cells, which would realize those dialogic human relations which his philosophical speculation led him to

34. *Kol Kitvei Y.H. Brenner*, Tel Aviv, vol. 2, 1960, p. 65.

interpret as the ethos of Judaism and its mission for mankind.[35] Buber's Zionism had an affinity to the thought of A.D. Gordon who envisaged the reemergence of an organic community in "cosmic relationship with nature." However, Gordon's ideal rested more specifically on a life of labor. He assumed that all the ethical and cultural attributes of the community would emerge spontaneously out of a life of labor. Hence, in contrast to Ahad Ha-Am's conception, it did not follow from that of Gordon that the cultural creativity of Eretz Israel was transferable to the Diaspora.[36]

The premises of Orthodox-religious Zionism were far more compatible with the idea of a spiritual center. Indeed, the name *Mizrachi* was partly an allusion to *Mercaz Ruchani* (Spiritual Center). Without a doubt, observant Jews could continue to live meaningfully in *galut*, though not so fully as in Eretz Israel. But the content of the center envisaged by *Mizrachi* was diametrically opposed to that of Ahad Ha-Am. Orthodox-religious Zionism could not countenance a national center divorced from traditional norms. Paradoxically, it was the *ultimate* eschatological vision, never relinquished by Orthodox-religious Zionism, which facilitated an *interim* vision of Zion as a safe refuge for secular and observant Jews alike, and as a center for the revitalization of every facet of life according to the Torah. Particularly in the conceptions of Rabbi Abraham Isaac Kook (Chief Ashkenazi Rabbi in Palestine from 1921 to 1935) was the motif of cooperation with the non-observant, in the face of critical Jewish distress, subsumed by the eschatological motif. Since in Rabbi Kook's eyes, the whole process of return through human effort signified *athalta di-ge'ulah* (beginning of redemption), a cloak of divine sanctity enveloped religious and non-religious alike, engaged in the upbuilding of Zion. Consciously or not, the secular *halutzim*, guided by the hand of providence in anticipation of imminent redemption, were thus fulfilling important religious precepts.[37]

Implementation

A survey of the contours of divergence over means to attain the objectives of Zionism would have to encompass the history of internal

35. See, for example, Martin Buber, *Paths in Utopia*, New York, 1950, ch. X; *Pointing the Way: Collected Essays*, New York, 1957, pp. 161–176.
36. Except in so far as those remaining in the Diaspora also turned to a life of labor. See "The Work of Revival in the Diaspora," *A.D. Gordon: Selected Essays, op. cit.* pp. 77–82.
37. See Zvi Yaron, *Mishnato shel Ha-Rav Kook*, Jerusalem, 1974.

Zionist politics as well as of the development of the *Yishuv* in Eretz Israel. It would also have to include the evolution of Zionist attitudes towards the Arabs in Palestine, which has not fallen within our purview.[38] In the context of this essay only the most salient divergencies over implementation of the Zionist program can be indicated.

Theodor Herzl's advocacy of diplomatic means for the attainment of Zionism was his most innovative contribution. He proposed that a charter be gained which would provide international sanction for the creation of a Jewish State. Once this was achieved, a rationally planned mass emigration of Jews to Palestine would be implemented stage by stage, until the Jewish problem was finally resolved. It followed from these assumptions of political Zionism that the old style of philanthropically-aided, small-scale settlement carried on by *Hibbat Zion* was not only futile, but—insofar as it assumed the appearance of infiltration without full legal blessing—detrimental to the achievement of Zionist goals.

Not long before Herzl's death the Zionist Organization suffered its first major crisis from within—the Uganda controversy of 1903. Not only was the Movement divided between those who favored consideration of Britain's tentative proposal of a territory in East Africa and those who refused to consider any territory other than Eretz Israel, but even when this offer came to naught, a faction led by Israel Zangwill formed the independent Territorialist Organization. After Herzl's death in 1904, it was the balance between political efforts and practical settlement activities in Eretz Israel which constituted the main controversy over means. Frustrated by abortive efforts to attain the elusive political charter, the so-called "practical Zionists" urged that intensified activities be launched in the areas of *aliyah*, agricultural settlements, land purchases and industrial development. After the Eighth Zionist Congress (1907), the "practicals" were in the ascendancy, virtually gaining control of the Zionist Executive at the Eleventh Congress (1911).

The aggregate of constructive means applied by Labor Zionists of all kinds provided the thrust for the Zionist Movement's practical work in Eretz Israel. However, the adherents of socialist-Zionism were split in their own camp, between those who purported to base themselves upon Marxist determinism and those who rested their socialist ideals on volitional and ethical grounds. The former con-

38. For such a survey see Walter Laqueur, *A History of Zionism*, London, 1972.

ceived a reordering of the Jewish situation as a result of deterministic socio-economic forces, which not only made any solution of the Jewish problem in the Diaspora impossible, but made territorial concentration in Eretz Israel the inevitable solution. They drew on the early ideas of Borochov who had formulated the theory that by a "stichic" process of emigration and flow of capital, the Jew would inevitably gravitate to Palestine as the haven objectively most suited for the establishment of a normal economy and class structure. The programmatic implications of this approach were that proletarian Zionism should be wary of indiscriminate cooperation with the "bourgeois" Zionist Organization and that it should maintain a vigilant eye on class interests while undertaking settlement in Palestine.

The alternative trend of socialist-Zionism drew upon the theoretical legacy of Nahman Syrkin, which allowed for volition and idealism in the attainment of its goals. Not inevitable processes of immigration to Palestine, but conscious acts of will would bring *aliyah* and build up the homeland. Not spontaneous processes of capital inflow, but the voluntary efforts of Zionist financial institutions would provide the funds to finance cooperative settlements and economic development. Syrkin's legacy also bequeathed a greater willingness to cooperate with "bourgeois" political Zionism, though not with its intention to build a Jewish State based on capitalism and private property. The Jews had a unique historic opportunity: forced to establish a society *ab initio*, they could be the first to build it in socialist form from the foundations upwards.

A dialectical tension between these trends of socialist-Zionism underlies the doctrinaire ideological disputes and the repeated unions and splits which punctuate the history of this important branch of the Zionist Movement. One major bone of contention was the balance between work in Eretz Israel and involvement in the politics of Diaspora countries. Closely related to this was the rivalry between Hebrew and Yiddish. Another was the balance between participation in the World Zionist Organization and affiliation with Socialist Internationals. Yet another point of controversy revolved around the forms of organization to be adopted: those of a "vanguard party" or of a broad "class party," and whether the party should be outside and above trade union frameworks or coextensive with them. Most decisive was to determine the balance between what came to be called "socialist constructivism" on the one hand, and "class struggle" on the other. The former implied setting the class struggle aside, to all intents and purposes, and undertaking the actual task of building the cooperative settlements and economic enterprises of a socialist society.

In practice, the realities of the situation in Eretz Israel were deciding factors. Neither "stichic" immigration nor capital invest-ments were forthcoming, and Jewish "conquest of labor" was painful-ly slow. Consequently, the general trend of socialist-Zionism in Eretz Israel veered, nolens volens, in the direction of establishing its own sources of labor in settlements and economic enterprises. In 1919, the fusion of Po'alei Zion, in which David Ben Gurion and Yitzhak Ben Zvi were prominent, with independent socialist-Zionists like Berl Katznelson, signified a victory for "socialist constructivism." The new party thus formed, Achdut Ha-Avodah (Union of Labor) strove to unite party and trade union in one framework, and sought to make the polit-ical party coextensive with the working class as a whole.

After the left-wing split from the World Union of Po'alei Zion in 1920, its less doctrinaire section, which included Achdut Ha-Avo-dah, went on to become the major tributary of the Labor Zionist main-stream. However, in Eretz Israel the other major segment of Labor Zionism, Ha-Po'el Ha-Tza'ir, which retained strong reservations about doctrinaire socialism, remained outside this framework, together with its Tze'irei Zion affiliates in the Diaspora. When Ha-Po'el Ha-Tza'ir finally united with Achdut Ha-Avodah in 1930 to form Mapai (the Workers Party of Eretz Israel), this became the mainstream party of Labor Zionism. On the basis of "socialist constructivism" and a pragmatic fusion of workers' needs with a strong sense of national responsibility, Mapai became the dominant group in the World Zionist Organization until the creation of the State of Israel and for almost three decades after.

However, purist ideological reservations continued to be a per-ennial source of dissonance. The Left-Po'alei Zion clung doggedly to the early theories of Borochov, while Ha-Shomer Ha-Tza'ir persisted in the independent line which had characterized it from its beginnings as a youth movement in Galicia. About 1927 it had taken a sharp turn towards politicization of the Marxist variety. It developed an indepen-dent avant-gardist party approach which insisted on a "revolutionary perspective," meaning that the ultimate prospect of class struggle, and indeed even revolution, be retained in principle.

After Chaim Weizmann came to the forefront of world Zionism by virtue of his preeminent role in the Balfour Declaration (1917), the major controversies over means revolved around his policies in regard to the British Mandatory regime in Palestine and his efforts, crowned with success in 1929, in mobilizing the financial support of non-Zionists within the framework of an enlarged Jewish Agency. The large, ideologically inchoate body of "general Zionists" whose organizational affiliation was mediated by the various Territorial Organizations rather than by the separate unions or parties, divided sharply over Weizmann's policies. Group A supported Weizmann's political policies and followed a pro-Labor line in regard to the development of Palestine, while Group B was severely critical of Weizmann's policies as well as of the hegemony of Labor Zionism in Palestine.

It was, however, the emergence of another, more cohesive group from within general Zionism which provided the crucial counterpoint to the alliance between Weizmann's political leadership and the increasing hegemony of Labor Zionism. This was the Revisionist Zionist Party founded by Vladimir Jabotinsky in 1925, the larger part of which split from the World Zionist Organization to form the New Zionist Organization in 1935. Jabotinsky reaffirmed and extended the political Zionist assumptions of Herzl and Nordau. He insisted on the primacy of political action over practical settlement activities. In the conditions then prevailing, Jabotinsky interpreted this to mean unequivocally maximalist formulations of Zionist aims, militant political demands and the mobilization of massive popular pressure against the Mandatory power. The Revisionists insisted, unsuccessfully, that the Zionist Organization officially declare its ultimate aim to be nothing less than the establishment of a Jewish State with a Jewish majority on both sides of the Jordan. The political demands advocated by Jabotinsky centered on the insistence that Britain unswervingly fulfil its obligations by conducting a "colonization regime." This meant special legislation and state controls, in order to forge ahead with massive, nonselective Jewish immigration, and development of Eretz Israel, irrespective of Arab objections. He held that it was an illusion to imagine that the Arabs would come to terms with Zionism until an "iron wall" of established facts and power forced them to do so. Although Jabotinsky's aggressive posture led some of his followers to resort to violent resistance to the British regime, the idea of a vast public petitionary movement against British policy, which relied on the force of moral pressure, was more representative of Revisionist intentions during his lifetime.

Fundamental incompatibilities of ideological conception separated Revisionism from socialist-Zionism. Jabotinsky espoused a

"monistic" conception of Jewish nationalism which rejected, in principle, any adulteration of the pristine national ideal by extrinsic ideological influences such as socialism. He condemned the idea of class
struggle as "an empty and dangerous lie," arguing that dualism of
ideals was both absurd and disastrous for the attainment of Zionist
goals. He insisted, in principle, that all issues concerning the socio-
economic system be deferred until the Jewish State was actually
created.

Weizmann, Labor Zionism and Revisionism occupied the center of the stage in the struggle over policies and means for attainment
of the Jewish State. In this respect, Orthodox-religious Zionism played
a largely adjunct role. It was supportive of Weizmann as well as of
pioneering *aliyah* and the gradual practical development of Eretz
Israel, in which its labor wing, *Ha-Po'el Ha-Mizrachi* cooperated with
Labor Zionists. Of a different order altogether was the influence of
Ahad Ha-Am and his idea of cultural Zionism. He leavened the intellectual content of Zionism with his controversial formulations of a
normative secularized Judaism. His ideas were a formative influence
in the development of secular Zionist education, but his cultural Zionism did not give rise to any particular party. To be sure, in the *Hibbat
Zion* period he had experimented with the creation of a secretive elite
order, *Bnei Moshe*, which devoted itself exclusively to effecting a
Jewish national-cultural renascence. But this venture was short-lived.
At the early Zionist congresses, his influence was also strongly felt in
the ephemeral Democratic Faction led by young Zionists like Weizmann, Buber and Motzkin, which opposed Herzl's methods, among
other things, on the question of Jewish culture. But apart from that,
Ahad Ha-Am's influence was very general, finding expression in
somewhat modulated form in practices as wide apart as general Zionist *Gegenwartsarbeit* (political and cultural work in the Diaspora) in
Poland on the one hand, and the religious-centered Zionist program of
Mordecai Kaplan in America, on the other hand.

Within non-Marxist Labor Zionism, the *He-Halutz* movement
and youth movements like *Ha-Shomer Ha-Tza'ir* and *Gordonia*, it
was not Ahad Ha-Am's cultural Zionism, but the conception of Zionism as a personal revolution in the life of each individual Zionist,
which had the profoundest formative effect. These movements not
only provided the thrust of idealistic pioneering *aliyah* to Eretz Israel
from World War I on, but also had a far-reaching effect on Jewish
youth throughout the Diaspora, mainly in Europe but also in new

lands of immigration like the United States, Argentina and South Africa. The ideas of A.D. Gordon and, to some extent, Martin Buber's, found expression particularly in the *Ha-Po'el Ha-Tza'ir* party and those sections of *Tze'irei Zion* in the Diaspora which unified with it in the *Hitachdut* (World Union of *Ha-Po'el Ha-Tza'ir* and *Tze'irei Zion*) in 1920, and ultimately became one of the constituent parts of *Mapai*. *Ha-Po'el Ha-Tza'ir* placed great emphasis on "conquest of labor" as the fulcrum of the Zionist restoration. It maintained reservations about socialist doctrine and emphatically rejected the idea of class struggle, which it branded as a product of assimilationist mentality, destructive of national regeneration. Not determinism and materialism, but idealism and the spiritual and therapeutic value of labor, were the avowed means by which *Ha-Po'el Ha-Tza'ir* sought to consummate Zionism.

Negation of the *Galut*

The antithesis between the desired Zion and the deficient *galut* is implicit in the Zionist idea through all the contours of divergence traced here. Yet the historical record on even so fundamental an implication of the Zionist idea as the negation of the *galut* reveals considerable divergencies and ambiguities. Ahad Ha-Am based his entire outlook on the assumption that the *galut* would continue to exist. However, he drew a perceptive distinction between subjective and objective negation. Subjectively, he negated the *galut*; it was "a thoroughly evil and unpleasant thing," a state of things to which he "would gladly put an end if it were possible." Objectively, he accepted the fact that Jews did and could live in the *galut*, and his conception of Zionism took this fully into account. Thus, subjectively, the attitude he espoused towards the *galut* was negative but, objectively, it was a positive one.[39]

This was not the attitude to *galut* which the premises of political Zionism evoked. Nor was it compatible with the assumptions of those who regarded Zionism as a personal transformation. The logical conclusion of these premises in combination was formulated by Jacob Klatzkin, who argued not only that "*galut* Jewry cannot survive," but also that even if it could, "the Judaism of the *galut* is not worthy of survival." Yet, even Klatzkin left some room for what Ahad Ha-Am called an "objectively" positive attitude to the *galut*. He, too, did not

---

39. *Ahad Ha-Am, op. cit.*, p. 213.

turn his back completely on the Diaspora. "We must look after Jewry in the *galut* to the best of our ability," he wrote. "We must cultivate a national culture in the face of realities and despite the inevitable course of developments." But he drew a clear line between affirmation of *galut* life as an end in itself, and its affirmation as a means towards transcendence of the *galut*. "*Galut* Jewry has no right to exist," he argued, "if it has the pretension of being an end in itself. But it certainly does have a right to exist if it conceives of itself as a means and a transition to a new existence. The *galut* is worthy of life for the sake of redemption from the *galut* . . . Without negation of the *galut* there is no basis for any affirmation of its worth."[40] The operative implication of this attitude for Zionism was that all work in the Diaspora was conditional upon its serving the ultimate purpose of building the national homeland, and, as it were, peeling off the layers of *galut* existence and absorbing them into the national homeland.

Despite the divergences between these two views, their operative implications were not entirely dissimilar. Both conceptions maintained the primacy of Jewish life in the homeland of the Jews and both allowed for efforts by Zionists to preserve Jewish life in the *galut* as well as circumstances allowed. Historically, this is in fact what happened. A very considerable part of Zionist resources was devoted to parochial work in the *galut*. This work, which came to be called *Gegenwartsarbeit*, revolved mainly around the ideas of national-cultural autonomy which had been formulated independently by Chaim Zhitlovsky, Nathan Birnbaum and Simon Dubnow around the end of the nineteenth century.

In the multi-national empires of Czarist Russia and Imperial Austria, their ideas became increasingly credible, in bourgeois and proletarian Zionist circles alike, so much so that a Zionist accommodation to the idea of attaining national autonomy for the Jews became well-nigh irresistible. Commencing with the adoption of work for Jewish national rights by the student socialist-Zionist group, *Renascence*, in 1903, one may discern a continuous interaction within East-European Zionist ideologies—between the pristine Zionist idea of a territorial solution through a return to Eretz Israel and the Diaspora-oriented idea of national autonomy. Indeed, attitudes to *Gegenwartsarbeit* became a major touchstone of ideological differentiation in the Zionism of Eastern Europe. These spread over a broad spectrum, from

40. Jacob Klatzkin, *Tehumim*, Berlin, 1925, pp. 81–82.

outright rejection of the idea as a facile delusion and travesty of authentic Zionism, to the opposite pole of virtually total neglect of all work
for, and in, Eretz Israel.[41] However, the common denominator of all
Zionist *Gegenwartsarbeit*, in contradistinction to the Diaspora nationalism of Dubnow or the program of the socialist Bund, was the ideological premise that this work was not an end in itself but rather a
means for the ultimate realization of a territorial Zionist solution. The
rationale for resort to this means was both tactical and substantive.
Tactically it meant that Zionism could not remain oblivious to the
attainment of local Jewish rights. If it were to ignore the needs of the
Jewish masses, anti-Zionist forces would gain hegemony in the Jewish
mainstream and Zionism would be relegated to an insignificant corner
of Jewish life. The substantive rationale was that attainment of the
greatest possible measure of national autonomy was important, first, in
order to mobilize the national energies of the Jewish population and
then, to organize them in the drive to Jewish territorial sovereignty in
Eretz Israel. This common approach was expressed at the Third Conference of Russian Zionists (Helsingfors, November 1906), which
resolved that work in the *galut* constituted "one of the most important
means for attainment of Zionism's aims, in that it strengthens the
resources of Jewry in the *galut* and imparts to it new cultural, material
and political means in its struggle for the creation of a normal national
life in Eretz Israel. . ."[42]

In Poland between the two World Wars, direct involvement in
local public affairs, general elections and Sejm politics absorbed the
greater part of the energies of the Zionist leadership, whether of the
left, the center or the right.[43] The arch protagonist of *Gegenwartsarbeit*
as an integral facet of Zionism was the General Zionist leader Itzhak
Grünbaum, who ventured so far into the thicket of Sejm politics as to
initiate in 1922 a "minorities bloc" of Jews, Germans, Byelorussians
and Ukrainians to attain common objectives of minority rights. As he
declared at the Fifth Conference of Polish Zionists in 1921:

> Both forms of our work, in Eretz Israel and in *galut*, are strongly inter-
> connected: just as it is impossible to demand national rights in *galut*

---

41. See Oscar Janowsky, *The Jews and Minority Rights 1898–1919*, New York, 1966.
42. *Ibid.*, pp. 106ff.; *Katzir: Kovetz le-Korot Ha-tnuah Ha-Zionit be-Russiyah*, Tel Aviv,
1964, pp. 98–99.
43. See Ezra Mendelsohn, "The Dilemma of Jewish Politics in Poland: Four
Responses," *Jews and Non-Jews in Eastern Europe 1918–1945*, Bela Vago and George
Mosse, eds., Jerusalem, 1974, pp. 203–220.

without the expectation of Eretz Israel in the future, so it is impossible to fight for Eretz Israel in the future, without the present battle here for our national rights. . . . We would be greatly in error, if we were to surrender to that view which demands that we leave everything and devote all our strength only to work in Eretz Israel![44]

It was the pioneering element, particularly as embodied in *He-Halutz* and in the various youth movements, which rejected *Gegenwartsarbeit* during this period. They contemptuously called it "sejm Zionismus," condemning it as a futile exercise in self-delusion, and, at best, considered it as an ephemeral palliative. Only as the "politics of hope" gave way to the "politics of despair" with the passage of the tragic 1930s, did the normative status of *Gegenwartsarbeit* retreat before preparation for pioneering work in Eretz Israel and the Revisionist call for absolute "liquidation of the *galut*." But there can be no doubt that it had mediated a far-reaching moderation of Zionism's intrinsic negation of the *galut* over a long period of East-European Zionism.

Elsewhere the position was different. *Gegenwartsarbeit*, as it was understood in Eastern Europe, was hardly suited to the situation in Central and Western Europe and totally inapplicable in the countries of the New World. Not that ideas of cultural autonomism failed to cross the oceans together with all the other elements of Zionist ideology brought by Jewish immigrants; but the societal structures of countries like the United States, Canada, Argentina and South Africa, as well as the great thrust towards acculturation which characterized the aspirations of the new Jewish communities, were incompatible with cultural autonomy for minorities.[45]

On the other hand, in those post-Emancipation Jewries Zionism's ideological negation of the *galut* underwent far greater modification than *Gegenwartsarbeit* had wrought in Europe: their unprecedentedly hopeful circumstances engendered a conceptual mutation of the Zionist idea itself. Although Herzl's ideas immediately found supporters in the New World among highly acculturated Jews, their confidence in the continued viability and freedom of Jewish life in their new homes imparted a vicarious quality which enabled them to identify wholeheartedly with his contentions, yet not regard them as directly applicable to themselves. Not that their confidence was total;

44. *Ha-Ve'idah Ha-Hamishit shel Zionei Polin*, Lodz, 1921, p. 14.
45. See Ben Halpern, *The American Jew: A Zionist Analysis*, New York, 1956, pp. 77-89.

it was precisely the element of doubt which distinguished them from those acculturated Jews who refused to countenance Zionism at all. The Zion which they vicariously sensed was absolutely vital as a haven for distressed European Jewry, was, they also sensed, a vital complement for their own Jewish future in the Diaspora. Zionism in the New World thus took a view closer to that of the precursors of Zionism—that Zion was not a *substitute* for the Diaspora, at any rate not for the emancipated New World Diaspora.[46] It was a *complement*, vital and indispensable, but only a complement nonetheless. No one epitomized this view more explicitly than Judah L. Magnes, precisely because he *did* settle in Eretz Israel. For Magnes did not refute either the feasibility or the desirability of preserving "Jewish religion and Jewish nationality" in America. "Zionism," he said, "is rather the desire for the live and unhampered and harmonious further development of Jewish nationality and Jewish religion. Zion is the complement to the fulfilment of America, not its alternative. . . ."[47]

True, it cannot be said that this conception of Zion in relation to *galut* was unique to Zionism in the New World. Much the same was also prevalent in Britain and in European countries such as France, Italy and Germany where, at least until the 1930s, confidence in the fulfilment of emancipation remained unshaken. The difference was a matter of degree: in those European countries the idea of a complementary Zion was neither as all-pervasive nor as durable as it was in the New World. It should also be noted that this mutation in Zionist ideology did not nullify the ideological clash with anti-Zionists or non-Zionists. Against the anti-Zionist's charge that Zionism imperilled emancipation, the New World Zionist insisted that it, in fact, complemented emancipation. Against the non-Zionist's highly conditional acquiescence to cooperate in the development of Zion, as long as it was less than sovereign, the Zionist affirmed the need for ultimate sovereignty. The Zionist insisted that Zion was not just a philanthropic enterprise; it was the vital prerequisite for meaningful Jewish survival in the emancipated Diaspora.

Still, this ideological mutation did modify the distinction between political and cultural Zionism in the New World. Even the early leaders of American Zionism, such as Richard Gottheil (first

46. For perceptive comments on this point of similarity see Judd Teller, "Zionism, Israel and American Jewry," in *The American Jew: A Reappraisal*, Oscar Janowsky, ed., Philadelphia, 1967, pp. 301–321.
47. Judah L. Magnes, *The Melting Pot*, New York, 1909, p. 8.

President of the Federation of American Zionists), who wholly supported Herzlian political Zionism in the World Zionist Organization,
intended for themselves something more akin to Ahad Ha-Am's cultural Zionism. Unlike Herzl, they did not assume that once a Jewish
State had been attained those who did not go to live in it would inevitably assimilate. Gottheil, for example, spoke of the Diaspora Jew's
position in terms of revitalization and normalization. Revitalization,
because "embodied in a physical center, . . . it will serve as a point
towards which the thoughts, aspirations and longings of Diaspora Jews
will converge and from which they will draw that sufficiency of moral
and religious strength that will better enable them to resist the
encroachment of their surroundings." Normalization, because the
relation to "the new Jewish polity" of those who continued to live in
the Diaspora would be "exactly the same as is the relation of people of
other nationalities all the world over to their parent home."[48]

Very much the same interweaving of political and cultural
Zionist themes is abundantly evident in the statements of Louis Brandeis: "Zionism seeks to establish in Palestine a legally secured home,"
but it "is not a movement to remove all the Jews of the world compulsorily to Palestine. . . . It aims to enable the Jews to exercise the same
right now exercised by practically every other people in the world: to
live at their option either in the land of their fathers or in some other
country."[49] Similarly, Horace Kallen identified himself with political
Zionism, yet his own distinctive contribution to American Zionist
ideology, rooted in the theory of cultural pluralism, was, in fact, a form
of cultural Zionism. It affirmed the centrality of the homeland in Zion
and, at the same time, provided a legitimate framework for the preservation of Jewish identity in America.[50]

Much the same applied in other countries of the New World. In
the extraordinarily strong Zionist movement of South Africa, the leadership, headed by Samuel Goldreich, unreservedly supported Herzl
and his successor David Wolffsohn.[51] Yet confidence in the permanence of South African Jewry remained quite unaffected and South
African Zionists really envisaged themselves as part of the Diaspora
periphery, sustained by the center in Zion.

48. Richard Gottheil, Zionism, Philadelphia, 1914, p. 207.
49. Brandeis on Zionism, op. cit., p. 24.
50. Horace Kallen, Zionism and World Politics, London, 1921, p. 78.
51. See Marcia Gitlin, The Vision Amazing: The Story of South African Zionism,
Johannesburg, 1950, pp. 141-145.

On the other hand, there were formative figures in American Zionism, notably Solomon Schechter, Israel Friedlaender, Harry Friedenwald and Judah Magnes, who, while not unsympathetic to the political Zionist endeavor, focused their attention almost exclusively on the implications of Zionism for the American Diaspora. Schechter looked upon Zionism as "the great bulwark against assimilation"; as an instrument towards the strengthening of a religiously-rooted Jewish life in America.[52] Even Israel Friedlaender, who did much to propagate Ahad Ha-Am's writings, was no less inspired by Dubnow's Diaspora-centered ideas. Though he attempted to synthesize these two views, Friedlaender's theoretical affinity to Ahad Ha-Am was more than offset by his actual preoccupation with the Diaspora.[53] Although these men were regarded by some contemporaries as adherents of Ahad Ha-Am's cultural Zionism, the identity of ideas was more apparent than real. Whereas a secularized interpretation of Jewish culture was of the essence of Ahad Ha-Am's conception, these American Zionists were almost all adherents of a religious interpretation. Unlike Ahad Ha-Am, who assumed that the religious mode of Jewish identity was in irreversible decline and regarded Reform Judaism as a manifestation of "slavery in freedom," they placed all their hope in what Zionism could do to regenerate their own religious mode of identity. Ahad Ha-Am was quite explicit on the distinction when he wrote to Magnes:

> When you talk of propagating "religious nationalism," I do not know what you mean . . . Do you really think of excluding from the ranks of the nationalists all those who do not believe in the principles of religion? If that is your intention, I cannot agree. In my view our religion is national—that is to say, it is a product of our national spirit—but the reverse is not true. If it is impossible to be a Jew in the religious sense, without acknowledging our nationality, it is possible to be a Jew in the national sense without accepting many things in which religion requires belief.[54]

There was also no real identity of ideas between Ahad Ha-Am and the American secular-minded Zionists. Horace Kallen and Louis Brandeis, for example, perceived Zionism as a replacement for outmoded religious identity and, in this respect, they were closer to Ahad

52. Solomon Schechter, *Seminary Addresses and Other Papers*, New York, 1915, p. 93.
53. See Israel Friedlaender, *Past and Present*, Cincinnati, 1919, pp. xxii, 159–184.
54. *Ahad Ha-Am, op. cit.*, p. 269.

Ha-Am than those who adhered to Schechter's views. Whereas Ahad Ha-Am was concerned with protecting the Jews from acculturation to the non-Jewish environment, the overriding concern of Kallen and Brandeis was to demonstrate the compatibility of Zionism with acculturation in America and with American democratic and "progressivist" ideals. The center-Diaspora relationship which they envisaged drew one-sidedly on the psychological dimension of the relationship posited by Ahad Ha-Am. They talked much of the "ennobling self-respect" which American Jews derived from Zionist upbuilding of Zion; but they stopped short of anticipating the deeper cultural dimensions which, in fact, were crucial to Ahad Ha-Am's thinking.

Mordecai Kaplan bridged the gap between the secular and the religious emphasis in American Zionism by virtue of his unique synthesis between secularist assumptions and religious behavior. This, in conjunction with his forceful affirmation of the centrality of Zion for "Judaism as a civilization" brought him very close to Ahad Ha-Am's cultural Zionism. Yet even in his case, the difference is substantial. Kaplan's affirmation of the Diaspora went far beyond that of Ahad Ha-Am, both in the religious orientation of his "Reconstructionist" Judaism and in his insistence on the parallel value of a Diaspora Jewish life "in two civilizations."[55]

In sum, the spectrum of divergence within Zionism on the relationship between Zion and *galut* was very wide, even before the creation of the State of Israel. At most, it may be said that subjective negation of the *galut* in Ahad Ha-Am's terms was the common denominator. The pioneering Zionist youth movements epitomized the extreme negative pole of the spectrum. They negated the *galut*, objectively as well as subjectively. They regarded *Gegenwartsarbeit* as a futile exercise, and they virtually turned their backs on the Diaspora. Only a little less negative was the kind of formulation articulated by Klatzkin. This was supportive of the *galut* only in the limited sense of making it transcend itself, a view not incompatible with *Gegenwartsarbeit*. The positive pole of the spectrum was the normative New World Zionist view of Zion as the necessary complement to an affirmed Diaspora. Considerably less positive was Ahad Ha-Am's affirmation of the Diaspora, provided it possessed a real measure of national cultural autonomy and drew upon the fully autonomous cultural center in Zion.

---

55. See Mordecai M. Kaplan,   *The Future of the American Jew*,   New York,   1948, pp. 129–130.

Aliyah as Personal Imperative

The act of *aliyah* was so intrinsic to Zionist ideology that no serious adherent of Zionism could regard it with anything but approbation and encouragement. In abstract principle, at least, all Zionists saw *aliyah* as a high ideal, and there were always some who considered it a personal imperative. In practice, however, the personal imperatives which engaged the vast majority of Zionists everywhere in the world ranged over many activities other than preparation for personal *aliyah*. These included fund raising, diplomatic endeavors, Hebrew education and publicistic activities. In practice, too, many adherents of Zionism, not excluding some of its leading ideologists, joined the immigration waves to the New World rather than the ascent to Zion. No doubt the most pervasive explanation for this seeming paradox lies in prosaic human factors and objective difficulties. Settling in Eretz Israel imposed infinitely greater human difficulties than did immigration to countries of the New World. Equally important were the adverse circumstances surrounding the entire Zionist enterprise, particularly the severe restrictions on Jewish immigration imposed by the British to appease militant Arab objections. They were a decisive obstacle to *aliyah* in the 1930s and 1940s when the Jewish situation in Europe deteriorated most tragically into the Holocaust catastrophe.

No less significant were internal weaknesses of the World Zionist Organization. In the critical years of the early 1920s, when the British Mandate over Palestine heralded an era of unprecedented opportunity for Zionist fulfilment, comparable to that later made possible by statehood itself, it was the financial poverty of the movement more than Arab opposition or British policy which hindered *aliyah*. Nowhere was this more evident than in the case of Polish Zionism, the major reservoir of *aliyah* in that period, on account of its strength and the abject condition of Polish Jewry. Applications for *aliyah* abounded, and the Mandatory regime headed by Herbert Samuel gave its blessing to a liberal policy which could have doubled the Jewish population in Eretz Israel within a few years. But it soon became painfully apparent to the World Zionist Organization, headed by Weizmann, that it lacked the financial resources to fulfil its guarantee to integrate so massive an immigration within the economic fabric of the *Yishuv*. Hence the paradox, that precisely at a time when the Polish deputies in the Sejm were shouting, "Jews go to Palestine," and when so many Jews were clamoring to go, the Zionist office in Berlin was anxiously urging Polish Zionist leaders to halt *aliyah*. Moreover, the world Zionist leadership in effect elicited the Mandatory regime's help in restricting the number of certificates considered necessary for immigration.[56]

Even apart from objective difficulties of this kind, Zionist ideology itself was not devoid of ambiguities on the question of *aliyah*. The very grandeur of the political Zionist vision tended to depersonalize *aliyah*, giving it the character of a vast social engineering project, to be implemented after the requisite charter to establish a Jewish State had been secured. For the individual exponent of political Zionism, personal *aliyah* was a remote prospect. Indeed, it was as if insistence on *aliyah* as a personal imperative would trivialize the grandeur of the Zionist enterprise. While Herzl himself had every intention of settling in Eretz Israel once the longed-for charter had been legally obtained, there is no reason to question the statement of Franz Oppenheimer, one of the leaders of German Zionism:

> When I was asked . . . to join the Zionist Movement I declined because I had not the slightest intention of leaving Germany. I was assured that it was absolutely not required. Then Herzl himself tried to win me over [to Zionism]. I made no secret of my position on Zionism, to which Herzl replied, "You are a good Zionist."[57]

Oppenheimer authentically characterized the equivocal place of *aliyah* in the political Zionist conception when he claimed that Zionism was "not a movement of Jews who desire to emigrate to Palestine, but a movement that desires the emigration of the Jewish People."

This conception was predominant among Jews of the Western world, especially those in the United States. From the outset, the adherents of political Zionism in America were explicit in denying that *aliyah* was a personal obligation. The first programmatic statement of the American Federation of Zionists capped its summary of Zionism's objects with the declaration: "And we hold that this does not mean that all Jews must return to Palestine."[58] Throughout the New World the normative attitude of Zionists towards *aliyah* was that it did not necessarily apply to them except as an act of altruistic service to

56. These events are documented in Ezra Mendelsohn's study, *Zionism in Poland 1915–1926: The Formative Years* (in press).
57. *Jüdische Rundschau*, 19, no. 25, June 19, 1914, p. 270.
58. Richard Gottheil, *The Aims of Zionism*, New York, 1899, p. 20

the cause, or as a somewhat idiosyncratic act of personal fulfilment. In the records of Zionist conferences, writings and journals in the English-speaking countries, the subject of personal *aliyah* comes up infrequently. It seems that Zionists in countries such as the United States, Britain or South Africa seldom incorporated the idea of *aliyah* as a personal obligation within their universe of discourse; at any rate, not until the emergence of Zionist youth movements in the 1930s and after World War II.

Even the victory of the more practical Zionist approach over the primarily political policy of the World Zionist Organization prior to World War I did not signify an ideological personalization of *aliyah*. This was not the issue, but rather the allocation of scarce resources for settlement activity as opposed to the deferment of such activity until the basic political objective had been achieved. Characteristic is the fate of a resolution relating to personal *aliyah*—in itself a rarity—presented to the Eleventh World Zionist Congress in 1913. It stated:

> Considering the overwhelming importance of the Palestine (oriented) principle in the Zionist Movement, the Congress declares it the obligation of every Zionist—especially whoever is in a financial position to do so—to become personally acquainted with Palestine, to establish personal economic interests there and to incorporate emigration to Palestine in his life program.

The protocol records that consideration of this resolution was postponed for lack of time.[59]

The conception of *aliyah* as a personal obligation was fostered mainly within the Labor streams of Zionism. Yet even in the ideology of socialist-Zionists the attitude did not lack ambiguity; their personal exemplification of *aliyah* was at times obfuscated by ideological contortions. Thus, during the period of the Second *Aliyah*, *Ha-Po'el Ha-Tza'ir*'s idealistic appeal to Zionists in the Diaspora to stop their "Sisyphean work in the *galut* . . . to cease discussions about 'realistic' work in Palestine—and come here to do real work!" was regarded with scorn by those *Po'alei Zion* leaders whose conception of *aliyah* was "scientifically" deterministic.[60] A particularly striking illustration of the impact of pure ideological considerations is in attitudes towards

59. *Stenographisches Protokoll der Verhandlungen des XI. Zionisten-Kongress*, 1913, pp. 346–349.
60. See Yosef Shapira, *Hapo'el Ha-Tza'ir: Ha-Ra'ayon ve-ha-Ma'aseh*, Tel Aviv, 1968, pp. 64ff.

the Fourth *Aliyah* in the mid-1920s. This new immigration, consisting mainly of middle class Jews—merchants, storekeepers, artisans—was precipitated by the deteriorating situation in Poland and by the closing of the gates to America. Yet, instead of being encouraged by all, this *aliyah* aroused severe criticism on the part of a formidable segment of the Polish Zionists headed by Itzhak Grünbaum's *Al Ha-Mishmar* Zionist faction and supported by almost all of the Labor Zionists, from *He-Halutz* to *Po'alei Zion*. The Fourth *Aliyah* ran counter to their conception of the qualitative upbuilding of Eretz Israel by selective, ideologically motivated pioneers. They felt that the wholesale transfer to Zion of "Nalewki" (a Jewish quarter in Warsaw) with its vulgar spirit of shopkeepers and *Luftmenschen* would divest Zionism of its ideological élan. The main proponent of the Fourth *Aliyah* was the centrist *Et Livnot* Zionist faction of Poland, which advocated the creation of a Jewish majority in Eretz Israel as speedily as possible, greeting the Fourth *Aliyah* as "the beginning of the fulfilment of our dreams." Nothing epitomizes the ideological character of the issue more starkly than the fact that the Left-*Po'alei Zion*, joined *Et Livnot* in applauding the "petit bourgeois" Fourth *Aliyah*. However, the paradox is more apparent than real: after all, was that *aliyah* not an indicator of the long-awaited "stichic" movement seeking the territorial base for the development of "normal conditions of production"?[61]

It was the vein of Zionist ideology based on the idea of personal regeneration and an existential search for self-fulfilment which unequivocably elevated the act of personal *aliyah* to the status of an absolute Zionist imperative. This vein prevailed mainly in the non-Marxist elements of Labor Zionism, particularly the *Hitachdut Ha-Po'el Ha-Tza'ir-Tze'irei Zion* and segments of the *He-Halutz* pioneering movement. Above all, personal *aliyah* became the preeminent ideal of the Zionist youth movements. In Germany, where the first Jewish youth movement, the *Blau-Weiss Wanderbund*, had been founded as early as 1912, many of the Jewish youth *Bunde* grappled with the ideal of *aliyah* for more than a decade before the rise of Hitler eliminated all alternative orientations; in Eastern Europe *aliyah* became the focal ideal of such youth movements as *He-Halutz Ha-Tza'ir*, *Ha-Shomer Ha-Tza'ir* and *Gordonia*. As the latter youth movements spread from their main centers in Eastern Europe as far as the Jewish communities in the New World, they disseminated the idea of personal *aliyah* to a

---

61. Ezra Mendelsohn, *op. cit.*

small but highly significant segment of the Zionist Organization. By the 1930s they also stimulated the development of indigenous youth movements in the English-speaking countries, for example, *Habonim*, which became committed to the idea of personal *aliyah*. Within the various senior Zionist Federations all over the world, however, the demand for personal *aliyah* as a touchstone of authentic Zionism erupted only sporadically and without much consequence. A striking instance of this phenomenon occurred in German Zionism some time before World War I. Its central figure was Kurt Blumenfeld, whose Zionist convictions, rooted in a post-assimilationist crisis of identity, broke radically with the vicarious political-cum-philanthropic version of Zionism then current in Germany. The radical innovation of Blumenfeld's version of Zionist ideology lay in his contention that *Deutschtum* was, in fact, so irredeemably alien to the essence of *Judentum*, that there could be no genuine synthesis of the two. Hence the individual Jew was fundamentally rootless in Germany and *aliyah* was really the only answer. Consistent with this position, Blumenfeld maintained that once a Zionist had reached this conviction, it was the better part of discretion to keep a *Distanz* from the ambience of German culture and politics in anticipation of his eventual self-fulfilment in Eretz Israel. Blumenfeld asserted quite bluntly that anyone who considered Zionism nothing more than a charitable effort to help the Jews of the East harmed the cause. Zionism's true goals could only be achieved by the kind of person who "recognized that the final fulfilment of his Zionism lies in the return to Eretz Israel, the Promised Land."[62]

This ideological radicalization was expressed in a resolution passed at the Posen Conference of the Zionist Federation of Germany in 1912, which stated that "it is the duty of every Zionist—especially one who is economically independent—to incorporate emigration to Palestine into his life's program." The old guard of German Zionists like Max Bodenheimer, Adolf Friedmann and Franz Oppenheimer were far from enamored of this new *Weltanschauung*. They reacted with a mixture of dismay and outrage at what they described, at best, as the wholly artificial and unrealistic phraseology of "youngsters intoxicated by their own ideas," claiming it was an unwarranted distortion of the Zionist idea which could do nothing but harm the Zionist

62. Kurt Blumenfeld, *Zionistische Betrachtungen*, Berlin, 1916, pp. 13, 14. The quote is from an article written in September 1910.

position in Germany. They found it intolerable to be expected to uproot themselves from their strong identification with *Deutschtum* and immigrate to Palestine.[63]

The controversy over the Posen resolution is indicative of the equivocal role of personal *aliyah* in Zionist ideology. Likewise, the aftermath of the resolution signifies its ephemeral and non-normative character. Neither then nor after the Balfour Declaration did it bring about the *aliyah* of German Zionists to any significant degree. It is possible that Blumenfeld and his circle did not literally mean what they said and sought no more than a rhetorical tactical device to shake the leadership out of its complacency; or else the emancipated and highly acculturated ambience of German Zionism simply proved impervious to such ideological innovation.

Thus the historical record reveals that personal *aliyah*, though implicit in all Zionist ideology and considered imperative by an important segment of its adherents, was not an unequivocal *sine qua non* for being a Zionist. For the most part, the issue of *aliyah* was not personalized as much as familiarity with the contemporary Zionist dilemma of personal *aliyah* might lead one to expect. Only after the creation of the State of Israel did the attitude of Zionists to personal *aliyah* become a crucial issue. Ben Gurion, with all the force of his public authority, uncompromisingly confronted the Zionist Movement with this issue. But he oversimplified when he invoked the historical record in order to accuse contemporary Zionists of deserting authentic Zionism since they had no intention of immigrating to Israel. "My Zionism and that of European Jewry during the fifty years before the Nazi Holocaust and the rise of the State," he declared, "was built on the conviction that we did not form part of the peoples among whom we lived, that we had no intention of remaining in exile, and that our deepest aspiration was to return personally to Zion."[64] Ben Gurion's own strain of Zionism was undoubtedly as he described it, but whether the same could be said unreservedly of all European Zionism, or even of the particular segment of socialist-Zionism with which Ben Gurion was originally associated, is questionable. In any case, it was definitely not the normative view of those strands of Zionist ideology

63. See Jehuda Reinharz, *Fatherland or Promised Land: The Dilemma of the German Jew, 1893–1914*, Ann Arbor, 1975, pp. 164ff.; cf. Stephen Poppel, *Zionism in Germany 1897–1933*, Philadelphia, 1977, pp. 50ff.
64. David Ben Gurion, "Zionism and Pseudo-Zionism," *Forum*, vol. IV, Jerusalem, 1959, p. 148.

which developed in the countries of the New World, and to whose representatives Ben Gurion now addressed his contentions.

The commanding force of Ben Gurion's challenge derived less from the historical record than from the revolution ensuing from the achievement of Jewish statehood. At last the gates of Zion were wide open and Israel was calling out of dire need, as well as in a spirit of offering, for the personal *aliyah* of every Zionist. The situation warranted a commensurately new response from Western Zionists, irrespective of their historical record on *aliyah*. If they could not be persuaded to settle in Israel out of fidelity to past convictions, they could at least be asked to do so by force of present necessity and opportunity.

When the expected response was not forthcoming, Ben Gurion could cogently argue that since "all Diaspora Jews in the free countries love Israel, seek the welfare of Zion and give their assistance towards rebuilding it," there was "no difference whatsoever between [so-called] Zionists and Jews who do not call themselves by that name." Hence, ideologically, and even organizationally, Ben Gurion drew the inference that the Zionist Movement had served its purpose and was now dispensable. Although his views were undermining the status of the World Zionist Organization, he compromised in practice, so that the Movement not only continued to function but also made successful organizational adjustments in order to enlist the full support of non-members within the expanded Jewish Agency. The central issue of personal *aliyah*, however, remains an unresolved source of dissonance between most Israeli and Diaspora Zionists, and continues to threaten the ideological viability of Zionism.

To sum up, if we return to the typological basis of this essay—the dimensions of diagnosis, vision and implementation of the Zionist idea—we will note that the question of personal *aliyah* is not the only controversial ideological issue remaining after the creation of the State of Israel. Considerable differences of opinion still persist over diagnosis of the Jewish situation. The question of whether the American Diaspora is *sui generis* or subject to the inherent defects of *galut* is still a bone of contention. In addition, divergent visions of end-goals are still vying with one another, particularly secularists versus religious Zionists. Even choosing the means to achieve agreed goals is a disputed issue, as is abundantly evident in Israel's controversies over the painful concessions and grave security risks involved in the pursuit of peace.

While the return of Jews to Zion and the restoration of Zion as a homeland for Jews has become a reality of Jewish life, other dimensions of that reality impede fulfilment of the Zionist idea. Thus, the maximalist political conception of Zionism, which strove to ultimately vest all Jewish life in the Jewish State, confronts the reality of a majority of Jewry still looking to its future in the Diaspora. No more fulfilled are the requirements of the alternative conception which sought the renascence of Jewish culture through an autonomous center in Zion. Ironically, it is precisely the Western Diaspora, which did not play a major role in Ahad Ha-Am's vision, that is called upon to relate to the center. Moreover, in an era of disenchantment with ideologies, at least in the Western world, it has been suggested that Zionist ideology is no longer capable of functioning in Jewish life, having been replaced by a broad consensus of pragmatic support for Israel.[65] In contrast, some of the foremost Jewish intellects of our time continue to grapple with the ideological implications of a continuing Diaspora situation lacking in the objective, generative impulses which formerly activated the Zionist Movement. In an incisive penetration of the ideological core of the contemporary issue, Nathan Rotenstreich has sought to define the status of the State of Israel vis-à-vis the continuing Diaspora, not by virtue of overriding concern for Israel's needs and safety, nor even by virtue of its actual centrality, but rather as a function of its inherent primacy for Jewish life as a whole.[66]

The future will tell whether such formulations can serve as the basis for new integrative conceptions of Zionism. In the meanwhile most Zionists agree that the establishment of the State of Israel has fulfilled the essential prerequisite for attaining the Zionist idea, but that the ultimate consummation of that idea remains as formidable a challenge as ever.

65. See David Sidorsky, The End of Ideology and American Zionism, in Study Circle on World Jewry (Hebrew), Moshe Davis, ed., Series 4, Jerusalem, 1976.
66. See Nathan Rotenstreich, "State and Diaspora in Our Time," in World Jewry and the State of Israel, Moshe Davis, ed., New York, 1977, pp. 329–339.

II

Diaspora Zionism: Achievements and Problems

The United States

Ben Halpern

A stereotyped view of American Zionism, shared by partisan critics and defenders alike, takes it to be uniquely different from the tradition of the rest of the movement. The American concept, allegedly invented by Louis Brandeis as a formula for avoiding charges of "dual loyalty," is said to deny that *aliyah* can solve any Jewish problems for Americans. Therefore, it reduces the Zionist obligations of Americans to no more than economic and political support of the *Yishuv*. Recent Zionist congresses and ideological conferences have regularly denounced such American Zionism as a betrayal of "classic Zionist" principles, since it does not foresee calamity, nor preach rescue through *aliyah*, for American Jewry. But that is a greatly distorted perception of both Zionism in America and the historical tradition of world Zionism.

Jewish Homelessness

The whole history of traditional Zionism shows a rough division between Herzlians, concerned with the "problem of the Jews," and Ahad Ha-Amists, concerned with the "problem of Judaism." Only the former thought in terms of a systematic "ingathering of the exiles" that would require the *aliyah* of all who wished to remain Jews, and certainly of all Zionists.

Traditional Zionism also shows a rough division between attitudes typical of Western countries, where Jews were effectively emancipated in the nineteenth century, and of Eastern countries, where they were not. Only Eastern Jews experienced the "problem of the Jews" directly. Western Jews merely witnessed it in the form of waves of immigrants from the East who had to be helped.

Some Westerners became Zionists because they believed that the problem of Eastern Jewry was not an accidental but an essential

45

expression of the Jewish condition, which they defined as one of national homelessness. The basic Jewish problem could be solved only by concentrating Jews from the most afflicted areas in their ancestral homeland, where they could build a free Jewish nation.

Certain consequences followed from this position for most Western Zionists. Since the basic Jewish condition was rendered more than tolerable, according to the consensus of Western Jewries, then *aliyah* was not relevant as a solution for whatever problems of inequality and discomfort still concerned them. If *aliyah* was contemplated or carried out at all in the West, it was generally conceived as an act of voluntary service, not of escape.

However, Western Zionists did not see their own emancipation as a solution for the fundamental Jewish problem, most starkly exemplified in the East. They tended toward a vicarious Herzlianism (unlike that of Herzl himself), dedicated to supporting the *aliyah* of Eastern Zionists in order to end the national homelessness of all Jews. Such a practical Zionism was capable of enlisting the cooperation of Western non-Zionists, since its ideological implications were not stressed.

In no Western country was there a uniform attitude among all Zionists disavowing the duty of *aliyah*. In Germany this issue was central in a debate where rival factions clearly defined opposite views regarding their German and Jewish national identities: a first generation, led by Max Bodenheimer, took the very view said to be uniquely represented in American Zionism; the other, led by Kurt Blumenfeld, assumed a personal duty of *aliyah*, and combined deep commitment to German culture with voluntary abstention from German public life.

In American Zionism, these same problems were faced in a pragmatic spirit without a major split between rival ideologies. Brandeis' dictum that a Jew had to be a Zionist to be a good American, his rather mild objection to phrases in drafts of the Balfour Declaration implying that Zionism might be based on the discontent of Jews with their current citizenship, his apprehension that it might jeopardize Jewish equality if he should resign from the Supreme Court to assume world Zionist leadership—all these expressed a vicarious, generally Herzlian type of Zionism. Yet Brandeis did not lightly reject the possibility of leaving American public life; on the contrary, he gave it conscientious consideration; and later, he gave the *halutz* movements of young American Jews—especially *Ha-Shomer Ha-Tza'ir*—his warm and fatherly patronage. His was a complex attitude, shared by many other American Zionists. Accordingly, the American *halutz* movement and societies formed to purchase land or invest capital for the settlement of American Jews in Palestine did not produce ideological upheavals: they were loosely integrated into the structure of American Zionism, without concern whatsoever for rigorous, ideological consistency.

Diaspora Nationalism

Parallel considerations apply to the Ahad Ha-Amist influence. East-European Ahad Ha-Amism, which was strongly secularist, was transformed into a religious ethnicism in the West. Martin Buber imbued it with mystical overtones for German Jewry, and Mordecai Kaplan made it over as a naturalist theology for Americans. Both used Zionism as an ethnic binder to stiffen the dissolving religious culture of Western Judaism. In this form, spiritual Zionism, too, was capable of attracting non-Zionists who defined their Jewishness as a religious identification.

Secularist cultural nationalism was a more controversial concept when taken up in the West. The Germans, under Kurt Blumenfeld's Zionist regime, approached the model of East-European, politically-oriented, Diaspora nationalism more closely than the American Zionist establishment ever did. At an earlier date, German Zionists (who included a large proportion of *Ostjuden*), took a leading part in the attempt to form a Jewish political party in Germany, similar to the Catholic Center Party. Such efforts rendered Zionism intellectually stimulating, but practically negligible in German Jewish communal affairs.

The American variant of Diaspora nationalism was both more effective and more tenuous. The campaign for an American Jewish Congress in 1914–16 may have arisen out of the autonomist theories of Russian Jewish immigrants like Nahman Syrkin, but it was taken over by fully Americanized Zionists. Its institutional principle, in the end, was Horace Kallen's pragmatist doctrine of cultural pluralism, which justified ethnic politics only at the level of a popular pressure group and ruled out a polity of ethnic autonomy on the scale of the Russian Helsingfors program.

These differences in theory and practice can easily be traced to the social and historical conditions that distinguished Germany from America. Both were nation-states; both had emancipated Western institutions. The nation-idea underlying the state was conceived in more exclusive and doctrinaire spirit in Germany than in America. In both countries, the Zionist movement combined a few near-assimilated local leaders with a predominantly East-European immigrant membership; but immigrants were a far larger, more autonomous component of the American than of the German Jewish community at large.

Another decisive difference is chronological. The German movement was a main support of Herzl's organization from the beginning, and assumed leadership after his death. American Zionism rose to a comparable position only during World War I, when the German movement lost its authority. The style of American Zionism was institutionalized after the movement had achieved its preliminary political goal in the provisions of the Balfour Declaration and the Palestine Mandate. The practical issues that dominated the ensuing years left a decisive stamp upon the highly receptive pragmatic temper of the Americans.

American Zionist Groups

What is truly different about American Zionism, more than the theories and practices just discussed, lies in the forms of organization it adopted. These were related to the overwhelmingly immigrant composition of American Jewry, to the needs of the period when American Zionism rose to major importance, and to the loose and open style of American organizational life generally.

The Zionist Movement, scattered all over the world, was never a homogeneous organization with effective central control and uniform discipline. In a federally united, non-conformist Protestant country like America, where the whole Jewish community was a loose collection of voluntary units, this Zionist weakness (or proclivity) was heightened. Each distinct stratum of American Zionists—of similar immigrant origins, sex or age group, political or ideological orientation—created its own cluster of Zionist societies, rather than entered into already established bodies. The movement developed layer by layer, by a sort of geological accretion rather than by organic growth.

The early Zionist movement in the United States provided a congenial milieu for the newcomers. It often took the form of a mutual benefit society, whether as a landsmannschaft or a fraternal order. Moreover, traditional functions and structures of European Zionism

were continued. All the members saved and collected money to purchase land in Palestine, hoping in many cases for their own eventual
settlement there. Some trained as agricultural laborers to this end.
They continued, not only to buy and sell the *shekel,* Jewish Colonial
Trust shares, Carmel wines and other products of the new *Yishuv,* but
to found Hebrew-speaking clubs, Hebrew periodicals, and Hebrew
schools. And when World War I broke out, they enlisted in the Jewish
Legion.

The first *Po'alei Zion* and *Mizrachi* societies in America were
near contemporaries of the beginnings of those parties in the Old
Country. Both elements devoted themselves, each in its own spirit, to
the creation and support of Jewish schools; they also played significant
roles in the formation of the New York Kehillah and the American
Jewish Congress.

The core of the American Zionist movement was the general
Zionist Federation of American Zionists (FAZ), later to become the
Zionist Organization of America (ZOA). Here, too, the members were
mainly immigrants. In later years, the more prosperous and Americanized among immigrant Zionists were those attracted to the ZOA.
From the first, their leaders included prominent native Americans,
and they consistently sought the support of wealthy, politically
influential, established Jews. This policy became more vital after
World War I reduced the strength of European Jewry and imposed
unprecedented economic and political responsibilities on American
Zionists. The immigration laws of the 1920s made it necessary to look
to native-born Jewish youth for new Zionist recruits. But neither the
older generation of native Americans nor the sons of immigrants could
be attracted to the meetings of Yiddish-speaking *landsmannschaft*
organizations. They could be drawn in only by encouraging new,
autonomous organizations constructed according to their own taste.

This goal was pursued, and in some outstanding cases
achieved, by setting up organizations which, from the point of view of
traditional Zionists, involved a limited Zionist commitment. Shortly
before World War I, the Federation of American Zionists adopted a
form of associate membership which exempted one from attending
frequent meetings and, in the case of women, did not even require
purchasing the *shekel.* Such associate Zionists were expected to
devote themselves to special, practical, Zionist tasks of greater scope
than could be entrusted to the older, poorer class of members. Out of
hese beginnings arose the Hadassah Women's Zionist Organization

and some other Zionist enterprises associated with the name of Louis
D. Brandeis. All Zionist sectors developed women's auxiliary organizations and autonomous youth groups. Labor Zionists as well as General Zionists adopted the characteristically American device of creating front organizations of influential "friends," from whom a full ideological commitment was not expected.

The Brandeis-Weizmann Controversy

The characteristic features of postwar American Zionism were
crystallized in a prolonged conflict in the 1920s between factions identified with Brandeis and Weizmann. Brandeis proposed to reorganize
Zionism as a loose association of territorial societies, each committed
to a specific practical task, with the World Organization's work in Palestine under central management by technical experts. On this basis
(continuing, in a way, the FAZ's associate membership scheme), he
expected to enroll "all Jews," including prominent non-Zionists, as
full members of the organization.

The difference between Brandeis' position and Weizmann's
was not as great as the rival battle cries suggested; nor—when Weizmann eventually won the accession of non-Zionists to the extended
Jewish Agency in 1929—was he, as sometimes alleged, simply adopting the very proposals about which he had once fought Brandeis so
bitterly. The real difference that divided them was a condition well
understood by Weizmann himself, at the time of the first split in 1919–
20. When Brandeis' plan foundered at the 1920 World Zionist Conference in London (and again in 1921), he felt able to renounce responsibilities to the Zionist Organization and make his own contribution
outside the established framework, through agencies of his own.
Weizmann at that time felt that he was the one man who could not
resign from the official leadership of world Zionism, and Brandeis
concurred in this judgment. Hence he could not cavalierly disregard
the cherished ideas of East-European Zionists (or, indeed, the preferences of Western non-Zionists), since his effective leadership
depended on their willing acceptance of him.

Weizmann's synthesis borrowed ideas from the Brandeis group
as well as from their East-European adversaries, while fully satisfying
neither, and proved in the end better suited to the preferences of
Western non-Zionists than Brandeis' proposals. An equal partnership
in building the National Home, offered to non-Zionists primarily
through their own existing organizations, was ultimately accepted; the

East-European alternative of general elections to Jewish democratic assemblies in each country, which would then elect the "non-Zionist" delegations to the Jewish Agency Council, could never have been. Brandeis' idea of entrusting competent technicians, without reference to their Zionist or non-Zionist views, with full executive authority to manage Jewish Agency functions succeeded in totally alienating the veteran Zionists; and it could hardly have been accepted by a man like Louis Marshall. Weizmann's alternative not only proved acceptable to Marshall, but, with minimal loss of the loyalty of old Zionists, achieved much of Brandeis' objectives.

A Foundation Fund

The main idea of the East-European camp which the Weizmann synthesis picked up was the *Keren Hayesod*, that rock of contention upon which the second and decisive Brandeis–Weizmann split occurred in 1921. It was intended that the income of this "foundation fund" which the Jewish People would raise over five years by "sacrificial" self-taxation (by tithing income *and* capital), would be available to the Jewish Agency for *all* its fiscal operations.

Brandeis vehemently opposed this scheme: (a) because Zionist budgets should now be based on economic (not political) considerations as determined by technicians (not politicians); and (b), because the "commingling" of donations and business loans in a common fund and the diversion of funds from one source (or budget line) to another were fiscally irresponsible, indeed immoral, practices that would corrupt the Zionist Movement and pauperize the settlers.

Weizmann, with the aid of Louis Lipsky, Emanuel Neumann and the rest of the "Opposition," made the *Keren Hayesod* the main business of American Zionism—at least of the ZOA—for the inter-war period. There was a severe crisis in the Zionist Movement in the late 1920s, brought on by the collapse of the land boom in Eretz Israel in 1927, but when restorative measures were accomplished in 1929, as the non-Zionists entered the Jewish Agency and the Brandeis group took over the ZOA, the *Keren Hayesod* and the politically-constituted Zionist Executive were accepted as the main instruments of the effort to build the National Home in Palestine. General Zionism in America was still further confirmed in its established pattern as the main fund-raising arm of the world movement, and this one activity absorbed the bulk of American Zionist energy and attention.

It has been claimed that a Brandeis credo, which renounced

aliyah and other Zionist features implying dual loyalty, was the cardinal element in the growth of mass Zionist membership; and the sharp decline in ZOA membership in the post-Brandeis era is cited in confirmation. But this decline set in before, not after, the Brandeis administration's defeat. The sharp fluctuations to which the American men's General Zionist membership is subject—as evidenced in both World Wars—depends on the image of the ZOA as the titular representative of American Zionism. So perceived, it attracts a floating mass of loosely committed adherents who join in times of crisis and emergency, and leave when the movement returns to its dull routine tasks. (The ease with which small committed cliques capture or lose control of such an organization is related to this fact.)

Jewish Cultural Influence

Other American Zionist organizations followed different patterns of growth, depending on the functions they were able to perform in the lives of their members. Strongly immigrant-based organizations like the old FAZ, the *Mizrachi* and *Po'alei Zion*, served as a congenial social milieu for small bodies of old-style Zionists. To extend their appeal to Americanized and native Americans these organizations had to serve other functions, related to their position in America.

One such function, recommended by Brandeis, was the adoption of special, practical Zionist tasks. The ZOA, which had to present the *Keren Hayesod* (or later, the United Palestine Appeal) as a general American-Jewish effort, did not draw such advantages from its connection with this fund as did the *Mizrachi*, the Labor Zionists and above all, Hadassah, from their special Eretz Israel projects and campaign. Women's organizations, including the Mizrachi Women and Labor Pioneer Women, were particularly strengthened, because of an image of greater personal involvement in the operations of their projects in Eretz Israel, and also because organizational work was itself functional for women.

All American Zionist parties produced literature and sponsored other methods that disseminated a certain Jewish cultural, as well as propagandistic, influence. *Mizrachi* was active in disseminating modern Orthodoxy, and helped foster religious schools, up to the university level. The Labor Zionists operated a Yiddish school system of their own. Under the Lipsky regime, the ZOA was run in good part by a group of journalists; their magazine, *The New Palestine*, featured a number of eminent contributors to the diversity of American culture,

notably Maurice Samuel and Ludwig Lewisohn. The Labor Zionist
Jewish Frontier in the 1930s, under Hayim Greenberg's editorship,
became a widely respected English-language Zionist platform, based
on broad cultural and political concerns. The Zionist writers were, of
course, virtually alone in American Hebrew letters, dominant in the
Orthodox Yiddish press, and a strong presence in the secular Yid-
dishist literary and popular organs.

Apart from such organizationally related channels, Zionist
influences were pervasively effective owing to the inherent relation of
the ethnic and religious aspects of Jewishness. *Mizrachi,* as noted, was
closely related to modern Orthodoxy, which had a wider, less well-
defined ambit. During the socially conscious 1930s, some social action
leaders of Reform Judaism were attracted to Labor Zionism, in which
they saw a revival of the prophetic ethical tradition. The widest, most
profound impact was that of Mordecai Kaplan, whose Reconstructionist philosophy reared a whole generation of Conservative (and many
Reform) rabbis in a new theologically liberal and ethnically rooted
Americanized Judaism.

Student Activities

Zionists were active initiators of student youth societies; and
given the resistance to Jewish separatism on American campuses,
their ethnic pride was essential for the creation of fraternities like Zeta
Beta Tau (which eventually became a general Greek letter fraternity)
and the Menorah Society, launched by Harvard Zionists for the general Jewish student body.

Continual efforts were made to organize and maintain Zionist
societies on the campus. Given the short duration of a college generation, and the strong inclination of students, particularly Jewish students, to ideological controversy, these organizations sometimes had
brief and stormy careers. The whole gamut of Zionist partisanship,
from *Ha-Shomer Ha-Tza'ir* in its Trotskyist phase to Irgunist Zionist
Revisionism, was represented; and since the conservative ZOA was
the main source of financial support for college Zionists, seizure of
control by a left-dominated college generation could precipitate the
succession to power of protagonists of the right.

Such volatility was evident not only among students in the late
1930s and 1940s, when ideological issues became salient for all Zionists. Ideological, *halutz*-oriented youth groups sprouted everywhere.

The war brought America into the center of controversy,

involving world Zionist, and world Jewish, leadership, and the battles of the Biltmore Program, the American Jewish Conference, the Weizmann–Ben Gurion and Wise–Silver rivalries were all fought out before the American public. Zionist ranks were multiplied out of a full commitment to political aims. Under these conditions, it fell to the Americans to stand for all Jewry, through Abba Hillel Silver, and do battle shoulder to shoulder with the *Yishuv* before the United Nations for the creation of the Jewish State.

A Free Jewish Society

Most contemporary American Zionist leaders were active before 1948. Members of the generation born later find difficulty in becoming integrated in the Zionist establishment, and often seek alternative frameworks where they feel able to express themselves more freely. The creation of Israel is a crucial event for both generations: the elders face it as a challenge of their Zionism conceived before the State, and the young as rendering such Zionism untenable. Young and old alike assume that what is being questioned is the stereotyped "American Zionism." But the crisis is not related to the myth, or indeed to the historical actuality of Zionism as it concretely developed in the past. It relates to any possible version of Zionism, in its essential meaning.

With the creation of the State, all Zionist ideological differences based on diverging estimates of the likelihood and appropriate methods for achieving a sovereign Jewish homeland—for example, the actual differences between Herzl and Ahad Ha-Am—became obsolete. But this only posed in sharper outline the issue between "Herzlianism" and "Ahad Ha-Amism" in the unexplored terrain of achieved statehood. The possibility of a radical solution of anyone's Jewish problem by *aliyah* was now available; and so, too, was the prerequisite for an Ahad Ha-Amist solution of the "problem of Judaism"—a free Jewish society now existed to produce an authentic Hebrew culture for the invigoration of the Diaspora.

The destruction of East-European Jewry made this new test of Zionism more acute, and also more complicated. American Zionism was challenged in particular, since it remained not only the largest, but the preponderant part of the surviving Diaspora. It could no longer vicariously identify with Zionist solutions for either the "problem of the Jews" or the "problem of Judaism," solutions which supposedly

applied to other Jews and not to America. American Jews themselves
became those to whom the old Zionist solutions would have to apply if
they were still valid. And the established tradition of American Zionism, at least in its mainstream, had already sharply discounted the
applicability of the standard Zionist theories to the special American
situation.

In the ensuing years it became clear, that for the foreseeable
future, Israel's extraordinary success in absorbing entire Diaspora
communities in its first years was not to be followed by a similar radical solution of the problems of other Diaspora communities. Beginning
with the Hungarian Jews, a series of beleaguered Jewries—Algerian,
Chilean, Argentinian, Russian and even South African—chose in dismaying numbers not to accept the redemption which Israel freely
offered them, but sought other asylums now open to them. In such
circumstances the American insistence that *aliyah* was not relevant to
their situation became almost superfluous. It was evident that the
great western Diaspora would continue to exist side by side with Israel
indefinitely; and the problem now was the Ahad Ha-Amist "'problem
of Judaism," of which America itself was the prime example. It soon
became evident that neither Israel nor the Diaspora was capable of
turning the Ahad Ha-Amist vision of a prophetic Hebraism into the
common, institutionally realized, cultural norm of World Jewry.

One way of dealing with this crisis was to demand that both
Zionist solutions, Herzlian and Ahad Ha-Amist, be fully realized:
every Zionist must seek *aliyah* and Israel must become the true center
of Diaspora life. True, this synthetic approach ignores its own self-
contradiction, for it implies simultaneously negating and positing the
golah. But, in any case, the Diaspora, including American Zionists,
chose a different approach—one subject to the same illogic. Instead of
trying to realize fully the two opposed solutions at once, it succeeded
in applying them simultaneously by diluting both. In place of *aliyah*,
pilgrimages, short-term service and tourism became meritorious acts,
quasi-Zionist *mitzvot*. Instead of an authentic Hebraic prophetism,
Israeli dance and arts and crafts became the common coin of Diaspora
Jewish culture.

Zionism of this sort was now accepted as a general commitment
not only of Zionists but of the total Jewish community, in America and
elsewhere. Moreover, the whole community rallied to Israel's support
in both fields that had been the chief traditional concern of American
Zionism: social-economic aid and political backing. The immense

economic and political pressures that weighed on Israel were met by a response that caused Norman Podhoretz to say at a critical moment that American Jews had all become Zionists.

The enrolled and active Zionists, however, declined rather than increased in number. When, after the reconstitution of the extended Jewish Agency, the whole organized Jewish community shared in responsibility for supporting Israel, only those who were vitally concerned with Israel's internal policies (or who, like Hadassah, had specific responsibilities in Israel) needed to be Zionist members. The left-of-center ZOA members renounced party organization; secular Zionists generally became less involved, leaving the field to the right wing and *Mizrachi*. This was the case, at any rate, until recently, in good part because old left-leaning, secular Zionists could not feel that their membership was essential at a time when a labor regime controlled Israel. Precisely this circumstance strongly concerned right-wing and Orthodox Zionists.

The situation described above, together with local grievances, produced a revolt among young radical Zionists in the 1960s. Their activist rebellion was based on theories as eclectic—not to say confused—as those of the Establishment. They were maximalist in every direction, without regard to consistency: at once Herzlian and Ahad Ha-Amist, at once negators and positers of the *golah*. They found their way into organized Jewish life and into Zionist affairs, in the classic manner long accepted in America; they formed obstreperous outsider organizations and so compelled the Establishment to coopt them, as individuals and as organized groups.

The coexistence of Israel and the *golah* has led in America to a recrudescence of mildly anti-Zionist theoretical attitudes, often combined with practical cooperation with Zionism. Israel as a secular society compels American Jewry to justify itself more specifically as a religious community. Yet the centrifugal straining toward autonomous self-assertion is counterbalanced by a powerful centripetal force. The adherence of American Reform and Conservative organizations to the World Zionist Movement is a recent indicator of this trend.

The involvement of all American Jews in Israel's fate cannot stop short at supportive concern for the external threats and economic difficulties it encounters. How Israel achieves its destiny through the social structures it erects and the cultural forms it creates are matters no less vital to the Diaspora, even if Israeli values cannot easily be transported or intimately shared. The Zionist Movement is still the channel through which such concern can be responsibly expressed.

Comments

ALFRED GOTTSCHALK

American Zionism, as Ben Halpern so clearly indicated in his paper, has undergone a number of metamorphoses. Essentially different in its origin from European Zionism, it sought, nevertheless, to replicate, in part, the traditional Zionist "problems" which ultimately stress the question of *aliyah*, the inevitable and historic tension between the centrality of Eretz Israel and the notion of an autonomous Diaspora. The manner in which one approaches these classic Zionist problems ultimately depends on the functional *a priori* concepts with which the arguments are submitted. American Jewry is still fighting phantoms of the past: how to engage most effectively the classic principles of Zionism which must clearly argue for the centrality of Israel as a center of centers. This would harbor the essential idea that only in the center of centers can a Jew, however conditioned by the Diaspora, lead a full, Jewish national existence.

American Jewry's encounter with these classic proposals has at best been problematic. Their lure to a politically emancipated community, maximally assimilated, living with the least problematic tension of any Jewry in the world today, has posed a special problem, so far elusive of solution. The traditionalist right wing questions, from a very fundamental religious posture, the legitimacy of Israel. What an enigma is the homage paid to Orthodox "royalty," who on principle will neither visit nor settle in Israel!

Despite the non-recognition of Reform and Conservative Judaism *vis-à-vis* their legal rights in Israel, these two Movements represent, ideologically and numerically, the most formidable alliance for Israel in the Diaspora. Ben Halpern writes of the division between Herzlians concerned with "the problem of the Jews" and Ahad Ha-Amists concerned with "the problem of Judaism." Through the attempted resolution of the problem of Judaism, the Reform Movement, representing the modernistic expression of contemporary

57

Jewish movements, has demonstrated in recent times positive attachments to Israel. The "non-recognition" in Israel of the Reform Movement represents in contemporary terms a moral scandal; this must be
rectified if American Jewry in its most emancipated dimensions is to
continue its positive and vigorous response to *aliyah* and the idea of
the centrality of Israel in Jewish life. Lack of clarity with regard to the
status of Reform and Conservative Jews in Israel, the stigma attached
to their non-recognition, can hardly stir enthusiasm in the Diaspora for
an activated program leading to increased *aliyah*, or variations
thereof, which would involve spending a period of time in Israel.

Each of the programs initiated by the Reform Movement during
the last decade represents the realization of dreams of those individuals who themselves spent significant periods in Eretz Israel before
and after the creation of the State of Israel; they sensed that the lure of
Eretz Israel could work only through personal exposure of individuals
to the Land and People of Israel. From an ideological point of view,
the Reform Movement, representative of the Jews in the Diaspora and
Israel, who committed themselves to live as Jews without surrendering
their modernity, initiated programs that would tie young people, particularly the potential leadership of the Reform Movement, to Israel.
The decision to initiate a mandatory year of study in Israel for all
Reform rabbis, now enlarged to include Reform Jewish educators,
social workers and cantors, did not stem from a new theology or from
official Zionist establishments; it came from people who were personally convinced that the replication of their Israel experience would
immeasurably enrich the understanding of their Jewishness and
would increase the dimensions of living as a Jew in the modern world.
Existentialist realities rather than elaborate organizational plans led to
the initiation of the "year in Israel" program at Ma'aleh Ha-Hamishah
and the establishing of Kibbutz Yahel; or, more recently, to a program
for the training of rabbis for the Reform Movement in Israel, and the
Movement's decision to join the World Zionist Organization. The
sense of Jewish life in Israel, if not the quality, has acted as an impetus
to the leaders of the Reform Movement to send their young people
and their leaders to Israel, not in a trickle but in a growing and mighty
stream. Only recently, and reluctantly, did the Israel Zionist establishment "recognize" our presence, or attempted presence in Israel. Imagine the anomaly of a Conservative or Reform religious Jew compelled
to feel alienation and separation from the so-called established religious life in Israel, while the secularist unbeliever, or non-believer,

feels completely at home; this, because the religious community and its established agencies exercise the most limited moral suasion over him, although he is compelled in matters of personal status to comply with the religious establishment.

The sense of alienation experienced by religiously-oriented, modern Jews, termed Reform or Progressive today, should, perhaps, represent an intolerable state for modern Israelis. For all those in Israel who are searching for levels of Jewish identification and religious Jewish commitment, the reversion to *mindless* traditionalism represents one of the great risks to Judaism in our time. In the midst of our enormous cultural and scientific thrusts, the call to reaffirm the old rather than confront the new, will lead emancipated Jews of Israel and the Diaspora to withdraw from present and future religious establishments as long as these establishments maintain a policy of exclusion rather than inclusion.

There are forces of modernity working upon our young people over which we have no direct control. The new society that is emerging in the world of tomorrow is one that will be more universalist and less particularist. Today there is global communism and global capitalism. There will emerge a pan-culturalism that will extend to the secular existence of future generations. The manner of differentiation will be evident in their private, psychic, esthetic and religious lives. The one place where Jews will be able to develop collectively that new psychic space, so to speak, will be Eretz Israel. There new forms of Jewish identification will develop in community, and new expressions of religious fealty will emerge. That is not to say that these will not, and cannot, emerge in the Diaspora. What is at stake with their concurrent emergence in the Diaspora is their Jewish quantification in relation to the secular existence which will submerge the Jewish psyche more and more.

It is fair to say that internal developments within Reform Judaism in America are approaching dimensions of a hidden revolution. The outcome of revolutions is usually not predictable, but I would venture to posit that the new radicalism in Reform and in other religiously unaligned Jewish radical groupings represents, under the guise of a new universalism, the greatest threat to Jewish identity. These unaligned young people come not only from the Reform and secularist movements, or from the irreligious and unaffiliated groups, but from the ultra-Orthodox as well. Their unaligned status represents the radical deviation. The other element at work within the revolution among Jewish youth, who do remain aligned, is the need to find an authentic dimension of their Jewish experience, rooted in, or emerging from, their tradition but not confined or entrapped by it. To the extent that Zionist establishments, which include many of the old guard, appreciate the need to face this problem, to that extent is there a chance of having these elements emerge victorious in the hidden revolution presently at work. To the extent that these needs are not recognized, to that extent is the risk of losing the present generation and the revolution increased.

It is the intention of those who are aligned with the modernistic expression of religious Judaism, called today Reform or Progressive, to recognize within the miracle that is modern Israel the Jewish dimensions of their own being. Students of Hebrew Union College in Jerusalem, members of Kibbutz Yahel and the second kibbutz that is presently in the process of being created, members of the Progressive Movement aligned with congregations and other social organizations in Israel, thousands of young people who are sent by the Reform Movement to Israel each year as students and as prospective settlers, those who come on their own seeking an open-ended expression of their Jewish spiritual dimension—all represent the avant-garde of the new Zionism which is in the process of being defined. A new Judaism is arising in Eretz Israel and in other related centers of Jewish life, a Judaism in which Zionism and modernity are inextricably and irrevocably bound together.

CHARLOTTE JACOBSON

Ben Halpern is undoubtedly correct in his analysis of the antecedents of the Zionist movement in the United States, its organizational forms and even the framework of its immigrant origins. *Aliyah* has not been high on the agenda of American Zionism even after the creation of the State of Israel. Indeed, *aliyah* did not achieve respectability in general Zionist circles until the last dozen years or so. It was downplayed all these years, not out of fear that the "dual loyalty" charge would be raised, but more simply because earlier Zionists, being themselves either immigrants or the children of immigrants, were psychologically and emotionally unprepared for yet another migration—even to the Jewish Homeland. The American Jewish community today is in its third generation, and while it may or may not be true that "what the children strive to forget, the grandchildren want to remember," it is true that the trauma of movement from one country to another with all the attendant strains and difficulties—language, culture, livelihood, social absorption, and such like—have receded into the background, far enough and deep enough for American Jews not to recoil from the very concept, as they did for so long.

The "fluctuations to which the American men's General Zionist membership is subject" is to a great extent a function of the image the men's movements created of themselves, as primarily political movers. As a result, the sharpest drop in their membership came when the State of Israel was born in 1948. The political job was done; political activity would be no longer needed. "Friends of Israel" of one kind or another—primarily for fund raising—could take the place of "Zionist" groups. The problem did not develop in Hadassah, for example, which not only retained its membership levels but grew steadily through the years, because it did not define itself in purely political terms. It had, in addition to political activity, two important sources of strength: a rich Jewish educational program, and serious Israel project commitments, strong enough to retain the loyalties of literally hundreds of thousands of women by giving them a sense of individual participation in the building of Israel.

Professor Halpern is correct in saying that "members of the generation born later (after 1948) find difficulty in becoming integrated in the Zionist establishment." However, this is not because of a particular perception of American Zionism, but because they see too much of the American Zionist establishment as pale counterparts of Israeli political parties (which themselves derive from Diaspora origins). Hadassah would once again bear me out: not being a reflection of Israel partisanship, it never had to struggle with the twists and turns of a party waging its battles in the arena of Israeli political life.

Professor Halpern refers to "a series of beleaguered Jewries" which chose "in dismaying numbers" to go to countries other than Israel, but gives no indication why they made such a choice; there is only the implication that it was a failure of Zionist ideology or Zionist organization. The fact should suggest not simply that the Movement is at fault, but that there are elements on the Israeli scene which weaken its attraction for so many Diaspora Jews. It would be simplistic to state the obvious fact that the quality of life in Israel leaves something to be desired. Certainly it is true that the hostility of the surrounding Arabs and the series of wars Israel has had to fight is a major contributing factor in the choice these people make. An increase in emigration from the Western countries, particularly from the United States, in the wake of the Israeli-Egyptian peace process would seem to confirm this analysis. I might add, too, that every "flare-up" of peace hopes produces a reaction among Israeli *yordim* (emigrants), too, and more of them have been returning to Israel.

Even before the so-called "peace initiative" was started, however there was a tendency towards affiliation with Zionism—with Establishment Zionism at that. American Reform and Conservative religious organizations joined the World Zionist Organization, the result of "a powerful centripetal force," in Professor Halpern's words. And they found their way into the Movement despite all the problems he cites.

Professor Halpern himself, in the final analysis, finds that "the Zionist Movement is still the channel through which [such] concern can be responsibly expressed." It would seem, then, that there is not the crisis in Zionism that he posits earlier in his paper. What I see is not a crisis, but another historical challenge and an opportunity to offer a viable Zionist ideology which can attract the younger generation of American Jews.

To do this, we must return to basics, to the major thrust of early Zionism, which was concerned with creating an ideal society in Eretz Israel: cooperation with Arab neighbors and the spiritual dimension of life in the Jewish State—Ahad Ha-Amism, if you please, but not reduced to mere "concern for Judaism"—a formulation which Ahad Ha-Am himself would have scorned as a distortion of his views. Indeed, he explained himself very clearly in words written in 1903-04:

> Palestine will become our spiritual center only when the Jews are a majority of the population and own most of the land . . . I am told every day that I am exclusively "spiritual," and that my ideal is to establish in Palestine a "heavenly Jerusalem" where unpractical idealists will sit and bask in the radiance of "divine presence." This is a lie, invented long ago by my opponents, which has gained currency. If that were really my ideal, I should not have given so much time and energy to the practical work of Palestinian colonization, nor should I have made a study, as I have done to the best of my ability, of the methods of agricultural settlement in Palestine.
>
> The truth is that one single word led to all the misunderstanding . . . Actually I called Zionism a "spiritual" movement only in relation to its end and purpose: that is to say, Zionism cannot put an end to the material Jewish problem, because not all the Jews can migrate to Palestine, and therefore the object of our movement is only to create for

our people a national center, the influence of which on the *Diaspora* will be spiritual only, in the sense that it will strengthen their morale, increase their sense of unity, and provide a suitable content for their life as Jews. But it is obvious that a national center cannot come into existence, and cannot create a new type of life, if it is purely spiritual. It must obviously include all the elements necessary to a nation, from agricultural laborers and craftsmen to the purest intellectuals.[1]

It would be the "pull" of Israel that would generate *aliyah*, not oppression or fear in the Diaspora; it would be cultural and spiritual pioneering, grafted on to physical pioneering, which would help create the society our early Zionists dreamed of and for which they made their sacrifices. The challenge is before us; it is up to us to promote an adequate response.

EMANUEL RACKMAN

Professor Halpern's analysis is concise and insightful. More ought be said, however, about the relationship in the future between American Judaism and American Zionism.

Until the seventies, the World Zionist Organization had only one party committed to Judaism as a religion—*Mizrachi*, and Judaism was understood to be *halakhic* Judaism. This was also true of the American scene. Leaders of American Zionism who were Reform, Conservative or Reconstructionist identified with parties other than *Mizrachi*, and their different conceptions of Judaism were not represented as such in Zionist forums. Perhaps they did not believe that Orthodoxy in Israel would ever mobilize more than a small minority of Israel's population and they temporarily deferred to the voices of the past or were content to let secularism prevail, hoping that Israel would develop its own indigenous religious orientation.

In the seventies there was a great change. The overwhelming majority of Reform rabbis were now Zionists, and within the Reform Movement itself, the non-Zionists, or anti-Zionists, had fallen from grace. Conservative rabbis and their congregations had always been Zionists—they were mostly the children or grandchildren of East-European immigrants who were Orthodox and, even if not members of *Mizrachi*, ardent devotees of the Jewish national renascence. They were sensitive to the fact that for all their unrelenting devotion to the

1. See *Ahad Ha-Am: Essays, Letters and Memoirs*, Leon Simon, ed. & tr., Oxford, 1946, pp. 282ff.

cause of Israel, their religious commitment was regarded as heresy by Israel's religious establishment.

At the same time, Jewish secularism was losing ground. American Jews were organized principally in synagogues; religious commitment and Jewish education were "a mile long and an inch deep" but almost every approach had to achieve respectability by calling itself Judaism. It was important to belong to a congregation and the congregation had to belong to a national congregational body and the national congregational body had to organize an international movement and the international movement had to seek recognition from the World Zionist Organization. At the same time there were centrifugal forces magnifying the religious pluralism of American Judaism even as centripetal forces were bringing all together into larger bodies which wanted a substantial share of the purse—the campaigns for Israel and local needs.

The implications for Zionism in general and American Zionism in particular are significant. First, American Zionism will have to deal hereafter with many more "lists" in Zionist elections. Not only political parties which have counterparts in Israel will submit candidates, but also the religious groups—at least three of them.

Second, because of the pressure of the American religious groups, the World Zionist Organization may be forced to play a role in the achievement of a so-called "religious pluralism" in Israel. That campaign has already begun. But it is really legal pluralism that is being sought. Israel has both religious pluralism and legal pluralism, but it is the latter pluralism that Reform and Conservative Judaism want to expand.

Third, the religious groups will generally seek to achieve Israel's recognition of the legitimacy of the Diaspora. They will be loath to yield to Israel the final word as to what is best for Jews and/or Judaism. They will seek to be equal partners in decisions affecting the destiny of our People and its heritage.

As all of this takes place in the arena of the most eclectic Judaism ever known in Jewish history, many Orthodox Jews will be leaving the Zionist Movement and alienate themselves from Israel and its fate. This sad process has already begun. It is especially Orthodox Jews and non-Zionist Reform Jews who are least dismayed that so many Russian Jews opt to go to the United States rather than to Israel. They feel that the United States is safer for religious commitment than Israel.

The alienation of many American Orthodox Jews from the Zionist Movement will also cause those Orthodox Jews who remain, to be less responsive to the views and programs of the non-Orthodox. The alienated will be those who generally favor minimum contact with the non-Orthodox and certainly non-recognition of their "heresies." Their separatism from the general Jewish community will induce an ambivalence in those Orthodox Jews who do not want to separate from their coreligionists. On the one hand, they will be committed to the notion that we are one People with an indivisible fate; on the other hand, they will require for the survival of their Orthodoxy the zeal of the extremists who will be manning most of their synagogues and schools. This dependency will make them less zealous and articulate in the cause of Jewish unity and less tolerant of religious differences as they fear the loss of their own children to the non-Orthodox camps. Very often such ambivalence causes their children either to join the extremists or to forfeit Orthodoxy altogether.

This is also a partial explanation for the fact that most Orthodox Jews in America are no longer identified with *Mizrachi.* The members of *Mizrachi* are by far outnumbered by those in the Hasidic as well as the *yeshivah* world. And among the few who remain organizationally and ideologically within the World Zionist Organization, one finds all the ideological divisions that one finds in Israel's Religious Zionist party—the *Mafdal.* Almost none have identified with the *Breira* group in the United States, but many of them are fervent supporters of *Gush Emunim,* while others are more inclined to seek a peace that is costly in territorial terms.

What must be reckoned with is that so illustrious a non-Zionist as the Rebbe of Lubavitch is encouraging support for the position of *Gush Emunim.* His proclamations hardly differ from those of Rabbi Tzvi Yehudah Hacohen Kook in Israel. His supporters all over the world are legion. Rabbi Joseph B. Soloveitchik, on the other hand, is far less militant—even dovish. Can one account for the different views by reference to the fact that, of the two, Dr. Soloveitchik is by far the more exposed to, and the more involved in, the non-Jewish spheres of living, so that the Diaspora has had more of an effect on him than on the "Rebbe" who sees issues almost exclusively within the written and oral traditions of Judaism?

One should not come to hasty conclusions. A psychological interpretation may be more correct. The Lubavitcher is by nature a militant—bold, courageous, defiant. Dr. Soloveitchik is by nature apprehensive, ambivalent, cautious. Both have hosts of admirers and many disciples, and the Orthodox Jews in America who remain within the Zionist Movement will reflect the two views.

One hesitates to speak about the future. It is very possible that American Orthodoxy will also produce an *aliyah* movement that will take advantage of the Israel government's subsidization of *aliyah* but will be hostile to the World Zionist Organization. Many American *yeshivot* have already made *aliyah*, although some damn the State even as they damn the Zionists. Too many of them could even endanger Israel's sovereignty—they often prefer a benign non-Jewish sovereign to a Jew alienated from Torah. This group is the American counterpart to Israel's *Neturei Karta*. But even among the Orthodox they constitute a tiny minority. Most of America's Orthodox Jews identify either with the Rebbe of Lubavitch or with Rabbi Soloveitchik or take a position between the two.

Both of these leaders are committed to the development of an American-based Judaism with at least as much status as that of Israel's Judaism. They do not demean Israel as a center but they deny its centrality. They feel confident that they can establish in the Western hemisphere another Babylon, which in many respects will be more representative of what they hold Judaism to be than Israel can possibly achieve. Israel, they feel, precisely because it spells state as well as land, is subject to many corrupting factors. The purer faith can live— at least until the Messiah comes—with the Divine Presence in the Diaspora. They love Jews too much not to identify wholeheartedly with Israel, its trials and tribulations. Occasionally they see divine intervention in Israel's miraculous history. But their principal prescription for Israel's survival is *teshuvah*—penitence—a return to God and *Torah*. Though few men understand the realities of the present situation better than they, the two prefer to be eschatological with regard to Israel's future, concentrating on the teaching of *Torah* and the propagation of the faith. The Rebbe of Lubavitch engages more in missionary work; Rabbi Soloveitchik appeals to the intelligentsia.

But most Orthodox Jews are practical—like other Jews and other people. Their Zionism, though based on the messianic ideal, involves a commitment to the preservation of the Jewish People and the Jewish heritage in the face of the challenges of the here and now. They support all movements for the propagation of *Torah*, and they welcome the thousands who, each year, return to the faith. However, they feel impelled to act quickly on behalf of the tens of thousands who are being lost through intermarriage and assimilation. They are convinced that only an Israel-centered Judaism can stem the assimilatory tide in the Diaspora. The *Torah* taught in New York may be superior to that taught in Zion, but Zion does more to revive the sense of Jewish identity in the multitudes everywhere than *Torah* by itself can possibly do now. Therefore, they want to join hands with all Jews who deem the centrality of Israel as a must for Jewish survival. They give to the UJA and buy Israel bonds; above all, they visit Israel and send their children there to study or work, in the *yeshivot* or in the universities, in the *moshavim* or in the *kibbutzim*. They are not so sanguine as to believe that survival of *Torah* in America is possible without the "ghettoization" which the Lubavitcher encourages and which Rabbi Soloveitchik does not like, but cannot prevent even among his own students, who are becoming increasingly rightist and separatist in their outlook. This is the view held by American Orthodox Jews who are still active in the Zionist Movement and regard Zionism not merely as a program for the establishment and securing of a Jewish State but as a program for the survival of the Jewish People and the Jewish heritage.

For those Orthodox Jews, the State itself has a religious significance not generally attributed to states. Since the State of Israel is a major instrument for a religious end—the survival of Jews and Judaism—it is endowed with a measure of holiness. The Rebbe of Lubavitch and Rabbi Soloveitchik may equivocate on this. Many among those who are not their committed disciples do not.

In any event, religious pluralism exists not only in American Judaism but in American Orthodoxy. Perhaps one should be grateful for it. Pluralism shows that there are people who still think for themselves and care.

MICHAEL WALZER

Background conditions of Zionist activity in the United States do indeed make the life of American Jews "more than tolerable," as Ben Halpern says, but, at the same time they make Zionism very problematic, as his paper also suggests.

The United States is first of all a modern and a liberal society. These words describe the triumph in theory, if not always in practice, of universal values: political secularism, religious tolerance, legal equality, cultural cosmopolitanism, the career open to talents. The triumph of these values has been a matter of long struggle. They have had to be fought for, and Jews have been in the forefront of that fight in the United States, as in the West generally. From some point in the middle of the nineteenth century, for all their marginality, Jews have never been marginal to the struggles of the political Left. And the outcome of those struggles has been, among other things, our own emancipation. Emancipation of Western Jewry has been, at least in part, an auto-emancipation—though of a special sort. Jews have been liberated, have liberated themselves, as individuals, not only from the physical constraints of the ghetto, not only from the legal discrimination and repression of Gentile governments, but also from the authority of the Jewish community itself. The emancipation of individuals was not possible in Eastern Europe (hence the power of both socialism and Zionism), but it is now virtually complete in the West.

This is not to suggest that Jewish participation in the struggle for liberal universality has been a kind of communal suicide. Western liberalism has taken on broadly pluralist forms, especially in the United States where Jewish organizational life flourishes. Since the community has no coercive power, it is possible for individual men and women to get up and walk out. It is also possible for them to drift away, to move toward the margins of Jewishness, even without knowing when they have actually separated themselves from the community. In a liberal and pluralist society Jewishness has no boundaries. This movement of individuals into an open and secular world is one form of assimilation, but there is another form, which is more characteristic of American Jewry and more directly relevant to our subject here.

"We are in grave danger," Hayim Greenberg wrote in 1951, "of becoming merely an ethnic group in the conventional sense of the term . . . No more Congregation of Israel, but only a group with a long and heroic history . . ." Now, more than a quarter century later, the danger looms larger, though it has not yet been fully realized. The very term *American Jews* is a sign that we are not yet merely an ethnic group. In the United States, there are Black-Americans, Italian-Americans, Irish-Americans, but there are no Jewish-Americans. Our Americanism is not hyphenated but adjectival; it modifies our Jewishness, perhaps in profound and extensive ways, but leaves its basic character intact, at least potentially. An Italian-American is not much of an Italian. An American Jew is still, or can be, very much a Jew.

Nevertheless, ethnicity is clearly the exilic form of normalization. As Israel is a state among the states of the world, so American Jews are one among the ethnic groups of a pluralist society. There is, however, an important difference in these two forms of normality: states have staying power, while in "the perspective of history," as Greenberg wrote, the acceptance of ethnicity "means to be without a future." Greenberg was writing before the recent period of ethnic affirmation and revival in the United States, but the "new ethnicity" does not contradict his argument. Ironically, ethnic affirmation has to a considerable extent been an imitation (first of all by Black-Americans) of the commitment and solidarity attributed to the Jews. We know, however, that this solidarity has sources and reasons which an explanation in ethnic terms cannot reach. Nor are we likely to retain our solidarity if, as Halpern suggests, "the common coin of Diaspora Jewish culture" is, or becomes, say, Israeli arts and crafts. For we have always traded in a different and infinitely more valuable currency.

The problem faced by American Jews, then, is precisely the Ahad Ha-Amist "problem of Judaism." It is a problem which has to do with religion, culture, education, the solution to which must have its starting point not in Zionism, that is, not in a merely political orientation toward the State of Israel, but in Jewishness itself. "'Zionism should be," Greenberg argued, "the natural product of an organic education to Jewishness." The question is whether it is possible, under American conditions, to seek a status beyond ethnicity, a more intensive particularity than that of other groups in American society.

In a limited sense, it is easy to give an affirmative answer. We already have a more intense connection to Israel than any other group of Americans has to any other country. And that intensity is virtually unchallenged in American political life today. For those Jews who anguished so fearfully over the perils of dual loyalty, the present situation must seem amazing. We may explain it in terms of the support that exists among American Gentiles for Israel as a Jewish State—support that has pluralist reasons (as befits a pluralist society): moral, strategic, evangelical, and so on. But I suspect that the willingness to tolerate our Zionist loyalties has to do, above all, with the willingness to tolerate us, and that, in turn, has to do with how similar to other Americans we have become. We are not, and we do not look like, dangerous people among our Gentile neighbors—not alien or exotic or, for that matter, chosen people. Whatever our peculiar feelings about Israel, we share the general moral values of our society; indeed, we helped create those values. By and large, we live by them. If we did not, things might be harder.

The real question is not about hardness but easiness. We are at ease in exile and, under the conditions of liberal emancipation, we have every reason to expect continued ease. But persecution, intolerance and isolation, it might be said, have always been the necessary spurs to Jewish commitment in the Diaspora. Even current intensity of feeling derives from the Arab threat to Israel's existence—a geographically distant but visible danger, echoing our memories of the Holocaust. But imagine peace, real peace, in the Middle East, and where would we be? Eating rye bread and blintzes, telling Jewish jokes, contributing (less and less) to the UJA, stumbling through the Haggadah at Passover, touring Israel in the summer? Most of us would continue to offer political support to Israel; a smaller number would be observant in traditional ways; more generally, we would be ethnic Jews . . . What else awaits us in the liberal and pluralist society of the United States?

A picture of this kind, however, is nothing more than the projection into the future of certain contemporary tendencies. It is not clear, in fact, that the actual experience of liberal universality and of mere ethnicity will prove all that satisfying. Universality is an empty space into which we must bring our own cultural belongings, and ethnicity is a way of travelling light—so that we may well arrive and find ourselves inadequately furnished for a long stay and a meaningful existence. It would not be surprising if the ethnic revival of recent years were one day superseded by a more genuine renascence.

Jews need not yield to current tendencies; we can also resist them. Zionism is the call to that resistance. To some degree, success depends upon the development in Israel of a new and vital Jewish life: that is what Zionists have always argued. But we can see today that resistance must also have an exilic basis, a ground of its own apart from Eretz Israel. For other American ethnic groups are not much enriched by the culture of the "home" country, however vital it is. Only a strong sense of our own identity as Jews, and of the value of that identity *even in America*, will enable us to receive from Israel something more than arts and crafts.

MORDECAI WAXMAN

There are more members of Zionist organizations in the United States today than at any time in the past and fewer Zionists. On the other hand, concern with Israel is almost universal among American Jews. This anomaly owes much to the way that Zionism was understood and promulgated in the United States, both before and after the creation of Israel. It owes perhaps even more to the nature of America and the Jewish relationship to the American scene.

In the early part of the century and up to 1948, most American Jews were either immigrants or the children of immigrants. Their primary concern was to integrate themselves into the American environment linguistically, culturally and economically. Fundamentally, they did improve their lot over the course of a generation, and while anti-Semitism was not absent, it did not take the virulent and violent form it did in Eastern Europe. Economic betterment and acculturation went hand in hand with greater physical security and political freedom. And so, at no time, was the original immigrant generation open to the possibility of settling in the Land of Israel. There were exceptions, of course, but the great majority of Jews in the United States had already done all the immigrating that they were going to do.

Moreover, the prevalent tone in American life early in the century militated against a clear proclamation of Herzlian goals for American Jews. America saw itself as a melting pot, in which ethnicity and cultural differences were ingredients—not to be preserved, but rather mingled together to produce a homogeneous American type. The school system considered it its function to contribute to this process and to put the American stamp on the immigrant youth. In this climate, political Zionism posed some theoretical problems, theoretical because no one really saw them as applying to American Jews and because no one really believed that a Jewish State would become a reality in his lifetime. The implicit issue involved in political Zionism led to frequent debates on the question "Are Jews a religion, a race or a nation," which were never really resolved. The term "people," which became common, provided a useful evasion, and the term "peoplehood," which was associated with Mordecai Kaplan and others, provided a useful theoretical formulation, although it was never really widely used.

While the outward political role and impact of the Zionist movements in this country were limited by American Zionist expectations and by the American scene, they did, prior to the 1940s, lay significant foundations for the future. They were active and vocal enough to convince the political world that Jews were concerned with Palestine; they were able, through the *Po'alei Zion* and the Jewish labor unions, to establish relations with the labor movement which proved increasingly important in later years. They succeeded in creating an awareness—in political, journalistic and some intellectual circles—of Zionism, of Eretz Israel as a place of social experiment, of a Jewish flag and of a Jewish People. In the public relations area, therefore, there was some fulfilment of the Herzlian vision of a changed image of the Jew.

It was in internal Jewish life, however, that the impact of the Zionist Movement was most marked. In the first place, Zionist parties, conventions and the Zionist Congress provided a political outlet for Jews who had not yet become significant factors in American politics. Here was a cause, with some semblance of a democratic process and with a Jewish Parliament, of a kind, on a national and international basis. All of these were relatively new in Jewish experience. They combined to make the Zionist Movement the most dynamic element in Jewish life in America at the time.

More significantly, if less obviously, Zionism resulted, in a variety of ways, in *kibbush ha-kehillot*, in the sort of conquest of the community which was a platform in the programs of European Zionism. In America, this was not a formally recognized and adopted program but rather the result of the activities of people who were engaged in key Jewish activities and brought a Zionist perspective to them. It was particularly manifest in the area of education. The movement of revival of the Hebrew language, which began with the Haskalah in Europe, was associated in the United States with the Zionist cause. While most Zionists were not Hebraists, all Hebraists were Zionists. This concern for the use of the Hebrew language, which expressed itself on the educational level of the schools as a method of teaching *Ivrit be-Ivrit*, became a dominant feature of the new curriculum being introduced by the young Americans who were building up the boards of Jewish education throughout the United States. They were largely products of the Teachers Institute of the Jewish Theological Seminary and were further associated with Dr. Benderly. Simultaneously, they were all Zionists. They brought in a new curriculum and created what was to become the dominant pattern of education in the community schools and in the afternoon Hebrew schools of the more modern kind. Substantially, it was a curriculum which emphasized Zionism and the Hebrew language and taught the conventional subjects from a nationalist and Haskalah perspective. Thus, starting from the children's level in many of the newer and better schools, the Zionist outlook was widely disseminated.

But the brand of Zionism being disseminated owed far more to

Ahad Ha-Am than to Herzl. The teachers of the new dispensation were largely products of the Haskalah, or derivations of it, and they saw Zionism, in many respects, as a movement of cultural renascence. There were two forms to this Ahad Ha-Amism, a secular and a religious one. Secular Zionists found in the concept of the Land of Israel as a place for the creation of a renewed Hebrew culture which would impinge upon the Diaspora, a reason for Jewish being and identification which they could accept, even while they rejected the religious outlook of Judaism. The religious version was perhaps peculiar to America, and especially to the Conservative Movement, the only one of the three religious bodies identifying itself with the Zionist idea from the very beginnings of both the idea and the Conservative outlook. Ahad Ha-Am and Zionism were thoroughly acceptable to the Conservative view, which stressed the needs of the Jewish People as well as God and Torah, in distinction from the Reform, which stressed God and ethics, and Orthodoxy, which emphasized Torah. The Ahad Ha-Amist position, that the Jewish national organism sought different forms in different eras to guarantee its existence and that, in the modern era, a dedication to the ethical should replace the religious, could be accepted with modifications by the Conservative Movement. It could, indeed, imply consciousness of peoplehood and a consequent dedication to Jewishness as a surrogate for religious feeling, while insisting that the form in which such commitment was expressed was religious, ritualistic and synagogal. At the same time, it could envision the cultural revival which would flourish in the Land of Israel in circumstances where the Jewish genius would be free to follow its national form as, essentially, a religious renewal.

Since 1948, the Zionist movement in America has lost much of the role it enjoyed in earlier years. The political role has been seized by Israel, which not only can talk foreign policy, but make it. In the U.S., the support of virtually every American Jewish organization for Israel has caused the Zionist movements to be only a few among many supporters of the Jewish State, and only a small fraction of the members of the Conference of Presidents of Major Jewish Organizations, now the recognized American representative of the Jewish community to the American Government on matters relating to Israel.

Fund raising, too, has passed beyond the ken of the Zionist movements. The major work of the UJA and of Bonds, and the efforts for various institutions in Israel now involve people who never were members of the Zionist movements.

The Zionist movements in America have thus substantially lost

their historical functions. The exception is Hadassah, whose membership has expanded greatly without really being committed to a Zionist
ideology, and whose role and function does not really depend on ideology. Since the Zionist movements, despite occasional restructurings,
have not generated new goals, and since *aliyah* which Israel continues
to insist is the essential Zionist function, is not now, and never has
been, on top of the agenda, the Zionist movements in America are
organizations in search of a role. Zionism elsewhere is in much the
same situation.

In this same period of the last thirty years, the American Jewish
community developed along lines which had been adumbrated
before, but which now sealed its destiny as an ongoing Diaspora community and negated the premises of both Herzlian and Ahad Ha-
Amist Zionism.

In the first place, it achieved a status unprecedented in Jewish
history. Ahad Ha-Am had described two states of the Jewish People in
his time. He characterized one as "slavery in the midst of freedom"
and deprecated the assimilationist tendencies of Western European
Jewry. On the other hand, he described East-European Jewry as being
in a state of "freedom in the midst of slavery." He did not envision a
state of *herut be-tokh herut,* of "freedom in the midst of freedom" as
applying to a Diaspora community. Yet it is precisely this status that
American Jewry has been enjoying for the last three decades. Its numbers, its general education, its affluence, its position in American life,
its political role and the number and variety of its organizations and
institutions, have given it a unique status. Anti-Semitism has diminished considerably, partly as a result of the Holocaust, partly as a
result of the existence of Israel, just as Zionist theory had predicted.
On the other hand, American Jews have been strengthened in their
Jewish identity precisely because of Israel's existence and have
played a significant political role in promoting the welfare of Israel,
which Zionist theory did not predict.

The "freedom within freedom" status of American Jewry has
had two unanticipated effects. The Zionist thesis that anti-Semitism
would force either the departure of the Jew to Israel or his disappearance in the Diaspora has not been borne out. The second is that the
Jewish world is, indeed, contracting as problems grow in various parts
of the world, but a significant number of the Jews from such countries
as Iran and South Africa and the U.S.S.R. are coming to the United
States and not to Israel.

Ahad Ha-Am's thesis has also been invalidated by events. The United States clearly has been able to produce a vital and varied Jewish culture of high quality, which has doubtless been influenced by the existence of Israel and by interaction with it, but which can stand on its own feet. Forty years ago, United States Jewry was, indeed, much dependent on European Jewry. In the intervening years, "the kids have become goats." More to the Ahad Ha-Am point, Israel has not yet produced the autonomous and creative Jewish culture which can be exported to the American Diaspora.

The major problem is that American Jewry, with all its secular trends, is organized in religious terms and around religious institutions. The character of religious Judaism in America is pluralistic. In the triad of religious outlooks, Orthodoxy is the smallest. Israel, on the other hand, recognizes and allows only varieties of the Orthodox outlook, discourages pluralism, and has made religion essentially a ritualistic, legalistic civil service instead of a potential moral and spiritual force. That sort of religion is not speaking to American Jewry and is incapable of speaking to it. Yet it is precisely new outlooks and a new spirit, born in an autonomous Jewish state, which American Jewry craves.

In the light of these considerations, what can an American Zionism or, indeed, any Zionism, espouse today which will make it once again an active and creative power in Jewish life?

One answer to the question is that Zionism must stand for something different and superior to what the bulk of the community— which already supports Israel—affirms. Its contention that it is differentiated by an insistence upon *aliyah* as the mark of Zionism may be accurate enough, but it neither generates enthusiasm for Zionism nor leads to *aliyah*. Indeed, an examination of *olim* from America probably will reveal that many of them were never formally Zionists. The only significant role for Zionism is to proclaim that it has an unfulfilled program other than *aliyah*, and, by advocating it, create the conditions which might promote *aliyah* from the West.

History has turned the original Zionist thesis on its head. Zionism originally contended that it was bent on establishing a normal nation which would make the Jewish People in its homeland like all the nations. Nonetheless, early Zionists recognized that the road to that normalcy was through their own abnormality, their willingness to create new social and economic forms, their readiness to recreate a language at grave emotional cost, their willingness to fashion their

children in a new and different image, and their commitment to sac-
rificing for the cause decade after decade. Once their abnormality had
achieved the miracle, most Israelis were prepared to revert to the normal. In consequence, the Jewish State has lost some of the awe of
wonder, of social idealism and of resolution to be unique, which characterized it in the past. The world thereupon betrayed it and refuted
Zionist theory by demonstrating that it was not prepared to treat Israel
as a normal state, but as a totally abnormal one. Israel has not solved
the Jewish problem; it has simply changed its nature.

Contemporary Zionism must revert to the religious thesis that
Israel is unique among the nations. "Israel," said Martin Buber, "is not
another example of the species nation; it is the only example of the
species Israel." In recognizing that Zionism belongs within the religious cultural dimension, the movement will necessarily address itself
to the Jewish quality of the State of Israel rather than solely to its
political existence. It will be asserting that the Jewish State is a place
in which Jewish social ideals are to be realized, in which the value of
the Jewish tradition is to be made evident, in which there will be an
attempt to deal with the major problems of Jewish existence, of Jewish
religion and of Jewish law adequate to the needs of the time. In a
sense, it will be reaffirming that which was the basic approach of the
American Conservative Movement. In the process it will be recreating
Zionism as a cause which is rooted in the history of the people and
carries messianic overtones translated into realizable objectives.

Whether fairly or unfairly, the Jewish People expects to see in
Israel a realization of ideal goals and a validation of Jewish history. It
is precisely because Israel came into being on the heels of the Holocaust and has done so much for the Jewish image and self-image that
most Jews are not prepared to see it lapse into the ordinary and be of
less than heroic stature.

There is another role for the Zionist Movement in our time
which arises out of unexpected circumstances. The interdependence
of Israel and the Diaspora is so great that, contrary to Zionist theory, it
represents a new fact to be dealt with. There is no reason to think that
it will diminish nor is there reason to expect that the American Diaspora will disappear in the perceptible future. What Israel does can
have a major effect upon the Diaspora and what the Diaspora does, or
fails to do, can vitally affect Israel. This is certainly true in the realm of
Jewish affairs and no less true of the impact of Israeli foreign policy
upon Diaspora communities. In consequence, there is a need for an

overarching body of the Jewish People in which there can be an exchange of opinion and a formulation of policy for the people as a whole rather than for a segment of it. Obviously, this is an especially delicate matter for which no prototype exists, but the problem of the Jewish People is a unique one. The nearest thing to a Parliament for the Jewish People is the Zionist Congress and its agencies. Indeed, prior to the creation of the State, it served such a purpose. Today, it and the General Zionist Council are essentially devoid of purpose and function, but the Jewish Agency Executive does dispose of the funds of the Jewish world. The mechanism for a significant body exists if its role and its mode of organization could be revised and its party structure abandoned. Passion and purpose might be revived and Zionism might again become a cause if the Zionist Movement became the agency through which the dispersed Jewish People, both in Israel and the Diaspora, could address itself to its collective needs and redefine the goals to which Jews should aspire in this new and exciting era of their history.

Latin America

Haim Avni

A classic conception of Zionism, one which is still widely accepted today, was formulated by Theodor Herzl and Max Nordau at the First Zionist Congress in 1897. Very simply, it held that Zionism is, in fact, motivated and strengthened by "the affliction of the Jews," providing the only solution to the catastrophes and physical dangers threatening the existence of the Jews everywhere.

The brutal "affliction of the Jews," which reached its nadir in the Holocaust, did show that the diagnosis of "catastrophe Zionism" was correct. However, with the emergence of open societies in the West and the development of a politically vigorous Jewish community in the United States, the reality of this Jewish affliction has receded. Those who based their Zionism exclusively on the lessons of this affliction were in a state of quandary: they had lost sight of other aspects of Jewish existence which have their origins in the non-Jewish majority societies.

One of these aspects, the legitimacy of the Jewish presence within the host society, comes clearly to the fore when we examine the situation of the Jews in Latin America.

Jewish Settlement in Latin America

The legal basis for Jewish existence in all Latin American countries—with the exception of the Dutch and British colonies in the Caribbean and Guyana—was in the process of formation even before the advent of any substantial Jewish presence there. Until the wars of independence giving rise to the Latin American nations in the first quarter of the nineteenth century, this sub-continent was *judenrein*—at least officially and legally. The few Jews who had succeeded in entering did so clandestinely or in the guise of Christians. Then, as a result of processes in which the Jews had no part, the constitutional structure of society in Latin American lands changed. Individual Jews were allowed to settle, unmolested, in those countries; and by the second half of the nineteenth century, conditions had been created for their open existence as a community. Thus the Jews who came to Latin America at the end of the nineteenth century and in the early part of the twentieth, found themselves in societies whose legal norms were no longer inconsistent with the existence of an organized Jewish community in their midst.

Even so, considerable variations may be noted in the legal infrastructure which determines the position of various Jewish communities in Latin America. In Argentina, which has by far the largest Jewish community on the continent, there is no full separation between Church and State. Mexican Jewry lies at the other extreme. The revolutionary constitution adopted in Mexico in 1917 not only established absolute separation of Church and State, but restricted the activities of the Catholic Church and drastically curtailed its influence. Between these two poles we find the other Latin American countries; in none of these can the Jews point to existing legislation directed explicitly against them. Notwithstanding certain limitations in several of the Latin American countries, we are dealing with legally emancipated and apparently prosperous Jewish communities.

Nevertheless, the mere legality of Jewish existence in a given region does not necessarily spell complete emancipation. For the Jews to achieve full equality—as individuals and as a community—another dimension is required.

Emancipation versus Tolerance

"Zionism is a return to Judaism, even before a return to the Land of the Jews," Herzl proclaimed at the First Zionist Congress. In making this statement he was not proposing to develop a "spiritual Zionism" of his own, but he did allude to at least two additional elements that were to become—and have remained to this day—pillars of Zionism: emphasis on Jewish national identity, and a proud declaration of intent to preserve it. The precise nature of this national identity, or essence, has been subjected to different interpretations by the various Zionist factions. But the Jew's uniqueness became a commonly accepted value, which was not the result of anti-Semitic attacks; it existed as a basic principle of Judaism before the era of legal emancipation and modern anti-Semitism.

The Jews' demand for full emancipation was linked, therefore, openly or implicitly, with the demand that non-Jewish society accept them *as Jews*—that is, in their uniqueness. A society which requires the Jew to cease to exist as a Jew in order to be accepted in its midst, is, in effect, a society in which the Jew has no place at all. Moreover, if the Jews are required to undertake certain acts and sacrifices not required of others in that society, then the concept of equality becomes meaningless.

While the anti-Semite is troubled by the Jews' actual existence, such is not the case as far as the more liberal elements of the majority are concerned. The attainment of full emancipation is possible only in societies whose religious, ethnic and cultural composition and self-image can be reconciled with the existence of a Jewish community in their midst. Only this kind of equality for the Jews as individuals and as a community is capable of making emancipation a "solution" to the local "Jewish problem." Wherever their membership in the society is made conditional upon relinquishing their Judaism, or even a part of it, the Jews can consider the equality they have achieved only as a temporary solution to their immediate problem, a solution implying continued exile rather than redemption.

This reality is exemplified in the status of several of the Jewish communities in Latin America.

Political Strife and Nationalism

The special situation of Latin American Jewry within the Diaspora was emphasized by Louis Pincus, late Chairman of the Executive of the Jewish Agency, in his opening address to the Zionist Congress in January 1972. He placed the Jewish communities in Latin America in a special category, midway between "living in lands of oppression and discrimination," and "living in free countries where democracy is the very foundation of their way of life, in which the Jews enjoy a degree of equality and a standing for which it would be difficult to find a precedent in the entire history of our exile." Pincus viewed the Latin American states as "countries in which the Jew . . . feels free and enjoys equality . . . , but these are countries undergoing social and economic crises that are raising forces liable to jeopardize the standing of the Jews living there."[1]

1. Opening Address to the 28th Zionist Congress, Jan. 18, 1972.

In this description and in his subsequent remarks, Pincus did indeed pinpoint the potentially disastrous situation of Latin American Jewry; and, in terms of "catastrophe Zionism," he based his conclusions on the prevailing politico-economic events of the day. But these events were at the time, as they are today, grounded in a more enduring ideological infrastructure; and it is precisely this ideological base that the Zionist Movement was bound to examine more thoroughly.

The political and economic tensions prevailing in the Latin American states have their roots in historical and contemporary processes characteristic of the Third World. Poor or little industrialization and agricultural production, heavy dependence on the markets of the United States and the other industrialized countries, all these are augmented by a socio-economic gap which in some countries is shocking in its dimensions and manifestations of undernourishment, starvation, and lack of education. Against such a background a stormy political struggle is waged between those in power and those who are trying to overthrow the existing order. In the course of this struggle, the rules and parameters of the democratic game lose their value, and so do the civil and political guarantees laid down in the constitutions. The stronger the forces trying to undermine the existing order, the more unsteady the position of those social strata of which the Jews are a part.

The effort to overthrow the existing order is based on historical and social arguments that ascribe all the woes of society to the acts and failures of the liberal governments that have ruled the Latin American states during the period of their political coming-of-age. Class-oriented selfishness and the blind worship of liberal ideas—so the argument runs—produced the subjugation of the national economies to the imperialistic interests of the "Anglo-Saxon" democratic powers in the nineteenth and twentieth centuries. The economic and political liberalism which Britain and the United States "exported" to Latin America is presented, in this context, as the source of all evil. The remedy for these ills is a "return to the sources," a reemphasis of that which is unique in Latin American society, a resurgence of nationalism. On this last point the contending camps are in effect joined: both the rulers and those who want their demise look to nationalism as their activating ideology.

These two elements—anti-liberalism and a narrowly defined nationalism—are in clear contradiction to the ideological legitimization of Jewish existence in several Latin American countries.

Exclusion from the Majority Society

Argentina, one of the most highly advanced countries in Latin America, has a well-developed industry and a substantial middle class. Its birthrate is among the lowest in Latin America, similar to that of the West, and the educational level is higher there than in the other Latin American countries. Argentina has attracted more immigrants than its neighbors; in fact, during the last 120 years, most of its inhabitants (or their ancestors) have been immigrants.

One might have expected that these factors provide Argentine Jewry with optimal conditions of existence in a pluralistic society and the recognition of its right to perpetuate itself in that society. In practice, however, Jewish existence is undermined by highly active anti-Semitic elements.[2] Close examination of the self-image of various groups within Argentine society in matters which do not directly concern the Jews, leads to the conclusion that the overwhelming majority of the population does not wish to be regarded as a multi-faceted society in which ethnic, cultural, and even religious minority groups preserve their separate status, even as they are accepted as full and equal members of that society. Some regard the Argentine Republic as Catholic, basing their stand on the country's constitution, history and population composition. Others perceive Argentina in the future as an ethnically and culturally monolithic state, to which each of the heterogeneous elements will contribute its share before merging with the others. The common denominator of both these conceptions is the assumption that Jewish existence, as a permanent feature of the country, is not consistent with the image they have developed of their society.

Mexico's position differs from that of Argentina. While its industry has undergone substantial development in recent decades, other factors—such as its largely backward agriculture, increased birthrate, hunger, and ignorance—have placed Mexico among the least developed countries on the continent. The Revolution of 1917, which ostensibly freed the masses from bondage, succeeded in restoring to the Mexicans their pre-Columbian heritage. The Mexicans' direct and positive relationship with Aztec and Mayan civilizations reinforced their natural hostility towards Europeans. To this

2. See Haim Avni, "Anti-Semitism in Latin America after the Yom Kippur War—A New Departure," *World Jewry and the State of Israel*, Moshe Davis, ed., New York, 1977, p. 53.

must be added their suspicion and resentment of the North American "Anglo-Saxons." The xenophobia rooted in these hostile feelings is expressed not only by a stringent and illiberal immigration policy, but also by the social ostracism of all outsiders as abetted by Mexico's constitution. The Jews, who arrived in the country only fifty years ago, are among the outsiders.

Thus the Jews in both Argentina and Mexico have this in common, that neither community can view its legal position in its country of residence as one of "redemption," that is, a satisfying solution to its Jewish problem. Even if we were to discount anti-Semitism, which is strong and pervasive in both countries, a full-fledged legitimate and permanent Jewish existence in their midst is not compatible with the self-image and self-definition of very large segments of the majority societies. This reality should be constantly kept in mind by Zionists in Latin America and elsewhere.

The New Marranoism

There are many indications that full acceptance of Jews in Latin American society hinges on the implicit condition that they divest themselves of their Jewishness. The essence of this Jewishness may be defined negatively; as long as the Jew is not a Christian (and above all, not a Catholic), the process of his integration into the majority society is not complete, despite the legalization of religious differentiation. In addition, the Jew is attached, whether he wants to be or not, to the Jewish ethnic group. Thus, while Jews may be accepted by the majority society and even attain prominent socio-cultural and political positions, the fact that they are Jewish is not forgotten—not by their friends, and certainly not by their opponents. To a large extent this applies also to the revolutionary movements, although most of their platforms or activities do not bear an explicitly marked Catholic religious element.

The basic condition of Jewish life in most Latin American countries is characterized by the absence of a definitive solution. Only one moral response can apply to this condition: Zionism. Only Zionist ideology and activity can bestow real meaning to the Jew's being different. Only Zionist commitment can preserve the Latin American Jew's awareness of his singularity and enhance his self-esteem even if he has decided not to go to Israel—but on these conditions: that he be

mindful of his true place in society, aware of the extent of his alienation and, above all, that he does not mistake exile for redemption.

An alternative to Zionism, but one which would be immoral, is
to surrender to the demand for obliterating Jewish particularity, leading to a modern version of Marranoism. The meaning of such a step, in
our day, need not be the abrogation of Jewish identity as a result of
brute force, but rather voluntary acceptance of the bases of the majority society for reasons of social convenience. The theories of assimilation existing in Judaism on both the Right and the Left are in line with
such a surrender, even when they are not designed to achieve the total
elimination of the Jew's uniqueness. As has happened elsewhere,
however, these theories are not necessarily in consonance with the
self-image and the monolithic tendencies of the majority societies.
Those professing such views are also exposed to pressures from the
non-Jewish environment, being led in the immoral direction of the
New Marranoism.

Under these circumstances, Zionism can have its appeal, in
most of the Latin American countries, by calling for the rebellion of
morality against immorality.

Legitimacy—A World Jewish Problem

In most Latin American countries, we cannot speak, therefore,
of a "post-Zionist" era, and it would not be right to say that Israel is the
source of the Jew's troubles in those countries. On the contrary, by its
very existence Israel is delaying and obstructing the quiet surrender of
the neo-Marranos to the demand for self-effacement. This has been
the cause of a certain amount of tension between the Jewish community and the majority society that demands its assimilation; and those
who justify yielding to this demand are liable to see the State of Israel
as the trouble source. But those who regard such a surrender as an
immoral act, as relinquishing the concept of the Jew's equal value as a
human being, will find of necessity that they are adhering to one of
Zionism's basic tenets.

Is this reality limited to Latin America? Are not some of its elements true also for Jewish communities in the English-speaking world,
as well as in Eastern and Western Europe? It might be of interest to
examine how much of the Latin American experience may be
detected in other societies also. Is the Jew, indeed, a legitimate (not

only a legal) part of the local national entity in which he lives, or is
there, in the fact that he is not a Gentile, an element that separates him
from the majority society? In the majority societies' laws, in their educational program and national holidays, are there elements that clash
with the Jew's fundamental beliefs and thus alienate him from the
environment?

We may speak of complete liberation, in the sense offered by
Zionism, only in those places where the Jew is not required to "pay"
for the equality granted him by falsifying his identity. Only an examination of the Jewish condition in the light of these criteria will enable
us to judge whether the position of the Jews in any particular country
is similar to that of the Jews in Latin America, or whether they are
indeed living in a "post-Zionist era."

Comments

NACHMAN FALBEL

Latin America should not be viewed as a unit from the Jewish communal point of view, and the case of Brazilian Jewry underlines some of the variations. The Jewish communities are not a uniform bloc sharing the same history and sociology. The countries on the South American continent differ from one another, the history of each presenting diverse elements as regards socio-economic, cultural and political aspects: Portuguese America (Brazil) differs from Spanish America, the South differs from Central America with its small republics. Moreover, a study of the composition of each community, its immigration processes and cultural integration, would clearly indicate that each must be examined separately if we wish to understand the nature and character of the local Zionist groups.

Zionism in Brazil

Zionism had its beginnings in Europe, a product of a Jewish reality not generally found in Latin America. It was a cultural heritage which the Jewish immigrant brought along with him from the old country, a part of his individual Jewish experience. Anti-Semitism in Europe led to frequent persecutions which culminated in the Holocaust. But "catastrophe Zionism" holds little meaning in a country like Brazil, where anti-Semitism never attained significant or threatening proportions, although its presence is felt from time to time in one area or another. It is clear that there is nothing to prevent a sudden change in the apparent stability maintained, in part, because of economic prosperity, and, partly, because of the strong political regime. But this premise, often advanced by Zionist emissaries, does not meet with widespread response among Brazilian Jews, because their daily lives do not reflect the possibility of such a change. Even the Holocaust has left little impression upon the younger generation.

We cannot say exactly when the first Zionist nuclei were founded in Brazil; but we do know that there were Zionist groups in the North of the country at the beginning of the twentieth century. The Brazilian Zionist Federation was founded in 1922 by delegates representing several Jewish organizations.[1] This was a time when the community was following two clearly opposing ideologies—Zionism and Communism. Their conflict was not restricted to the ideological plane; both aimed at conquering political positions and institutional influence within the community. An intense political-partisan struggle took place within the Zionist organization itself, each side finding its natural leaders either among the more active of the new immigrants or among the veterans of the community. Po'alei Zion was founded early in 1927 in Porto Alegre; soon after, its members took part in May Day celebrations, marching side by side with the Italian socialists. This act was undoubtedly displeasing to the majority of the General Zionists. Po'alei Zion wished to found Jewish schools where Hebrew would be taught even against the will of the parents, many of whom favored Yiddish as the language of instruction. This issue was debated between Zionists and non-Zionists, though some Zionists favored Yiddish as well as Hebrew.

Besides Po'alei Zion, other parties were active in the 1930s, running the gamut from Linke Po'alei Zion to Brit Trumpeldor (Revisionists). One of the first Zionist mass meetings, at which some 5,000 people participated, was held in Rio de Janeiro in 1929 after the Arab attacks on Jews in Eretz Israel, to demand active intervention on the part of both the Brazilian and British governments. By the eve of World War II the Jewish community in Brazil had a solid organizational framework which could handle communal affairs. But the political changes wrought by the Getulio Vargas dictatorship caused considerable interruption in the consolidation process of Jewish communal life. In 1940-41 the government decreed a halt to "activities of foreigners" and forbade the publication of journals and magazines in languages other than Portuguese, inflicting a heavy blow to Jewish cultural life and communal institutions, especially to the Zionist groups. This situation was in force until the end of World War II when the prohibition of Zionist activities was abrogated.

---

1. See Samuel Malamud, "Zionism in Brazil," Encyclopedia of Zionism and Israel, vol. 1, New York, 1971, pp. 156–158.

The Jewish Community After World War II

World War II did much to boost Brazil's economic development; the abundant raw materials of the country were essential to the Allied war effort. The Jews participated in the new burst of industrial and commercial activity, enjoying tremendous economic advancement. Economic prosperity of the Jewish community was followed by a deep spiritual change as the impact of the Holocaust made itself felt individually and collectively. It took years before the tragedy of the Holocaust was completely assimilated; but when the community did become conscious of what had happened, each and every person was ready to dedicate himself to the Jewish cause and to the creation of a Jewish State.

In 1945, when Zionism was renewed in the urban centers of Brazil, it became the driving force of Jewish communal life. In those tense years, the struggle in Eretz Israel against the British Mandatory power augured great changes for the Jewish People at large. No one could remain indifferent; historic decisions were in the balance. A considerable number of young Brazilian Jews aligned themselves with the reemerging youth movements, and the ideological characteristics of pre-war European Zionism again came to the fore. Those who did not affiliate with Zionist youth movements joined in other movements, among them groups with progressive tendencies.

The ideological polemics in the youth movements, Zionist or otherwise, were inflamed by the decisive events taking place in Eretz Israel. Several youth movements adopted a positive attitude to *halutziut* (pioneering), creating *hakhsharot* (preparation groups) in the style of the European *halutzic* movements. In consonance with their educational ideals, they intended to realize their nationalist dream in their own *kibbutzim* in Eretz Israel.

A positive consequence of this Zionist revival was the interest shown by young second-generation Brazilian Jews in the study of Judaism. This led to innovations in the traditional Jewish school curriculum; more time was given to the study of Jewish subjects; Yiddish was replaced by Hebrew; Jewish literature was studied in Portuguese, the only language understood by the new generation. Pioneering youth movements owed their success not only to the decisive historic moment but to the critical attitude of Brazilian youth to social problems in general. The development of Zionist-socialist ideology among Jewish youth epitomized the aspirations and ideals of their generation.

In 1945, the two most influential Zionist parties, *Po'alei Zion* and General Zionists, merged into a United Zionist Organization based on individual rather than group affiliation. The other Zionist organizations were revived and later came to be represented in the Zionist Organization of Brazil. Around 1946, public opinion was enlisted to support Zionism, and mass meetings were organized to draw attention to events in Eretz Israel. Soon a pro-Palestine Committee was set up, composed of influential intellectuals. The activities of the Zionist Organization of Brazil were of paramount importance when the United Nations debated the partition of Palestine. The Brazilian ambassador, Oswaldo Aranha, who presided over the United Nations General Assembly, played an important role in the adoption of the historic partition plan. To this day, the role of the Brazilian representative in the resolution is credited as a gesture identifying Brazil with the destiny of Israel. The political reality, however, is quite different; Brazil later voted in favor of the motion which condemned Zionism as racism.

From 1945 to the present, Zionism in Brazil has been strengthened in internal organization. Some of the pioneering youth groups founded *kibbutzim* in Israel, and WIZO and Pioneer Women have engaged intensively in Zionist activity within the Brazilian Jewish community. Contact with Israel and Hebrew culture has further developed through the presence of *shelihim* (emissaries) in all the areas of Jewish communal life, particularly in Jewish education.

Zionism Today

Although the present government is not inimical to national minorities, it has been calling for national cohesiveness. Zionism may thus seem to be creating a problem of dual loyalty for Jews. Recent economic interests have directed government policy to favor the Arab world. Arab propaganda, too, has been instrumental in spreading anti-Jewish and anti-Zionist sentiment, as is the case in Argentina. Anti-Semitism, commonly repudiated by enlightened citizens, does crop up in rightist and leftist circles. Thus the Brazilian Zionist movement and the Jewish community must cope with a situation in which many Jewish students have been influenced by the ideological climate in the universities and adopted the views of the New Left about Israel and Jewish nationalism. The gap has been widening between Jewish university youth and the Zionist leadership.

Unfortunately, the Zionist Movement has not yet found the way to meet this challenge. Accordingly, assimilation is gaining on two grounds. First, the Jew is anxious to become integrated into the society in which he lives and he enhances his economic and social position by minimizing cultural and religious barriers. The second, infinitely more dangerous and destructive tendency is the kind of assimilation which denies Judaism and Jewish values in the name of so-called higher social ideals. The traditional Jewish youth movement can no longer attract the Jewish student who seeks to satisfy his restlessness in non-Jewish associations and clubs. When differences between national identities diminish, mixed marriage increases at a frightening rate in a new generation which feels greatly bewildered and insecure in a changing world.

Zionism, as seen by Brazilian Jews today, is a movement concerned more with practical identification with the State of Israel and its day-to-day problems than with the desire to resolve the problem of *golah* and its historical-national destiny as formulated by the Zionist theoreticians of the early days.

JOSÉ A. ITZIGSOHN

My remarks focus on Dr. Avni's analysis of neo-Marranoism and the eventual validity, or lack of validity, of arguments relating to "catastrophe Zionism" within the Latin American situation, more particularly within the Argentine Jewish community. I believe that essential elements of catastrophe Zionism apply to the Jewish community in the Argentine, not because I fear a repetition of the Nazi Catastrophe, but because the Jewish community is still receiving distress signals. Moreover, surrender to neo-Marranoism is not just a matter of ethics; it also indicates inadequate preparation for collective and individual security.

The Jews arrived in Argentina at a time of the political predominance of the liberal and anticlerical groups who were interested in opening up the country to mass immigration of non-Catholic as well as Catholic elements. However, for long periods power was in the hands of conservative clerical groups, imbued with Fascist ideology or with a mixture of economic neo-liberalism and clericalism.

Even before the era of mass Jewish immigration, supporters of non-liberal tendencies manifested their opposition to the settlement of Jews in Argentina. Traditional anti-Semitism inherited from colonial

Hispanic tradition was followed by perverse European anti-Semitic ideologies and later by Arab propaganda. Baron de Hirsch encouraged persecuted Russian Jews to start a new life in a country free of anti-Jewish prejudice, but the newcomers were attacked in the influential daily press as well as by prominent literary figures. They were also opposed by the conservative clerical elements, although a spirit of integrationist optimism could be discerned among the Jews, as exemplified in the early works of Alberto Gerchunoff. Later, when immigration was no longer confined to the agricultural areas, hostile propaganda also became manifest in the large urban centers, particularly in Buenos Aires. Conservative forces concluded that Jews were the instigators of labor unrest. Violent anti-labor repression went hand in hand with anti-Semitic attacks. In 1919, during the so-called "Tragic Week" which occurred under the Populist government of Hipólito Yrigoyen, these anti-Jewish attacks reached pogrom proportions.

Nevertheless, these manifestations did not seem to dampen the predominantly optimistic hopes of the Jews, who identified with the democratic progressive tendencies, especially with socialism. In 1930, the middle-class Radical Party government, with its populist ideology, was overthrown by a military coup d'état. That event and others which followed had specific consequences for Jews: Jewish immigration from Europe dropped abruptly and anti-Jewish discrimination in public sectors became more noticeable. Naturally, global events such as the economic crisis of 1930 and Hitler's rise to power, also had their effect on the country. Pro-Nazi activity intensified in Argentina after the overthrow of the Spanish Republic and the outbreak of World War II. While important segments of the middle class also favored the Nazis, Jews still enjoyed the support of the remaining population. Still these were difficult years, characterized by many acts of overt aggression against Jews.

In 1943, a group of Fascist officers staged a revolt. For the first time there were signs of official anti-Jewish policy, even though it was instituted on a restricted scale in the provinces. Jewish teachers were dismissed from their positions, and it was officially forbidden to speak Yiddish under penalty of arrest. Some of the police even wore S.S. uniforms. The Nazi defeat put an end to that particular experiment. Perón came to power, and even though he adhered to the Fascist ideology of his predecessors, he was wise enough to adapt himself to the post-war situation.

Jews now turned in large numbers to traditional democratic

spheres and to Zionism. Paradoxically, while the war period had been a difficult time for the Jews of Argentina politically, they had strengthened their economic position considerably. Since Argentina was cut off from other industrial countries, it had been forced to promote light industry on a local scale. Jewish craftsmen and skilled workers played a major role in this development, even rising to become important business managers. Jewish youth entered the universities and the professions in increasing numbers; Jewish agricultural communities dissolved and Jews transferred to the cities. With this last phase, the Argentinian Jewish community acquired its present socio-economic features.

Perón's government, which came to power about the same time as the State of Israel was established, was one of the first to recognize the new state. Although the Jewish community strongly identified with Israel, and large numbers of young people went on *aliyah*, settling for the most part in the *kibbutzim*, most Jews felt secure in their familiar surroundings, believing that the changes which had taken place on the local and international scenes ushered in a period of relative peace.

The position of the Jews was inevitably conditioned by the attitude of the government in power. The ruling class was sometimes supportive of the Jews as individuals though not as a group. When the Fascists were in power, militant anti-Semitic forces came to the fore, Jews were assassinated or simply "disappeared." Many Jews emigrated to Eretz Israel; and after the fall of the first Peronist government, others became integrated in the political and social life of the country. But with each change in power, Jews were fearful of the consequences which would affect their position.

Obviously this succession of hopes, frustrations and fears, experienced over an extended period, has left its mark on the Jewish community. It is not surprising that one-tenth settled, or made an attempt to settle, in Israel. Nor is it surprising that many Argentinian Jews now live in Spain, in Mexico City, in the U. S. and elsewhere. Such a community is perhaps not a concrete example of "castrophe Zionism," but it can become just that if the situation deteriorates.

It is difficult to foresee the fate of Argentine Jewry. Today, those socio-economic sectors in which the largest number of Jews are found, are excluded from political power. Young people, deprived of local channels through which to express their discontent effectively, turn to personal activities. Under such conditions, neo-Marranoism is no longer characterized as semi-conversion; nor do other social and national objectives attract Jewish youth as they did when Perón was last in power. Neo-Marranoism now provides a way of escape from problems with which they are unable to cope. The problem is not only one of Jewishness, but also of political and social attitudes.

Neo-Marranoism is not adopted freely or deliberately; it is a choice made in reaction to danger portents. A solution to the problem is nowhere in sight.

MARCOS AGUINIS

In order to understand the problems facing Jewish communities and the Zionist movement in Latin America, certain aspects of Latin American life in general must be clarified, in addition to those raised by Haim Avni.

A longing for cosmovision has begun to ferment in this enormous sub-continent. Latin Americans, among them the Jewish population, have an urgent desire to achieve self-knowledge and assert their identity. With the Spanish conquest, Latin America developed a dual society: the masters were European and the natives became the oppressed. The ruling landowner class developed an aristocratic ideology maintained by absolutist racial and religious principles. This integral approach has persisted to the present, surviving in the right-wing nationalist groups.

Until recently, difficulties prevailing in Latin America were generally attributed to *internal* factors. It was assumed that problems arose from the primitivity of the continent and its superstitions, from its leaders, from the Indians and gauchos. If there was to be any progress, it was essential to eliminate that primitivity, a process which implied another *tabula rasa*: people and myths were wiped out; French, English and North American establishments were created; Italians, Spaniards, Jews, Arabs came to settle. There was a pressing need for integration, and although many hoped that a liberal party would be established, it was the ruling families who ultimately gained power by bribery and corruption.

The Problem of Jewish Status

From the beginning the Jews were a minority, distinguished by ethnic, linguistic, religious, and cultural characteristics. Jews did not demand special political rights; they were content to express the desire to maintain values derived from their historical distinctiveness.

The governments of Latin America, inspired by Europe and the United States, advocate freedom of religion. Yet, the Catholic Church does enjoy preferential status in many Latin American countries. Juridical tradition opposes the recognition of special rights for minority groups; communities of foreign origin are being integrated into the nation—but not as minorities. While Catholicism is, in fact, the majority religion, adherence to the Jewish religion is also permitted; Jewish traditions, Jewish ties with Jews in other countries and Jewish education are all products of the Jewish religion. A Jewish representative is not a spokesman for the Jewish minority; he is the representative of a nation whose origin or religious affiliation is Jewish. This definition is problematic for Zionist ideology in Latin America because it is not just a case of exclusive planning for an "exogroup"—the minority concept no longer holds for the immigrant Jews, as it did in Eastern Europe.

The Jewish communal position has undergone a number of changes. The immigrants understandably kept themselves apart from the rest of the population; but their children and grandchildren now ask themselves if maintaining that difference is still worth the effort. Those who fight assimilation today nostalgically recall with regret the generation of immigrants who did not question their Jewish identity. Indeed, these immigrants would have defended their right to be different with their lives. Today that right no longer interests the majority of their descendants—except when there is an attempt to violate that right.

The Jews and Latin American Society

The heritage of Latin America is Iberian and Catholic; it maintains an archaic monistic orientation. There is no desire to promote a mosaic of social structures; nor is there encouragement of differences which contradict the predominant culture. Today, people are tolerant. Tolerance, however, does not betoken acceptance but sufferance. Jews, without doubt, try to change tolerance into acceptance.

This is the reason that Jews have been developing neo-Marranoism; they have been attempting to conform to the majority society, although this compliance does not reflect their true inclinations. Neo-Marranoism is now exploring a new and subtle interpretation modeled on the Jewish community of North America, in the hope that Latin American countries will not oppose such an innovation. Such a model would imply increasing synagogue activity and encourage Jewish identification through participation in community centers.

Zionist Ideology

Zionism has been gaining ground throughout Latin America and each community today acknowledges its identification with Zionism. Zionism has also been granted official recognition, an achievement in many respects. Paradoxically, this achievement has not led to greater prestige. Indeed, it has inspired a certain fear and a progressive retreat from the changing reality.

The phenomenal interest shown by parents in their children's *aliyah* to Eretz Israel reflects the changing situation. Previously the younger generation had imposed Zionism on their parents, who were bound to maintaining Judaism in the Diaspora. Today the tables have been turned. Why are so many parents eager to have their children emigrate to Israel? Have they been overwhelmed by "pangs of conscience?" Unfortunately, the young people believe the real reason for the older generation's concern is a desire to remove them from the dangerous influence of local political parties. They argue that for older Zionists, Israel is no longer an ideal. Consequently, there is widespread distrust between the generations; attempts to clarify the situation come up against a barrier of disappointment and disbelief. Zionism without *aliyah* is not truly Zionism, although that is the kind of Zionism practiced by most Zionists today. *Aliyah* is not always a response to ideological impulses—non-Zionists, too, have come on *aliyah*. Is there a difference, then, between idealistic *aliyah* and mere immigration? The obvious contradiction no longer troubles us; we have learned to go along with it.

Israel believes that active Zionists should come on *aliyah*, or forfeit the right to call themselves Zionists. In the face of this dilemma, many Jews who do not plan to immigrate to Israel would rather cease to call themselves Zionists, in order to avoid being considered hypocrites. The absence of a catastrophic situation, to which Haim Avni referred, has reduced Zionism to "philo-Israelism." Rather than talk of a crisis in the Zionist movement in Latin America, one should talk of a crisis in its ideology.

ISRAEL EVEN-SHOSHAN

Jews from Eastern Europe brought Zionism to the new Latin American scene at the beginning of the century. As the sources of immigration ran dry, so did the Jews draw further and further from their traditional roots. The second generation of immigrants absorbed whatever East-European heritage their parents were able to transmit. The next generation already faced different conditions and problems; at best, Yiddish culture became their second frame of reference. For most Jews there had never been a religious alternative, not even for the first generation. The destruction of East-European Jewry caused the obliteration of the basic culture which formed the background for the Jewish community in the Argentine. Later, the establishment of the State of Israel, its accomplishments and triumphs over hardships and wars, became the focus—at times the only focus—of Jewish identity. In this way, Zionism became a substitute for the vanished Jewish roots. When Zionism "took over" the Argentinian Jewish community, the entire communal framework was altered. The militant anti-Zionist element (the strong *Yevsektsiya* group) withdrew from the community. The State of Israel created a new definition: every Jew who supported Israel was considered a Zionist. Instead of the Zionist minority who engaged in an ideological struggle with an indifferent, or even anti-Zionist, majority, the Zionist leadership now faced a pro-Israel majority. For some, Zionism meant *aliyah*, settlement in Israel.

Those self-realizing Zionists, foremost among them the young people, asked the established Zionist leaders for the meaning of their Zionism. No serious answer was forthcoming. As the central communal institutions of organized Jewry were taken over by the Zionists, a process of decline set in among the Zionist parties and the institutions which came under their control.

A parallel development was the shift of action and participation, especially on the part of the younger generation, from the various parties to the community centers. This new generation swelled the already large pro-Israel camp, and some of them, even while being aware of the criticism leveled at the older Zionist leaders, proclaimed their loyalty to the Zionist idea. The group was comprised, in part, of past members of youth movements who contended that Zionism symbolized the unity of the Jewish People and the centrality of the State of Israel for the Jewish People as a whole. In other words, if there is a center, there must also be a periphery. Although it would be ideal if the Jewish People were concentrated at the center, it is also possible to maintain Jewish existence at the periphery. Moreover, the periphery would also serve as a support for Israel, the center. These new leaders were able to gain substantial support from Zionist institutions in Israel and from several departments of the World Zionist Organization.

Today, a confrontation exists between an eroding community structure—the last vestige of the East-European influence—and a new form of organization largely conditioned by United States Jewry. Still, Argentinian Jewry, headed by "neo-Zionist" or "neo-Ahad Ha-Amist" leaders, has its own unique features and specific Latin American emphasis.

Does this situation indicate a weakening of Zionist control and the emergence of a leadership which does not consider itself linked to the Zionist establishment? The new leaders certainly do not feel a part of the Zionist establishment against which they contend. Moreover, the younger generation is not prepared to accept a "colonial" type of relationship between Israel and Diaspora Jewry. But it is no less true that the State of Israel gives content and direction to their basic Jewish existence.

The Zionist youth organizations are powerless against this new alignment. By virtue of their definition of Zionism they oppose the Ahad Ha-Amist approach. The recent political situation in the southern part of the continent has reinforced their conviction that Zionism calls for *aliyah*, a negation of the *golah*.

Even while an essentially qualitative regression was taking place, two new developments have enhanced Jewish youth activities, particularly in the Argentine: the successful youth programs organized by the institutions of Conservative Judaism, and the Zionist framework developed within the community centers.

The Conservative Movement functions by means of its Latin American Rabbinical Seminary and a network of counselors who work with many of the young people in Buenos Aires and its environs. In Argentina the movement defines itself as Zionist and takes pride in the fact that approximately 1,800 people have emigrated to Israel in the course of a decade of activity. It has been successful in motivating young people to broaden their knowledge of Jewish values and identify with their historical tradition.

A new kind of activity has originated in the youth sections of the large Jewish clubs in Buenos Aires, especially in the Hebraica and Maccabee clubs. Groups of 13 to 18 year-olds have been organized in the best classic youth movement tradition, under improved physical and organizational conditions. Even though the basic orientation of these youth sections is Zionist, their interpretation of Zionism differs from that of the leaders of the parent organizations. The youth, too, insist on *aliyah* as the realization of the Zionist idea. In fact, it is so defined in their educational program. However, demand is not for

collective *aliyah* but one directed exclusively to the kibbutz movement. It is an individual kind of *aliyah* which encourages its participants to pursue their university studies in Israel.

Thus, the scope of Zionist activity among the youth of Latin
America is far from showing signs of weakening. But the familiar picture of pioneer youth movements, engaged exclusively in Zionist
activity, has changed. In its place we see today a variety of youth
organizations, working through pioneer movements, community centers, neighborhood centers and modern religious movements—each
engaged, in its own way, in education that is essentially Zionist.

NATAN LERNER

Each wave of Jewish immigration to Latin America brought
with it the full spectrum of Jewish ideological belief and commitment,
including the various approaches to Zionism and socialism. While
Zionism as it had been known in Europe was part of the intellectual
and emotional baggage of the newcomers, its subsequent development
in Latin America is the result of two main factors: (a) the impact of
recent Jewish history, primarily the tragedy of the Holocaust and the
creation and progress of the State of Israel, on the younger generation;
(b) the relationship between local society and the Jewish minority in
the various countries during the last four or five decades.

In considering the first point, anyone familiar with Latin American Jewry will agree, that although small Zionist groups were in existence since the beginning of the century—especially in Argentina—it
was the shock of the Holocaust and then the joy accompanying the
creation of the State of Israel which impelled thousands of Jews,
including locally educated youth, to add their numbers to the Zionist
associations. Latin American Jews turned to Zionism under the dramatic impact of contemporary Jewish history, with its tragedy and
revival, and not because they were motivated by religion, Jewish education or philanthropy.

As for the second factor, environmental conditions have always
been a fundamental element in strengthening or awakening Zionist
ideology and determining the degree of personal involvement of those
who claim to adhere to that ideology. While solidarity with Israel is
largely emotional and ideological, fulfilment of Zionist *mitzvot*
depends, to a large degree, on the extent of Jewish integration into the
general society. Thus, it has been shown conclusively, that the Zionism of Argentinian or Uruguayan Jewish youth is quite different from

that of its Brazilian or Venezuelan counterparts.[1] Not only ideology and emotion, but other factors as well—standard of living, political stability, democracy or dictatorship, economic welfare and degree of modernization—play a major role in molding the attitude of the individual Latin American Jew *vis-à-vis* Zionism.

Two additional elements, closely linked and affecting the Jews directly, complete the set of influences that shape the philosophy and behavior of Latin American Zionists: anti-Semitism, and the possibility—or impossibility—of integration in society without being condemned to total assimilation or disintegration as a group.

Anti-Semitism must be examined against the general picture of weakening democracy, suppression of individual rights and growth of political violence. While suppression and violence on the South American continent do not have as their main or exclusive target a particular religious or ethnic minority, the Jews are singled out as easy victims in some countries, as a consequence of special local conditions. The situation in Argentina has in recent years become more alarming than is the case elsewhere in Latin America; indeed, it has resulted in international repercussions.

Since the 1930s, anti-Semitism in Argentina has been a recurrent cause for concern. "Routine" manifestations of anti-Semitism are not a new phenomenon in many Latin American countries, and outbursts of violence against Jews and Jewish institutions are not unusual; but anti-Semitism within the framework of general political instability and violence is not the same as "routine" anti-Semitism.

The Argentinian population as a whole cannot be blamed for the actions of an extremist and active minority, against which the Government did try to take some action. But anti-Semitism in the Argentine can no longer be considered the activity of a "lunatic fringe" which expresses itself in a wild "Stürmer"-like press and physical attacks against persons and institutions. It is now an integral part of the general political scene.[2] In this context, anti-Semitism in Latin America has been a major factor in bringing many Jews to Zionism.

1. See Itamar Rogovsky, in Haim Avni, *Zionism in Latin America* (Hebrew), Publications of Study Circle on Diaspora Jewry, Moshe Davis, ed., 7th Series, Jerusalem, 1976, pp. 21–26.
2. There are numerous statements by Argentinian leaders repudiating anti-Semitism, but, simultaneously they acknowledge the seriousness of some of its manifestations. President Videla, during his visit to the United States in September 1977, met representatives of Jewish organizations and spoke to the press on the matter.

An English language daily, the *Buenos Aires Herald*, commenting on the anti-Semitic campaign, examined the position of all the Jews in Argentina:

> Suspicion of Jews appears to have prevented Argentine Jewry from playing a larger role in the government of the country. Jewish politicians—unfortunately it is impossible to speak of Jewish generals, admirals and brigadiers—have had to make their entrance on the public stage in Argentina through the back door, so to speak. This might explain why Jews who have become prominent in public life have remained somewhat shadowy figures. . . . But it is not easy to explain why such un-Argentine attitudes as anti-Semitism and xenophobia (the former is merely an expression of the latter) should continue to exist with such virulence . . . (May 17, 1977).

The *Herald* editorial touches in a rather superficial manner on the essential problem confronting the Jews in Argentina and other Latin American countries. It points out that after a hundred years of individual Jewish contribution to many aspects of life, including public life, not only is the Jewish community subjected to anti-Semitic attacks but is still not accepted as an equal partner in the shaping of the nation. Besides right-wingers and extreme nationalists, there are segments of the liberal and general population who are not ready for a pluralistic society, in which descendants of immigrants who arrived in the country at various periods of its history are to be considered equals.

Assimilation, as total as possible, is what many Argentinians, including liberal circles, expect from the Jews. As *Newsweek* noted (August 1, 1977), quoting an unnamed Jew: "What anti-Semites are calling for is an ethnically pure, Catholic and monolithic Argentina. The line is the Jew has got to assimilate or get the hell out—or die." This view is valid, of course, for an extremist minority; Argentinian and Latin American enlightened opinion does not wholly share that attitude.

Latin America today is exposed to the strong influence of nationalist philosophies, on the Right as well as on the Left. There is an eagerness to consolidate unequivocal national identities on the basis of a monolithic culture that abolishes societal differences. Spokesmen oppose formulas of cultural pluralism; they reject manifestations affirming the individuality and diversity of minority groups, and deny the right of these groups to be different. In assimilation they see the ultimate destiny of each separate component of society; they have shaped a doctrine of *national essences—Argentinidad, Peruani-dad, Bolivianidad*, and so on—as ways of life demanding basic monolithism.[3]

Consequently, the individual Jew, who was educated in Latin America and has become identified with the general currents of life in his country, even while he is still conscious of belonging to the Jewish People, is at present exposed to a double pressure. Not unfrequently he must contend with anti-Semitic sentiment and, quite often, with the refusal of general society to admit legitimate and desirable forms of Jewish life such as exist in Western democracies. This is the Jew's position, at a time when general society is undergoing a crisis, the components of which are terrorism, subversion, violence and acts of repression.

Is such a situation likely to strengthen Zionism in Latin America? Hardly—unless affirmative, internally creative factors also play a role. The meaning of Israel as the fulfilment of the millenary Jewish dream, the enriching influence of Jewish education, the discovery of values that justify Jewish secular society, the efforts to attract Jewish youth to new forms of Jewish religiosity, the struggle to keep alive the prestige of the *halutzic* movement that brought thousands of Latin American idealistic youth to the kibbutz in Israel—all those elements are certainly important. No less important will be the image of Israel in the eyes of Latin American Jews. But, what will ultimately determine the place of Zionism in Latin American Jewry will be mainly the general development of the continent and its impact upon individual Jews.

3. We dealt with this subject in "Nationalism and Minorities in Latin America," *Patterns of Prejudice*, vol. II, no. 1, 1977.

British Commonwealth and South Africa

Great Britain

Schneier Levenberg

It is impossible to appreciate the situation of British Zionism today without taking into consideration its historical roots and development. The British Zionist movement consists of various trends. Some Zionists have always been attracted by practical work. A minority has been interested in cultural problems. Throughout the years, there were many ideological controversies and organizational rivalries from within and outside the movement—rivalries from which the personal element was never absent.

Early British Zionists

The first British Zionist was Sir Moses Montefiore (1784-1885). He paid seven visits to Eretz Israel, where he initiated many practical projects to further Jewish settlement. He was also a supporter of the new city of Jerusalem. The following was entered in his diary on May 24, 1839:

> Many Jews now emigrate to New South Wales, Canada, etc., but in the Holy Land they would find a greater certainty of success; here they will find wells already dug, olives and vines already planted, and a land so rich as to require little manure. By degrees I hope to induce the return of our brethren to the Land of Israel. I am sure they would be happy in the enjoyment of the observance of our holy religion in a manner which is impossible in Europe . . .

Prior to his death, he declared:

> I do not expect that all *Israelites* will quit their abodes in those territories in which they feel happy, even as there are Englishmen in Hungary, Germany, America and Japan, but Palestine must belong to the Jews, and Jerusalem is destined to become the seat of a Jewish Commonwealth.

Hovevei Zion

Kalman (Charles) Woorauch established a pro-Zion Society in London in 1884. He had come from Eastern Europe and was one of 26 delegates who assembled at the first Conference of *Hovevei Zion* groups in the city of Kattowitz in Prussia. Another representative from Britain was Zorah Barnett, who later became one of the builders of Petah Tikvah. Hayyim Zundel Maccoby (the Kamenitzer Maggid), who arrived in London in 1890, inspired great enthusiasm for the revival of Jewish life in the Land of Israel. A great scholar, a pious Jew, a man of considerable eloquence, whose addresses drew large audiences, Maccoby showed that Zionist ideas and strict Orthodoxy were compatible.

At first the movement was confined to the East End of Jewish working-class London, gradually spreading to the West End and attracting well-established Jewish personalities of British stock.

The English *Hovevei Zion* Association had some outstanding leaders, including its first head, Elim d'Avigdor, who was a prominent member of the Sephardi community. He enthusiastically supported the Jewish revival in Zion, declaring at a public rally:

> I am convinced that many wealthy co-religionists are willing to surrender cheerfully all their worldly possessions, and resign all their hopes of worldly aggrandisement in order to return with their brethren to the land of their fathers. We express the hope every Passover, "Next Year in Jerusalem." Is this utterance merely lip service or does it spring from our hearts?

By 1892 thirty-one *Hovevei Zion* "tents" had been set up in England, including three junior groups and a Women's Association. Members discussed many topics, among other things a proposal to train pioneers for Palestine (*hakhsharah*) and suggestions for spreading knowledge of the Hebrew language. Some of the leaders spoke about a "Jewish State." The character of the "tents" varied. Members of British birth or education conducted their activities in English, while the majority of the members used Yiddish. Several non-Jewish personalities supported *Hovevei Zion*, such as Laurence Oliphant, Col. Claude R. Conder, Sir Charles Warren and Father Ignatius, who spoke in eloquent terms about the revival of Israel and the rebuilding of Jerusalem.

Official leaders of the Anglo-Jewish community frowned upon Jewish national ideas, which they believed hampered the process of assimilation as the highest ideal of British Jewry; and the working classes, most of whom were new immigrants, were under the influence of socialist and anarchist groups and preoccupied with "bread and butter" problems. In addition, practical work in Eretz Israel seemed slow, and the political outlook for further Jewish settlement did not look promising. The various "tents" maintained their activities but encountered a great deal of apathy within their own ranks.

The Zionist Message

It was mainly among the foreign-born section of the community that Herzl found his supporters. Chief among them was Dr. Moses Gaster (1856-1939), the Haham of the Sephardi community, who combined scholarship and oratory with a strong personality. With each successive visit of Herzl to London his following increased. The First Annual Conference of the British Zionist Federation, which Herzl addressed in 1899, was attended by delegates from cities throughout the British Isles.

In spite of opposition, the Zionist Federation embarked on several practical tasks. One was the establishment of the Jewish Colonial Trust—the financial instrument of the World Zionist Organization (WZO). The sale of *shekalim* was another venture, which gave new immigrants a feeling of participation in the shaping of Zionist policy through Congress—the "Jewish Parliament." Members of the "Herzl-Nordau Kulturverein" in Whitechapel engaged in educational work. Zionist banners, Hebrew and Yiddish songs were a permanent feature of its gatherings. The decision to hold the Fourth Zionist Congress (1900) in London gave the British Federation a special place in the development of the world movement.

Various clashes dominated the Movement from the time of Herzl's death (1904) until the outbreak of World War I. The Jewish Territorialist Organization, founded by the writer Israel Zangwill (1864-1926), opposed the decision of the Seventh Zionist Congress

(1905) to relinquish the idea of the Uganda Project. There were differences of opinion about the leadership of David Wolffsohn, Herzl's successor; between "political Zionists," who adhered to the idea of a "Charter," and "practical Zionists," who urged settlement in Eretz Israel under all circumstances; between Po'alei Zion and the Zionist Federation. The Jewish Socialist Labor Party, which affiliated with the British Labor Party in 1920, played an important part in the Zionist political struggle, both in external and internal matters. In 1924 Po'alei Zion became an integral part of the British Zionist Federation. Conflict reigned between Mizrachi and the Federation, the former wishing to preserve its own organizational framework and independent educational activities.

Chaim Weizmann and Nahum Sokolow, both of whom lived in England for many years, had considerable impact on British Zionism. British Zionists played a central role in the achievement of the Balfour Declaration (1917) and in the political struggle during the Mandatory period (1922-1948); they were in the forefront of the fight for the establishment of the State of Israel, defying with great courage the policies of their own government. For many years, London was the major Zionist center in the Diaspora. Ha'olam, the Hebrew organ of the Movement, was published there, as were the Zionist Review and New Judea. The voices of the World Zionist Organization, then of the enlarged Jewish Agency (1929) and the reconstituted Jewish Agency (1970), were always well heard in Britain, serving as a link between Jerusalem and Anglo-Jewry.

British Jewry's response to the establishment of Israel may be described in one word—solidarity. Thirty years ago, solidarity with the new State was no simple matter, since the British Government refused to grant recognition to Israel.

Among the British Jews, however, response was immediate. Professor Selig Brodetsky, a prominent Zionist leader and President of the Board of Deputies, read a declaration greeting the new State of Israel. The Zionist Federation issued a manifesto, the Joint Palestine Appeal (now Joint Israel Appeal—JIA) set itself a target of £5,000,000. Young British Jews, who had fought with the British army in World War II joined the Israel Defense Forces during the War of Independence as part of Mahal (volunteers from abroad). Some of them remained in Israel. After a long political struggle, the British Government accorded de facto recognition to Israel on January 29, 1949; de jure recognition was granted on April 27, 1950.

The *Aliyah* Movement

British Jews who settled in Eretz Israel have made a vital contribution to the country's development. Out of an estimated 30,000 Jews of British origin in Israel, 10 percent live in *kibbutzim* and in *moshavim*. British Jewry today is not opposed to *aliyah* on ideological grounds, regarding it as a personal concern. There may be some opposition within the family, but there is no open discouragement.

During the last three decades, tourism to Israel has increased noticeably, bringing the reality of the country to countless British homes, Gentile as well as Jewish. This is a tremendous potential for Zionist work in various fields. Nevertheless, some Jews have never visited Israel for lack of financial resources, suitable opportunity or lack of interest. Many thousands of young people have taken advantage of the study courses arranged in Israel by various departments of the WZO. This would not have been possible without the youth organizations, which have enjoyed the support of the Youth Department of the WZO, the Zionist Federation and the Hillel Houses of B'nai B'rith. Fund raising for Israel has developed greatly and is represented mainly by the Joint Israel Appeal, the *Ahdut* and Young Leadership groups. The Appeal's weakness lies in its comparatively limited socio-economic base—mainly the affluent and middle class. Its difficulties in reaching the lower middle class are not due to lack of effort but rather to the complexities of the situation.

An important educational development is the network of Zionist day schools, which comprise more than 5,000 pupils. Knowledge of Hebrew has spread among the Anglo-Jewish community, but not to the degree expected 30 years ago, when it was hoped that the younger Jewish generation would become bilingual. Spiritual and cultural ties between Anglo-Jewry and Israel have not been as strong as the interest in the Jewish State's struggle for peace, its constructive achievements and internal developments.

Anglo-Jewry's reply to the notorious United Nations Resolution equating Zionism with racism was the establishment, early in 1976, of the Israel Solidarity Committee, which virtually represents all the major Jewish organizations. This committee has created an atmosphere of cooperation between leaders of the Board of Deputies, the Zionist Federation, the JIA and other bodies—an important achievement in itself. It is understood, however, that the Solidarity Committee does not deal with political issues or problems which are the exclusive responsibility of the various bodies concerned. It is a vehicle for carrying out concrete tasks on behalf of Israel or the Zionist Movement, when it is felt that a joint effort can serve a useful purpose.

The women's Zionist organizations are well coordinated: they are practical, project-oriented, conscious of the importance of fund raising as well as the educational aspect, and they display a sympathetic attitude to the *aliyah* problem. The Women's International Zionist Organization (WIZO), *Mizrachi* and Pioneer Women (*Na'amat*) do have a specific ideological outlook, but they are, on the whole, not affiliated with Israeli political parties.

Practical Zionism

The British Zionist Federation has always been proud of its practical achievements. It represents all Zionist groups except the Mizrachi Federation, which is a separate entity. But *Heads of Agreement*, signed on January 12, 1979, has provided for the establishment of a United Federation of Zionists to be operative from the end of 1979. It will include all groups and individuals at present within the Zionist Federation and the constituent bodies of the Mizrachi Federation. The merger—a result of long and protracted negotiations—will open a new chapter in the history of British Zionism. Its main significance lies in the organizational and representative spheres; as regards ideology, all groups remain autonomous. However, unity will enhance the prestige of the movement and should open up possibilities for change and advancement.

The affiliation to the Zionist Federation of the pro-Zion group—consisting of members of the Reform and Liberal religious groups—is another development; negotiations to the same end are now in progress with representatives of the World Sephardi Federation in Britain. Internal political issues play a certain part in British Zionism but differences of opinion on practical problems are not necessarily fought along party lines. Divisions on religious issues are hardly noticeable in British Zionism.

Some Jews are anti-Israel: they are active in pro-Arab organizations or maintain no contact whatsoever with Jewish bodies. Persons of Jewish origin also participate in the Trotskyite groups and the Communist Party but they are not active in the Jewish community.

Lack of opposition within the Jewish community has impoverished the Zionist Movement in the ideological sense. Paradoxically, it

is Arab propaganda which compels supporters of Israel to pay attention to the basic issues which played such a great part in pre-State
days. A minority in British Zionism with a sense of history appreciates
the importance of ideology and long-term planning. But British Zionists in the main are practical.

The universities, however, have become a battleground for pro-
Palestinians—supported in a violent way by Trotskyite groups—and
Jewish students; the issue is the attitude to Zionism. Since many of the
debates focus around political-ideological issues, Jewish students have
been impelled to take an interest in the history of the Zionist Movement. Thus, indirectly, the New Left has made a contribution to the
awareness of Zionism among those Jewish students who previously
paid little attention to ideological issues. Indeed, a growing number of
academics choose Zionist themes as topics of research. Jewish lecturers and professors who formerly kept aloof from Zionism are compelled by circumstances to take an interest in its origin and development. As in the case of anti-Semitism, which has always made assimilated Jews conscious of their identity, so the anti-Zionist campaign
today has its positive results: it leads some alienated Jews to an identification with Zionism.

Among the non-academic Zionist youth, there are many groups
whose ideological outloook follows closely that of the various Israeli
parties and organizations with which they are allied.

Many of the young Jews today are as "practical-minded" as
their elders. This does not necessarily mean that they are not interested in Israel, or that some of them will not go on *aliyah*; but they
show little interest in ideological or political issues unless these relate
to their political ambitions. Two factors may account for the present
situation: 1) the general trend against formal political affiliation, leaving people free to vote in elections according to their interests and
views; 2) the fact that the active elements in the Jewish community are
mostly middle class or even lower on the economic scale. This unorganized sector has little time or opportunity to make its voice heard,
especially on ideological or political issues. It is perhaps the best
potential for *aliyah*, but some persons are not sufficiently informed
about Zionism, and others are not easily accessible for receiving proper information.

The line dividing general pro-Israel activities from Zionism is
not clearcut, and this presents both advantages and disadvantages for
the Zionist Organization. On the one hand, since anything connected

with Israel is generally identified with Zionism, it enhances Zionism's impact. On the other hand, some Jews do not feel the need to affiliate with the Zionist Movement on the premise that "we are all Zionists anyway." This weakens the movement from within as well as from without. Official Anglo-Jewish bodies and pro-Israel committees are led by people who consider themselves Zionists; the same applies to those who engage in fighting anti-Israel propaganda.

No Jewish anti-Zionist or non-Zionist groups oppose Zionist ideology in organized fashion, except perhaps for certain Orthodox circles who may be pro-Israel but oppose the organized Zionist Movement. However, the influence of this particular sector is limited.

In surveying the long history of British Zionism it is not unreasonable to conclude that the future of the movement does not depend merely on individuals; it depends mainly on current prevailing conditions. The strength of the movement rests on its sense of history and continuing ability to adjust itself to prevailing conditions, whether adverse or opportune. There will also be individuals, as in the past, who will follow the specific "British road to Zion," paved by Sir Moses Montefiore in the middle of the nineteenth century.

Canada

Harold M. Waller

Since 1948 Zionism in the Diaspora has been facing a problem of self-definition in the era of Israeli statehood. Canadian Zionism is certainly no exception. The Canadian Jewish community consists of approximately 300,000 people, concentrated primarily in Toronto (110,000) and Montreal (115,000). The rest of the community is widely scattered, with clusters in cities such as Winnipeg, Vancouver, Edmonton, Calgary and Ottawa. The Jewish community is fairly cohesive and maintains a well-organized network of diversified programs and activities. Despite the proximity, common language and outlook similar to that of American Jewry, the Canadian community has tended to operate independently. It is an active community, well represented in international Jewish bodies.

Zionist Commitment

The vast majority of Jews identify with their own people in a number of ways, but the most prevalent forms seem to have become affiliation with Jewish organizations and contributing to Jewish causes. For many, the donation, especially to Israel, has become the major form of Jewish expression. Since the main campaigns are run by the fund-raising arms of the welfare federations and not by the Zionist organizations, it is possible for an individual to declare his solidarity with Israel and the Jewish People without Zionist involvement. No longer is it essential to participate in Zionist activities in order to support the Jewish State; the Zionist organizations have lost their monopoly on the bond between Diaspora Jewry and Israel. This development undoubtedly justifies a reexamination of the role of Zionism in Canadian Jewish life, but so far this has not been done.

In one sense, the term "Zionist" is losing its very meaning in Canada. If Zionism is taken to mean support for and identification

111

with Israel and with the Jewish People, and recognition of Israel's primacy in Jewish life, then virtually all Jews are Zionists, whether or not they are affiliated with a Zionist organization. On the other hand, if one insists on commitment to *aliyah*, then few Canadian Jews may be considered committed Zionists. The concept has lost much of its ideological content. Yet nearly every Canadian Jew is a Zionist, and what passes for Zionism now has become an integral part of Canadian Jewish life. That may well be a victory for Zionism, but victory in a battle that is no longer relevant. The challenge now is to define Zionist goals and then plan ways of achieving these goals. In the meantime Zionism suffers from the routinization of Israel in Diaspora Jewish life.

There are various ways to identify Zionists. One is to include only the official members of a Zionist organization. This would narrow the field considerably, but it may not be very helpful to do so because it is difficult to distinguish members from non-members in terms of attitude, behavior, or involvement. Formal affiliation with the Zionist movement does signify something beyond mere support for Israel, but the precise degree of commitment is often difficult to assess. Moreover, it is possible to be involved in Zionist-type activities without formal membership in a Zionist group. For example, an *oleh* need not have been a member of a Zionist organization in order to settle in Israel. However, since so little is known about "unofficial" Zionism, the present paper will be limited to a discussion of "official" Zionism.

Jewish Organizations

Zionist organizations have their headquarters in Montreal and branch offices in other parts of the country. Included among the constituents of the Canadian Zionist Federation (CZF) are Labor Zionists, Revisionists, Mizrachi-Hapoel Hamizrachi, Hadassah-WIZO, Friends of Pioneering Israel, Fédération Sephardie Canadienne and the Zionist Organization of Canada. The CZF has some 42,000 members, most of whom belong by virtue of their membership in one of the aforementioned groups.

The CZF is one of three key national Jewish organizations. The other two are Canadian Jewish Congress (CJC) and B'nai B'rith. In principle, Congress, which represents all Jewish organizations, is the dominant body in Jewish life: it is the spokesman for the community to the general public, to governments and to international Jewish bodies.

Congress has been referred to as "the parliament of Canadian Jewry"; it does, in fact, meet in triennial plenary sessions at which all types of Jewish organizations are represented. Generally, Congress bears responsibility in the following areas: education and culture, foreign affairs, community relations and politics. However, in several areas power is shared with one or both of the other two major organizations. For example, all three jointly sponsor the Canada-Israel Committee, to which the responsibility for public affairs involving Israel has been delegated. There is extensive cooperation between the major national organizations on matters of joint concern. There is also considerable maneuvering for position, as each organization tries to maintain its prestige through involvement in various activities. Each group is jealous of its own prerogatives and missions, assiduous in its efforts to assert its primacy or at least equality. This is especially true whenever new activities are initiated, in which organizational jurisdictions have to be defined.

Fund Raising and the Israel Connection

Much of the competition between the national organizations is virtually irrelevant, because powerful local welfare federations tend to centralize community government at the local level. These federations, newer and more active than the traditional national organizations, are more open to innovative approaches. But the key to their position within the community is their control over financial resources. Their fund-raising sections collect funds, while the federations themselves allocate funds. A relatively small number of very wealthy families, who provide a disproportionate share of the funds, also enjoy disproportionate influence.

Most fund raising is oriented toward Israel, mainly through the United Israel Appeal. Some observers feel that less money would be raised for local needs if the local and Israel campaigns were not unified. In a sense the fund raisers have appropriated the Israel connection for themselves. Fund raising and contributing do not demand a great deal in terms of Jewish commitment or practice, knowledge or participation. Emphasis on fund raising in Jewish life, therefore, enables a new leadership to emerge, one that is pro-Israel in its orientation but not necessarily preoccupied with traditional Jewish concerns and probably not very sensitive to classical Zionist values. Fund raising, not ideological in the Zionist sense, is a matter of supporting Israel for Israel's sake. In the sense that such support for Israel constitutes an integral part of Zionism, every fund raiser and contributor may be considered a Zionist. The only cost is monetary, and perhaps the time involved. But the contribution also brings indirect benefits, including social and professional contacts, enhanced status and prestige, recognition and influence. Thus for many people monetary contributions have replaced Zionist commitment as a way of identifying with Israel. Israeli officials are well aware of this development. Consequently, much of their contact with the Canadian Jewish community is through fund raising rather than Zionist activities. When a prominent Israeli visits Canada, his or her public appearances are likely to be under fund-raising, rather than Zionist, auspices. Undoubtedly this enhances collection efforts, but it also serves to legitimize the implicit claim of fund-raising organizations that they represent Israel in Canada. By the transfer of fund-raising responsibilities from Zionist organizations to welfare federations, the Zionists have relinquished one of their major claims, simultaneously enhancing the status of the fund-raising bodies.

At present, the CZF is involved in many aspects of community activity, but its areas of sole responsibility are few. Political work is shared with the Canada-Israel Committee, which probably plays a more significant role. The cause of Soviet Jewry is shared with the national committee. Education is primarily a local concern, despite the existence of a CZF education committee. *Aliyah* is almost all that remains. The CZF is, therefore, constantly forced to reassert its claim to equal participation in areas of shared jurisdiction.

The trend in Canada is toward increasing power for the federations and increasingly centralized community decisions. Mergers of the local operations of CJC in Toronto and Winnipeg with the local welfare federations, as well as the contemplated merger in Montreal, are probably indicative of the long-range trend. One may therefore anticipate that the CZF will continue to find it difficult to hold a dominant place for itself in Jewish organizational life. In a certain sense there is indeed a great redundancy in Jewish affairs. If an organization is to be considered vital to the community and its interests it must be able to contribute something unique, or perform a unique function. The CZF or rather its constituent bodies have seen many of their responsibilities and powers drift away to other organisms over the years as circumstances and power configurations have changed. Accordingly, Zionist organizations may have to reconsider their own role in relation to other community groups. In the meantime, organizational competition within the Jewish community is likely to remain intense.

The Nature of Canadian Zionism

The CZF sees itself as an organization that plays a vital role in Canadian Jewish life: to foster among Jews a sense of peoplehood that is directed toward Israel. In so doing the CZF believes that it ensures Jewish survival as well as strong identification with and attachment to Israel. Substantively, this approach to Jewish life may be different from that employed by other groups. Zionists would argue, therefore, that the uniqueness of the CZF's mission is to be found in its approach to certain activities rather than in the activities themselves. For example, education is primarily a local matter, with some CJC involvement. Religious schools are also influenced by the national religious organizations. In contrast, the CZF believes that its educational activities, implemented by the only national department of Jewish education in Canada, carry a uniquely Zionist content because of the ideological foundation. Thus the CZF undertakes to prepare school curricula from a Zionist perspective, sends teachers to Israel for in-service training, and operates a teachers institute in Canada. Similarly, the CZF contends that its information activities carry a unique orientation that differs from those conducted by the Canada-Israel Committee, for example. Furthermore, information activities of the CZF are directed toward the Jewish community, whereas the CJC is oriented more toward government, the media and the non-Jewish world. These examples illustrate the way in which the Zionist undertaking is justified by a specifically Zionist, not just a Jewish, approach.

The second most important Zionist activity is the encouragement of *aliyah*. The CZF, constantly innovating means to stimulate *aliyah*, puts much effort into this aspect of the program. Results have been steady but unspectacular; about 1,000 *olim*, including former Israeli residents, left in 1977. Other activities include Youth and Hechalutz, public programming, fostering of trade with Israel and promotion of tourism. In addition, constituent groups carry out their own programs.

The Federation reflects the traditional party-oriented ideological structure with its executive representing the various constituent organizations. However, some organizations are not particularly dynamic or consequential forces in community life. Therefore, the effectiveness of the CZF is less than might otherwise be the case. Some of the constituent organizations represent the interests and concerns of immigrants who came from Europe many years ago. In certain constellations, the membership has remained static for fifteen or twenty years. Other organizations rely very heavily on a small number of traditional leaders. When old guard leadership is combined with ritualistic adherence to ideological positions, the quality of ideological debate and discussion is not very high. There seems to be little attempt to formulate new ideological responses to changing conditions. In the early 1970s there was an attempt by younger members of the CZF, people in their thirties, to form a new non-party grouping, called Zionists of the Seventies. This group has sent delegates to Zionist Congresses, but it has never really established itself.

It should not be surprising that the largest and most active Zionist group in the country is one that deemphasizes ideology: Hadassah-WIZO. It has about 17,000 members and reaches into cities and towns with small Jewish populations. In addition to its traditional charitable, social, medical and fund-raising work for Israel, Hadassah-WIZO has also become active in intellectual pursuits, public affairs and political work. Consequently, it is a very forceful voice in Canadian Zionism and the commitment of its members certainly enhances the status of the organization.

In retaining an ideologically-based structure, it would appear that the CZF limits its growth and potential as a force in Canadian Jewish life. While the vast majority of Canadian Jews are Zionists, at least in a broad sense, the ideological politics of organized Zionism do not have widespread appeal. If anything, the trend is away from an ideological approach to Israel, especially among younger Canadian Jews who do not remember pre-1948 Zionist politics, or who did not grow up in a Zionist youth group. This trend is more in harmony with political life in North America generally; furthermore, such an approach lends itself readily to unity and coherence of purpose. In principle it should be an attractive option.

When considering ideological trends, it should be remembered that the existing parties are interested in perpetuating the partisan approach, mainly because the personnel involved thereby retain their importance. Thus it suits their interests if the CZF remains relatively weak. As things stand, a member's chief loyalty and identification is related to his or her party and not to the CZF. Thus the CZF may be seen as an umbrella organization with coordinating responsibility; it is also a spokesman to the outside world. But for the individual member, affiliation with the CZF is merely something that goes along with membership in one of the parties. Naturally the parties have an importance of their own, especially Hadassah-WIZO, but their activities are oriented toward the individual Jew and his relationship toward Israel—an important consideration but not the only one. However, when interpreting Israel and Zionism to the non-Jewish world, the CZF is more important than its constituents.

Israel Orientation

Although the various Zionist organizations play a role in enabling Canadian Jews to relate to Israel, there are many ways in which the relationship can be established without the organizations. It is not an exaggeration to say that identification with Israel unites Jews from coast to coast, that it is the common denominator of Jewish commitment which brings together Jews of all religious and political persuasions. This is a far more generalized type of commitment than that expected by traditional Zionist organizations. The fund-raising agencies have wisely utilized this fact in their activities, thereby converting the charitable imperative into the preeminent Jewish affirmation for thousands of Jews. Consequently, the Zionists can no longer claim to be the sole medium for this type of expression.

The foregoing analysis indicates that the place of Zionism in Canadian Jewish life is somewhat problematic. In its essence Zionism is integral to Jewish life. But in the organizational sense, it is becoming peripheral. Officially, the CZF remains an equal partner on the national community scene, along with CJC and perhaps B'nai B'rith. It participates in all the decision-making processes involving Israel, representation to the government, the sponsorship of the Canada-Israel Committee, etc. But it maintains that position more through the force of particular personalities than through organizational strength and vitality. Despite the present size of its membership, it appears that the CZF may run into future difficulties because of the weakness of several of the constituent organizations, some of which may coalesce in the course of time.

In the meantime, organized Zionism will continue its activities, probably with an increasing emphasis on education. Efforts are under way to ensure that Jewish schools in the country have a meaningful

Zionist program. However, Jewish schools are conventionally very careful to retain control over their own curricula, so that it is not clear how much of an impact Zionist education will have. Most day schools exist primarily because of their religious orientation; their Zionist orientation varies with the outlook of the leadership. The CZF can make Zionist material and curricula available, but it is difficult to predict to what extent it will be integrated into the schools' program.

Anti-Zionist Activity

The relationship of Zionism to non-Zionist or anti-Zionist groups is not very important in the Canadian context, such groups being virtually non-existent within the Jewish community. Traditionally, major community groups, such as CJC, were not particularly Zionist in their outlook, preferring to concentrate on domestic issues. But the world and the Jewish community have changed over the years, causing changes in community organizations as well. After the Six Day War, Israel was no longer considered an issue for Zionists alone but rather an issue for all Jews. Hence the concept of a Jewish organization at once important and non-Zionist has become meaningless.

Outside the Jewish community, some anti-Zionist activity definitely takes place. In English-speaking Canada it goes on mainly among Arab Canadians, while in Quebec labor leaders and leftists have taken the lead. Furthermore, some Quebec separatists have used Jewish opposition to separation as an excuse to link attacks on Montreal Jews to attacks on Israel. Since 1967 there have been attempts to relate the concept of independence for Quebec with that of self-determination for the Palestinian Arabs. Here the CZF and its affiliates have taken a determined stand, and so have other organizations in the community. Jews view anti-Zionism as a matter of concern for the entire community.

A matter of concern which reaches beyond the present for the Jews of Montreal is the effect that Quebec independence would have on Zionist interests. A distinct possibility exists that an independent Quebec would pursue a pro-Arab foreign policy. Major elements among the intellectual and political elite who already favor the Arab cause, are also partial to aspects of Third World ideology. Hence the Jews of Montreal would probably be impotent politically. Furthermore, it is not inconceivable that their ability to provide financial and other aid to their Israeli brethren would be seriously impaired.

Outlook for Canadian Zionism

The purpose and functions of Zionist organizations have to be reassessed in the face of realistic considerations. First, there was a time when some Zionist ideologies provided an alternative to the religious approach to Jewish identity. Jews were not just adherents of a religion; they were also a nation. Zionism, as ideology of nationhood could appeal to the diverse elements in the community and provide a sense of purpose. But in recent years, a form of secular identification, based on welfare federations and fund-raising agencies, has emerged. This secular identity incorporates those elements of Zionist ideology that most Jews are willing to accept. Moreover, since the approach to Israel is generalized and not partisan, it could be argued that Zionist organizations as presently constituted do not really fill a need.

Second, many of the functions traditionally carried out by Zionist organizations have been taken over by other bodies or by joint committees sponsored by Zionists and other community organizations. Such sharing of power and responsibility diminishes the status of the CZF. In addition, there are many ways for the individual to engage in Zionist activity without necessarily becoming involved in Zionist organizations. This consideration, added to the fact that virtually every Jew supports Israel morally, politically and financially, means that most Jews probably do not believe that the Zionist organizations provide them with anything that cannot be obtained from some other organization.

Third, very few Canadian Jews go on *aliyah*. The figure is well below one percent per year. One can hardly blame the CZF, which has a very active *aliyah* program. Rather, it reflects the well-known proclivities of North American Jews. Whatever the reason, the limited interest in *aliyah* and the unlikelihood of a dramatic increase in numbers (except, perhaps, if Quebec separates) raise serious questions about the value of the *aliyah* program. Interestingly enough, the political uncertainty in Quebec has resulted in the departure of at least a few thousand Jews from Montreal. Few have gone to Israel; most have emigrated to the United States or to other parts of Canada.

All this indicates that Zionist ideologies and party identification are not really relevant concerns in the life of most Canadian Jews. Hence the outlook for the Zionist movement in Canada is somewhat uncertain. As generations change, it is likely that Zionism will have to change also or run the risk of simply being incorporated into a vague

Jewish ethos. The process which is already under way has by no means run its course. The challenge now is to develop an ideology and an organizational structure that will retain unique characteristics for Canadian Zionism, thereby extending the viability of the movement and orienting it to the tasks of the future rather than to the struggles of the past.

Australia

Peter Y. Medding

This paper interprets "Zionism in Australia" broadly. It will explain the relationship of Australian Jews to the Holy Land, to the Jewish national idea, and to the independent Jewish State. It goes beyond details of the development of the organized Zionist movement in Australia and the attitude of Australian Jews to Zionism, although between 1920 and 1948 the two were more or less synonymous. The establishment of an independent Jewish State, of an autonomous Jewish national entity, significantly broadened and deepened the ethnic and national dimensions of Jewish peoplehood. It thus directly involved the basic Jewish self-conceptions of identity and meaning, and the important psychological dimensions of existence.[1]

Early Origins and Struggles

The miniscule Jewish community in Australia (numbering only 1,887 in 1851, 15,239 in 1901 and 32,019 in 1947) was connected with the Holy Land from the middle of the nineteenth century through the visits of various *meshulahim* (emissaries) who came to collect funds. To assist these activities was generally regarded as a philanthropic endeavor, deriving from the obligation of Jews everywhere to aid their less fortunate brethren. This feeling of universal charitable brotherhood, together with significant contemporary issues [2] was instrumental in raising questions about the nature of Jewish peoplehood. Thus, in

1. The effect of Israel upon Jewish peoplehood and the problems it creates for Jews is discussed in P. Y. Medding, "A Contemporary Paradox: Israel and Jewish Peoplehood," *Forum*, vol. 26, no. 1, 1977, pp. 5-16.
2. In Australia the most important of these were the debates over the relationship of Church and State, state aid to various forms of religious activity and the education question. These are fully analyzed in I. Getzler, *Neither Toleration Nor Favour: The Australian Chapter of Jewish Emancipation*, Melbourne, 1970.

the middle of the nineteenth century Australian Jewry was engaged in a *public* debate about the ethnic, religious and national components of Judaism. This debate, rekindled with the founding of the Zionist movement in Australia, did not cease until after the establishment of the State of Israel. The earlier debate encompassed both Jews and non-Jews, and it is significant that in countering anti-Semitic attacks, some established sections of Jewry responded by denying the existence of that national element of Jewishness which made Zionism itself possible.

The anti-Jewish view was clearly enunciated in terms of the integral connection between religion, nationality and citizenship. James Martin in the New South Wales Legislative Council in 1854 asked "whether they would allow a people who professed themselves to be a distinct and separate nation, to step in and share with them those privileges which were intended for British subjects alone and which were peculiar to the Christian auspices under which they lived."[3]

Australian Jewry responded in two characteristic ways to such attacks and to the more common argument that it would be wrong for a Christian state to extend aid to non-Christians. The first was to deny Jewish national separateness and distinctiveness, thus affirming the Jews' capacity for loyal citizenship and their willingness to undertake civic obligations despite their clear religious differences.

Another response was that of the communal leaders and probably the majority of Jews. It was a proud and public affirmation of Jewish peoplehood in universal terms, and a demand that Jews be accorded citizenship equality as a right.

Until the last decade of the nineteenth century the attitude in the Australian colonies towards most minorities was fairly liberal. The social ambience changed around the turn of the present century as nationalism took an exclusivist turn and Australia became wary of immigrants, if not outrightly prejudiced and xenophobic towards all settlers who were not of white British origin. Anti-Semitism became part of the public scene, and anti-Semitic stereotypes appeared in the popular press. It was into this kind of climate that Zionism, with its emphasis on Jewish separateness and distinctiveness and its aim of political sovereignty in Eretz Israel entered into the life of Australian Jewry.

3. Quoted in Getzler, *op. cit.* p. 46.

During the 1890s organized Zionism was taken up mainly by East-European immigrants, eliciting various kinds of reactions in the Jewish community. One view held that the idea of a Jewish homeland in Palestine was sheer fantasy and that resources devoted to it were wasted. Others, apprehensive that the position of Jews as British citizens of Australia might be compromised, were ambivalent or even completely opposed to Zionism. The more extreme attitude, most common among the more established English and Australian-born elements, held that support for Zionism implied that Jews were members of a separate race and unpatriotic. In their view, Jews were held together only by ties of religion and ethics, and they owed total national allegiance to their country of residence. Most outpsoken were the rabbis in Sydney who publicly opposed Zionism on the religious grounds that it was a secular movement which undermined the messianic teachings of Judaism.[4]

After the Balfour Declaration and the assumption of the Mandate for Palestine by the British, Zionism was taken more seriously. The Australian Zionist Federation, the first Jewish body established on an interstate basis, marks a significant change in the community structure. A new generation of rabbis, different from the Anglo-Jewish rabbinical leadership, was at its helm. Before 1939 these included Rabbi Israel Brodie (later Chief Rabbi of the British Commonwealth) who came from Britain but was of East-European parentage and spoke Yiddish, Rabbi Freedman of Perth and Rabbi Levy of Sydney.

More general support for Zionism as well as for Hebrew culture came from newly arrived East-European immigrants and those from Eretz Israel. When conflict developed between Britain and the Yishuv, the Australian Jewish community was divided. The patrician leaders and rabbis of the Anglo-Jewish establishment considered it unpatriotic to oppose British actions and criticize British policies. They frequently dissociated themselves and their communities from Zionist resolutions and activities critical of Britain. To speak of "a homeless Jewish Nation" which needed a national home in Palestine was to suggest that Jews elsewhere were aliens, that they were deprived of their civic equality; it would also create the specter of dual nationalities and loyalties.

The Anglo-Jewish patrician leadership consistently questioned

4. See S. Rutland, "The New South Wales Jewish Community 1880-1914," (B.A. Hons., Thesis, History Department), University of Sydney, 1969, pp. 88-89.

the right of the Zionists to speak in the name of the Jewish community. But the newly-formed representative bodies and their leaders solidly supported the Zionist position. The formerly dominant Anglo-Jewish patrician leaders were now out of touch with community views and clearly in the minority.

In fact, Australian Jewry's major representative body, the Executive Council of Australian Jewry (ECAJ), in conjunction with the Zionist Federation, made known its unequivocal support for a Jewish State, and consistently pressed its claims before the Australian Government. Some of the recent immigrants had become actively involved in the Labor Party and were thus instrumental in putting the Zionist case before the Minister for External Affairs, Dr. Herbert V. Evatt, who was Chairman of the United Nations Ad Hoc Committee on the Palestine Question. With the establishment of the State of Israel, most active opposition ceased, although in certain quarters a coolness to the Jewish State lingered on.[5]

Organization and Structure

By the time Israel became independent, Zionism had succeeded in gaining control of the community's official leadership. One could no longer be a major communal leader if one was opposed to Zionism, because this now meant opposing the State of Israel, although Zionist leadership or active involvement in the Zionist movement were not criteria for communal leadership. The overall outcome was complete integration of the general communal and Zionist leadership. Not only was this integration indicative of successful political organization in capturing the centers of communal power, but a direct and authentic reflection of Jewish public opinion which was unequivocally pro-Israel. Such feelings had been reinforced by the immigration of almost 30,000 Jews, most of whom had come from Eastern Europe after World War II.

The structure of Zionist activity throughout Australia follows a common pattern. In each state, the various forms of Zionist organization are combined within the local State Zionist Council. The state councils are joined together at the national level in the Zionist Federation of Australia; and parallel with this organization is a federally

5. The period after 1920 is dealt with in some detail in P.Y. Medding, *From Assimilation to Group Survival: A Political and Sociological Analysis of an Australian Jewish Community*, Melbourne, 1968, pp. 127–140.

organized appeal structure, Federal Keren Hayesod. Appeals for Israel and local purposes are separate, though closely coordinated. In theory the Zionist Federation is the senior body; it handles all political and representative functions and conducts most of the negotiations with the various Zionist bodies in Jerusalem, particularly with the Jewish Agency; the Keren Hayesod, however, maintains its own channels of communication.

Structurally, the Zionist movement in Australia, in common with other major Jewish organizations, has developed into a single all-embracing and united system, closely coordinated with the major representative bodies of the community. No dissident elements threaten internal or public unity. The Zionist movement is the spearhead of the organized community's activities on behalf of Israel and its connections with it.

The Zionist Movement in the Community

The establishment of Israel resolved the great debate in Australian Jewry about a Jewish State and eliminated the problem of dual loyalties and dual nationality. But after the initial euphoria subsided, other undercurrents and antagonisms came to the surface. While there was no open opposition to the State, there was considerable opposition to the Zionist Movement. Even as they admitted the primacy of Israel's overall interests, many local communal leaders denied the Zionist leaders the privileged position of being spokesmen for the Jewish community in matters affecting Israel. Similarly they refused to accept the local Zionist leadership's definition of Israel's needs and its relationship to local needs.

In 1948 tensions developed over another issue: should Australian Jewry encourage European Jews to immigrate to Australia? Some Zionist leaders argued that Jews should now be assisted to emigrate to Israel and that further Jewish immigration to Australia be actively discouraged. At a special ECAJ conference, the majority decided to allow the immigrants the choice, to give them full assistance if they decided to come to Australia, but to avoid offering any inducements for them to do so.

Differences also arose over the allocation of appeal funds. Proposals to tax all Jewish communal appeals for Israel to pay for local community administrative activities were regularly opposed in principle by the Australian Zionist movement. In all these disagreements the antipathies were directed not only at Israel but at the movement, which neglected local community needs in the belief that Jewish life outside Israel had little future. Indicative of this approach was the Zionist movement's attitude to Jewish education in Australia, which it encouraged mainly because it would strengthen Zionism and support for Israel.

In the community at large, apart from a few small groups which were opposed to the State of Israel on ideological grounds (the Bund in particular), these early tensions and conflicts were less felt. It soon became apparent that Israel had wrought a fundamental revolution in attitudes by giving psychological security to both the average Jew and the communal leader. A survey in Melbourne in 1962 found no active anti-Zionists, some Jews who were neutral, and the vast majority sympathetic to Israel. About 25 percent of the community were actively involved in Zionism and Israel.[6] The Six Day War completely eradicated any previous antipathies and tensions, significantly altering the status of Israel and Zionism in the communal structure. This was reinforced by the Yom Kippur War.

Many Australian Jews feel so deeply involved with Israel that it constitutes a central aspect of their identity as Jews. In the Six Day War large numbers of young people volunteered to go to Israel to assist in various ways. A survey conducted prior to the war had already demonstrated that just under half of those interviewed had a very high degree of involvement with Israel, that is, twice as many as in 1962, while about 30 percent had a moderate degree of involvement and only 20 percent had a low degree of involvement. Negative reactions did not surface at all.[7]

Unprecedented sums have been donated since 1967, increasing with a particularly dramatic jump in 1973. There was also a rise in the number of people going on *aliyah*: after 1967 an estimated 2,000 Australian Jews migrated to Israel, a high proportion when compared with other communities.

Since 1967 Israel has been the main item on which the Jewish community has participated in public political debate, sought media

6. *Ibid.*
7. R. Taft, "The Impact of the Middle East Crisis of June 1967 on Jews in Melbourne," in *Jews in Australian Society*, P.Y. Medding, ed., Melbourne, 1973, ch. 7; R. Taft & G. Solomon, "The Melbourne Jewish Community and the Middle East War of 1973," *Jewish Journal of Sociology*, vol. 16, no. 11, June 1974. Similar findings in Sydney were reported in S. Encel, *The Sydney Jewish Community*, University of New South Wales, 1972.

exposure, and made approaches to politicians. A professionally-directed office was set up for the first time by the representative communal leadership and the Zionists on an equal basis, even though the Zionist movement supplies most of the financial resources, and therefore has taken over most of the activities on behalf of Israel. While official approaches to the Australian Government still remain the province of the ECAJ, the partial displacement of other communal leaders by Zionist professionals and leaders has not proved to be an easy transition.

These changes reflect the increasing importance of the power of the purse in communal and representational matters. Systematic and professional fund raising, and the fact that substantial donors rose to leadership positions, have created a semi-autonomous Appeal body whose activities now overshadow those of the Zionist Federation even though still operating within its framework. These administrative changes symbolize in microcosm the changes in the community; in the last 25 years the Zionist movement has become more community-oriented, while the Australian Jewish community has become much more Israel-centered.

Zionism, Israel and Jewish Peoplehood

There can be no doubt that the role of Zionism in Australia has undergone fundamental change, paralleled by universal developments in the nature of Jewish ethnic identity and peoplehood. While Jewish religious practices and beliefs have declined in extent and intensity, the ethnic dimension of Jewish identity has risen in importance.[8] Zionism changed from a charitable endeavor into a central element in Jewishness, a fundamental facet of ethnic identity. Israel has become the permanent specific and self-explanatory focus and rationale of Jewish existence. With the establishment of the State, the post-Zionist era of Jewish history has begun insofar as Zionism is the movement of Jewish national liberation. In other words, Israel has created problems of identity for Jews outside it which must be faced squarely if we are to assess the import and future development of Zionism in Australia.[9]

Primordial feelings of Jewish peoplehood focus upon Israel

8. For further analysis of these questions see Medding, "A Contemporary Paradox," *loc. cit.*
9. The following discussion closely follows the argument in Medding, *ibid.*

because it is the only territory exercising any legitimate Jewish claims over members of the Jewish People. This means that Jewry outside of Israel has its sense of peoplehood continually reinforced by its various ties with Israel. The greater the pull of Israel, the less the claims for any kind of Jewish autonomy in the Diaspora—a feature of Jewish politics before Israel came into being as an independent sovereign Jewish political entity.

Australian society in general has changed over the last thirty years. The migration program has brought over 2.5 million immigrants, of whom less than 50 percent have come from the British Isles; large numbers have come from southern, central and eastern parts of Europe and increasing proportions from the Mediterranean region. Indigenous Australian nationalism has lost most of its exclusiveness, and thereby much of its distinctive character as a white British society dedicated to the preservation of the British way of life.

In a sense, Australia has become denationalized. Various forms of national cultural identity seem currently acceptable, and a dominant, or even desirable, pattern of Australian national identity is hardly discernible. These changes have direct implications for Australian Jewry beyond the specific and not unimportant fact that anti-Jewish prejudice seems to have declined. It may be useful to consider possible alternative strategies whereby Australian Jewry can resolve the tensions inherent in contemporary Jewish identity.

(1) *To denationalize contemporary Jewish identity.* This would involve reemphasizing the religious and cultural elements of the Jewish tradition and heritage. It would also mean sharpening the concept of the centrality of the Jewish People, from which all Jewish communities would draw their significance. While still the most significant Jewish communal entity, Israel would become secondary to the universal Jewish People. Its independence would be justified, not as an end in itself, but as one means among many of fulfilling the broader universal and human goals and aspirations of the Jewish People. Some of the leading exponents of this approach have tended to the position that over-concern with Israel and over-commmitment to its needs and interests have deprived Jewish life outside Israel of vital energy and support.

While such an approach might have some success in the United States, with its Jewish cultural and scholarly resources, it seems less feasible in the Australian Jewish community. Despite a widespread organizational and educational network involving larger proportions of Jews than in most other countries, Australian Jewry is distinguished by the derivativeness and poverty of its religious, cultural and intellectual resources.

(2)   To denationalize Australian identity. The basis here would be development of a high level of Jewish ethnic identity, while simultaneously maintaining Australian national identity at the minimally accepted level. As long as the migration flow continues (probably for another generation), and as long as the dominant values are working-class rather than middle-class, they will probably hold little attraction for the Jews. In this way tension may be avoided, but eventually a distinctive sense of Australian national identity is likely to develop. Nor would such a strategy avoid the inevitable tensions of direct conflict between Israeli and Australian policies. Some of the recent experiences of the Jewish community in relation to the Whitlam government, and Mr. Whitlam's reactions to the Jewish community's opposition to his policies, have given an idea of what might lie in store.

This approach also suffers from some of the limitations of the first approach. To be viable beyond immediate concern with Jewish and Israeli survival, that is to say, to develop a conscious and coherent Jewish ethnic commitment that can survive direct threats to Jewish existence will need intellectual and cultural resources beyond those presently available within the Australian Jewish community.

(3)   Dual Identities. This involves a combination of the previous two approaches. It would seek to promote cultural pluralism, in which the national identity aspect of Australian citizenship would be fully developed with a high level of Jewish ethnic identity and commitment. Tension would be controlled by keeping the competing identities in more or less separate compartments.[10] That would be suitable for those who are capable of living with marked ambiguity and uncertainty, but could be adopted only if it is accepted from the outset that such dual identities would prevent the development of both to their highest possible degree. This approach is unlikely as long as Australian national and cultural identity remains in its present vague and indeterminate state.

(4)   Synthesis: a new Australian Jewish identity? Such an approach would seek to synthesize elements of both forms of identity,

10. Compartmentalization as a means of coping with Jewish ethnic identity in culturally pluralist societies is discussed in P.Y. Medding, "Equality and the Shrinkage of Jewish Identity," in *World Jewry and the State of Israel*, Moshe Davis, ed., New York, 1977.

rather than keep them separate. It would have to be based upon con-
gruent cultural values, shared historical experiences, complementary
national and cultural symbols, and joint participation in the social
structure on the basis of equality and mutual respect. Under such conditions Jews highly committed to Jewish identity might find it possible
to develop a new Australian Jewish identity, especially suited to and
influenced by the Australian cultural environment.

The current obstacles to such a development loom large. No
common historical actuality can be counted on to provide the foundation of such a synthesis.[11] Similarly, while Jewish social participation
takes place mainly within predominantly Jewish social circles, such
experiences and shared values are less likely to develop. However,
conditions might arise in the future which would facilitate such a synthesis. Australia at war or under siege for a long period of time would
be one such possible basis.

Conversely, there are obstacles within the Jewish community to
such an approach. Those who are devoted to Jewish cultural symbols
and values are usually the least likely to favor such a development.
Israel also stands as a constant reminder of all that is distinctive and
non-shared, and reinforces the special sense of intimate Jewish peoplehood, thereby rendering a new synthesis highly improbable.

Zionism and Israelism

The preceding analysis reveals a phenomenon which we
observed in microcosm in the small Australian Jewish community and
must be examined more closely in relation to its universal implications
for Zionism. This is the phenomenon of almost universal support
among Jews for Israel—Israelism. What needs further analysis is the
relationship between Israelism as a contemporary form of almost universal Jewish loyalty and Zionism. In short, is Israelism today synonymous with Zionism? How does it relate to the classical Zionism of the
pre-State era? Can one be an Israelist without being a Zionist?

11. As Erikson has said, "The alternative to an exclusive totalism is the wholeness of the
more inclusive identity." Applying this to the American Negro he asks, "If the Negro
wants to find that other identity which permits him to be self-certain as a Negro (or a
descendant of Negroes) and *integrated as an American*, what joint historical actuality
can he count on?" E. H. Erikson, "The Concept of Identity in Race Relations," in *The
Negro American*, T. Parsons and K.B. Clark, eds., Boston, 1965, p. 247. See also
pp. 227-253. By transposing Jew for Negro, and Australian for American in the citation,
the full impact of the argument is received.

Before 1948, it can be argued, Zionism and Israelism were more or less synonymous terms. To seek and to support the establishment of a Jewish State was Zionism; to oppose it was anti-Zionism. At that historic juncture, to support the establishment of the Jewish State meant to affirm the national aspects of Jewish peoplehood when they were not universally recognized, and to oppose those conceptions of Jewishness which were solely in religious terms and those which sought the complete national identification or integration of Jews within their countries of residence. To endorse the idea of a Jewish State was Zionism; all the other ideological arguments, conceptions and proposals were merely commentary, insofar as they were either a justification of the idea of and need for a State or, alternatively, conceptions about how the State should be organized.

But with the establishment of Israel, a more discriminating criterion than mere support is necessary, if for no other reason than the ease of support and the futility of opposition to reality and established fact. That is to say, the meaning of Zionism has changed in the face of Israelism. Today, by supporting Israel one affirms universal Jewish peoplehood in its national aspects without being a Zionist. It is even possible to conceive of political support by Jews for Israel on various grounds while simultaneously rejecting the incorporating aspects of Jewish ethnic identity and peoplehood.

To make the distinction clear, the concept of Zionism must therefore be understood in more precise and carefully conceived ideological terms. One way is to suggest that Zionism refers specifically to the acceptance and endorsement of the goal of independent Jewish majority existence in a sovereign state as the *ultimate* expression of Jewish peoplehood in political and national terms. It is the desire to encapsulate this goal within clearly delineated national boundaries, with the independent sovereign State as the vehicle for fulfilment.

Thus the major distinguishing criterion of Zionism is the conception of the role of the State of Israel as a value in its own right in determining the nature and meaning of Jewishness and Jewish peoplehood. The State is not merely a form of organization characteristic of all contemporary political systems in every society, but it is seen as a vehicle endowed with specific qualities and values, which *adds* real meaning to Jewish existence, which *only it*, as a sovereign majority political entity, is capable of providing.

Outside of Israel, those Jews who accept this outlook and who therefore relegate Jewish minority existence in the Diaspora to secondary significance in the Jewish national framework of things would be considered Zionists, even if they did not go to live in Israel. Support for Israel on emotional grounds would by this definition not be considered Zionism. Nor, paradoxically, would participation in the Zionist Movement in whatever capacity, as long as this participation did not derive from the type of commitment we have outlined above. Similarly, those who deny the special contribution to the Jewish People and Jewishness made by a sovereign state embodying majority Jewish existence, could not be regarded as Zionists, however rich their Jewish cultural or religious life and contribution to the Jewish People. Nor would going to live in Israel alone be a sufficient criterion, unless it were *aliyah* motivated by considerations such as the above. Moreover, Jews living in Israel who are loyal citizens of the State but do not recognize its contribution to the meaning of Jewishness and Jewish peoplehood would not be regarded as Zionists, whereas those who do recognize it, even as part of a more complex or all-embracing value system, would be.

The irony of history is such that the victory of Zionism in achieving the establishment of a Jewish State has led directly to the decline of Zionism as a major motivating and energizing force in the life of the Jewish communities outside Israel—a position it previously occupied despite strong opposition—and its replacement by Israelism which now enjoys almost universal support. In this, Australian Jewry is not an exception.

South Africa

Marcus Arkin

By world standards, South African Jewry is a relatively small community of approximately 116,000 souls. It has become heavily urbanized, with some 60,000 concentrated in and around Johannesburg, a further 25,000 in the Cape Town area, and the balance divided mainly among the other large cities, such as Durban, Port Elizabeth, and Pretoria.

It is by no means easy to decide what it means to be Jewish in a South African context, or to classify the various elements of "Jewishness" and discover the manner in which these are expressed by those who regard themselves as Jews. There can be no question that sentiment plays an extremely important role, especially with regard to the basic question of Jewish survival and the State of Israel. In fact, since it has always been legitimate for Jews in South Africa to be deeply involved in their national liberation movement, an ever-increasing proportion have expressed their identity in Zionist rather than orthodox religious terms. In other words, Zionism in South Africa has provided an anchor for Jewish ethnicity.

Hence, in terms of the scope of activities and the number of persons involved in its affairs, the Zionist movement in South Africa forms the backbone of communal life. Local Israel United Appeal contributions per capita are among the highest in the world; since 1948 the rate of *aliyah*, relatively, has been at least five times greater than that of the United States; and the South African Zionist Federation probably is the largest and most complex Jewish communal organization in the entire southern hemisphere.

What are the circumstances that have fashioned such a unique territorial Zionist situation?

Zionist Action

In contrast to the situation elsewhere, the South African Zionist Federation (SAZF), established in 1899, is a highly effective umbrella organization for all communal Zionist activities, including fund raising. The Women's Zionist Organization (with some 18,000 members), the Maccabi sports association, the Jewish National Fund, and the Zionist youth movements are, in fact, integral departments of the Federation and subject to its overall discipline. From its headquarters in Johannesburg and through its six provincial offices, the SAZF disseminates knowledge of Israel to the Jewish community and the general public through lectures, seminars, films and publications; it publishes its own weekly newspaper, *The Zionist Record*, maintains the most specialized and best-stocked libraries of Jewish books and journals in the country, while its cultural officers and its audio-visual programs reach even the most isolated communities.[1]

The encouragement of *aliyah*, naturally, is given top priority by the SAZF. A successful *aliyah* movement functions countrywide under the Federation's auspices, and in Israel itself the SAZF maintains a network of offices to assist South African *olim*.

Perhaps the most important factor accounting for the strength and all-embracing nature of the SAZF is the manner in which fund raising for Israel's human needs has always been an integral part of the Federation's activities. This means that the biennial Israel United Appeal (IUA) campaigns reach out to the entire Jewish community, without undue concentration on wealthy donors. This has positive Zionist educational effects. It is noteworthy that no deductions are made for local communal needs.[2]

It has been argued from time to time that the IUA should no longer be an integral part of the Federation, since an injustice is being done to major contributors who are in a situation of "responsibility without power,"[3] though there is little evidence that these contributors feel aggrieved in any way. In effect, such proposals would transform

1. A documentary entitled "It is No Legend," which depicts the manifold activities of the SAZF, was selected by the South African Tourist Department for its entry at the 1977 Antwerp Festival of travel and tourism films.
2. The one important exception in this regard is subsidization by the IUA of the Jewish day schools; this is done with the knowledge and support of the Jewish Agency to ensure that future generations will be imbued with a Zionist outlook. In short, it is an investment in the future financial support of Israel's needs.
3. See, for example, a report of the Johannesburg IUA Chairman's remarks at a "top donor" banquet, *Zionist Record*, Sept. 16, 1977.

the IUA into a closed shop run by a small coterie of wealthy donors—a development wholly foreign and iniquitous to the Zionist traditions of the country; to date the Federation has been sufficiently steadfast in resisting such pressures.

Spectrum of Attitudes

In view of this unique and effective Zionist structure in South Africa, what are the prospects for mass fulfilment of the basic Zionist ideal of *aliyah*? To provide even a tentative answer, several misconceptions concerning the Jewish community within the context of the local environment must be removed.

Outside observers without firsthand knowledge of the socioeconomic and political realities of contemporary South Africa are apt to display simplistic attitudes toward the country's complex problems.[4] The population reflects an incredible patchwork of ethnic strains, languages, and modes of living, which has led to tremendous contrasts in rates of progress, with spectacular economic development in some regions and a state of primitive backwardness in others. Undoubtedly, part of the prevailing earnings-gap between white and black stems from discriminatory legislation coupled with the need to raise the productivity of the non-white labor force. Failure on the government's part to take timely and decisive remedial action has helped produce the volatile situation in the black townships which has been so prominent in the world press from mid-1976.

It would be misleading to suggest that the Jewish community is in the vanguard of forces urging political change. Jewish participation in recent general elections—insofar as it can be meaningfully assessed—is indicative of a wide spectrum of attitudes, ranging from a belief in preserving the *status quo* to an awareness that the country's future may be at risk unless some major socio-political transformations are introduced without delay. By no stretch of imagination, however, can South African Jewry be regarded as a "community under stress" and therefore particularly responsive to the attractions of *aliyah*.

Hence, while individuals continue to emigrate (as they have done over the last three decades), chiefly to North America, Australia

4. See, for example, Julius Nyerere, "America and Southern Africa," *Foreign Affairs*, July 1977; R. P. Stevens, "Israel and South Africa," *Middle East International*, March 1977; B. Beit-Hallahmi, "South Africa and Israel's Strategy of Survival," *New Outlook*,

and Israel,[5] the great majority are likely to remain in the country of their birth and hopefully play a constructive role in ameliorating South Africa's problems.

A Dedicated Zionist Youth

Where does the Zionist movement stand today in relation to the Jewish youth of South Africa?

The day school movement has been highly successful at both primary and secondary levels. In some centers, such as Port Elizabeth and Durban, more than 70 percent of all children attending school are pupils of the Jewish day schools; in the larger cities, the proportion is smaller but nevertheless impressive. Through the Zionist Federation pupils have for many years been enabled to participate in *ulpanim* (Hebrew study groups) in Israel. In addition, the Judaica courses offered within the schools themselves have a basic Zionist content.

Moreover, using the Federation as its agent in South Africa, the Jewish Agency provides subsidization for the day school movement. This has proved to be a worthwhile long-term investment in *aliyah* and young Zionist communal leadership. Although the day schools are controlled by a separate board of education, a fruitful partnership has been evolved between the schools and the Zionist Federation.

The practical consequence of this partnership is the production of a whole new generation with no inhibitions about the centrality of Israel in Jewish life. These products of the day schools do not experience any *galut* phobia concerning divided allegiances or dual loyalties: their responsibilities as South African citizens in no way inhibit their dedication to the cause of the Jewish State, nor has such dedication been questioned by the public at large.

The four *halutz* Zionist youth movements (*Habonim, B'nei Akiva, Betar* and *M'ginim*[6]) taken together have an approximate membership of 7,000. These movements all suffer from a common leadership problem: in recent years, as the military call-up period has been progressively extended with fewer deferments for university studies, the age level of the *madrichim* (leaders) has steadily fallen. This has inev-

---

5. Since 1970, and especially since the Yom Kippur War, the number of Israelis migrating to South Africa has exceeded South African Jews proceeding on *aliyah;* there are now indications that this trend may have been reversed. See *Sunday Times* (Johannesburg), Oct. 16, 1977, p. 11.
6. Youth wing of the Progressive Reform Movement.

itably had an adverse impact on the depth and caliber of the programs. South African participation in extended youth courses in Israel has also been gravely impeded. Nevertheless, the movements—through their popular summer camps, winter seminars and regular weekly gatherings—play a vital role in furthering Zionist education, particularly among children who do not attend Jewish day schools. Their activities are coordinated and subsidized on a national level by the Zionist Youth Council, a fully integrated department of the Zionist Federation.

The number of Jewish students enrolled with South African institutions of higher learning in any given academic year is a matter of guesswork (it varies from 5,000 to 7,000); yet it is almost certain that the proportion of students within the Jewish segment is considerably higher than that of any other ethnic group.

To what extent does this very important part of the community identify with matters of Zionist interest? If the yardstick of participation in the activities of the various student Jewish associations (SJA) is employed, the answer must definitely be pessimistic. In fact, there is an inverse correlation between the size of the Jewish student population and active membership of the relevant SJAs. However, this criterion is misleading: both the universities of Cape Town and Witwatersrand (Johannesburg) are essentially commuter institutions, where the great majority of students attend lectures but participate only marginally in extra-curricular activities. Thus, although the larger campuses reveal a somewhat disappointing picture of organized Zionist involvement, that by no means implies a general apathy towards matters concerning Israel.[7] In fact, on the basis of family background and the social circles in which the students move, it would appear that the majority are indeed conscious of their Zionist heritage but find outlets of expression away from the campus itself.

Moreover, Jewish students are not under the same kind of pressure as, for example, their counterparts in Britain: there are no organized New Left or pro-Palestinian elements at the local universities. But how do Jewish students react to the obvious moral dilemma which many of them experience as upholders of Jewish ethical traditions in a country of racial discrimination based on color? The tendency has been for them to express their views as individuals or through other

7. Postgraduate students from South Africa in recent years have always constituted a substantial portion of those enrolled at the International Graduate Center for Hebrew and Jewish Studies in Arad, Israel.

student organizations rather than on the platform of the South African
Union of Jewish Students. In general this has also applied to the leadership of the youth movements, though *Habonim*, particularly, has
been torn between its loyalty to the common discipline of the Zionist
Movement and its own egalitarian-socialist outlook.[8] In contrast to the
general body of students and youth leaders, most Jewish academicians
tend to be apathetic. Under pressure, they will identify with matters of
Zionist concern but normally their involvement is minimal.[9]

      Accordingly, any notable upsurge in *aliyah* from South Africa
will take place only if absorption facilities, economic conditions and
the overall quality of life in Israel show steady improvement. This
would lead to a deflection in the normal outward movement from
English-speaking countries to the Jewish State. In this regard, therefore, the Jews of South Africa should be expected to perform notably
better than their coreligionists in Britain or the United States, except
for that minority motivated essentially by their superior Zionist background.

The Zionist Dimension

      In the broader field of South Africa-Israel relations, the local
Zionist movement has played a notable role in promoting closer ties
between the two countries. The relationship has caused a certain
amount of soul searching and misgiving among Israeli commentators,
some of it based on spurious moral grounds, since before 1973 the
Jewish State maintained close ties with certain Black African territories which had records of political tyranny far worse than anything
experienced in South Africa.[10] Outside critics—especially in the Third
World—cannot be expected to understand this relationship, since it is
the product of historical forces; it stems from the fact that Zionism has
always been the primary cultural expression and group concern of

8. Inevitably, the public affairs committee of the Federation considers the possible
impact on Israel-South African relations in its broadest context when considering what
official line to adopt on any particular issue.
9. See my comments in "How Jewish are our Jewish Academics," *Jewish Affairs* (Johannesburg), March 1974, pp. 18-20.
10. See, for example, Asher Maniv, "Israel's South African Connection," *Israel Star*,
Sept. 17, 1976 (originally published in *Davar*); and Michael Wade, "Bypassing Africa—
and History," *New Outlook*. Nov. 1976.

South African Jewry, coupled with the sympathetic and positive attitudes of Afrikaner statesmen which predate the Balfour Declaration.[11]

Zionism in South Africa has helped create the appropriate climate for the burgeoning of "the Israel connection." To what extent has Zionism in South Africa, in turn, been influenced by the forging of these close links? The answer lies mainly in the field of public relations. There can be little doubt that the present cordial ties have been of positive assistance to the energetic band of Zionist workers in their many-sided efforts to promote the cause of Israel.

The Federation's information programs about the Jewish State now reach a much wider audience because the general media have regular news and feature items concerning Israel which have whetted the popular appetite for films, lectures and books of an in-depth nature.[12] This has led, also, to the establishment of close liaison with the local chapters of Christian Action for Israel, members of which aim to further the Zionist cause in a practical way. And the Federation works very closely with the South Africa-Israel Chamber of Economic Relations.

On the other hand, there is growing awareness in local Zionist circles that not nearly enough energy has been expended on the presentation of Israel's image to the twenty million people comprising South Africa's Black, Colored and Indian communities. The first halting and belated steps are currently being taken to establish closer contact with non-white church leaders, newspaper editors, university principals and others who mold opinion, but great care must be exercised in this regard to ensure that the movement remains aloof from local political issues and controversies.

For the foreseeable future, the community is likely to remain embedded in the local demographic pattern, but as a diminishing segment.[13] At the same time, it is extremely difficult to forecast future trends in a situation where so many variables are at work. Still, the Zionist dimension and links with Israel could in all probability assume added significance.

---

11. G. Shimoni, "Jan Christian Smuts and Zionism," *Jewish Social Studies*, Summer 1977.

12. In any single month, the Federation's mobile audio-visual unit visits several church groups, women's organizations, military camps and schools.

13. Over the last forty years, emigration, assimilation and intermarriage have reduced the community from 4.5 percent of the white population to 2.8 percent.

Western Europe

France

Doris Bensimon

The attitude of the Jews of France towards Zionism has become set in an unfavorable sterotype. The structural weakness of the Zionist Organization of France is deplored, as is the reluctance of the French Jews to contribute to the upbuilding of the State of Israel by political support and *aliyah*. This negative image, which has its roots in the past, is no longer entirely justified. In tracing the evolution of the attitude of the Jews of France towards Zionism and the State of Israel, certain developments must be considered.

Revolutionary France in 1791 was the first country to grant civic and political emancipation to the Jews. In reality, however, this emancipation was not realized through legislation; it was achieved after a struggle which lasted through the nineteenth century, even into the twentieth. The Jews of France were called upon to prove by their daily actions and political involvement that they were full-fledged citizens; in other words, they had to assimilate. It is not surprising, therefore, that French Jews are particularly sensitive to fluctuations of French policy in the Middle East. In the realization of the Zionist program, France has at times played an important and positive role; at other times its role has been ambiguous or even negative.

These considerations have been somewhat modified by the fact that since the nineteenth century French Jewry has been developed by successive waves of immigrants, each new wave reviving a Jewish community threatened by assimilationist tendencies. The immigrants' attitude towards Zionism has sometimes been more positive than that of earlier established French Jews. These points should be borne in mind if we are to understand how the Zionist movement evolved in France.

From the Birth of Zionism until World War I

Political Zionism had its beginnings in Paris at the time of the Dreyfus Affair. Although Herzl had been a great admirer of France, his faith was deeply shaken by the anti-Semitic manifestations that followed the trial. He published his *Judenstaat* in February 1896, one year after Captain Dreyfus was publicly stripped of his military rank. Eighteen months later, in August 1897, the first Zionist Congress was convened in Basle.

Herzl did not wait for the publication of his pamphlet to broach his scheme with influential personalities. In June 1895, he met with Baron Maurice de Hirsch, banker, philanthropist and founder of the Jewish Colonization Association, who declared that the ambitious plan was doomed to fail. One year later, in July 1896, Herzl discussed the project with Baron Edmond de Rothschild, who was at the time generously aiding the settlements of the First *Aliyah* in Palestine. Rothschild, too, dismissed the idea of a Jewish State.

Both Hirsch and Rothschild, who represented the French notables of their time, were aware of the tragic plight of the Jews of Eastern Europe and the problems connected with their emigration. Still, they rejected Herzl's plan. Although they were giving away part of their wealth to help establish Jewish colonies in Argentina and even in Eretz Israel, they could not comprehend the idea of an autonomous Jewish State, imbued as they were with the principles of the emancipation of the Jews and their integration into French society. These views were shared not only by most of the important French Jewish organizations of their time but also by the native-born Jewish population. It should be remembered that the Alliance Israélite Universelle founded Mikveh Israel, the first agricultural school in Eretz Israel, as early as 1870.[1]

In fact, most French Jews were indifferent to the Dreyfus Affair. On the whole, they regarded the wave of anti-Semitism it aroused simply as a reemergence of the past. They chose to face the hostility by proving they were full-fledged French citizens, loyal to France in every way. During this period, however, more and more Jews were coming to France from Central and Eastern Europe. Among these immigrant intellectuals Herzl found his closest collaborator, Dr.

1. The "Alliance" was founded in Paris in 1860, its goal being to strive "everywhere for the emancipation and moral advancement of the Jews." For this purpose, it established an important network of schools in many countries.

Max Nordau, and the Marmorek brothers who became his staunch supporters.

In 1899 the latter founded the first French Zionist newspaper, *Echo Sioniste*, published almost uninterruptedly until 1921. In 1901, Alexander Marmorek called the first meeting of the Fédération Sioniste de France, whose members were recruited for the most part from among the Jewish immigrants. Its impact was not particularly significant, although a few French-born Jews did join, notably the journalist Bernard Lazare, a staunch Dreyfus defender. Born into an assimilated Jewish family, Lazare was deeply impressed by Herzl's *Judenstaat*. He participated in the Second Zionist Congress (1898) and founded *Le Flambeau*, the organ of socialist-Zionist Judaism.

While Zionism was not favorably considered in French Jewish circles, some non-Jews became keenly interested in its message. In 1860, Ernest Laharanne, of the secretariat of Napoleon III, wrote "La Nouvelle Question d'Orient: Empires d'Egypte et d'Arabie: Reconstitution de la nationalité juive," in which he advocated the return of the Jews to Palestine with the aid of the French Government. Hess quoted excerpts of this pamphlet to support his own ideas. Philosopher and politician Leon Bourgeois, who served as Prime Minister of France in 1895-96, was also sympathetic to the Zionist idea. He was active in the *Ligue Franco-Sioniste*, founded in 1915 by French non-Jewish and Jewish intellectuals, liberals who fought in defense of man and considered Zionism a political movement which would liberate Jews from oppression.[2]

Until the eve of World War I, the attitude of French diplomacy to Zionism was determined by the competition among the Great Powers for dividing the Ottoman Empire legacy. French diplomats considered Zionism a utopian dream, often accusing the Zionists of being agents of German imperialism despite Max Nordau's mediation attempts. This official position strengthened the negative attitude of French Jews toward Zionism.

From the Balfour Declaration to World War II

From World War II onwards, there was an upsurge of French diplomatic activity in the Middle East. In 1916, under the Sykes-Picot

2. See G. Weill's article on "Zionism in France" in *Encyclopedia of Zionism*, vol. I, p. 357.

Agreements ratifying the partition of the Ottoman Empire, Palestine was to be divided between France and Great Britain. Since this plan did not satisfy France, French diplomats were eager to contact representatives of the World Zionist Movement, and in 1917 Paris became the center of negotiations with regard to the creation of a Jewish national home in Eretz Israel. Nahum Sokolow was particularly instrumental as an intermediary between the World Zionist Movement and the French Ministry for Foreign Affairs; but French Zionists, including the Conseiller d'Etat and author André Spire (born to a Jewish family from the Lorraine), also did their utmost to enlist French Government sympathy. The establishment of a Jewish National Home under British Mandate was discussed at the Paris Peace Conference in February of 1919. Orientalist Sylvain Lévy, President of the Alliance Israélite Universelle, stated in a report that Eretz Israel could not possibly absorb the thousands of Jews who would wish to take refuge there. He also brought up the problem of dual allegiance. A true native Frenchman, Lévy opposed the emergence of a "privileged class of citizens who would participate in the elections in their own country, and at the same time would also have similar, if not identical, rights in a far-off land."[3] Until the establishment of the State of Israel, Lévy's view was the leitmotif of French anti-Zionists. Indeed, the fear of being accused of dual allegiance has not yet disappeared entirely from French Jewry's psyche. At the same meeting of the Peace Conference, however, André Spire was able to put forward the nationalist views of Chaim Weizmann, of Nahum Sokolow, and of Menahem Ussishkin.

During the inter-war period the French Jewish community continued to be divided. The majority, consisting of the native-born, were indifferent, even hostile, to Zionism. At most, they supported the Jewish National Home in Eretz Israel as a refuge for persecuted Jews of other lands. The minority, who lived in Alsace-Lorraine and had better communal organization than Jews in other areas, belonged to the Zionist Movement and abetted the work of the halutzim with contributions and other services, but very few actually settled in Eretz Israel. Zionist ideas were more readily adopted by the immigrants from Eastern Europe who were now coming to France in increasing numbers. But even among this group, there was no consensus. Most were determined to settle in France and become integrated into

3. André Chouraqui, L'Alliance Israélite Universelle et la renaissance juive contemporaine: Cent ans d'histoire, Paris, 1965, p. 225.

French society, if not in the first generation, then at least in the second. Moreover, the Yiddish-speaking immigrants were being courted by other ideological trends, like the Bund or even the French Communist Party.

Still, it was mostly among the East-European Jews that the leaders of the Fédération Sioniste de France were recruited, as was the case with the various political movements represented in the World Zionist Movement.

This period between the World Wars was marked by intensive institutional activity. The large international Jewish organizations like the Jewish National Fund, Palestine Foundation Fund (*Keren Hayesod*) and WIZO were represented in France. The Zionist youth movements and political parties—General Zionist, Socialist-Zionist, Mizrachi and Revisionist—also operated in France. In fact, it was in Paris in 1925 that the World Union of Zionist Revisionists was founded by Vladimir Jabotinsky, whose sympathy for France's Middle East policy as opposed to the pro-British tendencies of the World Zionist Movement is well known. The Fédération Sioniste de France extended its activities to French territories in North Africa. The Zionist press in French and Yiddish also developed rapidly, counting some fifty newspapers and periodicals.

World War II and the Liberation of France

During the German occupation of France, the Zionist organizations went underground, clandestinely saving Jewish children from Nazi clutches and helping the French resistance movement. Zionists and non-Zionists alike joined in the struggle against the Nazis.

Scarred and traumatized by their experiences, the survivors set about rebuilding the Jewish community of France after the Liberation. Many now joined the Jewish organizations. Others prepared for *aliyah*, among them such prominent figures as Robert Gamzon, founder and leader of the Eclaireurs Israélites de France (French Jewish Scout movement) which had played a key role in the Résistance. Until the establishment of the State of Israel, France became the converging point for "illegal" immigrants to Eretz Israel. Zionism now had the support of the French government and could rely on public sympathy.

French Jews welcomed the establishment of the State of Israel with great enthusiasm, some of them contributing generously to its upbuilding, even though they had suffered great material losses in the war. But as the sad memories of persecution and the emotional impact of the creation of the State of Israel receded, French Jewry reverted to the pre-war conflicts between Zionists and anti-Zionists. The number of Zionists decreased, and by the end of 1950s and early 1960s, little trace of enthusiasm remained. Once again, the gatherings organized by the various Zionist organizations were attended only by aging Jews who hailed from Eastern Europe.

By now, however, the community had better organized institutions, which soon had to cope with the massive influx of Jews from North Africa following decolonization. Between 1955–56 and 1962–63 the number of Jews in France rose from 200,000–250,000 to over 500,000. After Israel, France was the focal point of immigration for the Jews of North Africa. French Jewry has become the largest Jewish community in Western Europe.

The Present

The majority of North African Jews have quickly integrated into the economic, social, and cultural life of France, and it would be mistaken to regard these immigrants as a potential source of *aliyah*. However, it should be understood that Jewish consciousness is still very strong in Maghrebi circles, especially among first-generation immigrants whose emotions are quickly stirred by an event—good or bad—related to Israel. The Six Day War and the Yom Kippur War changed the attitude of a considerable part of French Jewry towards the State of Israel. Demonstrations of sympathy for Israel, fund-collecting campaigns as well as keen intellectual interest have pervaded the life of the Jews of France regardless of their origin. The Zionist movement of France now consists of some 50,000 members, although only approximately 18,000 registered members actually voted in the election of delegates to the 1978 Zionist Congress. The *Am Ehad* list, supporting Begin's government, had tremendous success (over 12,000 votes), while the *Avoda* list, which had obtained a large majority in the previous elections, suffered huge defeat. Although they belong to the Zionist Movement, the Jews of France claim to be unfamiliar with its political factions. Yet they always support the Israeli government whatever its policy. For the first time in the history of the Jews of France, a relatively substantial *aliyah* movement took place immediately after the Six Day War, but the burst of enthusiasm was short-lived, and immigrants to Israel not infrequently returned to France.

The most striking feature of this period, undoubtedly, is the changed attitude of the large Jewish organizations to the State of Israel. All these organizations, whether formerly non-Zionist and even anti-Zionist, now support Israel wholeheartedly. They also cooperate more fully with the Jewish Agency. Many activities take place to aid Israel: lecture halls are filled to capacity, Hebrew classes are organized and the Zionist movement recruits many new adherents. Still, the picture is not as harmonious as it appears.

Even among Israel's sympathizers, support is not wholehearted. Close personal contact with Israel and frequent visits cause the shortcomings of Israeli society to be known and discussed. North African Jews are particularly sensitive about the position of Maghrebis in Israel.

Though declaring themselves to be pro-Israel, many of the French Jews will seldom admit to being Zionists. This is undoubtedly a form of self-censorship imposed as a result of the negative attitude of a substantial segment of the French Left and the effects of Arab propaganda, so that Zionism is a term which is frowned upon in certain Jewish intellectual circles. Reluctance to declare oneself a Zionist may even derive from ideological motives. On the one hand, the desire to assert one's French loyalty and belie accusations of dual allegiance is primordial, a feeling strongly shared by the majority. On the other, the ideological content of Zionism is not really known or understood. French Jews support Israel because it symbolizes Jewish survival. Although the majority of the Jewish community is pro-Israel, a fact confirmed by surveys and opinion polls since 1967, approximately fifteen to twenty percent of the Jewish population in France remain aloof and sometime express hostility. Thus, Israel both unites and divides French Jewry.

Like French Zionism, the French Jewish community itself is composed of many ideological strands. All the political trends of the World Zionist Organization and all the Zionist youth movements are represented in France, even though there are not many active adherents to such "organized" Zionism. The various groups are further in conflict because of the political cleavages in the World Zionist Movement. Until the new Likud government came to power in Israel various trends of the Zionist Left as well as the *Bene Akiva* had a certain following among French Jewish youth, but at present, *Betar* is attempting to assert itself. Tension has always existed between the Zionist Left and Right in France; the Israeli elections in 1977 and the elections to the Zionist Congress of 1978 certainly did very little to cool passions. Furthermore, since the main Zionist objective is to prepare for *aliyah*, leadership is too often entrusted to *shelihim* (emissaries) who follow instructions from Jerusalem and do not adequately understand or are not sufficiently attuned to the realities of French Jewry.

The impact of organized Zionism is even less effective among the adult population. While left-wing intellectuals do not hesitate to declare their solidarity with Israel in times of danger, they refuse, for the most part, to be actively involved in organized Zionist groups. The accesssion to power of the *Likud* party in Israel has not only emphasized this tendency, but also deepened the cleavage between Right and Left, between the religious and the non-religious.

Zionist Renewal

The Zionist movement in France is undergoing an institutional crisis. The same leaders have held their positions for some thirty years. A new generation of involved Zionists is determined to stand up to the old Zionist establishment, calling for "Zionist Renewal" ("Renouveau Sioniste"). In 1977 they organized the "Assizes of French Judaism" and drafted a charter proclaiming the political and spiritual centrality of the State of Israel in the life of the Jewish People. They demand "an efficient, younger, and more coherent Zionist leadership, democratically elected." Such elections were held, in fact, to choose delegates to the 29th Zionist Congress.

The difficulties facing French Zionism are not only structural but ideological as well. Political and ideological awareness of Zionism is experienced only by a minority and there is ambiguity regarding the distinction between pro-Israel and Zionist, as explained above. Thus, in France today, identification with Israel, is shown in mass rallies, in which thousands of people are mobilized, initiated by *all* the Jewish organizations. Similarly, fund raising is organized by the United Jewish Appeal of France, a non-political body which is not involved in the internal quarrels of the Zionist Movement. This almost unanimous involvement of the organized French Jewish community in support of Israel is the most significant development of the last decade. It has gone beyond the traditional cleavage between Left and Right and between the religious and the non-religious; but at the same time, it lacks definite ideological content and is confined to tourism, financial and economic aid or manifestations of solidarity with Israel in times of danger. It does not go out of its way to promote *aliyah*.

The pro-Arab policy and anti-Israel attitude of the French government are a cause for concern and uneasiness not only for the Zionist movement in France but for the Jewish community as a whole. While some Jews serve as cabinet ministers, there are also many Jews among the leaders of the French Left which, except for the Socialist Party and the Left Radicals, is not sympathetic to Israel. No scientific study has ever been undertaken on how the French Jewish community votes in political elections. On the whole, Jews learn the views of the political leaders towards the problems of the Middle East from the press. With the exception of the Communist Party, all the large parties try to win the Jewish votes to their cause. One cannot speak of a specifically Jewish vote in France, although there seems to be a marked preference for the Socialist Party and for the Center when the latter is opposed to the government in power. The attitude of the parties towards Israel does have some influence on Jewish voters, but it is not the only criterion which determines their final decision.

Although the majority of French Jewry proclaims its solidarity with Israel, assimilationist tendencies still persist. Before all the harm caused by the Stalinist regime became public knowledge, the influence of the French Communist Party was strong in Jewish circles, especially among the Yiddish-speaking immigrants from Eastern Europe. Nowadays this influence is on the decline, since these immigrants have grown older or died. The North African Jews, who make up the majority of the French Jewish population, rarely sympathize with the Communists. Unfortunately, young Jews of every origin, especially the students and young intellectuals, are attracted to the generally pro-Palestinian extreme leftist or anarchist groups. This sometimes creates ideological problems for them. It seems that a considerable sector of Jewish youth is particularly sensitive to the ills of Western society, and their characteristic alertness of mind leads them to play an important role in the more outspoken extreme-Left movements in an attempt to cure these ills.

Obviously these young Jews also reject any effort to provide them with a Jewish education. In spite of all the attempts of the last twenty years, this remains French Jewry's weak point. For over a century the Jews of France and Algeria attended state and secular schools. There are some Jewish day schools, attended by about three thousand youngsters from the more traditionally observant families. Some parents send their sons to Talmud Torah schools to prepare for bar-mitzvah. According to the most optimistic estimates and taking into account participation in youth movements, Zionist and communal groupings, a maximum of 35 percent of French Jewish youth are exposed to some kind of Jewish education. This education is primarily religious in the day schools and Talmud Torah schools where a strong bond exists between religious identification and a positive attitude towards the State of Israel. The young people who have been given some Jewish education are conscious of being Jews, and they may wish to try a new experience—perhaps even go on *aliyah*.

Prospects

In the last twenty years, and possibly even as long ago as the end of World War II, French Jewry has undertaken to build new structures and active organizations, at least on the communal level. The arrival of the Jews of North Africa in the 1960s has given French Jewry a new lease on life. It is undoubtedly in the Maghrebi circles that Jewish consciousness is the strongest. The Six Day War and the Yom Kippur War have generated in a large majority of the Jewish population of France, regardless of origin, a sense of solidarity with the State of Israel.

But even in their solidarity, French Jews do not accept Zionism unconditionally. On the contrary, they are critical observers of the State of Israel, even more so because of their familiarity with the conditions in Israel through frequent personal contact. This critical turn of mind is shared by all French Jews in spite of their different backgrounds. It is no less acute among the more recent immigrants, who happen to be Maghrebi Jews, than among earlier immigrants or early settlers. Indeed, the majority of North Africans demonstrate their feelings for Israel with greater emotion than others, though some fifteen years ago they chose France rather than Israel as their haven. They are now well integrated into French society, both economically and socially.

The Jews of France are thus very much like most of their counterparts in the West. They will go on supporting Israel in its struggle for survival and peace, but as long as open anti-Semitism does not break out, *aliyah* will not increase. Certain elements particularly conscious of their Jewishness may decide to make their home to Israel; but the movement will not involve the Jewish masses unless there is a major political crisis. Finally, it is essential that ideological content of Zionism be reformulated in line with the times so that it will influence the Western Diaspora population to a much greater extent than it has in the past.

Comment

DAVID LAZAR[1]

Zionism in France today is no longer an institutionalized, action-oriented ideology, which stresses *aliyah* in its program. There is a Zionist Federation and people who define themselves as Zionists, but there is also a widening gulf between them and the way in which the majority of France's Jews conceive their commitment to Israel.

Three major factors account for the weakening of Zionism in contemporary France: first, the special ethnic-demographic changes which have taken place in the Jewish community over the last twenty-five years; second, the inability of Zionist institutions to adapt themselves to the changing social status of the Jewish population; finally, the weakening of the ideological component of the Israel-Diaspora relationship.

Since France has always had a tradition of intellectual liberalism combined with an extremely ethnocentric culture, it was possible for Zionism to enlist the support of the East-European immmigrants. These became the pillars of French Zionism, bringing with them the political drive and temperament they used to militate for a Jewish State. Zionism was sustained, institutionally and in writing, by those who remained more at home with Jewish values even when secularized, than with French culture. To a certain extent, their Zionist commitment was reinforced by the socio-cultural obstacles that hindered their complete integration into French culture. Yiddish, not French, was the language of those leaders. Immediately after World War II, and again in 1948, some of them went to Israel. Those who remained still stand at the helm of institutionalized Zionism in France. They have maintained their power by acting as a permanent and loyal counterpart to the Zionist establishment in Israel; they uphold the political party system underlying the Zionist Congress and Executive,

1. Acknowledgment is made to R. Ascot, A. Borenstein, E. Bouskila, H. Bulawko and M. Chiche, with whom the problems in question were discussed.

the very party system which perpetuates their privileged position, and they conveniently ignore the fact that, over the years, they have become "generals without troops."

Organized Zionism in France experienced a drastic diminution of its role after 1948, when the State of Israel was established and the Zionist Movement became increasingly marginal. Decisions on policy were no longer taken by Zionist leadership and institutions in the Diaspora. Fund raising, including the Appel Unifié Juif de France (United Jewish Appeal) is organized by the Fonds Social Juif Unifié (FSJU). Aliyah is handled by the Jewish Agency and the Israel Government. Zionist leaders have lost their moral appeal since, for the most part, they are trapped in the paradoxical situation where they do not even care to hide their determination to remain in France. Jewish education, both religious and secular, was never in the hands of the Zionist Federation to begin with. In France, the Conseil Représentatif des Institutions Juives de France (CRIF), not the Zionist leaders, issues political statements, editorializes in the Jewish Telegraphic Agency bulletin and occasionally organizes a delegation to discuss matters of interest to the Jewish community with French statesmen.

Political action in France has been supported, even initiated, by the Israeli political parties. These bodies are not part of, nor are their actions credited to, the French Zionist movement, whose platform thus has no solid basis. The shali'ah (emissary) from Israel carries much more authority, both moral and practical, than any of the local Zionist institutions. The Zionist movement in France has been unable to make a serious appraisal of its role, leadership and means of action, let alone create a cultural center for the dissemination of information and the promotion of ideological seminars. Instead, squabbling among the Zionist parties has tended to further weaken the movement's impact on the Jewish community.

The demographic composition of French Jewry changed radically in the late 1950s, particularly in the early 1960s. The arrival of over 300,000 Jews from North Africa added fresh blood to the community, both numerically and in the way of commitment to traditional Jewish values. But these Jews did not call themselves Zionists and did not join any of the Zionist parties. Accustomed to a compact, traditional community life in their countries of origin, most North African Jews had little interest in Zionist politics. Their attachment to Israel was transmitted through family communal traditions, being "natural" or "instinctive" rather than intellectual or analytical. Interestingly enough, just as the East-European immigrants in previous generations had generally remained somewhat alienated from their adopted country, so the Jews from Morocco and Tunisia did not completely identify with France (nor were they even French nationals as were the Algerian immigrants). But whereas the East-European Jewish immigrant had found in organized Zionism a structure with which he could identify, the North African Jew arriving in France in the "post-Zionist era" related himself directly to Israel. For him, attachment to Israel is essentially sentimental, his affirmation of Zionism consisting of visits to Israel and participation in demonstrations and rallies on behalf of Israel. A relatively large number of North African Jews understand and even speak Hebrew. In the second generation, especially among the students, this attachment expresses itself in apparent resistance to leftist temptations and, more actively, in countering pro-Palestinian movements both in the high school and on the university campus. Yet even this group does not feel the need to intensify its commitment through study or leadership training.

The communal organizations have changed since 1967. The weeks of traumatic anguish preceding the Six Day War and the war itself engendered a strong feeling of identification with Israel. The leaders of the Consistoire became more outspoken both as regards support for Israel and criticism of French policies in the Middle East. When President De Gaulle voiced his notorious claim about the Jews being an "elite people, self-assured and domineering," Chief Rabbi Jacob Kaplan asserted that even in the "one and indivisible" French Republic, Jews had a right collectively to defend Israel.

While the communal bodies did not profess to be Zionist, they sensed the new attitude of the rank and file who supported Israel. The slogan adopted in the early seventies by the FSJU, "a strong community to help Israel" is an indication of the change. While it could not satisfy staunch Zionists because it asserted the primacy of the Diaspora community, it did suggest that the community must work hand in hand with Israel. This was borne out in the manifesto entitled *La Communauté Juive dans la Cité* (published by CRIF, Jan. 25, 1977). The chapter on "Links with Israel" states that "the Jewish Community of France recognizes in Israel the privileged expression of Jewish being."

While Israel's centrality has become self-evident to all but a fragment of French Jews, identification of one's own destiny with Israel's through personal *aliyah* has not taken place on any large scale. 1968 was a peak year for *aliyah* from France when many Jews, among them intellectuals and professionals, settled in Israel. It is not clear, however, how many in that group were genuinely motivated by the Zionist ideal prompted by the Six Day War and its aftermath and how many were repelled by De Gaulle's policy or desired to leave France after the events of May 1968, when most of the New Left supported Palestinian terrorism.

This brings us to the role of the Israeli institutions in the upbuilding of Israel-Diaspora relations. The classic Zionist "negation of the Diaspora" has been replaced by a more tolerant (and pragmatic) approach, in which the *golah* has become Israel's chief reservoir of support and immigration. Jewish education, leadership training, and strong communal organization are, therefore, in Israel's best interests and partly its responsibility.

If Zionism is to survive in France, if it is to help French Jews combat the effects of assimilation and halt the drift away from the community, it is necessary to act without delay, particularly in the fields of education and leadership training. Indifference, complacency and belief in continued stability should not be allowed to conceal the very real dangers to Jewish collective survival.

Italy

Sergio DellaPergola

Historic Background

Jews settled in Italy well before the Roman destruction of the Second Temple.[1] This unique time perspective is interwoven with the development of Jewish identity among Italian Jews and has affected to this day their perception of worldwide Jewish affairs, including Zionism and the State of Israel.

The spiritual link with the Holy Land was an obvious and integral component of early Jewish identity in the Italian peninsula. There were commercial exchanges, and, later, travel to the Holy Land and even settlement there. Many Jews who left Italy following various expulsion decrees by the Spanish rulers, came to the Holy Land. Indeed, in 1555, about ten percent of the Jewish population of Safed were of Italian origin.[2]

Along with the process of modernization and secularization that followed the Emancipation, the whole pattern of Jewish identity was weakened. At the beginning of the twentieth century, assimilation was clearly spreading, at least among the educated and upper social strata.

The beginnings of modern Zionism in Italy were intimately connected with a return to religion.[3] Some local rabbis were among the first official leaders of Zionism, though others sternly opposed the new movement. From the beginning of the century and during the

1. For the comprehensive historical background, see Cecil Roth, *The History of the Jews of Italy*, Philadelphia, 1946, and Attillio Milano, *Storia degli ebrei in Italia*, Turin, 1963.

2. Bernard Lewis, *Notes and Documents from the Turkish Archives: A Contribution to the History of the Jews in the Ottoman Empire*, The Israel Oriental Society, Oriental Notes and Studies, no. 3, Jerusalem, 1952.

3. Dante Lattes, "Le prime albe del Sionismo italiano," *Scritti in memoria di Leone Carpi: Saggi sull'Ebraismo Italiano*, D. Carpi, A. Milano, A. Rofe, eds., Jerusalem, 1967, pp. 208-218.

inter-war period, a group of well-educated, middle-class Jews from assimilated families were involved in a movement for "integral" Judaism. This movement called for *hazarah biteshuvah* (to return to the precepts and moral commitments of Orthodox Jewry) and a return to Zion. Although numerically small, this group, whose foremost leader was Alfonso Pacifici, exercised profound intellectual and spiritual impact on Italian Jewry and its institutions. It was an idealistic trend that emanated more from a local elaboration of universal Jewish themes than from direct contact with Orthodox Jews in other European countries, and aroused strong political opposition, both from within the organized Jewish community and without. Indeed, the movement challenged the nationalistic mood that was developing with the Fascist regime with which much of the integrated lay Jewish community leadership was in tune. This "Italian way to Zion" was totally incompatible with Fascist internal policy, though Mussolini was briefly interested in Zionism's international aspects in the framework of his Mediterranean and Middle East policy.[4]

Another Zionist group, oriented towards pioneer settlement of Eretz Israel, had no serious impact on the predominantly middle-class Jewish community. Its adherents believed that Zionism had been designed for "other" persecuted European Jews, not for the "happy" and integrated Italian Jews. This attitude also implied an almost total withdrawal of Italian Jews from Zionist party politics. Consequently, after the relatively significant *aliyah* in the wake of the Fascist racial laws of 1938, and even after the *aliyah* of younger people after World War II, Italians in Israel remained conspicuously aloof from local power struggles. The fact that Italian Zionism derived much more from Italian humanism than from other European Jewish sources and traditions may explain why no Italian political figure attained significant elective office in the State of Israel. The outstanding exception of a politically identified Italian Zionist leader was Enzo Sereni, but his great potential was cut down too early, in 1944, when he was killed following a Jewish parachutist action behind German lines.[5]

The Holocaust and its aftermath radically altered the face of Italian Jewry. About 40 percent of the existing community were wiped out by extermination, baptism and emigration. On the other hand, relatively large immigration from other countries—Eastern and Cen-

4. Sergio I. Minerbi, *L'Italie et la Palestine 1914-1920*, Paris, 1970; Meir Michaelis, *Mussolini and the Jews*, 1978.
5. See Ruth Bondi, *The Emissary*, Boston 1977; *Per non morire: Enzo Sereni*, U. Nahon, ed., Milan, 1973.

tral Europe, and subsequently from the Middle East—brought a kind
of population substitution. While Italian Jewry retained its overall size
(45,000 in 1938, 28,000 in 1945, 37,000 in 1978, including temporary
residents), its cultural composition changed rather dramatically. With
the reconstitution of the Jewish community after World War II, the
previously banned Zionist Federation could now function as a focus
for Zionism in Italy, along with a network of other central and local
Jewish institutions.

Antagonistic Forces

Today, Italian Jewry is a small, demographically declining,
aging and assimilated, economically unremarkable minority in a rapidly changing society that is far from having achieved a satisfactory
level of economic and political equilibrium or stability.[6] Although
virulent forms of anti-Semitism have generally been uncommon
among the Italian people, various acute forms of prejudice and potentially dangerous forms of opposition to the Jews do exist. These negative forces derive essentially from four anti-Semitic sources [7]:

(a) Fundamentalist Catholicism, which is evident from the ten-
acious insistence of certain sectors of the Church on established
themes, such as presumed deicide or ritual murder. Though a recent
document promised to renounce conversion as a means of redeeming
Jews, the Church's interests concerning the Holy Christian Places, and
especially Jerusalem's future status, have led to an ambivalent attitude
with regard to Jewry, and Zionism in particular.

(b) Neo-Fascist racist attempts to keep alive a tradition that was
not deeply rooted in Italy, but nevertheless had a very destructive
effect during the final period of the Fascist regime, virtually from
1934-1945.

(c) The spread of Marxist anti-Zionism and its gradual penetration into non-Marxist political and academic circles. Support for the
Palestinians and a negative approach to Zionist policies and, in part, to
the existence of the State of Israel, may lead indirectly to an attitude of
suspicion towards Jews in general, both in the large bureaucratic
Communist Party, and in smaller, radical and extreme-Left groups
where the internal structure is less formally established.

(d) Arab or Moslem nationalism is manifest among the thousands of Arab students and political activists residing in Italy, who are

6. Sergio DellaPergola, *Anatomia dell 'ebraismo italiano*, Rome, 1976.
7. Alfonso Di Nola, *Antisemitismo in Italia, 1962/1972*, Florence, 1973.

supported by an efficient and powerful propaganda bureau in Rome; added to this is the growing dependence of the Italian economy on Arab energy sources and industrial investments.

Public opinion polls in Italy have shown much greater support for Israel than for the Arabs. On the other hand, most of the mass media, including the important press and state radio-television network, are anti-Israel in varying degrees. The current, rather superficial support for the Jewish cause might well shift in the near future towards a widely shared feeling of opposition among the populace.

Italian society itself today experiences an unprecedented process of disintegration in the previously established pattern of law and order. A fundamental reshaping of the political system has been in effect for over thirty years under the Christian Democratic Party. Some of the forces ideologically opposed—at least potentially—to the Jews, in fact oppose the existing societal equilibrium in the framework of which the Jewish communities and institutions are a minute but clearly identified component of the Establishment. In recent years, the astonishing decrease of national cultural identity in general Italian society is incompatible with the emergence of a small counter-stream of Jewish nationalism.

Institutions—Jewish and non-Jewish

Faced with this heterogeneous alignment of antagonistic forces, Italian Jewry may well turn to several other channels of corporate response:

(a) The Italian Jewish community is one of the very few communities in the world where the institutional framework is not based upon voluntary membership. The organized Jewish community is the officially recognized instrumentality for the preservation of Jewish interests in Italy. Even so, it limits itself to local issues concerning Jews; only occasionally does it discuss international Jewish and Israeli affairs. However, the community has but limited political impact on the Jews.

(b) Voluntary Jewish activities proliferate along with this formal and centralized communal organization. In relation to Zionism, there are two kinds Jewish institutions:

(i) organizations committed to Zionism, such as the Zionist Federation, ADEI (WIZO's Italian branch), the Jewish National Fund, *Keren Hayesod*, branches of various other departments of the World

Zionist Organization, pioneer youth movements and Italian "branches" of Israeli parties;

(ii) organizations committed to Italian Jewish goals, such as B'nai B'rith, ORT, OSE, Maccabi, the now leftist Italian Jewish Youth Federation (FGEI) and a score of other local associations, as well as the Jewish press.

Actually this distinction is more formal than real, since these institutions may have organic links with Israel and there is a great overlap between the active personnel of both groups. Interestingly enough, there is a growing mood of detachment from recent Israeli policies, as a consequence of which some officially committed Zionist circles may turn to a more Italian-based orientation for their activities. The majority of officially recognized Zionists in Italy are probably opposed to the Israeli government that came to power after the 1977 elections.

(c) The established network of Jewish schools, with comprehensive day schools in Rome and Milan and smaller primary schools in other towns, deserves special mention. The current climate of *contestazione* (deliberate disturbance) has penetrated the Jewish school, too—though much less than the general Italian school—introducing a radical-leftist political outlook as well as growing support for the Palestinian cause. Jewish youth who are not exposed to Jewish education are even more affected by these trends.

(d) Finally, there are some institutions not specifically directed to the Jewish population. These include a small number of mixed, Jewish and non-Jewish organizations, like the Italy-Israel Friendship League, Friends of the Hebrew University, the *Unione Democratica Amici di Israele* (UDAI) and Left for Israel. Among other objectives, these groups aim to promote support for Israel in general, or within very specific political and cultural sectors of Italian society.

On the whole, the framework, or rather the multiplicity of frameworks outlined above, lacks the power, the cohesiveness and the financial means to act effectively on current Jewish issues, more particularly, on Zionist issues. It is even more distressing that no central strategic, or long-term planning agency exists, or that the central body, the *Unione delle Comunità Israelitiche Italiane* (UCII) does not fulfil this task. It may well be feared that in the event of danger for Italian Jewry, or for Jewry in general, existing institutions may not be able to cope any more efficiently than they could during the late 1930s and early 1940s. The habit of considering problems in general, social

terms, rather than in a broad Jewish perspective, is too deeply rooted
to have changed since the establishment of the State of Israel. There is
hardly any coordination between local Jewish communities, between
Zionist and non-Zionist organizations, or between Jews of different
political backgrounds. Attempts at linking Italian Jewry with broader—though weak—European Jewish groups have met with little
response. While there were demonstrations in support of Israel during
critical periods,[8] no such manifestations were evident on other issues
of Jewish interest, such as the plight of Soviet Jewry. Fund raising was
at its peak, but here, too, interest and support were short-lived.

Israel—Unifying and Divisive

Jewish identity is perceived mainly in relation to religious patterns, as a consequence of historical developments, especially of the
pressure exercised in Italy by the Catholic Church over a society with
little tradition of pluralism. While certain aspects of Judaism linked to
religion and liturgy have been preserved, other components of the
Jewish inheritance have been lost. With the decreasing impact of religion on contemporary society in general, no compensating national
component of Jewish identity has emerged. The trauma of Fascist
experience has led to the eclipse, perhaps even the end, of nationalist
ideology among the social strata in which the Jews were concentrated.

The influence of the State of Israel as a central pole of identity
for Italian Jews did grow after the Six Day War. Many regard Israel as
a haven for a time of crisis in Italy, and the percentage of those who
are establishing second homes in Israel with a view to the future is on
the increase. Frequently, it is the more religious who recognize the
centrality of Israel for the Jewish People. But the attraction exercised
by the State of Israel and Zionist ideology, often on a sentimental rather than on a rational level, has controversial facets. More than religion, Israel probably creates controversy and divisions among the
Jewish community no less than it unifies. The emotional reaction of

---

8. During the Yom Kippur War this was evident, especially in Rome, when many Jews
of the ghetto gathered together spontaneously on October 16, the same date on which in
1943 the Nazis carried out their mass roundup of the Jews of Rome. See Itzhak Sergio
Minerbi, "Western Europe: Overview," The Yom Kippur War: Israel and the Jewish
People, Moshe Davis, ed., New York, 1974, p. 192. In 1977, Jewish demonstrations followed an Italian proposal to grant amnesty to Herbert Kappler, the German colonel
chiefly responsible for the Fosse Ardeatine massacre in 1944.

some Jews who have not approved of Israel's governments reveals the existence of a deep and complex bond with Jewry, even though it may lead, in extreme cases, to a deliberate severing of links with the community, and even to assimilation.

Several diverse ethnic-cultural groups may be discerned in Italian Jewry, each having its own pattern of Jewish identity. Jews born outside the country may, consciously or subconsciously, drop some of their Jewish traditional habits and norms, considering these an obstacle to their integration into Italian society. For the second generation, born or educated in Italy and rapidly shifting from the socio-occupational structure of their parents to professional and managerial occupations, different perceptions of Judaism and Zionism are often a central element in the generation gap; this has been eroding the earlier Jewish traditional family structure. Other immigrant groups may consider their presence in Italy as a temporary experience: many Libyan Jews, for example, who came to Italy after the Six Day War, subsequently emigrated to Israel, while other foreign-born Jews proceeded to various Western countries after staying in the country for a while.

Veteran Italian Jews in the splinter communities outside Rome constitute the upper social and most assimilated stratum of Italian Jewry. This group's essentially secular attitude finds its correlate in the highest rate of exogamy, suggesting that ultimately there is little chance for survival as a consequence of the demographic erosion in this sector of the community.

The Jews of Rome—at least those who descend from the most ancient component of Italian Jewry—are still emotionally linked to the area of the ghetto where four centuries of Jewish history took place. Israel deserves a position of real privilege in the Jewish identity of the old-time Roman Jew, but it may be said in all fairness that its role is secondary as compared to the principal identification pole represented by the *Urbe* (Rome), its society, history and folklore.

Italian *Aliyah*

Such deep differentials in Jewish identity among the various strata are obviously reflected in Italian Jewry's perception of Zionism, more particularly *aliyah* to Israel.[9] Quantitatively small, Italian *aliyah*

---

9. Sergio DellaPergola and Amedeo Tagliacozzo, *Gli Italiani in Israele*, Rome, 1978.

has involved a much higher proportion of the local community than is the case with most other Western Diaspora communities. The total number of immigrants from Italy was approximately 2,800 (1,600 Italian-born) during the period of the British Mandate in Palestine (1919-1948) and 44,800 (3,200 Italian-born) from the establishment of the State of Israel to the end of 1977.

It has been a selective immigration, with a more-than-average representation of well-educated professionals and ideologically (including religiously) motivated persons. Certain local communities with a richer tradition of Jewish cultural life—especially Florence and Trieste—have been the most prominent in Italian *aliyah*. On the other hand, Roman Jewry, because of its Jewish identity patterns and its overwhelming occupational concentration in trade, has not been conspicuous in Italian *aliyah*, having also registered higher rates of return migration to Italy. On the whole, however, Italian *aliyah* has been successful in its attempt at integration in Israel. It has applied for relatively little help from public authorities, has contributed its professional abilities to the revival of the Land and the State of Israel, and has become deeply rooted in its new social and cultural setting.

The more exacting circumstances related to direct persecutions, typical of the later years of the Fascist period, have lost force in recent years, although they have not completely disappeared, as a delayed determinant for *aliyah*. A similar decreasing trend is evident, though at a much more moderate rate, with regard to the impact of such typical ideological factors as the desire to live in a society characterized as pioneer, egalitarian, or traditional-Jewish. On the other hand, psycho-sociological individual factors, family reasons, and above all, growing feelings of dissatisfaction with current Italian society in general, and with minority status in particular, are increasingly becoming the determining forces of Italian *aliyah*. Economic factors have played a marginal role, even during the most difficult years of the Fascist persecution.

The desire to live in a Jewish state emerged at all times as the dominant determinant of Italian immigration to Israel. The individualistic character of Italian *aliyah* should be stressed again: most new immigrants came independently from movements and organizations, even without previous formal Zionist activities and commitments. One should not think that the majority of Zionists in Italy today are committed to *aliyah*. Theory and practice are not identical, but they may coexist.

Survival—Challenge

To be a Zionist in Italy today implies assertion of alignment and solidarity with World Jewry. This affirmation should not be limited to a special relationship with the State of Israel and its Jewish population. In the current unsound conditions of Italian society in general, and of increasing assimilation and demographic erosion in the Jewish community, Zionists are in the vanguard, declaring themselves ready to fight, or at least ready to identify with those who are prepared to fight. At times this attitude closely resembles wearing a yellow badge when one is not really required to do so. Indeed, one of the most difficult eras for Italian Jewry seems to be imminent. This calls for a mobilization and wise administration of available forces. Italian Jews, especially Italian Zionists, cannot face the inevitable challenges alone, any more than other small Diaspora communities.

The development of a meaningful and organic tie between Italian Jewry and the State of Israel or, alternatively, other Jewish communities in the world, cannot be left exclusively to the local community. Help from outside is required, especially from Israel which, at least potentially, should have the resources, the manpower and the planning abilities to enhance Jewish life in the Diaspora. The degree of success in developing such a network of relationships during the next few years will dictate to a large extent the possible survival of Zionism and Jewry in Italy.

The Netherlands

Joel S. Fishman

Historic Background

To a large degree the evolution of the Zionist movement in the Netherlands reflected the influence of local conditions which prevailed during the nineteenth and twentieth centuries. One factor which affected all ranks of Dutch society, both Jewish and Gentile, was the great disparity between rich and poor: extremes of wealth influenced social relationships. While the Zionist movement generally found adherents among the Jewish middle class, the possibility of its expanding and encompassing wider circles within Dutch Jewish life was hindered as a consequence of social attitudes which split the community along lines of wealth.

A second factor was the reinforcement of tendencies toward the isolation of Dutch Jewry vis-à-vis the other Jewish communities of Europe. The provinciality of the Dutch rabbinate during the nineteenth century further weakened ties of culture and affinity with the great centers of world Jewry. While the close of the century witnessed the resurgence of open and violent antisemitism in many parts of Europe, whatever expression the antisemitic movement took in the Netherlands it was not of such a nature as to make life unbearable and hazardous for Dutch Jewry. Consequently, the relevance of Zionism and its aspirations were viewed as: 1) having more of a theoretical than immediate importance; and 2) as promising relief for others, primarily the East-European Jewish communities in distress.[1]

---

1. For background information on the formation of the modern Dutch rabbinate, see Benjamin de Vries, "Joseph Tzevi Halevi Dünner," in Leo Jung, *Guardians of Our Heritage*, New York, 1958, pp. 339–344. On Dünner's social ideas, see S. de Wolff, *Geschiedenis der Joden in Nederland: Laatste Bedrijf*, Amsterdam, 1946, pp. 50–51. For attitudes of Dutch Jewish leaders toward the Jews of Eastern Europe, see Ludy Giebels, *De Zionistische Beweging in Nederland 1899–1941*, Assen, 1945, p. 93. A reason for Dutch Jewry's support of Zionism was its opposton to East-European immigration. *Note*: The form "antisemitism" given here conforms with the usage of J.H. Parkes.

From the inception of the Dutch Zionist movement at the turn of the century, its leaders were influenced by nineteenth-century philanthropic and optimistic ideals of universal progress: the fulfilment of the Zionist dream was viewed as a goal to be achieved through an evolutionary process which was part of the general development of Western civilization. Opposing the cultural influences of both socialist and religious Zionism, they argued for an unqualified political Zionism to the complete exclusion of both the socialist and religious approaches. They also advocated maintaining a distance from local Jewish affairs or any endeavor which would strengthen the community, considering such participation as undesirable compromise which would distract members from the central issues.

Like the religious community, the Netherlands Zionist Federation was generally ruled by the satisfied and the wealthy (although it would ultimately attract increasing numbers of university-educated intellectuals). Through the years, Zionism in the Netherlands found its largest following among the small midddle class rather than in the mass of the Jewish proletariat who, if they took an interest in political matters, were more likely to choose socialism.[2]

After 1933, a reorientation took place, initially on the theoretical level, with the appearance of the writings of Fritz (Peretz) Bernstein, the German-born Zionist thinker who came to the Netherlands. Bernstein served as both secretary and president of the Dutch Zionist Federation, and from 1930 to 1935 was chief editor if its weekly, the Joodsche Wachter (The Jewish Watchman). He advocated a more nationalistic and activist orientation. The younger generation of the Zionist student movements and the Jewish Youth Federation adopted his approach and its influence extended to all the youth movements. Its program championed tarbut (Jewish national culture) to the exclusion of Dutch culture, and an exacting personal Zionism which required aliyah and halutziut (pioneering). The vitality of this movement was enhanced by the presence of German-Jewish youth and pioneering youth of East-European origin who arrived in the Netherlands throughout the 1930s.

Adherents of this more uncompromising form of Zionism were substantially younger than the established leadership and more maximalist in their politics. Historic circumstances would place members of the group into positions of leadership within the wider Dutch

2. S. Kleerekoper, "Het Joodse Proletariaat in het Amsterdam van de eerste helft van de twintigste eeuw en zijn leiders," Studia Rosenthaliana, vol. III (1969), pp. 208–233.

Jewish community during the formative years, 1944 to 1948. In general, the events of the 1930s had a beneficial and stimulating effect on the Dutch Zionist movement. Zionism, in part conceived as a response to racist antisemitism, gained renewed vitality as a result of fresh manifestations of organized anti-Jewish feeling. In the early 1930s, the membership of the Dutch Zionist Federation was about 2,000; in 1936—3,487; and in 1939—4,246 (in 1936, some 1,200 went on *aliyah*).[3]

World War II and After

The Holocaust profoundly altered the Dutch Jewish community both quantitatively and qualitatively. Generally speaking, only the professional classes survived; the popular classes, the proletariat of Amsterdam and The Hague, disappeared forever, while the formerly self-sufficient communities of the countryside could no longer sustain themselves.

When the extent of Jewish losses became known, there was definite intensification of Zionist feeling. Zionist membership was 2,800 in a Jewish population of 25,000–29,000. Leadership of both the Dutch Zionist movement and the Jewish community fell into the hands of the local activists, and a serious reexamination and questioning of prewar Jewish life became the order of the day. The policy of the Zionist activists was not necessarily representative and their views may not have been universally shared. Nevertheless, their maximalist approach had its advantages, and for a brief period, the frustrating situation in which the Jewish community found itself after the war lent plausibility to arguments against continued life in the Diaspora.

On September 2, 1945, the basic Zionist program was articulated in a motion presented at the first postwar meeting of the Netherlands Zionist Federation. It stated that "with the coming peace of the United Nations, the Jewish People more than ever have the right to demand an integral solution to the Jewish Question." This implied the maximalist program of an unpartitioned, unreduced, Jewish State which would include all of Mandate Palestine. The Chairman, Dr. A. Büchenbacher, articulated the view of the Netherlands Zionist Federation that there should be no further *Galus Arbeit*, Jewish work which

---

3. The relationship between the rise of antisemitism in the 1930s and increased interest in Zionism is noted in Giebels, *De Zionistische Beweging*, pp. 170–171.

would build up the Diaspora, but that with the destruction of European Jewry, it was now necessary to concentrate on Jerusalem, the one remaining Jewish center.[4] The Zionist program was strongly Israel-oriented, interested in the world political situation. Its main objective was to persuade Dutch Jewry that there was no longer a future in the Netherlands, to promote *aliyah* to Eretz Israel through legal or illegal means, and to unapologetically champion Jewish rights within the Netherlands.

A noteworthy aspect of the Zionist program was the adoption of the principle of action to be undertaken within the Jewish community. From the start the Zionist Federation managed to gain control over the *Nieuw Israëlietisch Weekblad*, the community's newspaper, even placing one of its prominent leaders, a Marxist and atheist, on the board of the Amsterdam religious community. The Zionist Federation endeavored to teach conversational Hebrew and reorient the educational system toward Eretz Israel, to democratize the Jewish establishment and promote a positive Jewish consciousness and self-esteem.

In May 1947, the Zionist Federation undertook one of its most ambitious acts by establishing an independent "Court of Honor" to try, in the name of Dutch Jewry, the former chairmen of the wartime Jewish Council, A. Asscher and Prof. D. Cohen. In January 1949, it declared the two guilty of collaboration with the Nazis. The direct influence of the activists was temporary, however. Faithful to their own principles, most of the Zionist leaders emigrated to Israel after 1948. They had provided leadership and direction at a time when it was sorely needed. Their departure had the effect of removing an important nucleus of talent and gave an opportunity for leadership to proponents of other approaches, not necessarily committed to immediate *aliyah*.

The success of Zionist activism in the Netherlands immediately after the war represented an unusual situation which should be understood as part of the polarized world which brought it into being: the background of the 1930s and the German occupation, the Cold War, the deep conviction among Zionist leaders that no further compromise, spiritual or political, was possible, and that the only solution to the Jewish Question was the immediate establishment of the Jewish State. The shock of the Holocaust and World War II resulted in a

4. In "Algemene Vergadering van den Nederlandschen Zionisten Bond," *Nieuw Israë-lietisch Weekblad*, Sept. 7, 1945.

sharp challenge to the long-accepted assumptions and values of an earlier generation which had been committed to life in the Netherlands. Before the war, the presence of these activists could be observed on the fringes of the established community, but they did not become a fully developed force in the community until the postwar era. The reorientation in the Jewish community along maximalist Zionist lines took place in the minds of the few, and ultimately expanded to include its leadership and institutions. Such a departure from past tradition resulted directly from the impact of the Holocaust and hastened the community's realignment in favor of the Zionist cause.

Israel's development has had a profound impact on Jewish life in the Netherlands. The Dutch community, no longer as self-contained as in the prewar years, basked to a considerable degree in the reflected glory of the State of Israel. As a result of the post-World War II *aliyah*, almost every Jewish family has relatives in Israel. Thus the bonds between the two communities have become closer through the years. For the Jews of the Netherlands, Israel offers an alternative to a life constantly threatened by demographic depletion and assimilation. No longer a dream, Israel has become a part of the lives of virtually the entire Dutch community; the manner in which Dutch Jews regard themselves and their surroundings has been profoundly changed by this fact.

The Last Two Decades

The trend of development of Zionist sentiment in the Netherlands in the late 1960s and 1970s has not been encouraging. A number of factors come into play: a growing secularism among Jews, parallel to that in Gentile society; ignorance on the part of many Jews of Jewish history, culture and religion; and the adoption of new lifestyles, resulting in weakened patterns of communal identification, cohesiveness and discipline. These tendencies have a destructive influence on Dutch Zionism, contributing to a low level of participation in Zionist activities, despite a moderate rise in membership in recent years. Today, Zionism in the Netherlands no longer represents a movement, as in the past, rather an affiliation comparable to nominal membership in one of the religious communities. Some would even argue that the significance of Zionist affiliation lies in its attraction as a secular Jewish movement, appealing to elements unable to find a spiritual home elsewhere, particularly the intermarried. And in this respect, an observation by M. Snijders made some twenty years ago retains its validity: "Membership in the community is no more an expression of religiosity than membership in the Zionist Federation is an expression of a resolution to go to Israel. In both cases, the desire to belong somewhere is stronger than the conviction."[5] By and large, the Zionist Federation has attracted secularly-oriented middle-class individuals and, despite attempts to improve the situation, its membership represents mainly an aging, stolid segment of the population.

The shift from active participation in the Zionist movement to largely passive affiliation has led, occasionally, to static introspection and confusion. In the earlier days, many held that Jewish life in the Diaspora was doomed and that it was urgently necessary to support the *Yishuv* in its struggle for independence and dignity. At present, many are confused by events in Israel, particularly in the light of the fact that open identification with Israel is not as fashionable in Gentile society as it was, for example, in the mid-1960s. The Yom Kippur War was a great shock, as were the scandals of the Rabin era and, more recently, the advent of the Begin cabinet which marked the end of the *entente* (of a sort) between the Socialist governments of the Netherlands and Israel. Positive identification with Israel has now become a more difficult proposition than in the past, sometimes giving rise to dilemmas of mixed loyalties.

In addition, two related developments must be considered: the rise of the welfare state and the decline of nationalism. Within the cosmos of the welfare state and its mentality, the well-adjusted individual represents the ideal of personal fulfilment. For better or for worse, the appeal of Zionism cannot really be addressed to well-adjusted individuals. On the contrary, much effort has been expended to make Jews in the Diaspora conscious of an inherent disharmony with their surroundings and, by this process, motivate them to emigrate to Israel. Likewise, the decline of the ideal of the nation-state has brought about a decreased preparedness to make personal sacrifices or a real political commitment to such a cause. In consequence, Dutch Zionism had tended toward an intellectualization of the Jewish condition—as if it were someone else's problem and not one's own—resulting in doubt, hesitation, inaction, and the reluctance to take a forceful stand on the Jewish State and its advancement. Similarly, the weak-

5. M[ax] L[eonard] Snijders, *Joden van Amsterdam*, Amsterdam, 1958, p. 10.

ness of Dutch Jewry in protecting its own interests within the body politic has long been evident.[6] What is significant with reference to Zionism is the abnegation of political responsibility when related to an ideology specifically bound to giving the Jewish People, as such, the dignity of political existence and its collective expression through the founding of the State.

A recent symptom of this general condition has been the rejection of the political meaning of Zionism and, generally, a flight from political responsibility. This tendency is expressed in the condemnation of politics in the Zionist Movement and the alleged politicization of all aspects of Israeli public life. While such views may have their merit, what is really meant is that in Dutch political life, where patterns of differential behavior have long been the rule, active political initiatives on behalf of Israel make people uncomfortable, because they are "political."[7] Such flight from political responsibility tends to paralyze constructive responses in the face of recurring expressions of anti-Zionism and antisemitism in the news media.

Strangely, many Dutch Jews are unable to perceive danger from antisemitism. Even within quarters professedly committed to Israel, there exists a willingness to accept virulent anti-Zionism as a legitimately tenable position. Furthermore, the question of an appropriate response has become more complicated in view of the change in the Dutch government's traditional policy toward Israel. Although much water has gone under the bridge since the sunny days of the *fin de siècle*, the situation in the Netherlands has its parallel with the dilemmas faced by such Western European Jewish communities as those of Germany and France when confronted with militant antisemitism. The inability to respond, and hesitation to admit the existence of the problem, are noteworthy.

Moreover, the Zionist Federation no longer enjoys a special place in the community. A former president, J. J. Meijers, has stated that since all forms of Dutch communal life are nominally Israel-centered, the Federation has lost its unique position in offering a solution

6. See M. H. Gans, *Memorbook*, Arnold Pomerantz, tr., Baarn, 1977, p. 755 and *passim*; L. de Jong, *Een Sterfgeval te Auswitz* (sic), Amsterdam, 1967; and H. Daalder, "Joden in een verzuilend Nederland," *Hollands Maandblad*, Jg. XVII, no. 335, October 1975, pp. 3–12.
7. See R. M. Naftaniel, *Zwartboek: De Arabische Boykot en Nederland*, The Hague, 1978; and M. Kopuit, "Manipulatie van Cidi brengt boycotbrochure in opspraak," *N.I.W.*, February 17, 1978, pp. 3, 7.

to the Jewish Question not found elsewhere.[8] Further, it is also note-worthy that the leadership ranks of the Zionist movement are now coming from the Progressive community rather than from the tradi-tional Ashkenazi community; this is a pattern which may be observed in other areas of Jewish life where the three communities cooperate, namely the struggle for Soviet Jewry and Jewish social work.

In the field of education, the Zionist Federation sponsors the informal teaching of modern Hebrew in the local Jewish school sys-tem in Amsterdam and in *ulpanim* (study circles) throughout the coun-try. The *ulpan* system, which disseminates both modern Hebrew and Israeli culture, has been of real importance and rather successful. The Zionist Federation, however, now estimates that seventy percent of the enrollment are non-Jews.

In this brief examination it must be recalled that Dutch Jewry has a low birthrate, intermarriage has been so high that no one has any idea of its real dimensions, and recently the divorce rate has risen. These underlying demographic factors must influence the present and future prospects of Jewish life in the Netherlands, including those of the Zionist Federation. Perhaps the question should be asked, if behind the polite banter of self-criticism, introspective analysis, and critical comment about the Israeli way of doing things, there may be a growing disharmony between a nominal allegiance to Zionism and its principles which offer fulfilment within the framework of building and supporting Israel.

8. "Openings rede uitgesproken door de Bondsvoorzitter Dr. J. J. Meijers tijdens de 75e Algemene Vergadering van de Nederlandsche Zionistenbond op Januari 21, 1978."

Sweden

Fritz Hollander

The first Jews were legally admitted to Sweden about 200 years ago. They came mainly from Germany and from areas which today belong to Germany but were then Danish. Few descendants of these first immigrants retained their Jewish identity. By the end of the nineteenth century assimilation had led to intermarriage and the inroads of Reform Judaism had resulted in cultural impoverishment. The Jewish School in Stockholm was closed in 1870. Practically every mention of Jerusalem and Zion was removed from the prayer book, or at least from the translated pages.

The East-European Jews who settled in Sweden altered the character of the Jewish community, and it was mainly from them that the Zionist movement took shape. Zionism became organized in 1901, when the first "club" was formed in Malmö. Although Sweden still has a State Church, a law passed in 1963 now permits citizens to remain religiously unaffiliated. Until then, anyone who left his religious community was compelled to join another. For this reason, many Jews who had no strong sense of Jewish identity preferred to remain in the Jewish community than convert to another religion. Before 1953 the Jewish community had the right to exclude Jews who were not Swedish citizens. This meant that new immigrants could not have any influence in the community until several years after their arrival. This law also explains why many East-European Jewish immigrants were not members of the official Jewish community before World War I. These immigrants did play a very important role in the elections to the Stockholm rabbinate in 1913. The veteran leadership had already decided to choose a Reform rabbi when the East-European "Zionist" Jews insisted that the community elect a spiritual leader with a Jewish national outlook.

The scholar and Hebraist, Professor Marcus Ehrenpreis, former Chief Rabbi of Bulgaria, was elected in 1913. Still, Zionism remained insignificant in Sweden. Although Ehrenpreis participated in the founding of the Hebrew University in Jerusalem in 1925 and was a member of the Zionist Organization, it was not until the last years of his long life that he became an active Zionist.

During the 1920s, support for Zionism increased somewhat. Hebrew clubs and a Zionist newspaper, *Judisk Kronika*, were established. The eminent historian and writer, Hugo Valentin, scion of an old Jewish family was elected President of the Swedish Zionist Organization and his prestige reflected on the Zionist movement. In general, though, the assimilatory tendencies of the past continued until the late 1930s, when the Swedish anti-Semites' support of Hitler jolted the Jewish community into action. The first *hakhsharah* (pioneer training) groups were established mainly for young refugee immigrants from Germany although some young Swedish Jews joined as well. A Jewish youth organization and a university students club had been in existence since the 1920s. While not openly Zionist, these clubs were not anti-Zionist, as was the official community. The first genuine Zionist youth movement, *Zerej Mizrachi*, was founded in 1934, through the initiative of the Chief Rabbi of Finland, Dr. Federbusch. It consisted of Jews who had come to Sweden after 1933, as well as native-born youth—mostly children or grandchildren of immigrants.

Following Hitler's rise to power, but before World War II, Sweden admitted Central European Jewish refugees—Germans, Austrians and Czechoslovakians. The small Zionist organization, now strengthened by the immigrants, was thus able to play a more active role. Zionists were influential in organizing the Central European refugees into a self-help association, *Immigranternas Självhjälp*, shortly before the 1938 *Kristallnacht*. That year, young German Jews were brought to Sweden by Youth Aliyah and trained for future settlement in Palestine.

The first great rescue effort of World War II was undertaken by Dr. Adler-Rudel, whom the Jewish Agency had sent from England. He succeeded in enlisting all of Swedish Jewry to pay for the transportation of young German *halutzim* (pioneers) from Denmark to Sweden. The project ultimately saved the lives of every member of the group. Other rescue work undertaken by the Zionist Movement was carried out mostly under the aegis of a neutral committee, and later on under the auspices of the Swedish section of the World Jewish Congress. Some of its members negotiated the release from the death camps of thousands of Jews. Rescue action for Danish Jewry in the autumn of

1943 originated outside the official Jewish community, but later on Swedish Jews took part in the project. Raoul Wallenberg's mission to save Hungarian Jews and the plan to send food parcels to Bergen-Belsen and Theresienstadt, were initiated by the World Jewish Congress and by leading Zionist members.

As a consequence of these rescue acts, the Jewish population of Sweden increased from 6,000 to approximately 25,000. After the war, most of the Danish Jews returned to Denmark, some refugees returned to their countries of origin, and many went to Eretz Israel. Another Jewish publication, *Judisk Tidskrift*, founded by Marcus Ehrenpreis and continued by Hugo Valentin and Franz Arnheim, served as a platform for ideological debate.

Shortly before the establishment of the State of Israel, the leaders of the official Jewish community and of the Zionist Organization decided to combine their efforts. They founded a joint committee for defense, which later became the *Keren Hayesod* or, as it is called in Sweden, *Förenade Israel-Insamlingen*. A number of young Swedish Jews went to Israel to help in the War of Independence and Swedish pilots who brought badly needed weapons from Czechoslovakia to Israel at the outbreak of the war were paid from funds collected from Swedish Jewry.

Nevertheless, inter-party strife continued to weaken the Zionist Organization in Sweden until it was reorganized into a Federation in the late 1940s. A representative of the World Zionist Organization was sent to Sweden to explain to the Jewish community that practical work in the Diaspora was more effective than wrangling over ideology in Israel.

One of the first acts of the Federation was to revive and reactivate the defunct youth organization. A scout organization was created, then *B'nai Akiva* as a successor to *Zerej Mizrachi*, and later on, *Habonim*. Another significant project was the formation of the *Hinnukh* (Education) organization and the establishment of a Jewish kindergarten and day school. Even though *Hinnukh* virtually had the same leadership as the Zionist Organization, it was set up as an independent body in order to attract Jews who were not active Zionists. *Hinnukh* had the support of the incumbent Chief Rabbi, Professor Kurt Wilhelm, but was bitterly opposed by most of the official Jewish community. As late as the early 1950s, the majority of the community council (*Fullmäktige*) declared that they were against a Jewish kindergarten, a Jewish school and a Jewish center. Some members even went so far as to say they opposed Jewish sports clubs, arguing that such separate organisms would be creating a new ghetto. Such was the official community attitude, but the refugees, especially from Eastern Europe, who were not yet members of the community, supported the work of the Zionists and the *Hinnukh* organization.

Remarkable developments were gradually taking place in the community which strengthened the local Zionist movement. The older assimilatory circles were willing to support Israel on social grounds but were against intensifying Jewish work in Sweden itself. On the other hand, the Zionists and their supporters, earlier reproached for having no interest in local work and for thinking only of Israel, became passionately involved in the development of Jewish culture and education in Sweden. A bitter fight developed once more about the election of a new rabbi. An anti-Zionist candidate was supported by the assimilatory faction, but as had happened in 1913, another rabbi, proposed by the Zionists, was elected. It was felt that in a large community such as Stockholm, unity might be endangered if the rabbi was anti-Zionist.

After this Zionist victory, the Jewish Center of Stockholm came into being. On the insistence of the Zionist group *(Judisk Samling)*, the by-laws of the Center provided that the Center be open to every Jew. Its Board was to be composed of three groups: one third—and no more—appointed by the politically influenced council of the Jewish community, one third by the *Hinnukh* organization and their friends, and—most important—one third elected directly by the Jewish youth organizations which met in the Center. The young people were thus allowed a direct say in Center policy, giving the older and younger generations an opportunity to work together. Though non-Zionist in principle, the Center always maintained an excellent relationship with the Zionist Federation. When Polish immigrants who came after 1967 wished to keep up their own Polish-Jewish culture, the Center leadership made it possible for them to do so. Now the active members of that group take part in the general Jewish cultural and Zionist activities throughout Sweden.

The Swedish Zionist Federation has been organizing low-cost charter flights to Israel to enable most Swedish Jews to visit Israel and also encourage non-Jewish tourism. When the Nobel Prize was conferred on S.Y. Agnon and Nelly Sachs in 1966, the Zionist Federation, together with the *Hinnukh* organization, established a Jewish youth foundation *(Stiftelsen Judiska Ungomsfonden)*, to further Jewish education. This foundation was especially helpful in supporting the settlement of a large group of Polish students, who came to Sweden and Denmark in 1967 and later, in the wake of anti-Semitic developments.

Shortly before the outbreak of the Six Day War, the Zionist Federation initiated a Solidarity Committee for Israel, supported by practically all the Jewish organizations in Sweden. *Aliyah* to Israel has continued steadily throughout the years, not only of East-European immigrants to Sweden but also of a number of Swedish-born Jews. However, the very success of these *aliyah* efforts makes it necessary to fill the gap in the younger generation. The Stockholm Jewish community's Summer Camp, *Glamsta*, in addition to the camp activities of *B'nai Akiva*, developed into an important instrument for Jewish education and contact with Zionism and Israeli culture. It is open to young people from Jewish communities all over the country.

There are between 15,000 and 20,000 Jews in Sweden today, of whom 25 to 30 percent are Federation members. Although membership campaigns have not been unsuccessful in recent years, only 700 voted in the elections to the last Zionist Congress. Zionism in Sweden is not strongly involved in the party affiliations of Israel. The relatively large Jewish organizations, like Maccabi, the Scandinavian Youth Organization and the Scandinavian Jewish Student Organization, are allied with either the Swedish or the Scandinavian Zionist Organization. Although a major change has occurred in the community, most of the Zionist work is still done in cooperation with institutions that are not directly Zionist-affiliated. Nevertheless, the leading members, even some of those who were previously ardent anti-Zionists, are today Zionists or closely related to the Zionist Movement.

Soviet Russia

Michael Zand

In the past decade, the *aliyah* movement of Soviet Jewry has been the only Zionist movement that succeeded in bringing a substantial number of Jews to Israel. Moreover, it has engendered widespread solidarity throughout the world with the plight of Soviet Jewry, a contribution which should not be underestimated.

Aliyah Figures

The Jewish national revival in the Soviet Union in the late 1960s and 1970s did not develop according to classical Zionist theory. According to the Soviet census of 1970, the Jewish population of the U.S.S.R. numbered about 2,150,000. It consists of three different groups, each with its own specific pattern of Jewish identity.[1] The smallest group includes the Oriental Jews of Georgia, the Bukharan Jews of Central Asia, and the Mountain Jews of the Caucasus. In 1970 this group numbered about 120,000 (6 percent of Soviet Jewry). From 1971 until September 1977, approximately 43,000 of them came to Israel, representing 35.8 percent of the entire *aliyah* movement from the Soviet Union in those years. In the Georgian community, the percentage of those who emigrated is as high as 70; only one percent settled elsewhere than Israel.

The second group consists of Jews from the territories taken over by the U.S.S.R. during World War II: from the Baltic Republics, from Northern Bukovina and Bessarabia which became Soviet in

1.   The figures for the various groups are given according to the official Soviet publication of the census (*Itogi vsesoyuznoy perepisi naseleniya 1970 goda*, vol. IV, Moscow, 1973); with regard to the Oriental Jews my calculation is based on language indications in this and the previous (1959) census. The numbers of those who left the U.S.S.R. for Israel and other countries are based on Z. Alexander, "Immigration to Israel from the U.S.S.R.," *Israel Yearbook on Human Rights*, Vol. 7 (1977), tables pp. 319-335.

1940, and from the Carpatho-Ukraine ceded to the U.S.S.R. in 1945. (Jews who now live in the western regions of the Ukraine and Byelorussia, formerly eastern parts of Poland which became Soviet in 1939, are regarded as internal Soviet migrants and are not counted in this group.) In 1970, the group numbered 270,000 (13 percent of all of Soviet Jewry). About 55,000 have emigrated to Israel, representing 45.8 percent of all those who came on *aliyah* from the U.S.S.R. between 1971 and 1977.

The third and largest group consists of European (or, in accepted Jewish terminology, Ashkenazi) Jews of that area of the U.S.S.R. contained within the pre-1939 borders. In 1970 this group totalled 1,770,000 (89 percent of Soviet Jewry). Of this number only about 22,000 have emigrated to Israel, or 18.3 percent of Soviet *aliyah* for the years 1971 to 1977.

Identity Patterns

These statistical data help us to understand the varying Jewish identity patterns. According to Eliezer Schweid, the contemporary Jew experiences his Jewishness in various ways: as a religious or cultural experience, or as an occurrence of fate.[2] The first two patterns—the religious and the cultural—lie within the framework of Jewish civilization as defined by Mordecai Kaplan: "Judaism as otherness is something far more comprehensive than Jewish religion. It includes that nexus of a history, literature, language, social organization, folk sanctions, standards of contact, social and spiritual ideals, esthetic values, which in their totality form a civilization."[3] The third pattern, Jewishness as an occurrence of fate only, cannot be defined in terms of Jewish civilization.

The Oriental Jews of the U.S.S.R., the first group mentioned above, live in areas where the Soviet regime, during the first decade of its existence, tried to put down the aspirations of the local populations to maintain their independence. All through the 1920s, the Communist Party used elaborate methods to weaken the resistance of these populations to Soviet rule. One of the most important facets of this policy was to demonstrate respect for local traditions, including a measure of religious tolerance. As a result, religion was less undermined there than in the Slavic parts of the U.S.S.R.

2.   See E. Schweid, *Emunat Am Yisrael ve-Tarbuto*, Jerusalem, 1976, p. 152.
3.   Mordecai M. Kaplan, *Judaism as a Civilization: Toward a Reconstruction of American Jewish Life*, New York, 1972 edition, p. 178.

This was also true for the Jewish religion in these areas. Efforts to secularize the Oriental Jewish community were less successful than the regime had expected.[4] Although it would be an exaggeration to say that this group fully retained its religious tradition, the religious base is still strong, and it provides the main pattern of Jewish self-identification for the members of this group. Since longing for the return to Zion is repeatedly stressed in the religious tradition, it has been the main incentive for the Oriental group's participation in the Jewish dissent movement in the U.S.S.R. Thus, members of this group not only account for the highest percentage of Jews who leave the Soviet Union, but also the highest percentage of those who settle in Israel.

As for the second group, namely Jews in the territories taken by the U.S.S.R. during World War II, some historical data should be stressed to define their main pattern of Jewish self-identification. In the period between the World Wars, the areas in which these Jews lived were centers of intensive Jewish political and cultural life. Political parties of every shade of the ideological spectrum functioned actively; a large network of Hebrew and Yiddish educational institutions flourished in Latvia, Lithuania and Besarabia; Yiddish and Hebrew newspapers were published in these areas, and also some in German (in Czernowitz), Rumanian (in Bessarabia) and Hungarian (in the Carpatho-Ukraine).[5]

As early as 1940, the Soviets attempted to paralyze Jewish public and cultural life in their new territories by imprisoning countless Jewish intellectuals After World War II, especially during "the black years of Soviet Jewry" (1948-1953) they intensified their efforts to eradicate all Jewish self-expression that survived. Despite persecutions, however, Jewish consciousness and group identification persisted. When large-scale Jewish dissent began in the 1960s, Kishinev and Vilnius were the first places to resume Yiddish theatrical performances

4. See M. Altshuler, "Ha-Pe'ilut ha-Tarbutit ha-Sovyetit be-Kerev Yehudei Gruziyah," *Behinot*, no. 6, 1975, pp. 103-127; M. Zand, "Kultura gorskikh yevreev kevkaza i kultura bukharskikh yevreev v sovetskiy periyod," *Yevreyskaya Kultura v Sovetskom Soyuze*, Jerusalem, 1974.

5. For more details on Latvia, see *Yahadut Latviyah: Sefer Zikkaron*, Tel Aviv, 1953; M. Bove, *Perakim be-Toldot Yahadut Latviyah*, Tel Aviv, 1965; on Lithuania: *Yahadut Litah*, Tel Aviv, 1971; B. Kagan, "Hinnukh ivri be-Litah," *Ha-hinnukh ve-ha-Tarbut ha-ivrit be-Eiropah beyn shtei milhamot ha-Olam*, Tel Aviv, 1957; specifically on Vilnius: I. Cohen, *History of the Jews in Vilna*, New York, 1943; on Bessarabia, see *Pirkei Bessarabiyah*, Tel Aviv, 1952; *Al Admat Bessarabiyah*, 3 vols., Tel Aviv, 1959-63; on Bukowina, specifically on Czernowitz, see *Geschichte der Juden in der Bukowina*, M. Gold, Herausgeb., Bd. 1-2, 1958-62; Zoharia-Goldhammer, "Chernovzi," *Arim ve-Immahot be-Yisrael*, Tel Aviv, 1950, pp. 85ff.

despite the many difficult obstacles imposed by the authorities. Riga became the main center of revived—though hardly intensive—Zionist activity. The self-identification reflected in the statistics cited above includes a preference among members of this group who leave the U.S.S.R. to come to Israel rather than go to other countries.

As for the third and largest group—"authentic" Soviet Ashkenazi Jewry—its unhappy history is well-known, but a brief survey is required from the viewpoint of Jewish identity. Before 1917, the Jewishness of the greater part of this group consisted of a sense of belonging to a specific civilization characterized first and foremost by religion. At the same time, the socio-cultural secular patterns were also given expression in Hebrew, Yiddish and Russian. By the end of the first decade of the Soviet regime, however, all Hebrew cultural activity was banned. In the second decade, virtually all efforts to maintain some kind of Jewish culture (especially writing) in Russian came to an end. While Yiddish was still allowed at first, the number of Yiddish schools and cultural institutions decreased rapidly from year to year. In addition, synagogues were shut down, religious leaders and their adherents persecuted. By the eve of World War II most members of the group were already secularized. For the overwhelming majority of the younger generation, Russian language and culture had become the basis of their education, their Jewishness a mere biological fact.

Those who still adhered to Jewish culture lived in what had been the Soviet Ukraine, Soviet Byelorussia, and some parts of Russia, until they were liquidated by the Nazis during World War II, and by the Soviet authorities in 1948. The surviving Yiddish cultural institutions were shut down, as were the publications, while poets, writers, journalists and actors were arrested and executed, or imprisoned in Gulags.[6]

Patterns of Jewish Experience

By the beginning of the post-Stalinist era, the overwhelming majority of Ashkenazi Russian Jews no longer had any active contact with Jewish civilization, experiencing their Jewishness only as an occurrence of fate. Schweid distinguishes three subpatterns of Jewishness as fate: fate as a source of pride, fate as a curse, and apathetic reconciliation to fate. The first two evoke active behavior, the latter presupposes passivity.

6.   See Y.A. Gilboa, The Black Years of Soviet Jewry, New York, 1971.

Those who considered their Jewish fate a source of pride came to the conclusion that their place was not in the U.S.S.R., where Jews are a governmentally discriminated minority, but in the Land of their own People, in Israel. Those who looked upon their Jewishness as a curse attempted to assimilate. To achieve complete assimilation under Soviet law, one's personal papers must indicate that neither he/she nor either of one's parents are Jews. In many branches of employment, a person of Jewish origin cannot "achieve" the designation of non-Jew, unless he/she is the child of a half-Jew who has opted for official designation as a non-Jew and is married to a non-Jew. In other words, it takes three generations to assimilate officially. Hence the only solution for the Jew who wishes to become assimilated completely and immediately is to leave the U.S.S.R. for a country where ethnic affiliation is not officially prescribed. Naturally this precludes Israel. Such people, therefore, attempt to gain admittance to a multi-ethnic country, primarily the United States. For those emigrants who reconciled themselves to their Jewish fate, the main preference has been the Western democracies, where there is political, juridical or economic freedom.

The Dissidents

In the final analysis, it would seem that political and juridical considerations have been the main incentive for Jewish participants in the general dissident movement of Soviet intellectuals. Since they did not have a clearly defined positive attitude to their Jewishness, they went along with the mainstream of the exodus. The statistics relating to this group—the largest in Soviet Jewry, who accept their Jewishness only as fate—show that as many have gone to other countries as to Israel. This demonstrates that the assimilationist tendency is at least as strong as the desire to settle in Israel. When the main flow of immigration was directed to Israel, those who were only apathetically reconciled to their Jewish fate went there, but following the present-day mainstream, they are now proceeding to other countries.

The *Aliyah* Movement: First Period

The period between World War II and the Six Day War in 1967 may be considered as the prehistory of the Soviet *aliyah* movement. Chronologically, the Holocaust was the first catalyst of what later became the Jewish national movement in the Soviet Union. Those

Jews who lived in the areas incorporated into the U.S.S.R. in 1939-40
and in the western parts of Soviet Union itself in its pre-1939 borders
were victims of the Holocaust. The survivors—Jewish soldiers who
served in the Soviet army, returnees from the interior of the U.S.S.R.
to their prewar residences, those whose relatives had been extermi-
nated—all felt that they were the remnants of a people without homes
and roots, unwanted in areas where their forebears had lived for
hundreds of years.

The establishment of the State of Israel in 1948 produced a
surge of Jewish national feeling among both the older and the younger
generations of Soviet Jewry. While it might be exaggerated to state that
all Jews were filled with enthusiasm over this event,[7] many were
deeply moved by it. Nevertheless, those who dared to attempt to trans-
late their enthusiasm into deeds were few. Petitions were sent to the
Soviet authorities, to Stalin himself, requesting that young Soviet Jews
be allowed to volunteer for the Israeli army. Several underground
groups began to occupy themselves with Jewish education; some
Hebrew writers tried to renew their literary activities and organized
themselves secretly.[8] Some tried to make their way to Israel by cross-
ing the Soviet borders illegally. Almost all the participants in these
activities were caught by the Soviet Security Service and sentenced to
long terms in prisons and *Gulag* camps. There they came in contact
with veteran members of Jewish political and cultural organizations in
the areas taken over by the Soviet Union in 1939-40. They were joined
by Jewish intellectuals sent to the work camps during "the black
years" (1948-53). Many active participants in the subsequent *aliyah*
movement were former inmates of the *Gulags*.

The *aliyah* movement, which began in the wake of the Six Day

7.   Cf., for example, the following statements: "I come from Central Russia and know
mainly the Jews in Leningrad and the North. I can testify that for them the establishment of the State of Israel was nothing more than a pleasant fact of historical, not
personal, significance." (Sophia Tertakovsky, translator of European belles-lettres into
Russian, an *olah* from the U.S.S.R., as quoted in *News Bulletin* of the Scientists Committee of the Israel Public Council for Soviet Jewry, no. 135/136, June 30, 1978, p. 15). Or:
"But then in May, 1948, the hall resounded with enthusiasm . . . there was loud
applause even when Vyshinsky jeeringly spoke about a state where people read from
right to left. What do I care about this Israel? I have lived without it and will continue to
do so. As for my country, my institute, that's another matter." Victor Perelman, *Pokin-
utaya Rossiya* (Russia Abandoned), 2 vols., Tel Aviv, 1976: v. I, *Illiuziy* (Illusions),
p. 123.
8.   See the memoirs (published posthumously) of an outstanding member of this group,
Zvi Preygerzon (A. Zioni), *Yoman ha-Zikhronot (1949-1955)*, Tel Aviv, 1976, and
Y. Slutsky's introduction to these memoirs, pp. 5-24.

War, intensified the national aspirations of those who defined their Jewishness in religious or in social and cultural terms, even of many who considered their Jewish heritage a product of fate. That event infused pride into the hearts of a considerable number of Jews who had remained Jewish out of apathy. They felt that Israel's astounding victory removed a grave threat to the very existence of the Jewish People after the Holocaust. By providing the Arabs with generous military aid, the Soviet Union had demonstrated that it was on the side of those who so virulently tried to do away with the Jews. It became quite impossible for Jews with any national consciousness to continue to live in such a country.

By the end of 1968, the Soviet government granted permission to 230 Jews from the western periphery, most of them elderly, to go on *aliyah*. They had applied for their exit visas before the Six Day War. Using this as a precedent, Jews sent a torrent of requests for exit permits to Israel. Throughout 1969, the authorities continued to renew previously cancelled visas and granted permits to some 3,000 persons who had applied before 1967, but new applications by middle-aged people from almost all parts of the U.S.S.R. were denied. By the end of 1968 and during 1969, the *aliyah* movement was reinforced by a number of Jewish participants in the democratic movement. In those same years, a relatively wide network of *ulpanim* (Hebrew classes) was established clandestinely.

Letters from Jews requesting permission to leave for Israel were circulated in *samizdat* publications, reaching the media in the West by the end of 1969 and rousing world public opinion. The first two Jewish *samizdat* journals, *Iskhod* and *Iton*, were founded in 1970.[9] *Iton* was the organ of VKK (Vsesoyuzny Koordinatsionny Komitet— the All-Soviet Coordinating Committee), a committee of activists. Both journals appeared anonymously until the beginning of 1971, when most of their contributing members emigrated to Israel.

During the summer of 1970, the authorities attempted to intimidate Jews who requested exit permits for Israel by sending them to prison. When the first Leningrad "hijackers" trial was held in December of the same year, the courts in Leningrad and in Moscow were

---

9.   A large part of this material has been published in the series *Yevreyski Samizdat* (Jewish Samizdat), vols. I-II Jerusalem, 1974. To date, 21 volumes of Jewish *samizdat* material have been published by the Center for Research and Documentation of Eastern European Jewry at the Hebrew University of Jerusalem.

picketed, and a wave of sharp protests that had not been anticipated by Soviet authorities came from abroad. During the time of the trial and immediately afterwards, there was a flurry of applications for exit permits to Israel.

In February 1971, *aliyah* activists began to employ the sit-in, a tactic never before used in the U.S.S.R. These demonstrations gathered momentum in March, and fairly large groups received permission to leave for Israel within a relatively short period. For the first time the authorities gave in; the Jewish dissidents, backed by world public opinion, had their way.

The *Aliyah* Movement: Second Period

The second *aliyah* period lasted from March 1971 to the end of 1973. Only 1,000 Jews had been granted exit permits in 1970; in 1971—13,000; in 1972—31,700; in 1973—34,700.

Most of the applicants received their permits after waiting two to three months, especially those in areas which came under Soviet rule during World War II and those in the Oriental Republics. Their participation in the *aliyah* movement was expressed in the very act of applying for exit visas to Israel, and in taking part in some activities before and after applying for their visas until these were granted. Thus, the participation of relatively large numbers in the *aliyah* movement makes it the most extensive of the dissident movements and groups of the 1970s.

A special group emerged during this period, providing the *aliyah* movement with leaders. They were the *otkazniki*, or "refuseniks," for the most part intellectuals who were denied permission to leave the Soviet Union, usually under the pretext that they had access to classified information. In the first period of the *aliyah* movement, denial of visas had been the rule; now it was the exception. According to various estimates, about 1,000 to 1,200 were denied exit permits every year between 1971 and 1973.

In 1971, three trials were held in the provinces, obviously in order to intimidate the local Jewish population and prevent the movement from spreading. In August 1972, the authorities introduced a new measure, the education tax: the more educated the potential emigrant, the more he was required to pay to emigrate. Since even the well-paid professional could not accumulate the necessary sum, this was intended to make emigration impossible. But after this measure provoked outraged reaction abroad, it was eventually suspended in March 1973.

Jewish *samizdat* activities persisted. New journals came into existence: *Vestnik Iskhoda* (actually a continuation of *Iskhod*) from 1971 and then *Yevrei v SSSR*. Two new struggle tactics were introduced—collective hunger strikes and seminars convened by dismissed scientists and scholars. Both proved effective.

The *Aliyah* Movement: 1974-1977

Three main characteristics of the period, which began after the Yom Kippur War, may be emphasized.

First, there was a steady decline in the number of emigrants from the U.S.S.R. during the mid-1970s. As we indicated, 34,700 left the country in 1973; in 1974—20,066; in 1975—13,900; in 1976—14,260; there was a slight rise in 1977 to 16,700. Various reasons for this decline have been suggested, but at least one fact is indisputable: contrary to Soviet implications, the potential of Jewish emigration has not yet been exhausted.

Second, the homogeneous Jewish dissent movement, strictly speaking, had now split into two factions: those who, as in previous periods, wanted to go on *aliyah*, and those whose principal desire was to leave the Soviet Union, not necessarily in order to make their homes in Israel. In 1971, out of a total of 13,000, only 58 persons preferred countries other than Israel; in 1976-77, the distribution between the two groups was almost equal. Various explanations have been offered for this development, but I would suggest the most important reason to be that recent emigration includes a far larger percentage of Jews from the central parts of the U.S.S.R. than in the previous periods. As mentioned above, their attitude to Jewishness is far from positive; hence their motives for leaving the Soviet Union are different. The weakening of the *aliyah* incentive evidently did not go unnoticed, as the Russian authorities decided in 1978 to crush the movement through imprisonments and trials of the few remaining leaders.

The third characteristic of the period is the deep concern of the leaders of the *aliyah* movement to disseminate Jewish culture among the Jews remaining in the U.S.S.R. It is hoped that these Jews may be encouraged to foster their heritage, saving them from becoming dissociated from the Jewish People. Eventually they might become motivated to go to Israel.

Ideological Principles

As for the ideology of the *aliyah* movement, it could be defined as "home-made" Zionism. Jabotinsky's "feuilletons," published in *Odesskiya Novosti*, and relatively widely read in his day, were (by an oversight of the Soviet censorship) still found in libraries until 1969-70. The modern reader was startled by the resemblance between the Russian Jewish reality at the time the "feuilletons" were written and the present. But even this impact was more psychological than ideological. Herzl's *Der Judenstaat*, published in Russian translation in 1918 and read by a limited number of people, was considered a classic. Ahad Ha-Am, also in Russian translation, was categorically rejected. Ber Borochov, A.D. Gordon, and Berl Katznelson were scarcely known, not even by those who were concerned with shaping their Jewish national *Weltanschauung*.

The main ideological principles of the *aliyah* movement, formulated at its inception, are still valid. The first principle was expressed in the words of the Bible: "Let my people go" (Exodus 7:16). It became the slogan of supporters of the movement throughout the free world. In the anthem of the movement, this verse was extended: "Let the Jewish People go to their homeland; let my People go in the path of God; let my People go home." Thus, the right demanded by the *aliyah* movement, and which it won to some extent with the help of its supporters in the free world, is the right of an ethnic group to return to its national territory.

Another principle underlying the *aliyah* movement is that it concerns itself exclusively with the Jewish problem in the U.S.S.R. Any other aspect of the internal situation preoccupies it only insofar as it is relevant to this problem. The *aliyah* movement must help every Soviet Jew who so desires to return to the Homeland—but the movement's adherents respect Russian culture, the Russian people and the other ethnic groups in the U.S.S.R., among whom they grew up. It does not interfere in the country's internal affairs because its participants do not consider the Soviet Union their country.

Underlying all these efforts is the urgency to establish the unquestionable legality of the struggle of the *aliyah* movement. The movement does not violate any Soviet laws, or any international laws signed by the Soviet Government. Where there is violation of such laws, the Soviet authorities do the violating. It is paradoxical that Jews who wish to leave the U.S.S.R. for their own country must wage a struggle within the Soviet Union for implementation of Soviet laws and international laws signed by the U.S.S.R. Government.

The fourth principle, elaborated in the movement's latter period, could be formulated thus: Jews who lived in the U.S.S.R. are a part of the Jewish People. They have the right to learn their own language, study their own civilization, practice their own religion.

The Positive Role of the *Aliyah* Movement

The *aliyah* movement is one of many national dissent movements in the Soviet Union. All the other minorities, such as the Crimean Tartars and the Meshkis, have their own territory in the Soviet Union, even if they were compelled to leave it. These people are also struggling to regain possession of their territory. The uniqueness of the *aliyah* movement lies in the fact that it is one of the very few minority national movements whose national territory lies beyond the borders of the U.S.S.R.

It should be noted that the Jewish dissident movement modeled itself, to a certain extent, on the democratic movement and employed similar methods of action, such as sending petitions and letters of protest to the authorities. During its early years the Jewish *samizdat* was closely modeled on the democratic *samizdat* (a considerable part of the Jewish *samizdat* consisting of translations of works of Jewish interest from Hebrew and from European languages). The *aliyah* movement was supported by the Russian liberals, mainly by the Soviet Human Rights Committee, whose favorable attitude to the Jewish question in the U.S.S.R. and to the Jewish dissident movement is well known. It should not be forgotten that certain *aliyah* movement documents were examined from the legal aspect by the Human Rights group before being publicly circulated.

The *aliyah* movement is the only dissident movement in the U.S.S.R. which has achieved its goal, at least in part. Its success demonstrates that if a movement possesses clearly defined principles, is relatively large, wins over world public opinion and is determined to persevere against all odds, it can attain its objective even in the autocratic Soviet regime.

Today, the *aliyah* movement in the U.S.S.R. is experiencing one of its most difficult phases, as its main reservoir—Jews conscious of their heritage and proud of it—is drying up. The emigration movement, led by "non-Jewish Jews" (to use Isaac Deutscher's expression), is gathering momentum and gaining the support of non-Zionist Jews in the free world for whom it serves as a kind of moral alibi. Soviet authorities are aware of this and try to crush the movement by sending its leaders to prison. The perpetuation of the Jewish movement in the U.S.S.R. as a part of the World Zionist Movement depends largely on whether the Soviet Jew who is apathetic to his Jewish fate can be transformed into a Jew who is proud of it. Under present circumstances, this can be achieved only by making him feel that he has a share in the Jewish experience. This is the task which Israel and Jews of the free world must constantly see before them.

Comment

Zev Katz

The situation of Soviet Jewry changed in the last two years of the 1970s. After several years of decline in both the number of Jews leaving the Soviet Union and the number of Russian *olim* to Israel, a sharp upward trend became manifest. In 1978, 29,000 Jews were allowed to leave Russia, 12,000 of whom immigrated to Israel—a rise of 72 percent in the first category and 45 percent in the second as compared to 1971. A record number of Soviet Jews—about 51,000—were allowed to leave the U.S.S.R in 1979. The number of those who came to Israel increased to 18,000.

At the same time, the direction and composition of the Jewish emigration from the U.S.S.R. were altered. Although the absolute numbers of Soviet Jews coming on *aliyah* was higher in these two years, the overall number in 1979 was only somewhat more than half the total for 1973, when about 33,000 *olim* had arrived. At the beginning of the decade, almost all Jews leaving Russia had gone to Israel, but in 1979 only about 35 percent did so, the remainder emigrating to Western countries, mainly to the United States. At present (early 1980), the percentage of Soviet Jewish emigrés going to the West has stabilized at about the above level, partly because Soviet visa authorities insist on "invitations" (*vyzovs*) only from first-degree relatives in Israel, and partly as a reaction against the growing tendency to emigrate to the West.

Let me bring up to date the situation of the three major groups delineated by Professor Zand. Almost all of the Oriental Jewish communities continue to go on *aliyah*. However, the number of Georgian Jews leaving is rather small at present, since the majority already have settled in Israel, and the remainder are deeply integrated in their place of residence (e.g., Party members, strongly assimilated or those in army service). The number of Bukharan Jewish immigrants is not large for similar reasons (and the overall percentage of this community

who left for Israel altogether is small). Many Oriental-Jewish *olim*
now come from the Mountain Jewish (Tat) community, from such
places as Baku, Derbent, and Makhach-Kala along the Caspian Sea.

An important element among those now leaving the Soviet
Union comes from the "new territories" incorporated by the U.S.S.R.
during World War II—especially from Moldavia (Bessarabia), Bukovina (Czernowitz), and the Carpatho-Ukraine (Munkach). The exodus of
Jews from Lithuania and Latvia, which is almost total also continues.
But while in the early 1970s almost all the emigrants from the "new
territories" went to Israel, now about one half or more are emigrating
to the West.

The third emigration movement has grown especially quickly
within the third group, the "authentic" (or "core") Soviet Jews of Ashkenazi origin. Jews have begun leaving many provincial towns in
Byelorussia and the Ukraine, as well as in Russia itself, e.g., Gomel,
Bobroisk, Zhitomir, Perm. Over 90 percent of Jews from the big city
centers (Odessa, Moscow, Leningrad, Kiev) choose to go to the West.

Altogether, during the past decade, the first period of large-
scale Jewish emigration from the U.S.S.R., about 225,000 left Soviet
Russia, 150,000 of whom settled in Israel and the other 75,000 went to
the West. The increase in the number of those granted exit visas in the
last two years was accompanied by an increase in the number of those
applying to leave. Many who had been reticent to apply for emigration, or were afraid to do so, have been encouraged by the large numbers of those allowed to leave. The average number of "invitations"
sent monthly in 1979 reached 15,000–18,000. The total number of
applicants is currently estimated at 400,000. In percentages, therefore,
about 10 percent of Soviet Jewry (in terms of the 1970 census figures)
left the U.S.S.R. in the past decade, and about 20 percent more are
presently seeking to leave.

Another major development, which asserted itself by the end of
the 1970s, is the appearance of an embryonic network of Hebrew
ulpanim and semi-legal seminars on Jewish culture, as well as a more
intense campaign for legitimate Jewish cultural activity in the U.S.S.R.
While Jewish *samizdat* was already manifest, semi-"open" study
groups and seminars for Hebrew and Jewish studies are a more recent
development. To be sure, such Jewish activities take place only in
private homes in a quasi-clandestine manner. The authorities are well
aware of them, and limit their interference to minor harassments and
warnings "not to widen the circle." In some respects, therefore, these

activities are "tolerated." A number of foreign—including Israeli—scholars visiting the U.S.S.R. have been able to meet with these study groups in Moscow, Leningrad, Riga, and Vilnius. The number of "students" at Hebrew *ulpan* circles in the main towns of the U.S.S.R. is estimated at about 1,000. The needs of this growing movement for Jewish culture in the Soviet Union are also served by the continuous appearance of such publications as *Tarbut* (Culture) and *Yevrei v SSSR* (Jews in the U.S.S.R.). While most of those engaged in these activities are long-term refuseniks, who consider teaching Hebrew, and Jewish research and writing both as a mission and a profession, since they have been cut off from their previous professional activities, a minority are Soviet Jews who continue their normal work and do not intend to leave (at least not at present). However, both groups insist on an active struggle for Jewish cultural institutions in the U.S.S.R.

Finally, among recent developments, the Soviet authorities have made several minor "concessions" concerning Jewish cultural expression. A new Yiddish musical theater was inaugurated in Birobidzhan, and tours a number of cities of the U.S.S.R. The Moscow Jewish religious community has been allowed to publish a religious calendar in Russian which contains some material on Jewish holidays and on famous rabbis, as well as explanations of the important prayers. *Sovietish Heimland* has announced plans for publishing a series of booklets in Yiddish which will amount to a "library of contemporary Yiddish literature." The Moscow Institute for Teaching Nationality Languages announced a position for a researcher in the methodology of teaching the Yiddish language in schools, as Yiddish is apparently to be introduced as a voluntary subject in some Birobidzhan schools. Altogether, these measures are possibly designed to counter the growing pressure for emigration and to make a favorable impression abroad.

Professor Zand rightly stresses the "religious base" of the Oriental Jewish communities which has resulted in the highest percentage of their emigration and *aliyah*. It is worthwhile to point to another specific characteristic of these communities—they have undergone much less modernization and Westernization than the Jews from the "core" Soviet territories and from the "new" Soviet territories. This may have had a decisive influence both on their decision to leave and on their overwhelming choice of Israel as their destination. Traditional religious attitudes and an earlier stage of socio-

cultural development might, in this case, have been related, and reinforced one another. The Oriental Jewish communities were capable of
preserving their religious traditions because of their family structure
and the lesser impact of modernization. For the same reasons, they
were able to maintain a strong sense of "natural-naive Zionism." The
highly modernized and industrialized northern countries of the West
offer a discouraging prospect to the Georgian or Mountain Jews. They
have no close family there; nor are they familiar with the language
and culture. On the other hand, in Israel they have family and friends
who emigrated earlier. Israel is also closer to them in terms of culture,
climate and, of course, religion.

For the highly assimilated, modernized "core" Jews from the
big cities, the position is largely reversed. The metropolitan centers of
the West are closer to their experience than Israel. They often have
family and friends there; they know Western languages; but they do
not know Hebrew. And they believe that the professional and material possibilities are better there. It appears also that at least some emigrants leave the Soviet Union and go to the West for assimilatory reasons: they failed to assimilate in the Soviet Union because of persecution and discrimination; now they have decided to go to the West in
the hope that they will at last be allowed to be assimilated and to
forget that they were born Jews.

A final comment relates to Professor Zand's central argument,
in which he points out that "in the past decade, the *aliyah* movement
of Soviet Jewry has been the only Zionist movement that succeeded in
bringing substantial numbers of Jews to Israel." The national Jewish
movement in the Soviet Union developed into a major force shortly
after the Six Day War as an indomitable and courageous mass movement. Not only did it base itself upon an openly asserted Zionism ideology; but it was also a mass movement, *hagshamah*, realizing the ideology in terms of an almost total emigration to Israel. Such are the iro-
nies and complexities of historical developments, that what at first was
an extremely Zionist movement later unleashed an "escape to the
West" mass movement. As the image of Israel lost its post-Six-Day-
War glory, and the difficulties of absorption in Israel became widely
known, so, in a parallel way, did the attractions of the West grow. The
Soviet Zionists thus became a minority in their very own migration
movement.

A balanced analysis, however, might question whether Soviet-
Russian Zionism can appropriately be compared with that in the coun-

tries of the West. In this matter, one may possibly draw the line between Jewish communities developing in normal and beneficial conditions, and communities which, for various reasons, had to uproot themselves from their habitat and move elsewhere urgently. Recent Jewish history has seen a number of cases of the latter situation. In some such communities there was only a very small Zionist minority. Yet at times of uprooting, it was able, with the help of Israel, to carry large numbers of Jews to Eretz Israel. Such was the situation, for example, of the Jewish community in Bulgaria or Iraq in the past. Moreover, since 1967, many thousands of Jews have come to Israel from various countries in the West, although no major crisis prompted them to leave. This is mentioned for balance, not to lessen appreciation of the immense achievements of the great Zionist *aliyah* from the U.S.S.R. The *aliyah* movement has focussed world attention on the plight of Soviet Jewry, and has brought to Israel a "substantial number of Jews"—not a minor feat.

Islamic Lands

North Africa
(Tunisia, Algeria, Morocco)

Michel Abitbol

Political Zionism began in North Africa between 1897 and 1900, when Dr. A. Valensin, a young physician from Constantine in Algeria, was appointed by the Zionist Executive Committee to be the Movement's representative in the three countries of the Maghreb.

Since conditions for Jews were different in each country, the development of Zionism in each varied as well.[1]

Zionist Beginnings in the Maghreb

In Algeria the Jews were emancipated in 1870, when the Crémieux Decree granted French citizenship to most of them. This change in their legal status led to cultural assimilation, even though they also had to contend with extreme anti-Semitism on the part of the local European population; liberals and conservatives, anarchists and churchmen were all anti-Semitic. Anti-Jewish ferment reached a peak in 1897 when serious physical attacks on Jews took place in most of the cities.

Word of these disturbances reached the participants of the first Zionist Congress, which M. Attali of Constantine attended as the delegate from North Africa.[2] But the Congress did not evoke any effective

---

1. The present article is based primarily on documents in the Central Zionist Archives (CZA). Research on Zionist activity in North Africa is still lacking. D. Bensimon-Donath devotes one chapter to the topic in her book on African Jews in Israel, *Immigrants d'Afrique du Nord en Israël*, Paris, 1970, pp. 45–78.
2. *Protocols of the First Zionist Congress* (Hebrew), 1897, p. 53.

response among the Jews of Algeria, except for the community in Constantine. A letter sent to Theodor Herzl by a local youth association stated, in part: "The initiative you have taken to realize the Zionist idea in practice has aroused great enthusiasm in Constantine. The Zionist idea has spread among the members of our community who, like their brethren in Russia and Romania are being persecuted. Your action has the full support of all the Constantine Jews who see it as the only solution to the Jewish problem."[3]

In Tunisia, a French protectorate since 1881, the authorities wished to avoid the complications encountered in Algeria and refused to extend French citizenship to the Jews; but they did encourage French education in the community, which also preserved its traditional institutions. The first Zionist group was organized immediately after the First Zionist Congress.[4] Individuals began to set up groups all over, and by World War I, Zionist associations had sprung up in all large cities of Tunisia.[5]

Before the French established their protectorate of Morocco in 1912, a considerable part of the community maintained close ties with other parts of the world. The early Zionist associations in Morocco appeared in the coastal cities which were exposed to European influence. In central Morocco Zionist activity began in 1908 with the establishment of *Hibbat Zion* in Fez, which also extended its activities to the two neighboring cities of Sefrou and Meknes.[6]

While a certain receptiveness was necessary for Zionism to become implanted in Morocco, in the other two countries it was the preservation of tradition which led to the Zionist awakening. In Algeria, conservative Constantine, not more modern Algiers or Oran, was the only Zionist center for a long time. In the outlying towns—Bône, Sétif and Tlemcen—Zionist institutions were established by individuals or groups who considered Zionism an effective defense against assimilation.[7]

In Morocco the Zionist idea was colored by the religious concept "the beginnings of redemption." In 1910, when it was suggested to

---

3. CZA Z1/279, 12.9.1897.
4. *Protocols of the Third Zionist Congress*, 1899.
5. See CZA Z1/321, for the establishment of the Zionist Association in Sousse by the local rabbi; see also Z1/288: 19.10.1898; Fédération Sioniste de France, Année 1918–1919, *Rapport Général*, pp. 7–8; *Jüdische Rundschau*, 7.11.1919, p. 183.
6. CZA Z2/309: 8.9.1909; Z2/511: 22.6.1910.
7. On the beginnings of Zionist organization in Algeria, see Fédération Sioniste de France, *op. cit.*, p. 6; CZA Z4/2574 (General Report), 17.7.1921.

the members of the groups in Fez and Meknes that they join the *Mizrachi* Federation, they agreed, but the Zionists of Fez found it difficult to grasp that among the supporters of the Zionist idea were some who "publicly" opposed the view that it was necessary "to protect our holy religion so that nothing be done within the Zionist movement that is counter to our religion."[8] For this reason, rabbis occupied a dominant place in the early stages of Zionist organization in North Africa.

Cultural Barriers

People who held important positions in the general community were also members of the Zionist groups. This was in keeping with the accepted values in society and facilitated fund-raising activity for Jewish causes.

The Zionists of Fez asked the Zionist Organization to appeal to one of the European powers—Great Britain, France or Germany—to take the *Hibbat Zion* group under its protection.[9] In pre-protectorate Morocco such requests were quite common. Groups benefitting from patronage attained not only a considerable measure of physical security to protect them from the authorities and the Moslem masses, but also a feeling of honor and prestige. Indeed, to be a subject, or enjoy the protection of a European country was a sign of socio-economic success. The request was turned down by David Wolffsohn on the grounds that the Zionist Organization had to be extremely careful not to do anything that might be construed as intervention in the internal affairs of any country.

Until well into the 1920s contact between the local associations and the Zionist Organization was hampered by the language barrier. Propaganda material in Yiddish and German was sent to the local activists who knew only French, Arabic or Ladino. ". . . Your letter remains an unsolved riddle," writes the secretary of *B'nei Zion* in Beja to the Executive Committee of the Central Zionist Organization. "In my name and in the name of our association I ask you not to write us any longer in a foreign tongue, but rather in our holy tongue dearer to us than gold."[10] Activists in North Africa were asked to contact the editorial board of *Ha-Olam* in Vilna for material in Hebrew. As early as 1900 a request for competent *shelihim* (emissaries) had been sent to

8. See, for example, CZA Z2/511: Meknes, 15.9.1910.
9. CZA Z4/2011 (1920).
10. CZA Z3/751.

the Executive Committee but it was not until much later that any positive response was forthcoming.[11] No less serious was the failure of the central institutions to properly explain the essence of Zionism and its activities.

At the same time, letters from the central offices constantly stressed the need to increase the sale of *shekalim* and shares in the Jewish Colonial Trust. Indeed, the chairman of *Ahavat Zion* in Safi wrote to Herzl in exasperation: "We know about the holy shekel that everyone has to buy, but is it true that Zionism is founded on the shekel, and that only by virtue of buying the shekel once a year a man earns the right to be called a Zionist . . . ?"[12] It is not surprising, therefore, that the Zionist undertaking should appear to many as no more than a charitable project. For a long time this depleted image was a serious obstacle to the dissemination of the Zionist idea in North Africa.

The Zionist associations developed on the basis of traditional attachment to Zion and the longing to end the Exile. It could be safely assumed that few individuals were aware of the secular character of political Zionism which maintains that Jewish existence among the Gentiles is a problem that can be resolved by human and political means, not necessarily by divine decree or a messianic miracle. Indeed, political Zionism developed in spite of the expected failure of all suggested solutions to the Jewish problem, including emancipation. This conception was far removed from the thinking of the North African Jews, who, for the most part, knew little about emancipation. Furthermore, the emancipation they knew, or would come to know, did not always involve assimilation to the point of canceling out Jewish identity. Religious identity remained well anchored in day-to-day reality, despite changes.

Alliance Israélite Universelle

In North Africa the Zionist groups faced serious competition— the Alliance Israélite Universelle, a well-funded Jewish organization favorably regarded by the authorities and which aspired to ease the distress of the Jewish population in its own way. But the Alliance was not merely a philanthropic organization. Its activity had an ideological

11. CZA Z3/979: 24.4.1913. For additional examples see also Z4/2574: 17.7.1921 (Algiers); Z4/10310: 8.7.1936 (Tunis).
12. CZA Z2/309.

foundation which also proffered a practical alternative to Zionism: as against the centrality of Eretz Israel the Alliance put forward the centrality of France, its culture and values. The Alliance believed the Jewish problem could be resolved locally—at least in countries under French rule—through the Jews' social and cultural integration into the general life of their countries of residence. It comes as no surprise, therefore, that early Zionist spokesmen attacked the "dark alliance" between the Alliance Israélite Universelle and the consistories at every opportunity.[13] Nor did the Alliance leaders remain silent. From time to time they leveled serious charges against Zionism, describing it as an anti-French movement which adversely affected France's aspirations in Palestine. Zionists would argue back, as evidenced in Ch. Sharshavsky's pungent article in *La Voix Juive* (1921):

> Alliance Israélite Universelle . . . what you want is not emancipation of the Jews, but their assimilation and suicide. The time has passed when individuals with honors and wealth could exploit their social standing to act as the procurators of an entire people.[14]

One of the major problems was the Zionists' inability in North Africa to make any real inroads among the modern and educated elements who were under the influence of the French model developed by the Alliance and the consistories. Paradoxically, Zionism's adherents came almost exclusively from the traditional elements who could not really understand its ideals. Only during World War II did the situation change, when the Jews suffered from the racist legislation of the Vichy representatives in North Africa and felt that France had let them down.

Between the Two World Wars

The Balfour Declaration and the decisions reached at the San Remo Conference aroused considerable enthusiasm among the North African Jews. An atmosphere of redemption prevailed, manifested by thanksgiving prayers, public meetings, a religious-messianic awakening, and an intensification of Zionist activity which included preparation for *aliyah* and increased *shekel* sales.

In Morocco, many new Zionist societies were established in

13. Bensimon-Donath, *op. cit.*
14. *La Voix Juive*, 1921, p. 14.

Marrakesh, Rabat, Mazagan, Oujda and Casablanca.[15] In the 1920s
there was also a significant breakthrough in the northern region under
Spanish control. Many families began to make their way to Eretz
Israel. In 1920 the *Kol Mevasser* group in Sefrou requested that its
emigrants settle in agricultural communities or near Arabs since they
were accustomed to such conditions. In Mogador, entry visas to Palestine were obtained from the local British consul for all residents who
wished to emigrate.[16] But many *olim* returned to Morocco after they
were not allowed to disembark at Jaffa.

In Algeria, even as the Jewish population generally remained
indifferent to Zionism, several circles did support the Zionist idea—in
Tlemcen, Media, Mostaganem and Ferryville.[17] In 1920, *Shivat Zion*,
or Union Sioniste Algérienne in Algiers, had 270 members. According
to L. Smadja, its leader, it was not particularly active.[18] He wrote:
". . . The wealthy and influential Jews of Algiers are totally dissociated from Zionism . . . Our group is composed of the poor, of
laborers and employees from the backward classes. We hope later to
succeed in attracting the wealthy and honorable as well . . . , those
same elements who contend that since they are first and foremost
French they do not have to take an interest in Zionism. They are all
selfish, stingy and cowards."[19]

As a result, most of the efforts of the emissaries who later came
to Algeria concentrated on eliminating the psychological and ideological barriers between the consistory leadership and Zionism. While
such efforts were doomed to failure, Leo Zussman did succeed in 1923
in enlisting the support of the consistory leaders in Constantine for the
establishment of a local branch of *Keren Hayesod*.

In Tunisia sound foundations were laid between 1917 and 1922.
By 1920 the twelve existing Zionist associations joined to become the
Tunisian Federation. The new organism was officially recognized by
the authorities—a rare achievement which enabled the movement to
enjoy freedom of action and freedom of expression (exemplified in its
two journals, *La Voix Juive* and *Le Réveil Juif*). Unlike in Morocco,
the Jewish elite in Tunisia was not hostile to Zionist activity. For exam-

15. See, for example, CZA Z4/2669: 24.9.1920 as well as the letters by the Hadida brothers in Casablanca Z4/2149: 21.1.1923.
16. CZA Z4/2149 (1924).
17. CZA Z4/2331 (1920).
18. CZA Z4/575: 31.8.1919.
19. Fédération Sioniste de France, *op. cit.*, p. 6.

ple, when the Zionist Federation made a public announcement in 1922 to launch the first *Keren Hayesod* fund-raising campaign, it was endorsed by all the community leaders, including the Chief Rabbi, Moshe Sitruk, and the president of the community committee at the time, A. Bessis.[20]

In the mid-1920s Zionist activity was on the decline throughout North Africa as a result of the increasing westernization, or, more accurately, "Frenchification" of many Jews. Moreover, the traditionalist elements from whom the movement had until then drawn most of its members, gradually left Zionist circles.

Problems Confronting Zionism

One of the many expressions of the modernization process among the Jews of Tunisia and Morocco, especially among the Alliance students, was the struggle to obtain French citizenship. In Tunisia, from 1923 on, this struggle was marked with partial success when Jews could obtain citizenship on a selective basis. That was not the case in Morocco, where the problem of attaining citizenship remained the focus of inter-communal quarrels and of deliberations between the community and the authorities. Restrictions in education and employment caused hundreds of young Jews to go to France to complete their education and sometimes also to acquire the much desired French citizenship, more readily granted in the mother country than in the protectorate. All this led to both a quantitative and qualitative decrease in the number of educated young people who might have been drawn into Zionist activity. They were, in any case, being attracted to other ideologies, such as socialism and communism.

The authorities' hostile attitude in both Morocco and Tunisia must also be noted. While the French were more tolerant in Tunisia than they were in Morocco, in principle, they opposed all political activity on the part of subjects in the two countries.[21] They stated explicitly: "Our policy toward the Jews in North Africa must be

20. See *La Voix Juive*, 10.7.1922, and the report by Dr. Buchmil to the administrative committee of Keren Hayesod: CZA Z4/2486: 16.2.1923.
21. On France's attitude towards Zionism in North Africa, see H. Gaillard, "Le Sionisme et la question juive en Afrique du Nord," *Renseignements Coloniaux*, Jan.-Feb. 1918, pp. 3-7. The hostile attitude of the French authorities is also evident in a report prepared by a French official in the Protectorate administration in Rabat on Zionist activity in Morocco. With all its distortions and errors, this is an important document. See Etienne Coidan, *Le Sionisme au Maroc*, Rabat, 1948.

related to our policy towards the Moslems. We must oppose Jewish nationalism to the same extent that we oppose pan-Islamism and pan-Arabism . . . [With regard to the Jews], we can achieve our aim in cooperation with the Alliance Israélite Universelle." In addition to being concerned over the hostile Arab reaction to Zionism, the French tended to see the Zionist Movement and its central institutions as pro-British.[22]

As early as 1919, the French opposed the establishment of a Zionist group in Casablanca on the grounds that "it is not necessary to establish contact with foreign elements in order to improve the situation of the Moroccan Jewish community." Four years later, they banned all Zionist activity in the Fez region, and in 1924 banned distribution in Morocco of the newspaper Ha-Olam. All fund raising for Eretz Israel was stopped; only the sale of the shekel was permitted, but even that activity was transferred from the community to the French consulate in Jerusalem.[23]

Several additional factors must be considered:

1. North African Zionism was a "non-realization Zionism." It lacked the dimension of aliyah, even though North African Jews were traditionally attached to Eretz Israel. Moreover, the inability of the central Zionist institutions to meet requests for immigration certificates, both for the traditionalists and the front-line activists, caused great disappointment, and Zionist activity was adversely affected.[24]

2. Since Zionism engaged more in fund raising than in education, it was naturally very much influenced by economic fluctuations. As a result of the economic crisis in the Maghreb countries in the early 1920s, shekel sales decreased.

3. North African Zionism in the mid-1920s also suffered from a dearth of distinguished leadership and from poor organization.

4. Suitable emissaries were not always sent to North Africa. Dr. Asher Perl, one of the principal leaders of the movement in northern Morocco, described the qualities required of an emissary to North Africa as follows: He should be "a scholar, a speaker of our language (Sephardic pronunciation), able to speak fluent Arabic and French (or Spanish) clearly, a person whom God has graced with a fine tongue to teach our brethren that God will not abandon us forever, that He will

22. CZA Z4/2486: 11.1.1924.
23. On all these developments see Z4/2011 (1924). See also S5/3496: 10.3.1938.
24. See CZA Z4/3262: 16.6.1927; 9.1.1928; 27.1.1928; 8.2.1929; also Z4/10310: 26.7.1936.

restore us and have mercy on us; a man of the Torah who knows not only how to address an audience but also to read in synagogue and to dispute with the rabbis and sages . . ."[25]

The central institutions were aware of the difficult situation, but they concentrated their efforts in one country, Morocco, to which, in 1924, they sent Jonathan Thurtz. To him may be attributed the first achievements of the movement in Morocco.

The first problem confronting Thurtz was to legalize Zionist activity in Morocco. Although he was not successful in his efforts to obtain for the movement a status similar to that of the Tunisian Federation, he did succeed in persuading the French government to adopt a more tolerant attitude towards Zionist activity in Morocco. In this he was supported by distinguished figures in French public life, such as Léon Blum, J. Godard and R. Cassin. The change was effected after the movement in Morocco was declared a branch of the French Zionist Federation.[26]

In 1926 Thurtz founded a periodical, *Avenir Illustré* which gradually became the major organ of Moroccan Jewry. While adopting an extremely cautious policy towards the French regime, the paper brought its readers news from the Jewish world and the Zionist Movement, reported on settlement in Eretz Israel, distributed background articles on the Zionist idea, and published selected excerpts from the writings of Zionist leaders. As was to be expected, the great success of *Avenir Illustré* irritated the assimilationists who began to publish an opposition paper, *Union Marocaine,* in 1931. Their attacks helped more than they hindered the dissemination of Zionist ideology among educated youth. Furthermore, the Zionists' organizational ties with the French Federation enabled local activists to receive material published in France; there were also frequent visits of emissaries and lecturers from France. Jewish settlement in Eretz Israel was not presented as a Zionist aim which required the effective participation of every Jew but rather as a symbol with a universal lesson: the Jews in Morocco should keep abreast of what their brethren in Eretz Israel were doing. They themselves were not expected to settle in Eretz Israel; they were only being asked to provide financial support. "It is

25. CZA Z4/3262: 8.1.1928. Confidential report on Zionism in Tunisia. See also Z4/2486: 16.1.1925.
26. Z4/3245: 31.5.1927.

not only American gold we want but also Moroccan gold," *Avenir Illustré* wrote candidly in one of its editorials.[27]

Negative French Attitude

Judging by the number of *shekalim* sold, however, or by the results of fund-raising activities, little gold flowed from Morocco to the central funds. The reason for that was not only the depressed economic situation of the community but also the negative attitude of the French authorities to all fund raising not intended for purely charitable purposes.

Although Thurtz fully enlisted his newspaper in the service of Zionism, he also managed to establish a central organization. In most of the large cities, branches were established whose activities were devoted principally to the Jewish National Fund. Only in Casablanca did the movement extend its activities beyond fund raising, such as teaching the Hebrew language and organizing youth activities.

In Tunisia this period was characterized by intellectual ferment and stormy debate among the various Zionist groups, when the organizational foundation established immediately after World War I was dissolved. To improve the situation, several emissaries and teachers were sent from Eretz Israel to the large Tunisian cities.

The Triumph of Revisionism

In the elections held June 19, 1927, an astonishing development took place, which influenced the character of Zionism in Tunisia until the 1950s: the Revisionist list received an absolute majority in this election and in all subsequent elections until the establishment of the State of Israel.

The Revisionist movement began in Tunisia as a result of a series of articles written by Vladimir Jabotinsky for *Le Réveil Juif* in the mid-1920s. Jabotinsky's keen thought, nationalist phraseology, his frequent references to Mediterranean *blood* and Spanish *hidalguia* (aristocracy), and his warm letters to sympathizers, captured the hearts of Tunisia's Zionists who had been more than disappointed by the indifference of the central organizations.[28]

27. *Ibid.*, "French Morocco" (General report) 1928.
28. On Revisionism in Tunisia see CZA Z4/3245: 23.6.1927; Revisionist Propaganda in North Africa: Z4/3262: 31.8.1934; see also Jabotinsky's congratulations to the members of the movement after their victory in the elections, *Le Réveil Juif*, February 9, 1927.

The central institutions, in total disregard of the new developments, continued to recognize the non-Revisionist leaders as the
heads of the Federation, even though they lacked public support and
possessed little or no leadership ability. As a result, the Tunisian federation seemed to be an organization which lacked initiative. But it
would be a mistake to evaluate all Zionist activity in Tunisia in this
way: exciting work took place outside the formal framework, among
the youth and the educated whose numbers were steadily increasing
at the time. A *Ha-Shomer Ha-Tza'ir* group was established in 1930 as
part of the local Hebrew Scouts Association. This new group may have
checked the influence of the Revisionist movement and the Betar
organization, but its revolutionary ideas—sometimes distorted by its
rivals—aroused vigorous public opposition. After four years of activity, most adherents left the movement. On the eve of World War II, the
Revisionists, numbering about 3,000, were the strongest Zionist force
in Tunisia.

After World War II

Several factors were responsible for altering North African
Zionism beyond recognition in the post-World War II period:

a) The enormous impact of the Holocaust led to a nationalist
revival among the Jewish intelligentsia and to a substantial change in
the attitude of the institutions to the Jews of the East;

b) the negative impression left by the Vichy regime brought
about a drastic change in Jewish attitude to France. Even the Alliance
Israélite Universelle retreated from the pro-French stance that had
characterized it until the war;

c) the events in Eretz Israel caused a change in relations
between Jews and Moslems in North Africa as well as in other Arab
countries;

d) the struggle for independence was beginning in all of the
North African countries, and the Jews feared that France would withdraw from the region.

As a result of these factors, the Zionist movement had a firmer
foundation. No longer was it occupied only with *shekel* sales and sporadic activity, but with intensive preparation for *aliyah*. The link with
the central institutions was restored in 1943, several weeks after the
Allied landing in Algeria and Morocco and immediately after the German withdrawal from Tunisia.

In Algeria, the entry of the American army did not lead to the rescinding of anti-Jewish legislation enacted during the Vichy period. The Crémieux Decree, revoked in 1940, was not put into effect again despite repeated pleas, until 1943. All the Jewish organizations demanded to have their rights restored. For the first time, the Algerian Zionists successfully established an umbrella organization which dealt in an effective way with information, leadership training and *aliyah*. In Algiers alone, some 400 Jews joined the Zionist Federation immediately after its establishment, and 25 additional associations were created in the outlying cities of Blida, Miliana and Cherchell, as well as in the Oran and Constantine areas. All the members participated in Hebrew lessons and in various cultural activities.[29]

The major obstacle to the expansion of Zionist activity derived precisely from the restoration of the Crémieux Decree in October 1943. French citizens again, the Jews of Algeria discounted everything that befell them during the war, and renewed their loyalty to France. Leading the struggle for the restoration of rights was the Comité Algérien d'Etudes Sociales, made up of the local Jewish intelligentsia. This organization became a vigorous opponent of the Algerian Zionist Federation.

With the outbreak of Israel's War of Independence, several Algerian Jews joined *Mahal* (Foreign Volunteers Corps) and some subsequently settled in the country. At the Zionist Congresses held in the 1950s, the Algerian Zionists were always represented. But Zionist ideology failed to penetrate Algerian Jewish society. When Algeria achieved independence in 1962, there was almost a mass migration of Algerian Jews to France, while an indifferent attitude prevailed towards Zionism.

The link between Jerusalem and the Tunisian Zionist Federation was reestablished in June 1943, about one month after the German retreat. Two years later Tunis became the North African center of the pioneering movement *Tze'irei Zion* branches in Sousse, Gabes, Bijouta, Beja and Jerba.[30] Although its ultimate goal was to found a North African kibbutz in Israel, it created a broad pedagogical and cultural platform in the interim. Most of the members were from middle-class families, steeped in French culture. They had severed all their ties with the Jewish masses who continued to live in the ghetto.

In 1944, the Federation, with an eleven-member committee,

29. See M. Ansky, *Les Juifs d'Algérie*, 1950, pp. 261–281.
30. CZA S5/795: 17.6.1945.

renewed its activity, which now consisted of the Jewish National Fund, *Keren Hayesod*, youth and information. But sharp differences among the various organizations arose, making regular work impossible. The major point of contention was the distribution of *aliyah* certificates. In 1945, for example, the Revisionists demanded that most of the certificates be handed over to Betar members since the majority of Tunisian Zionists were Revisionists. But Betar received only three of the 40 available certificates.[31]

These problems notwithstanding, the judgment of a visitor from Eretz Israel is revealing: "It may be said that whatever is Jewish in Tunis is Zionist, beginning with the Jewish newspapers, *La Voix Juive* and *La Gazette d'Israël*, and culminating with the important aspects of communal activity."[32]

In Morocco, the situation of the Jews remained critical, despite the American presence after 1942. Attacks against the Jews took place until 1945, inspired by Vichy French officials. That year, the local Zionist organization renewed its activity as a regional federation of the French Zionist Organization, although, in fact, it retained a direct and autonomous link with the central institutions. It was headed by the same individuals who had engaged in Zionist activity before the war, except for Thurtz who had emigrated to the United States. The Moroccan Zionists not only aspired to help establish the Jewish State, they also worked toward the material and spiritual rehabilitation of the local Jewish population and the intensification of Hebrew education among the young,[33] often in cooperation with the Alliance Israélite Universelle. Many of the more active Zionists were also involved in the philanthropic institutions which provided aid to European refugees. Most of the movement's work with youth organizations concentrated on various associations of Alliance school alumni, particularly the Karl Netter Club in Casablanca which became in every way a Zionist club. From its ranks the first *aliyah* groups of *Tze'irei Zion* were enlisted.

A New Life in Israel

In post-war Morocco, as in Tunisia, Zionism in all its ideological variants was aimed only at a small number of urban youths who

---

31. *Ibid.*, The Zionist Federation in Tunis.
32. CZA S5/795: 7.2.1946.
33. *Ibid.*, By-Laws of the Moroccan Regional Federation (paragraph 2).

had received a French education. Logically, their number would have increased as the educational network expanded. But after the dramatic declaration of the establishment of the State of Israel, young people began to turn towards Eretz Israel in the thousands. Training groups were established throughout the Maghreb. In addition to *Tze'irei Zion Dror*, which was associated with the *Haganah*, these movements became active—*Ha-Shomer Ha-Tz'air, Habonim, B'nei Akiva* and *Betar*. Although these groups did not always cooperate with one another or with the local Zionist federations, they did work together to prepare North African youth for *aliyah*.

In the first year of the State, less than 8 percent of all the *olim* reaching Israel were of North African origin. By 1952 this had increased to more than 14 percent. Between 1952 and 1956, when the countries of North Africa were engaged in their struggles for independence, this *aliyah* took on mass proportions. Indeed, in 1955, North African *aliyah* to Israel was as much as 87 percent of the total *aliyah*. The vast majority of the *olim* came from Morocco; by the end of the 1960s, two-thirds of the Jews had left Morocco to settle in Israel. Only half of the Jewish emigrants from Tunisia had come to Israel, while the number from Algeria was even less.

True, Zionist activists from North Africa had come to Israel during the 1940s and 1950s. But their number was small, and there is little or no record of how the mass *aliyah* was absorbed. Joining kibbutzim and outlying settlements, they could not assist in the establishment of suitable frameworks for absorption. Moreover, a wide social and cultural gap separated them from the mass of *olim* of the 1950s who had come, in response to emissaries from Israel, from the outlying areas of North Africa—the Atlas Mountains and the southern reaches of Morocco, Tunisia, Algeria, and Libya. These rural Jews had been far removed from the centers of Zionist activity in their former countries. However, Zionist ideas had slowly begun to penetrate the urban periphery, so that patterns of absorption and, to a certain extent, the image of North African *aliyah*, had already been established, not only in the consciousness of the Israeli public but also in that of the thousands of North African immigrants who for various reasons chose to settle elsewhere.

Yemen

Yehuda Nini

If we wish to speak in grand generalizations, we may say that *aliyah* from Yemen never really ceased since the day Jews were expelled from their own Land. The early *olim* from that country generally blended into the larger Jewish population of Eretz Israel. Only when a substantial group came to settle in the 1880s did the Yemenite Jews establish themselves as a distinctive community.

A hasty investigator might conclude that this *aliyah* from a stronghold of Islamic traditionalism was motivated by a desire to escape the yoke of the oppressor. A more detailed examination will show that the question of *aliyah* from Yemen is too complex for a single, unambiguous answer to suffice. "The yoke of the oppressor," in particular, can be no more than a partial cause, since it affected at most the Jews living in San'a, the capital.

The great majority of Jews were scattered over more than 1,200 settlements outside Yemen's capital. This geographic distribution resulted partly from the fact that Jews practiced certain crafts and professions which constituted auxiliary services to the Muslim peasants. Many of the latter had preserved the pre-Islamic tribal laws under which the Jew was considered *jar*, a status superior to that granted to Jews as a protected minority under orthodox Islamic Law. Persecution, expulsion, and occasionally death, threatened only the Jews of San'a, where the ancient tribal laws had lost much of their force.

The dominant motivation for Yemenite *aliyah*, from the 1880s onwards, was religio-messianic. When they learned of Jewish plans to resettle Eretz Israel, Yemenite Jews were impelled, after many centuries, to cast off the humiliations of their condition, feeling that the return to Zion was imminent.

The Surge of the 1880s

It is often thought that Yemenite Jewry was totally cut off from the rest of world Jewry. This was partially true until the British conquest of Aden in 1839. After that, there was an improvement in the situation of the local Jewish community, with certain families achieving economic prominence. Their trading connections brought them into contact with Jews in other lands. By the 1850s they served as a link between Yemenite Jewry and the Board of Deputies of British Jews, and from 1860 they were also in touch with the Alliance Israélite Universelle. One feature of an interesting correspondence between the head of the San'a Jewish community and those two organizations is the hint that many Yemenite Jews would come to Eretz Israel if they were to receive assistance.

In 1875, Yosef Ben-Shelomo Masud met with Israel Dov Frumkin, owner of the newspaper *Havatzelet* in Jerusalem. Frumkin heard what Masud had to say about the situation of the Jews in Yemen and told him about plans for resettling Jews in Eretz Israel. What had been mere possibilities for Frumkin turned into certainties for Masud. On his return to Yemen he brought the good news of the purchase of Eretz Israel by wealthy Jews. The impression produced by this news was subsequently reinforced by reports of other travelers reaching Yemen from Eretz Israel. At the time, the Jews of San'a were living under religious, economic and social pressures applied by the Ottoman authorities. The combination of these pressures, together with rumors of the prospective redemption of Eretz Israel, stimulated the *aliyah* of 1881–1882.

That *aliyah* began in May 1881, reaching its peak by October of the same year. But in November, letters were already being rushed from Jerusalem to delay the immigration movement. Among the *olim* themselves, there were some who advised a temporary halt, while others urged their relatives to come settle in Eretz Israel despite the difficulties. The movement was still going on, with brief interruptions, when the World Zionist Organization was created at the First Zionist Congress in Basle in 1897. While Herzl took an interest in the condition of Yemenite Jewry, both he and other leaders in the Zionist Movement were preoccupied by more complex matters. The massive emigration of Jews from Eastern Europe was presenting the Zionist Movement with such weighty problems that it saw no urgency in the *aliyah* of Yemenite Jewry. Indeed, there was some justification for

this. At a time when East-European Jewry was threatened with
pogroms and even annihilation by murderous anti-Semitism, it clearly
held priority over those who were not in such danger.

The Controversy over "Yemenite Labor"

The Zionist Movement first became interested in *olim* from
Yemen in 1908–1909. Immigrants from Northern Yemen joined the
Jewish settlements in Judea and Sharon, attracting attention by their
endurance in the face of hardship and the shortage of agricultural
work. The fight for Jewish labor led the Jewish workers' organizations
to think that the Yemenite Jews could play a part in the uncompromising struggle between Jewish and Arab labor. This led to the initiative
of Arthur Ruppin, Ya'akov Thon and Rabbi Binyamin (Yehoshua
Radler-Feldman), later joined by Yosef Aharonovitch (after he had
modified his viewpoint), to despatch Shemuel Yavne'eli (Warshavsky)
to Yemen to encourage *aliyah* on the part of potential agricultural
workers.

Yavne'eli set out on his mission in 1911. By then the controversy
over "the Yemenite laborer" was already at its peak. It had been
started by Yosef Aharonovitch, who opposed replacing the Arab
laborer with the Yemenite laborer out of two considerations. The first
was a moral one: as he put it, how could one use *olim* from Yemen as
mere tools in the conquest of Jewish labor? Were they not considered
as human beings just because they did not rise up against social
exploitation?[1]

The second consideration was national. In the labor of Yemenite *olim* he saw an even greater danger than in Arab labor:

> . . . We are creating a competitor even more dangerous than the pre-
> vious one. Against the previous competitor we fought with the devoted-
> ness of the Jewish worker, with the quality of his work, with the profit
> which he brings to the settlement in the present and in virtue of the
> national idea in the future. But against this competitor we have no right
> and no power to fight, for he has the advantages which we listed above,
> and he makes the existence of the young people who come from abroad
> completely impossible . . . Of course, those who support replacing the
> Ashkenazi workers with Yemenites are perhaps right in their own
> terms, but even if this displacement were desirable for us in all respects,
> it cannot be put into effect, because these young people—"the surviving

1. *Pirkei Ha-Po'el Ha-Tza'ir*, vol. 3, Tel Aviv, 1938, p. 225.

remnants"—who are drawn to Eretz Israel do not generally find any
other source of sustenance than work in a settlement, and if we make
the work impossible for them we shall not only have to close the gates to
newcomers, but we shall also have to expel the veterans, who will be
unable to come down from that wage which they have already attained
through so much toil.[2]

Here we see that Jewish nationalism as an ideological and
political issue necessarily affected the order of priorities in *aliyah*. The
tendency then was to think in terms of selecting what that ideology
considered the best available tools for solving the Jewish national
question. As noted, Aharonovitch subsequently altered his position
and supported the mission of Yavne'eli, his fellow-member in
Ha-Po'el Ha-Tza'ir. In the meantime, however, the controversy had
spread to *Po'alei Zion*. At a meeting of the latter's council Rahel Yan-
nait echoed Aharonovitch's original views:

> Surely the chief thing is not merely to exclude the Arabs and replace
> them with Jews, but to reinforce the Jewish workers on the land and
> enable them to exist and develop. The Yemenite does not lift up the
> worker, but brings him down.[3]

This provoked a bitter reaction from Yaakov Zerubavel:

> A few years ago we were all excited by the coming of the Yemenites to
> Eretz Israel. And now, on the contrary, it is claimed that, together with
> the Arab worker, the Yemenites are also excluding the Ashkenazi work-
> ers, and they are being almost subjected to propaganda. The source of
> the error lies in the wish to solve precisely the question of the Jewish
> worker in Russia or somewhere else, and since this element cannot, for
> the time being, penetrate into the agricultural economy, there is from
> our viewpoint no value in penetration by other Jews. Yet in our world
> view the chief thing is to solve the Jewish national question in general,
> and for that world view there is no difference between the Ashkenazi
> and the Sephardi elements. The chief thing is to create here a Jewish
> society existing in its own right, and if the Yemenites can bring that into
> being—that is something good.[4]

The most resolute statement in support of the Yemenites came
from David Ben Gurion. He was aroused by the injustice done to them
in Rishon le-Zion at the founding of a workers' *moshav* Ganei Yehuda

2. *Ha-Poel Ha-Tza'ir*, 1910, no. 4.
3. *Ha-Ahdut*, 1911, nos. 1–2.
4. *Ibid.*

(Nahalat Yehuda). The conditions governing this *moshav* were as follows: 1) every member was allotted seven dunams; 2) all members would receive equal plots of land: 3) of the 350 dunams assigned to the *moshav*, 60 dunams were set aside as a Yemenite *moshav* for 20 settlers. Ben Gurion retorted with biting sarcasm, asking the members of the *moshav* committee:

> Let the members of the committee, who were chosen to work out a plan for the workers' *moshav*, explain these three things to us. 1) What is the meaning of the word "member"? Is this an honorary title reserved only for those aristocrats who have a Russian passport, or can any worker crown himself with this title? 2) For what reason must a special *moshav* area be divided off for those of Yemenite origin? 3) Why does a "member" need seven dunams when three dunams are sufficient for "Yemenites"?[5]

Shortly afterwards, Ben Gurion also advanced a positive argument, from both the national and the political standpoints, in defense of Yemenite *aliyah* and its penetration into the settlements. From the national aspect, this penetration was "a phenomenon of the first importance in the life of the *Yishuv*, because here is the key to a radical solution of the question of Jewish labor." Politically, this *aliyah* was important because "through the incoming of the Yemenite workers, our political position is reinforced, too; through them we enrich our settlements with Ottoman subjects."[6]

The efforts of Ben Gurion and others eventually brought about a change in the official attitude of *Po'alei Zion*. The party's ninth congress, which met in 1913, finally extricated it from its confusion over the issues of *aliyah* from Yemen and the attitude *vis-a-vis* Yemenite labor. It adopted the following resolution: "The immigration of Yemenites is not a solution to the question of agricultural laborers, but as a solution to the question of work for the laborers themselves, it is a positive and important phenomenon for the *Yishuv* in Eretz Israel."[7]

It was this soul-searching dispute within the Jewish workers' organizations which—directly or indirectly—brought about the interruption of *aliyah* from Yemen before World War I (and further impeded it during the British Mandate). In March 1912, the Palestine Office of the Zionist Organization felt obliged to request Yavne'eli to

5. Letter in *Ha-Ahdut*, 1912, no. 20.
6. *Ha-Ahdut*, 1912, nos. 25–26.
7. *Ibid.*, 1913, nos. 27–28.

tell all the potential *olim* to postpone their departure. Even though *Po'alei Zion*, at least, eventually took a more positive attitude, its resolution of 1913 came on the eve of World War I, which halted *aliyah* from Yemen for about six years.

The Mandatory Period

The creation of the British Mandate and the Jewish Agency reopened the possibility of *aliyah* from Yemen but also created fresh difficulties. There were two main obstacles for Yemenite Jews (most of whom had but limited financial means) to surmount: the acquisition of a permit distributed by the Jewish Agency and the expenses of the journey to Eretz Israel. The number of permits for workers without capital was often arbitrarily restricted by the Mandatory authorities, while the distribution of permits by the Jewish Agency was influenced by the preference of the Jewish political parties for their own members in Eastern Europe. *Aliyah* policy was being dictated by considerations which, at that time, were pushing the Jews of Yemen to the bottom of the list.

Fearing that the delay in their *aliyah* might be due to doubts about their practical worth to the *Yishuv*, the Jews of Yemen sent letters in which they sought to prove their usefulness. But the scale of priorities dictated by the policy of the Mandatory government and by the political party structure in the *Yishuv* hampered any large-scale *aliyah* from Yemen. By 1929 the appeals from that country began to become truly desperate. Would-be *olim* who had succeeded in slipping across the border into the British colony of Aden were living in complete destitution; out of desperation, they were willing to become indentured to the institutions of the *Yishuv* if only this would bring them to Eretz Israel. Such a letter was written to the Zionist Organization by my late father, David Ben-Shimon Nini, and other members of a group of *olim* under his leadership who were waiting in Aden. It appeals as follows:

> . . . It is your duty to redeem our souls and rescue us from death, as we cannot establish ourselves in these lands, for they are of proven harmfulness . . . And bring us up to your holy camp, to Eretz Israel, may it be rebuilt . . . ; and when we reach your holy camp, even if you take dominion over our bodies we shall not delay . . .[8]

8. Letter apparently written in Autumn 1929.

In an attached letter my father described the sufferings of Yemenite Jewry, especially the "edict concerning orphans" whereby Jewish orphans were seized by the authorities and brought up as Muslims. He also expressed astonishment at the policy of selective *aliyah* applied to Yemenite Jewry, that is, the young people were told they could come but the aged were excluded. Aroused, he wrote:

> . . . Now you astonish us, sirs: how can permits be issued to the young men and not to the old? And it is written in the Torah of Moses "With our young and with our old we will go" . . . Of such an edict we have not heard either in days of old or in later days. He who has two sons, young men, and he is old . . . will you take the sons from the town of Aden and leave the father . . . to knock on doors?

It was hard for Yemenite Jews to acquiesce to the separation of families, hard for them to understand a policy of *aliyah* which—on account of the policy of building up the *Yishuv* in a planned way— gave preference to young people. The patriarchal character of the Yemenite family, together with the commandment to honor one's father and mother, made this policy incomprehensible to them.

The struggle of Yemenite Jews to come to Eretz Israel continued into the 1930s, and the institutions of the *Yishuv* were increasingly faced with a dilemma. On the one hand, there was the policy of preferring *halutzim*, but on the other, the problems of Yemenite Jewry remained and increased in intensity. Thousands of potential *olim* stranded in Aden, who had braved countless dangers when they crossed the border, began by their very existence to constitute a pressure on the representatives of the *aliyah* department of the Jewish Agency. This situation went on until shortly before the creation of the State of Israel. It should be noted, however, that many Yemenites, probably some thousands, managed to come on *aliyah* either by financing their trip themselves or by joining their relatives in Eretz Israel. All told, about a third of Yemenite Jewry—some 16,000—came to Eretz Israel during the Mandatory period.

After World War II, the Jewish Agency and its *aliyah* department began to become more active on behalf of Yemenite Jewry. Frameworks for absorption were set up in Aden for preparing and directing *aliyah*. With the creation of the State of Israel, the gates were opened to Yemenite Jewry and "Operation Magic Carpet" was launched. While even at this stage voices were heard both in favor and against,[9] it is to the credit of the Zionist Movement that those in favor prevailed and the omissions of all the previous decades were at last made good.

9. Yisrael Yeshayahu informed me that it was Ben Gurion who, at a crucial meeting in the summer of 1948, personally overruled all objections and thus once again came to the rescue of the Yemenite Jews.

Iraq

Hayyim J. Cohen

From the beginning of Zionism in Iraq in 1898, the movement was not officially recognized by the authorities (except for one brief period), and its activity had to remain inconspicuous. The Ottoman authorities banned political activity in general, especially that of minority groups. Iraq's isolation from the rest of the world also helped limit the development of the Zionist movement there. Moreover, before World War I, many of the 80,000 Iraqi Jews were scattered in small communities, except for the 50,000 who lived in Baghdad. Even the latter community was too small to organize a full range of Zionist activity, with publicity, education, *aliyah* and the training of pioneer youth.

But the Zionist movement's greatest weakness stemmed from the fact that, before World War I, the Jews of Iraq were legally considered equal citizens before the law. The attitude of the authorities and the local population was also mostly tolerant in practice. Pogroms or severe persecutions of Jews were unknown. These conditions explain why Zionism was the concern of only a few people in Baghdad and Basra. Activity consisted chiefly in reading Zionist literature, conducting talks on Zionist topics, and providing elements of Zionist education.

The Period of British Rule

An important change occurred with the British occupation of Iraq in 1917. During the early years of British rule, the Jews won considerable improvement in their economic and educational position, as well as in their political status. Some entered parliament, a few filled senior posts as judges and ministerial heads of departments, and Ezekiel Sassoon even served as the first finance minister of the new state.

219

Jews were able to maintain religious and educational institutions of their own and to enter state educational institutions without limitation.

Moreover, in March 1921 the "Zionist Society of Mesopotamia" received a permit from the British High Commissioner in Iraq. The permit was revoked a year later, but the head of the Society, Aaron Sasson (known as "The Teacher"), was permitted to continue his work until 1929 on the explicit condition that the Society's activity would have to remain as inconspicuous as possible.

Despite this relative freedom to conduct Zionist activity, a strong Zionist movement did not develop at that time. Partly this was due to the fact that there was still no persecution of Jews, but the main reason was that the leaders of the Jewish community were afraid of irritating the Muslim population and therefore preferred that Zionism be contained. Jews could go on *aliyah* or collect money for Jewish national institutions in Palestine, but not overtly. Accordingly, the heads of the Jewish community in Baghdad requested Aaron Sasson to give up his Zionist activity. He refused, resigned his teaching post and set up a private Hebrew school, in which he propagated Zionism among his young pupils. The apprehensive attitude of the community leaders led to the creation of a group of young activists whose commitment to Zionism was total. On the other hand, after 1926, the rabbis stopped publishing appeals to Iraqi Jews for contributions to the Jewish National Fund and to other Zionist institutions.

The attitude of these institutions, including the World Zionist Organization, was also a cause for the weakness of Zionist activity in Iraq at that time, since they were chiefly interested in raising money. Indeed, the Jews of Iraq gave generously in relation to their numbers. For instance, in 1920–25 they contributed £4,060 to the Jewish Foun-tion Fund (*Keren Hayesod*); this represented a *per capita* contribution twice as high as that of Polish Jewry, and in 1920–22 they contributed £32,187 to the Jewish National Fund, which was *per capita* 90 times as high as the contribution from Poland. Moreover, hundreds of Iraqi Jews bought plots of land in Eretz Israel near Atarot (Qalandia) through their Zionist Society.

Not only were Zionist activists in Iraq not called upon to encourage *aliyah*; they were sometimes requested to do everything possible to restrict it. Only a few immigration certificates were allotted to Iraq each year. Nevertheless, during the Third *Aliyah* (1919–25), 1,000 immigrants arrived from Iraq, and a further 2,500 came during the Fourth *Aliyah* (1924–28). In both cases, these numbers represent about three times the immigrants *per capita* of Polish Jews in the same period.

At that time, almost all the Jews of Iraq studied in Jewish schools, reading the Torah and other Hebrew texts; but Hebrew as a living language was hardly taught. Zionist activists sought to import teachers from abroad. But the Zionist institutions in London and Eretz Israel failed to help; the few teachers who did reach Iraq went of their own initiative. Zionist activity could possibly have been expanded in Iraq if emissaries had been sent from Eretz Israel not only to raise money, but spread Zionist education. Nevertheless, given the political and economic conditions of Iraqi Jewry at the time, it is doubtful whether Zionist activity could have been fundamentally changed.

An Independent Iraq

In 1932 Iraq gained its independence. After the death of King Feisal in 1933, and the accession to the throne of his son Ghazi, the position of the minorities deteriorated. All Zionist activity was banned in 1935, the last of the teachers from Eretz Israel was expelled, and the importation of Zionist and Hebrew literature into Iraq was forbidden. A year earlier, a number of Jews were dismissed from the state administration, although there was no purge of Jewish senior civil servants; it also became more difficult for Jews to obtain state employment. Moreover, the number of Jews admitted to secondary or higher state educational institutions was limited.

It was always possible, by using influential connections, to circumvent such restrictions, which had not been sanctioned by law. But Jews began to feel that their attempts to find a place in independent Iraq would be unsuccessful. This feeling was aggravated when the isolated murderous attacks upon Jews developed into a pogrom in June 1941. Although this was the only pogrom in Iraq, some 180 Jews were killed, including women, children, and old people; a further 800 were injured, and Jewish property valued at least at one million pounds sterling was destroyed. In reaction, many Jews sought to reach Eretz Israel, but only a few received entry certificates or managed to enter illegally.

Some of those who remained behind believed that the pogrom, which had been staged at a time of political crisis in Iraq, was not necessarily a portent of the future. On the other hand, young Jews forced to remain in Iraq, were determined to prepare against the possibility of another slaughter. Several secret organizations came into being: *No'ar Ha-Hatzalah, Ahdut Ve-Kidmah* and *Adat Yehudim Hofshi'im.* These groups did not merely acquire arms and train with them, but also distributed broadsheets calling upon other Jews to do likewise. In 1942, Shaul Avigur and other emissaries set up underground branches of *He-Halutz* and the *Haganah* in Iraq.

This combination of events changed the nature of Zionist activity in Iraq, as is illustrated by the following differences:

1. In the earlier period, such activity was open or only half-concealed, whereas now it went completely underground; anyone discovered to be a member of the movement faced imprisonment, or even a death sentence, after a law banning it was passed in 1948.

2. Earlier Zionist membership consisted mostly of older people; the activists were hardly interested in recruiting young people who had little money to contribute. Now members, and even the activists, consisted mainly of young people.

3. In the earlier period, the chief aim had been to collect money, whereas now there were three aims: Zionist Hebrew education, defense of persons and property, and *aliyah* by any means.

4. Previously, the activists had been local Jews, heads of families, who engaged in organizational activity during their leisure time; now there were *shelihim* from Eretz Israel, experienced in underground activity; they devoted all their time to the cause, and recruited many young, single people who were, for the most part, not yet earning their own living.

The conditions under which the Zionist underground had to work were very difficult. Acquiring and storing arms and training were not easy. Training endangered parents as well as the underground members themselves. Without the silent consent of their elders, who were well aware of what they faced if the young activists were found out, this armed underground clearly could not have operated at all.

The U.N. decision in November 1947 to partition Mandatory Palestine gave rise to street demonstrations in Iraq, with demands that the government send troops to crush the Zionists. Demonstrations and press incitement also took place against the Jews of Iraq who were regarded as traitors. The *Haganah* in Iraq had to prepare for the day when the Jewish State would be proclaimed. On the eve of that day it ordered all its members in Baghdad, Basra and Kirkuk—three cities in

which it had members—to take up positions with their concealed
arms. However, the military regime, proclaimed in Iraq on the very
same day, prevented disturbances.

The threat of death hung over the members of the underground. Between 1948 and 1952 three Jews were executed, one on a
false charge, and the other two for belonging to the underground. Others were killed by torture while in detention, and hundreds more were
tortured and given long prison sentences for supporting the Zionist
cause.

Many members of the *Haganah* also belonged to *He-Halutz*,
which recruited youths from the age of fifteen. Members of *He-Halutz*
learned Hebrew in secret and sought to keep in touch with events in
Israel. Because of the lack of Hebrew textbooks, they were forced to
tear each book into a number of parts, so that beginners could use
pages which the more advanced groups had already studied. But it
was dangerous even to learn Hebrew. A group would meet in a different place each time and its members would arrive for their lesson
individually and at short intervals, so as not to arouse the suspicion of
the authorities.

Emigration to Israel

The principal aim of these underground organizations was
aliyah. This was especially pronounced when anti-Jewish feeling
raged in Iraq. But it was precisely in such difficult periods that new
young recruits swelled their ranks, and then the leaders could not permit *aliyah* of those who already knew Hebrew since they were needed
in Iraq to train new groups. In any case, it was almost impossible—
especially in the late 1940s—for Jews to leave Iraq. At first they
exploited every means, including forged passports, to leave. Later,
they could only slip across the frontier illegally, or travel across the
Syrian desert in the lorries of Arab smugglers. Some young people
even made the journey on foot.

In August 1947, fifty young people came on an American plane
which had been chartered as a so-called commercial flight. They
assembled under cover of darkness near the runway of Baghdad air-
port and, when the plane took off with its doors open, they quickly
climbed in unnoticed. A month later, another group left in the same
way.

Even though some two thousand members and their families

were involved in the underground movement, its existence was not revealed to the Iraqi police. There were virtually no informers and captured members did not reveal important facts even under torture.

Despite all the Zionist underground activity, there was little success in preparing members for pioneering in Eretz Israel or, with one exception, for agricultural work. In the small Jewish community of Kirkuk, members of *He-Halutz* worked on a plot of land. But it was not easy to explain to the Muslim population the reason for Jews engaging in agriculture. Partly because such work aroused suspicion, and partly because of doubts as to the suitability of Jewish youth for agricultural work, the only preparation for Eretz Israel which they received through the Zionist movement was some knowledge of the Hebrew language. This was perhaps one reason why only isolated individuals were absorbed into the kibbutzim. Another reason was that the young people who came to Israel with their parents had to support them, since the older people had difficulty in finding work without being able to speak Hebrew.

The greatest achievement of the Zionist movement in Iraq was to bring the overwhelming majority of local Jews to Israel. It has been said that the Zionist idea existed in every Jewish community, but that it only came to the fore when the non-Jewish population began to oppress Jews. Other Jewish communities came to Zionism only after many pogroms. In Iraq one pogrom was enough.

Iran

Amnon Netzer

Zionism as an organized national political movement aiming to establish a Jewish State in Eretz Israel, began in the Iranian Jewish community around the time of the Balfour Declaration, two decades after the Basle Congress of 1897.[1] According to a report by Yehudah Kopeliovitz (Almog), who came to Iran in 1928 as a *shaliah* (emissary) from Palestine, a Zionist committee had already been set up in the city of Hamadan in 1912. This may have been the result of the numerous conversions among the Jews of that city to the new Bahai religion.[2] But organized Zionism in Iran actually began after 1917. News of the Balfour Declaration was brought by a *shaliah* from Petrograd a week after its proclamation.[3]

An End to Isolation

Contact had been established with Jewish institutions in Europe in the latter half of the nineteenth century, chiefly with the Alliance Israélite Universelle (in 1865) and the Anglo-Jewish Association (in 1873). These organizations were responsible for first steps toward improving the political and legal status of Iranian Jewry.[4] The first Alliance school was established in Teheran in 1898; it was followed by others in the major cities of Iran. As a result, local Jewry became aware of events taking place in the Jewish world at large.

Since Jewish education had been controlled by the Alliance for a long period, Jewish schools in Iran adhered to the pattern of the

1. Little or no research has been done on the Zionist movement in Iran. The present article is based on a paper delivered on May 31, 1977, at the Iran Conference held at the University of Haifa.
2. For Kopeliovitz's report see the Central Zionist Archives in Jerusalem (CZA).
3. CZA Z4/2004.
4. See *Bulletin de l'Alliance Israélite Universelle* (BAIU) and *Anglo-Jewish Association Report* of the period.

central organization in Paris: they emphasized French culture and disregarded Zionist aspirations. When the first Zionist organizations were established, local leaders faced a confrontation with the Alliance. Alliance students were detached not only from their Jewish roots, but from Persian culture as well. Thus they were not on the same standing as educated Persians. These limitations could have prevented them from entering organized Jewish life and government institutions, which were undergoing modernization. Fortunately, the situation was saved by the increasing intervention of Jewish community leaders, parents, and Zionist activists in the program of studies of the Alliance schools in various cities.[5] With regard to Zionism, the most important thing to be noted about this confrontation is that the Jewish community was roused from its passive state.

Another significant event preceding the awakening of Zionism in Iran was the Constitutional Revolution of 1905-6, which granted equal rights to religious minorities in certain spheres of political, legal, social and economic affairs.[6] Little documentation exists relating to the influence of this reform on the Jewish community and the widespread political agitation which accompanied it.[7] It is also difficult to assess how much the Jews of that period regarded themselves as part of the Persian nation, or to what extent they felt a part of the Jewish People. Yet it cannot be doubted that the new rights granted them, including the right to send their own representative to Parliament, were unprecedentedly beneficial.

Promotion of Hebrew

Early in 1918 the Iranian Jewish Youth Cultural Society was established, and its activities included the study of Hebrew, a subject neglected in the Alliance program. A committee of twelve was chosen to deal primarily with the promotion of Hebrew. It set up a "Society for the Promotion of the Hebrew Language," which published several books, among them a *History of the Zionist Movement* in Judeo-

5. A heated argument on the subject can be found in the Jewish local paper, *Ha-Geulah*, Nos. 16-19, Sept. 3-Sept. 22, 1921. As a result of this interest a "Comité Scolaire" was established.
6. This revolution was carried out mainly under the leadership of the bazaar merchants, a group of clergymen and a few intellectuals.
7. Dr. Habib Levi, an active Zionist of the 1920s, speaks of two Jews who took an active part in the Constitutional Revolution. See his *Tarikh-i Yahud-i Iran*, vol. iii, Teheran, pp. 841ff.

Persian by one of the leaders of the community, Aziz ben Jonah
Naïm.[8] In order to gain the recognition and support of the Zionist
organizations in Europe, the heads of the community decided early in
1919 to change the name of the group to *Ha-Histadrut ha-Siyonit be-
Faras* (Zionist Federation in Persia—ZFP). With this, Zionist activity in
Iran officially began. The ZFP then published a weekly newspaper,
Ha-Geulah,[9] linking the Jewish communities throughout the country
and maintaining an ongoing relationship with world Jewry.

The Zionist movement started in Iran with enthusiasm and
included among its activities the sale of *shekalim*. But two severe
blows caused it a major setback. In the election campaign for the Fifth
Parliament (1923–26), Dr. Loqman, the hitherto unchallenged Jewish
representative, was opposed by Shmuel Haïm, a young man from the
city of Kermanshah. The new candidate attracted many followers by
his criticism of both the Jewish establishment and the Iranian regime
which, despite constitutional changes, still discriminated against the
Jews.[10] Strong efforts on the part of the ZFP to stop Haïm's open, and
dangerous, criticism of the government, were of no avail. Another federation was founded under the new representative's leadership, split-
ting Zionists into two warring factions. Iranian Zionists became so
involved in internal affairs that they neglected their contact with the
European movement. The disputes finally led to the tragic events,
which ended in Haïm's death.[11]

The second major setback for the Zionist movement resulted
from the internal policies of Reza Shah. On ascending the throne,[12] the
new ruler was determined to unite the Iranian people and wage a war
of extinction against separatist forces within the state. He prohibited
all organized political or party activity connected with organizations
or groups outside the country. Although his main targets were Communists and the separatist groups in various regions of the country,

8. Naïm died in 1946. Mention should also be made of Solomon ben Cohen Zedek (d.
1964), the most brilliant and active personality in the Iranian Zionist movement; he
published books on Hebrew language and grammar.
9. The paper was published from December 1920 to June 1923 under the editorship of
Aziz Naïm.
10. To promote his cause he established a weekly newspaper *Ha-Haïm* (rival to *Ha-
Geulah*), which appeared from July 1922 to November 1925.
11. Shmuel Haïm was arrested in 1926, accused of conspiracy against the regime and
executed on December 15, 1931. A study of his life is in preparation.
12. He led a successful revolt in February 1921; subsequently he served as Minister of
War and Prime Minister. Finally, in December 1925, he was crowned King of Persia.

Zionist activity was also affected. Zionism became officially prohibited in Iran, although the prohibition was never strictly enforced.

Traditional Background

From their first contact with world Zionism, Iranian Jews approached it from the religious source. They did not see Herzl as the founder of a modern nationalist movement, but as a contemporary prophet, moved by supernatural powers. When the mandate for Palestine was given to Britain, emissaries to Iran were asked if Herbert Samuel was king of the Jews. For centuries the Jews of Persia had no part in determining historic processes and, more recently, they had no opportunity to develop party or political consciousness.

The religious and ideological movements peculiar to Western Jewry were foreign to Iranian Jews. They were not extreme in their religious observance, as were certain Jews in Eastern Europe, nor were they familiar with the Conservative and Reform Movements. With regard to Zionism, they knew little of the schools of Jabotinsky and Ahad Ha-Am. The Zionist aspiration had always been part of their lives in a religious sense. Nevertheless, Zionism, the need of the hour for a European Jewry split by religious differences, secular trends and various ideologies, was no less a watershed for the Jews of Iran. The growth of Zionism stimulated their self-image, which was at a low level indeed. In spite of the rights granted them by Persian legislation of 1906 regarding representation in Parliament, for years they did not dare to send a representative of their own, but asked a Muslim priest to appear on their behalf.[13] Anti-Jewish riots broke out in numerous cities,[14] and in 1925, the Jews were still paying the poll-tax required in order to live in a Muslim land.

The depressed economic condition of the Iranian Jews at that period was extreme. In the 1920s more than 90 percent lived in poverty, a condition prevailing until the mass emigration to Israel in the early 1950s. Even though the strong rule of Reza Shah prevented the organized uprising of religious Muslim groups against the Jews, there is little doubt that the Jewish community was still considered an undesirable foreign body.

13. The first Jewish representative to sit in Parliament was Aziz Simani who soon resigned because of the hostile atmosphere; his place was taken by the Muslim religious leader Abdullah Behbahani.
14. A description of the anti-Jewish riots in Kermanshah at the beginning of 1909 appeared in the report of the British Consul in White Book, Cd., 4733, p. 126.

By the 1930s Iran's commercial, professional, and cultural relations with Germany were extensive, so that with the outbreak of
World War II the danger to Iranian Jewry was evident. The situation
changed with the Allied conquest of Iran in August 1941. In spite of
economic and political difficulties, Zionist activity was revived.

Early Persian *Aliyah*

An immigration committee was established as part of the Zionist federation, which organized *aliyah* activity. Many Persian Jews
who hoped to escape the difficult political and economic situation in
the 1920s, emigrated to the Land of Israel. Among them, however,
were some families who took this step because of their Zionist ideals.
There is written evidence to show that half of the Jewish population of
Iran was ready for *aliyah* despite the opposition to Jewish immigration
in high government circles.[15] But this *aliyah* did not occupy an important place in world Zionist activity. As a result it was unorganized and
unplanned, a fact which may have had a detrimental effect on *aliyah*
in later years. The Persian immigrants who went to Jerusalem or Tel
Aviv suffered from unemployment and spiritual as well as material
want. They also had a language difficulty. The Persian Jewish organizations which already existed in Eretz Israel were not strong enough
to give effective help to their countrymen. If the World Zionist Organization had paid attention to these *olim*, a local leadership might have
been trained and a good part of the *aliyah* directed into viable projects
such as the establishment of kibbutzim and other agricultural settlements. Because of the difficulties they encountered, many *olim*
returned to the familiar ghettos of Teheran, Isfahan, and other cities.
A vivid account of the Iranian *aliyah* of those years appeared in the
New Judaea:

> Among the many groups of immigrants entering Palestine are also Per-
> sian Jews. Few other immigrants suffer so much for the sake of reaching
> Palestine or obtaining their right to the Holy Land at a price as high as
> theirs. It is already fifty years since they started coming to Palestine
> from distant Iran. Losing all their posessions, often their health, on the
> way, they arrive destitute in the land of their desire. They know neither
> Arabic nor European languages, and little Hebrew; and after having
> suffered the persecution of the fanatical Shi'ite Moslems they come to a

15. See *The New Judaea*, March 12, 1926, p. 642.

country which is utterly strange to them. Iranian Jews seem to be the stepchildren of Palestine's new Yishuv.[16]

The report goes on to praise their Zionist idealism as well as their success in agriculture and industrial work, areas hitherto unknown to them. Nevertheless, by the time the State of Israel was established, 30,000 Iranian Jews were already living there.[17] It was presumed that this important nucleus would be able to help those of its countrymen who emigrated to Israel soon after 1948. But the early settlers were not in a position to do so.

When Reza Shah was exiled by the Allies in 1941, he was succeeded by his young son, Mohammad Reza. Under cover of the Allied occupation, more than 20 political parties and about 70 daily and weekly Iranian newspapers appeared. The Jews also began to take part in the political life of the state. Several Jewish newspapers appeared as well as notices announcing Zionist conferences and other functions.[18] Moreover, with the Allied occupation, Jewish soldiers and officers from the United States, Great Britain, and Russia who came to Iran, strengthened and encouraged local Jewry. Many Jewish refugees from Russia and Poland were brought to Teheran and required immediate care. A branch of the Jewish Agency office there, with the cooperation of the Joint Distribution Committee and local Jewry, began energetic rescue activity among children who had been orphaned by the war, as well as the elderly.[19] *Shelihim* and rescue workers from Palestine also reorganized Jewish communal institutions. The activity of the Jewish Agency was made possible because of the Shah's sympathetic attitude. Realizing that they would not always be able to rely on the conquering forces, the Jews were careful to cultivate their relations with the royal court and government circles. Their political activity had already provoked strong antagonism in rightist and religious newspapers, which accused them of being an opportunist foreign body within the state. It was urged that they be eliminated. With the withdrawal of the occupation forces in 1946, anti-Jewish riots erupted in several cities, the most serious in Mashhad. But the Shah and the government remained sympathetic to the Jews.

16. *Ibid.*, June 11, 1926, p. 754.
17. This number takes into account both natural growth and illegal immigration. See also *Hed ha-Mizrah*, Jerusalem, October 20, 1941, p. 10. A rather different statistic is given by Moshe Sicron in *Ha-Aliyah le-Yisrael*, Jerusalem 1957, pp. 6–8.
18. See, for example, the weekly, *Yisrael*, no. 11 Teheran, June 7, 1946.
19. This valiant operation is described by Moshe Yishay, *Tzir be-lo Toar*, Tel Aviv, 1950. Mr. Yishay was the Jewish Agency representative.

Having succeeded in establishing friendly contact with the Iranian administration, emissaries from Israel were able to rescue persecuted Iraqi Jews. Thousands of Iraqi Jews were provided with Iranian documents and flown from Persia to Israel.

In spite of the good relations which then existed between Iranian authorities and the Jewish minority, and the positive relations between Iran and Israel, Zionist activity continued to be officially prohibited. Iran's Muslim population is larger than that of any other country in the Arab world. In spite of their cultural and political reservations regarding the Arabs, many Iranians felt a religious identification with the rest of the Muslim world in regard to the Arab-Israel conflict. The Jews of Persia were aware of this, taking care not to engage openly in Zionist activity.

Identification with Israel

Although reaction of the Persian Jews to events in Israel was not as immediate as in Western countries, war, or incidents such as occurred in Entebbe, brought an enthusiastic response, which, however, was not translated into action. The political weight of the 80,000 Iranian Jews (before 1978) among a population of 35,000,000 was, at best, marginal, especially as the Jews, like other religious minorities (Armenians and Zoroastrians), did not take part in parliamentary elections.

Until recently the Jews of Persia enjoyed affluence and economic freedom, yet always moved in an atmosphere of fear and insecurity. They feared danger to Israel, but even more immediate was their uncertainty regarding the stability of the Persian regime. Young Jewish intellectuals did not relate to Israel in a religious framework. Many of them, organized in groups, wished to see Israel as a model country.[20] News of defeat or failure would shake them to the core. In their eyes, the State of Israel must satisfy all the moral aspirations for which the People of Israel has struggled.

Among the young people, an undercurrent of acculturation, if not total assimilation, was felt, especially in Teheran, where three-quarters of the Jewish population were concentrated. Economic prosperity, professional and educational opportunities, as well as improved living conditions, led to better relations with Muslims.

---

20. The Jewish Student Organization in Iran was the only student organization allowed in the country.

Many were cut off from their Jewish roots by the modernized social and educational structures weakening the bonds of family and group life. Their Judeo-Persian culture was neglected since the beginning of the century. Yet their acculturation was held in check by the image of Israel, by the opposition of the older generation, and perhaps even more, by the fact that they were not completely accepted in Muslim society.

Postscript

Since January 1978, Iran has undergone socio-political upheavals, as religious groups asserted themselves against the Shah's regime and system of reform.[21] In January 1979, the Shah was forced to leave Iran, and two weeks later, the Ayatollah Khomeini rose to power. Since then, Iran has adopted a strongly anti-Israel line, Zionism being attacked almost daily on the radio and in the press as "the only dangerous enemy of Islam, Iran, and all the deprived nations of the world."

The new regime, called the "Islamic Republic of Iran," began large-scale arrests of the "enemies of God and the most corrupted on the earth," many of whom were shot after quick "trials" in "revolutionary courts." On May 9, Habib Elghanayan, formerly the president of the Jewish community, was put to death, charged, among other things, with being a Zionist and supporting Israel.

The future of the "Islamic Republic of Iran" is unclear, as is the fate of the Jewish community there. Whatever the shape of the future regime, the Jews are divided in their views as to the place they will occupy in Iranian society. Those who feared to remain in a country governed by Islamic law found ways of emigrating. By the end of 1979, about 25,000 Jews had left Iran: some 15,000 emigrated to the United States and Europe; some 10,000 came to Israel, most of them as "temporary" *olim*.

21. See Amnon Netzer, "Problems of Cultural, Social and Political Integration of Iranian Jews," *Gesher*, 1–2 (96–97), Spring–Summer 1979, pp. 69–83 (in Hebrew).

III

Zionism and the State of Israel

Elements of Zionist Ideology and Practice

Eliezer Schweid

Ideology is a structure of principles, an assessment of a situation and an analysis of the ingredients of that situation, as well as a proposal for a solution combined with suggestions as to ways and means of implementing that solution. As such, ideology is an integral part of any national or social movement bent upon action.

Today there is opposition to laying down hard and fast ideologies; instead, the tendency is toward "pragmatism." This opposition, which undermines the Zionist Movement's ability to act and to educate, stems from two factors. The first is the blatant moral and practical failure of a cluster of ideologies characteristic of certain socio-political movements which prevailed from the end of the nineteenth century to the middle of the present century. This group of ideologies based itself on the historical-deterministic *Anschauung* and by its very nature crystallized into dogmatic, fanatical, and dominance-seeking patterns. The second factor is the characteristic inclination of an affluent society to avoid long-range unequivocal commitments.

The critique of ideologies arising from the first factor is completely justified. But it does not apply to all ideologies. It may be said that the pragmatic, anti-ideological approach is itself an ideology the validity of which is worthy of examination on its own merits. In any case, there are ideologies that are not based on historical determinism and are not dogmatic and fanatical. Zionist ideology is an example of this. It based itself on a determination of principles in the area of Jewish national life, on an analysis of the tragic situation of the Jewish People in modern times, and on proposals for action—and ways and means of implementing that action—to rescue the Jewish People from tangible processes of oppression, disintegration, and paralysis of its creative force. The second factor is a focus of danger which must be fought by educational means. Otherwise it is apt to debilitate the Zionist Movement in mid-fulfilment.

My premise is that the Zionist Movement is far from having achieved its objective. It must mobilize the Jewish People's forces for the upbuilding of its homeland in Eretz Israel—a task which cannot be accomplished without an ideology that defines its objective in detail on the basis of principles and an assessment of the situation, and points to the ways and means for its attainment.

The Elements of Classical Zionist Ideology

Zionist ideology accepted a number of assumptions anchored in the sources and the living tradition of the Jewish People. From these sources and tradition it accepted that the Jews are a nation whose lack of full national life is a temporary product of *galut*; the categorical rejection of *galut* life; the aspiration for full national redemption; and the link to Eretz Israel as the Jewish People's homeland and to Hebrew as its national tongue. At the same time, the Zionist Movement is an unmistakably modern movement—a movement that crystallized in the Jewish People's social, cultural, and political reality in Western civilization since the dawn of the modern era, and whose ideology clearly reflects this.

Zionism as a modern political movement is based on an analysis of the transformation in the Jewish People's situation after the onset of the modern era. With the crystallization of the centralistic national state and the rise of secularism, a dual problem arose: on the one hand, "the problem of the Jews"; on the other hand, "the problem of Judaism."

The "problem of the Jews" derives from the fact that the sociopolitical framework in Europe was unable to provide a place within it for the Jews as a distinct group. Of course, it might have been able to accept the Jews as a separate religious denomination. But this would have meant that the Jews were to conceive and live their religion in terms and modes paralleling Christianity. This, in turn, would have meant that Judaism was to forsake its unique character as an all-embracing national way of life.

The Jews might also have been accepted as a national minority. The trouble was, however, that nowhere were the Jews concentrated in a particular region where they were a majority and could exercise the linguistic-educational and socio-cultural autonomy of a recognized national minority. Thus, the acceptance of the principle that the Jews should be granted equal civil rights was accompanied by the

unequivocal demand that as a national group Jews should assimilate
into the majority in each of the European states in which they were
living. Jews who did not wish to give up their distinctive national or
religious identity could not accept this. Therefore, they had the alternative of forgoing Emancipation and immuring themselves within the
thick walls of Orthodoxy, or of seeking Emancipation outside the
existing political frameworks, in a separate national framework of
their own.

Yet even those who accepted the demand to assimilate ran up
very quickly against the stiff opposition of the majority society; and
anti-Semitism, with its full variety of overt and covert manifestations,
confronted them with the alternative: to try and overcome the opposition of the majority environment by identifying with the forces of
progress (liberal-democratic or socialist), or to create an independent
framework.

Zionism, then, was created by those who refused either to
assimilate or to immure themselves in Orthodoxy, on the one hand,
and on the other hand, by those who encountered anti-Semitism and
did not believe that the forces of progress would solve the problem of
the Jews at all, or in good time. Zionism arose out of an assessment that
the problem created by the separateness and distinctiveness of the
Jews from the socio-cultural-political order that had taken shape in
Europe could not be solved within that order, and that if it was not
solved in a separate political framework the Jews would be the victims
of increasing oppression, discrimination, and violent persecution.

In addition, there was "the problem of Judaism," whose focus
was the confrontation with secularist European civilization. This civilization posed to the Jewish People the challenge of free scope for
creation in every sphere of life. This was not *ab initio* inimical to
Judaism as a faith and as a way of life. However, it offered an attractive choice that was very difficult to take without forsaking that which
is unique in Judaism—especially in view of the fact that in the *galut*,
Jewish creativity had become concentrated in the distinctly religious
sphere, while other areas of creativity were neglected.

Here, too, collective Jewry faced mutually contradictory
choices. There was the possibility of opting for rigid seclusion in the
religious way of life as it had crystallized over the ages. To the Zionists
this choice implied total spiritual petrification. There was also the
option of spiritual-cultural assimilation. To the Zionists this meant
total surrender of the individuality that was so precious to them.

Zionism rejected both of these choices and decided to accept the challenge of secularist civilization while at the same time seeking to preserve the individuality and continuity of Jewish civilization. It concluded, however, that all this was not possible as long as Jews existed as dependents within alien societies and cultures. *Galut* could not provide the Jewish People with an adequate basis for original creativity. From this came the "negation of *golah*" so intrinsic to Zionism—not merely because of the material poverty, oppression, persecution, and discrimination that the Jews were suffering in Exile, but also because of the spiritual, intellectual, and creative suffocation. The Jewish People had to return to its homeland in order to guarantee a basis for new and total cultural creativity.

The Zionist Movement contained various streams with various emphases in the quest for a solution to "the problem of the Jews" or "the problem of Judaism." But these two factors merged in the Zionist Movement as a whole, and they are what defines it as a national renascence movement, renascence meaning return to the starting point, to the basis of the life of all "normal" nations, to the homeland (Eretz Israel), to the national tongue (Hebrew), to the primary sources (history, the Bible), and out of them to build a social, economic, and cultural basis for a healthy national life.

In sum, Zionist ideology assumed that the Jews are a nation with a distinctive culture of its own; that in the *galut*, especially in the modern era, the Jewish nation was unable to cope with the problems of its existence on its own responsibility and with any chance of succeeding, for in *galut* there was no escaping oppression and discrimination, on the one hand, and assimilation or paralysis of the independent creative forces, on the other. The Jewish People was entitled to live in its national homeland, like any other nation, and there was no solution for its whole constellation of problems except its return to Eretz Israel, where it could fully revive its national life—politically, economically, socially, linguistically, and culturally.

The Uniqueness of Zionism as a National Movement

Here it is in place to emphasize the difference between Zionism and other national movements in both the nineteenth and the twentieth centuries. European nationalist thought certainly had a strong influence on Zionism. Yet Zionism did not arise as a direct result of this influence, but only after it became clear that it was the political crystallization of European nationalism that had created, and even sharply intensified, the "problem of the Jews."

Zionism faced a one-time task. It had to bring a scattered people home; revive its national language as a vernacular and as a language of total creativity; lay societal and economic foundations, at the same time transform the Jewish collectivity's occupational patterns; crystallize social and daily-life forms; and create political frameworks. In order to do all this, Zionism could not remain merely "Zionism." It needed the direction given by an all-embracing social and cultural *Weltanschauung*. This is the source of Zionism's diversification. Notwithstanding agreement on the above-mentioned principle, there was always fierce debate on the principles that would guide implementation. To this day there is no conclusive answer as to what the character of the future Jewish national culture will be. This is one of the gravest issues confronting Zionism today.

The Significance of the Establishment of the State of Israel

The transformation that took place in Jewish history with the establishment of the State of Israel is anchored in a number of structural changes—some gradual, some sudden and unexpected—that preceded this event and became part of its background. I refer mainly to the completion of the process of Emancipation in some European countries and in America, and to the Holocaust.

People who speak of the Holocaust as a decisive factor in the establishment of Israel, with respect both to the readiness of the powers to support its establishment and to the motivation of the Jews themselves, tend to overlook the equal importance of the completion of the Emancipation process—in Europe as an aspect of the background to the Holocaust; in America as an aspect of the Jewish People's manifestation of its capacity to shoulder the heavy burden of establishing the State and then sustaining it.

A reexamination of Zionist ideology necessitates consideration of the sweeping change that has taken place in the situation of the Jewish People. This examination makes it possible to see the recognition of the Jewish People's right to an independent state in its Homeland as a part of the general process of recognition of the Jews' right to complete emancipation. This leads to an understanding of the State of

Israel's problems against the background of the recognition of its right to exist—or despite that recognition—as the essence of the problematics of Jewish existence in a post-Emancipation situation.

This means that with the establishment of the State of Israel, the Jewish People has, politically speaking, a "national home." It can now cope with its problems on the basis of solid group organization, and in this manner can assume—like other nations—responsibility for its fate. With the establishment of the State there is also crystallization of the change that has taken place in the character of the *golah*. A majority of the Jewish People now lives in countries which grant full and equal civil rights to the Jews; even the Soviet Union, which does not recognize the right of the Jews to be Jews, recognizes their equal rights as citizens. Most of the characteristics of *golah*, as portrayed in classical Zionist ideology no longer exist. Economically, socially, politically, and culturally speaking, even with respect to mood and pride, the Jews have undergone a total transformation. This transformation is the background against which the State of Israel came into being and which it has continued to consolidate.

At the same time, it has become clear that Jewish survival, even in this post-Emancipation reality, is not exempt from extremely grave dangers, from the standpoint of both the threat of total physical annihilation and the threat of cultural-spiritual disintegration.

Is Zionism the answer to these questions? In order to answer this, we have to examine two important issues. First: whether and to what extent the establishment of the State of Israel is the ultimate, quintessential expression of the Zionist idea. Second: whether and to what extent *golah* is still *golah* as defined by classical Zionism.

Was the Establishment of the State of Israel the Fulfilment of the Zionist Idea?

Upon the establishment of the State of Israel, there was a widespread feeling among the Jewish People that the Zionist Movement had attained all its objectives. To be sure, Israel still had to be built up and strengthened, but this was the task of the State and it would be accomplished through the links the State would forge with all sectors of the Jewish People. But the Zionist undertaking, as such, had been consummated.

This idea was never "officially" accepted as a crystallized ideology. However, it became one of the foundations of the policy that shaped social action in the State of Israel and the relations between the State and the Jewish People. Within Israel this expressed itself in the ideology of *mamlakhtiut*, (sovereignty), a centralistic policy which transferred all responsibility for the upbuilding of the Land and social, educational, and cultural development from voluntary public movements to state agencies. Practical expression was thus given to the assumption that the State, represented by its agencies, was the fulfilment of the Zionist idea. With respect to Diaspora Jewry, this practical expression came in the form of the State taking over from the Zionist Movement the matter of Israel-Diaspora relations. Here the premise was that these are relations between Jewish centers that exist side by side and assist each other but do not interfere in one another's "internal affairs," and the emphasis was on inter-agency encounter—that is, the encounter between Diaspora Jewry's financial establishment and the State of Israel's governmental establishment. Again, this was a pattern of relations that replaced the concept of a Jewish People engaged in the upbuilding of its homeland with a concept of the Jewish People leaning on and helping its political center that was already built up.

This development expressed a "natural interest" of both Israel's state leadership and Diaspora Jewry's institutional leadership. It reflected the usual dynamics of establishments striving for power and sovereignty. However, it did not properly express the interest of the Jewish People, and did not reflect what the situation of the Jewish People both in Israel and in the Diaspora called for.

As to the situation in Israel, it is clear that the State is at a stage of upbuilding and consolidation which is far from having completed the Jewish People's social, cultural, and political renascence as conceived by classical Zionism, or even as required in order to cope with the problems facing the Jews today. Consequently, Israel falls short as a state in its ability to fulfil, *vis-à-vis* the Jewish People, the tasks that states generally are expected to fulfil *vis-à-vis* their nations, in the following respects:

1. Only a relatively small portion of the Jewish People lives in Israel, and the country's population is too small relative to what it requires to withstand the dangers threatening it and successfully fulfil its role as the Jewish Homeland. To do all this, it must grow considerably and become the largest Jewish center, even the center containing the majority of the Jewish People.

2. The over-concentration of Jews in a few population centers

while too many areas remain unpopulated has resulted in imbalances in the relative density of the Jewish and Arab populations in various parts of the country and left vast areas completely devoid of settlement, even within the "green line" (Israel's pre-Six-Day War borders). This situation is fraught with many dangers to the existence of the State.

3. There is inadequate basis for a self-sufficient economic life, one that would enable the Jewish population to sustain itself on a level vital to the survival of a modern state, even from the viewpoint of its requirements in all the occupational sectors essential to the State's economic development and survival. As long as Israel has to depend on outside foreign aid and on Arab labor in essential occupations, Israel as a state is not functioning properly *vis-à-vis* the Jewish People and cannot independently cope with the problems of its survival.

4. Inadequate social infrastructure: here there has even been some retrogression, due to the difficulties involved in the absorption of the mass *aliyah* that came in the years immediately after the establishment of the State and the centralistic tendency that contributed so much to the disintegration of the country's social-communal infrastructure. The State of Israel's capacity to properly fulfil its task *vis-à-vis* the Jewish People is seriously undermined by the very acute intergroup tensions inside the country and by Israeli society's resistance to assuming tasks that are of a social and not a state nature.

5. Inadequate cultural infrastructure: at the center of this problem is the lack of consensus as to the Jewish essence of the State of Israel and how it should be expressed in public life. The problem is manifested in the intensifying conflict between the so-called religious and the so-called secularist elements, a conflict that is threatening to cause a rift. But the core of the country's socio-political problem is really the encroaching spiritual wasteland that verges on "inward" assimilation and the severance of Israeli society's affinity to the demographic and historic totality of the Jewish People.

6. Inadequate infrastructure of international relations: here I refer not only to the Arabs' refusal to accept Israel's existence or even its right to exist, but also to the position of other countries, even friendly ones, which do not regard the State of Israel as a political framework as valid as any other national state. I also have in mind the ambivalent attitude to Israel that is rooted in certain fundamental ideological and religious positions in Western society.

In all these respects the State of Israel is not yet a perfect

achievement of Zionism but rather an important step towards fulfilment, a beginning on the long way ahead.

Is the *Tefutzah* (Dispersion) a *Golah* (Diaspora)?

The Jewish situation differs from country to country. I think
there is no debate over the definition of the Jews in the Arab lands,
where they are persecuted and discriminated against, as people in
exile. Neither is there any debate concerning Soviet Jews, who are not
permitted to express their Jewish distinctiveness, as a *golah* Jewry.

The debate arises when we come to the Western democracies,
especially the United States. There the Jews are not persecuted, are
not discriminated against, are able to live in freedom and dignity,
advance and achieve in the society and culture in which they live, and
even express their Jewishness in the organizational, educational, and
cultural spheres. Are such Jews "in *golah*"?

Those who answer this question in the negative contend that
many characteristics of *golah* as defined in the Zionist concept of "negation of *golah*" no longer obtain among the Jews of the "free world."
The question, however, is whether it is the characteristics of a particular situation in the history of the *golah* that defines *galut*. There is no
doubt that life in the *golah* has been characterized by many negative
features: the threat of physical extermination, oppression, degrada-
tion, discrimination, distortion of the structure of social and cultural
life. All these have been features of *golah* life, but they do not define
golah—just as life in the Homeland is not defined as a life without
negative features and problems. *Golah* means inner restriction which
brings on other restrictions and pressures and which then manifests
itself in the total or relative helplessness to cope with them. But it
exists also in periods of tranquility, though many individuals are not
always sensitive to it.

This leads me to my contention that *golah* does not necessarily
mean the plight of the individual; it means the collective plight of the
nation. The individual shares this plight as a member of his people, to
the extent that he identifies with his people and that the surrounding
society identifies with his people. That is why many individuals may
not be sensitive to the gravity of their people's plight and do not consider themselves, as individuals, in *golah* though their people is a
golah-people.

How, then, shall we define *golah*? It means a people dispersed outside its homeland in groups that are unstable minorities within other nations. It means existence without the territorial, social, and political basis for independent action and for full cultural creativity of its own. Thus, the *golah* situation expressed itself in the limited ability of the Jewish People to react independently—react by mobilizing all the organized institutional resources normally available to a people—to threats to its existence. *Golah* also means assimilation into the surrounding society and culture, resulting in the diminution of the scope of independent creativity and increased participation in the creativity of the host nation.

It should be said here that assimilation has always characterized Jewish existence in the *golah*, though the degree of assimilation has always varied according to the degree of internal Jewish resistance and according to the Jewish People's capacity to maintain, even in *golah*, some degree of independence or separateness.

If this is *galut*, then the Jewish People is in *galut* even in the Western democratic countries. In these countries, too, the Jews are a minority, within an overwhelming majority of other peoples. In these countries, too, the possibility of the Jews functioning as a people responsible for its own fate is extremely limited, and, moreover, the Jews are caught in a momentum of rapid assimilation. The fact that many, perhaps even most, individual Jews are not troubled by *galut* because they are living successfully and comfortably as Americans, Englishmen, Frenchmen, etc., is no proof that there is no *galut* in these lands. On the contrary, this may be testimony that the *galut* situation has advanced so far as to threaten the very existence of the Jewish People in the not-too-distant future. For it seems that most individual Jews are *not* sensitive to the pain of collective Jewry. They do not identify with this pain sufficiently, even if they do not deny its existence altogether.

There is no doubt that the existence of the State of Israel has changed something in the *galut* situation of that part of the Jewish People that is not living in its homeland. Israel has provided the Jewish People with an instrument for common action and a symbol of Jewish unity and national will. Israel has also given the Jews of the Dispersion not only a sense of Jewish pride and independence but also the possibility of expressing themselves as Jews in independent action aimed at advancing the collective well-being of the Jewish People.

On the other hand, neither is there any doubt that the fact that the majority of the Jewish People is not living in its homeland puts *galut* dimensions on the existence of the State of Israel and the Jewish collective living there. So long as the entire Jewish People is not living in its homeland, all sections of the people share equally in the advantages of homeland and the defects of *galut*. As far as Israel and its Jewish population are concerned, this is evident also in the State's weakened position in the international arena—the State in this respect being a focus of the plight of the as-yet-unredeemed Jewish People—and also in the process of "inward-assimilation" in Israel itself.

What this means is that no sector of the Jewish People can extricate itself from the *galut* situation, whether by Emancipation or by Auto-emancipation, independently of the other sectors. So long as the aim of Zionism has not been fulfilled *in toto*, the Jewish People will, in different manners in different countries, be a *golah* people.

The Tasks of Zionism Today

We have seen that in spite of the great transformation that the Jewish People underwent after World War II, the Zionist analysis remains essentially correct. In the new political, social, and cultural reality, the *golah* situation has become more acute. Furthermore, the Jewish People will not be able to cope properly with the threats to its survival, well-being and independent creativity unless it returns to its homeland and fulfils the potential of a people living in its own land not only in its political aspect but also in the social and cultural aspects.

Notwithstanding Israel's achievements and all that it has contributed towards a positive change in the situation of the Jewish People, it is still not the fulfilment of Zionism as a movement aspiring to the revival of the Jewish People on its own soil. It may be added that perceiving a partial achievment as though it were the fulfilment and acting according to this perception endangers the partial achievement, or strips it of all meaning and content.

If the State of Israel and the Jewish People do not do their utmost to consummate the Zionist undertaking, the State of Israel will be faced with the danger of disintegration and assimilation, its influence on Diaspora Jewry will diminish, and the assimilation process in the Diaspora will intensify. This is the subject of the debate between the Zionist and the non-Zionist outlooks within the Jewish People today. A Zionist stance is not defined by a positive attitude to the State of Israel and not even by a willingness to help the State economically and politically, but by the recognition that the Jewish People must invest all its strength and resources in the upbuilding of its homeland as the only solution to the problem of *golah*. A positive attitude and assistance to the State of Israel is not a Zionist attitude if, at the same time, it aims at preserving Jewish life in the *golah* as a life with a value and a future of its own. Even if we prefer this attitude to one of turning one's back on the Jewish People and its fate, we must not blur the issue and we must struggle to turn the Jewish People in the above-defined Zionist direction.

What are Zionism's practical tasks? First and foremost, inten-sifying *aliyah* until the State of Israel becomes the largest center of Jewish population. The stabilization of the Zionist achievement requires that the State of Israel shall have not only a clear and unchal-lengeable Jewish majority in the long range, but also a majority of the Jewish People. To achieve this we need a full-scale revival of settle-ment, which alone can make *aliyah* a truly Zionist *aliyah*. An *aliyah* that is absorbed into existing settlements, especially the overpopulated urban centers, does not contribute as much as *aliyah* can and ought to contribute to the upbuilding of Eretz Israel. *Aliyah* that increases the number of Jewish settlements on the soil of Eretz Israel will continue to be *aliyah* in the full sense—the homecoming of Jews to their Land—long after the people involved have "ascended," and its significance will be not only a quantitative one—i.e., in increasing the country's Jewish population, potential military manpower, and the number of settlements—but also, above all, in its contribution to strengthening the country's socio-economic foundations.

This applies also to Israel's present Jewish population, especial-ly to the younger generation. Zionist *aliyah* can be the task of people born and living in Eretz Israel. A young person who chooses his occu-pation and place of work not only in terms of his talents and personal benefit—material or spiritual—but also in terms of Eretz Israel's upbuilding needs as the Jewish People's Homeland—such a person is an *oleh*, a Jew coming home in fulfilment of his tasks as a member of the Jewish People. And a renewed full-scale settlement movement is one of the most important expressions of the change needed among the Jews of Eretz Israel.

It certainly is not necessary here to spell out the details of the economic task: achieving independence in the sense of a body eco-nomic providing a livelihood to its workers, and of a community of workers prepared to live on a standard that their labor makes possible.

In the context of the Zionist *Anschauung*, however, one ought to stress the value that is at the base of economic independence: labor. The Zionist Movement fought for a change in the attitude of Jews to manual labor in agriculture, industry, and the crafts, and it had notable achievements in this respect. It transpired, however, that these achievements were not sufficient and not stable, so that today the struggle has to be renewed for a positive attitude to manual labor in all areas. Educating the public to regard labor as a primary expression of social responsibility and not merely as a matter of livelihood is a national task of prime importance.

Changing the attitude to labor is a foundation of social health, but social health is itself a task. This task must be seen in the context of Zionist thought, because the State of Israel's social problems are a product of the failure to absorb previous *aliyah*, and they are endangering future absorption of *aliyah*. Moreover, the restoration of the Jewish People as a nation living in its homeland means the creation of a decent social order. And a decent social order means a society that values its individual members and gives them a feeling of home, a sense of belonging, and self-respect. All this predicates the right of every person to work and create, to provide for himself on a standard of basic equality with his fellows, to get help from his fellows when he is in need and help them in their need, and to be assured of his fellows' concern for his general well-being.

Towards this end, a halt must be put to the centralizing process that is stripping society of its responsibility for education, mutual aid, and cultural life, and communal organization must be renewed. At the same time, the process of widening the economic gap must be halted, a more equal and just economic standard must be guaranteed for all, and the processes of democratic action must be strengthened so as to assure maximal public influence on and control of governmental agencies.

The renewal of Jewish national life in the Jewish Homeland means the revival of Jewish culture in all its scope and distinctiveness. To be sure, this should be emphasized: Zionism, based on identification with Judaism as a total national-cultural experience, has no concept of its own concerning Judaism as a *Weltanschauung* and a way of life. As such, Zionism tolerates different, sometimes even mutually contradictory, approaches, as long as they have a basically positive approach to Judaism as a national-cultural experience and aspire to renew Jewish national-cultural creativity.

In this connection, the fulfilment of Zionism means laying the foundations for Jewish education and creativity. In classical Zionist ideology, it became a commonplace assumption that this foundation is a Jewish majority society—a society preserving the continuity of the identity of Jewish individuals with their nation, the affinity to Eretz Israel (not merely as a territorial base for political independence but as a cultural-historical symbol), the speaking of Hebrew, and the affinity to the Jewish primary sources, especially the Bible, as the basis of all Jewish education. There have been many achievements in this respect, but there is a growing feeling that even in the State of Israel there is a rapid process of assimilation, and that a great deal remains to be done with respect to the Jewish essence of Israel's cultural life. There are four main reasons for this that must be dealt with:

1. The secular Zionist's ambivalent attitude to his People's heritage, which he regards mainly as a "religious" one.

2. The need to cope with the political, economic, and military exigencies involved in the realization of Zionism, which led to pragmatic compromises on all the issues involved in the debate on the essence of Judaism.

3. The growing pace of technological development, giving impetus to the desire for material achievement.

4. The belief that distinctive Jewish spiritual creation would be a natural product of the existence of an independent Jewish society living in its own Land and speaking its national tongue.

Zionism, then, expected the problem to solve itself. What happened was that it gradually intensified. The rift between the "religious" and the "secular" not only did not close but even widened. This happened both as a result of the problems involved in maintaining independence and because of the decreasing mutual information and mutual understanding between the two camps: there was an intensification of self-seclusion in the Orthodox camp; the rejection of general cultural values by the "religious"; and a growing spiritual impoverishment among the "secular."

It is no longer possible to postpone intelligent treatment of the problem as a clear Zionist task: the task of laying the foundations of the knowledge and understanding of the Jewish sources, on the one hand, and of the cultural creativity of the "secular" camp, on the other; achieving a consensus on the Jewish nature of public-national life in the State of Israel; and, above all, encouraging every Jewish community to interpret, each in its own way and according to its perceptions, the Jewish meaning of its way of life and to express this interpretation in intellectual, literary, and artistic creativity, and even in life styles. If the renewal of communal life is a central social task, the crystallization in these communities of a Jewish way of life, according to the variety of conceptions existing in the Jewish People, is the central cultural task.

Finally, there is the political task: to overcome the opposition to Zionism that exists in various camps (Christendom; the Socialist camp); to strive for an understanding with the Arab world on the basis of a just solution of the problem of Palestinian nationalism; and, thus, to attain a peace settlement that will enable the State of Israel and the Zionist Movement to devote their full strength and resources to the task of physical reconstruction and cultural renascence.

Zionism and Arab Nationalism

Zionist ideology necessitates facing up realistically to the problems generated by the conflict between the Jewish People and Arab nationalism, and proposing a basis-in-principle for the resolution of the conflict. This problem confronted the Zionist Movement almost at the outset of its practical work, but it went through various stages, being generated by the Jewish People's return from its various dispersions to its homeland and occurring in a time of national awakening that went from the countries of the West to the lands of Asia and Africa.

Zionism's ideological point of departure here was, and still is, the claim of the Jewish People's historical right to return to Eretz Israel and rebuild it as the Jewish national homeland. This claim is based on the following premises:

1. The continuous, unbroken connection of the Jewish People with Eretz Israel: Even in Exile the Jewish People's affinity to Eretz Israel was a basis of national memory, hope, and unity. Furthermore, this affinity was expressed in a continuous representative Jewish presence in Eretz Israel, especially but not only in the "holy cities" (Jerusalem, Hebron, Safed and Tiberias), and in the observance of numerous religious precepts symbolizing this connection.

2. The fact that in none of the lands of Exile was the Jewish People allowed to live as a nation: It remained alien and, for the most part, oppressed and discriminated against, yet deprived of the opportunity to resume its independent national existence in Eretz Israel.

3. The fact that the Jewish People's national-religious nexus

with Eretz Israel was very well known to the nations to which the Jews were subject and which occupied Eretz Israel at different periods. This was known to them from their religions—Christianity and Islam, whose attitudes to Judaism and Jewry were at the root of the fate of the Jews living in their midst, a fate that is not paralleled by that of any other nation. This unique, unprecedented affinity of an exile-people to the Land from which it was in exile existed also in the consciousness of the nations that were responsible for the continuation of the exile situation.

4. The fact that when the Zionist Movement launched its practical work, Eretz Israel was a vacant land, nationally speaking, and open to large-scale settlement without displacing the existing Arab population, so that it was possible to implement the return of the Jewish People to its Land in perfectly legal and moral ways.

There is no doubt, however, that the implementation of the Jewish national right in Eretz Israel limited the possibility of implementing such a right where the country's Arabs were concerned—if they were to come and claim this right. Neither is there any doubt that the implementation of the Jewish national right spurred the country's Arabs to define themselves as a Palestinian Arab nation and to demand national rights.

This is the root of the conflict.

The Zionist Movement contends that it was morally entitled to demand for the Jewish People the least that any nation is entitled to for its existence—a homeland; in this case, a land that is in any case the Jewish People's historical homeland—and towards this end to limit the possibilities of the implementation of any Arab right, which has already been implemented in a number of countries and in a vast territorial expanse. For in this respect, too, and not only in terms of history, the Jewish People's right is greater.

Nonetheless, the Zionist Movement must recognize the national rights of the group calling itself the Palestine Arab Nation the moment this group claims these rights, and must be ready to agree to a solution involving the implementation of some of these rights—to the extent that such a solution does not undermine the State of Israel's own existence.

The basis for a solution, then, is the mutual recognition of national rights, mutual readiness not to insist on the full implementation of these rights, and reaching a territorial or political compromise based on this mutual recognition.

The State of Israel and Diaspora Jewry

A new platform has to be drawn up defining the relations between the State of Israel and the Diaspora. Until the establishment of the State, the Zionist Movement—especially those Zionists who went to Eretz Israel to live and build there—operated on the basis of a radical "negation of *golah*" which anticipated that, once the Jewish State was established, *aliyah* and assimilation would eventually cause the *golah* to disappear.

After the establishment of the State, the Ahad Ha-Amist ideology gained influence, an ideology that spoke of Center and Perimeter. What in fact developed, however, was the concept of coexistence of different centers helping each other. This concept, as I indicated above, was not an essentially Zionist one. The Zionist concept is the one that sees Eretz Israel as the center, though not in the sense of dominant leadership but in the sense of partnership in the national undertaking. The leadership of Eretz Israel Jewry and of the State of Israel has to be a product of this partnership. It must also leave much more scope than it has left in the past for the independently organized initiative of Diaspora Jewry. It must also open itself much more than it has done in the past to the opinions and influence of Diaspora Jewry as to how Eretz Israel is to be rebuilt as the Jewish People's homeland and center.

All this means that the process of upbuilding Eretz Israel and concentrating the majority of the Jewish People there has to be seen as a long-term process whose duration and shape cannot be foreseen. As far as we are able to see today, a considerable Diaspora will continue to exist and the State of Israel will have to continue to rely on it for help and for the constructive elements that will come from there. By the same token, the Diaspora will have to rely on the State of Israel's help and leadership. Therefore, the State of Israel and the Zionist Movement must assume much greater responsibility than heretofore for the survival of the Diaspora in its organizational and socio-cultural frameworks of Jewish identity. They must also invest much more money and manpower than they have heretofore invested in broadening and deepening Jewish education and strengthening the communal frameworks in the Diaspora. All this does not imply "affirmation of *golah*." All it implies is responsibility for the Jewish People and concern for the broad foundations needed for the continuation of the Zionist undertaking. Such activity doubtless generates considerable tension and may even cause the crystallization of the conflict of interest between the needs of Jewish survival in the Diaspora and those of Eretz Israel's upbuilding. This tension must be faced, and an effort made to develop an authoritative Jewish leadership that will responsibly consider programs of action and always come up with the right answers.

The concept of Eretz Israel as the Jewish People's center, in the sense I have mentioned, requires broadening and deepening the links between Diaspora Jewry and Eretz Israel Jewry. This means, first of all, cultivating new leadership groups, besides the political and organizational-financial leaderships. I refer especially to youth leadership and intellectual leadership: teachers, writers, scientists who will deepen the contacts between them. Efforts must be made to reach the masses, too, and create forms and channels of contact within the communal organizational frameworks.

All this necessitates a change of direction in the activity and the organizational structure of the Zionist Movement in both Israel and the Diaspora. It must become once more a people's movement, educating and setting the tone in social and spiritual life.

The Subjects of Zionist Fulfilment

The assumption that Zionism was fulfilled with the establishment of the State found its practical expression in the concentration of all the tasks involved in the upbuilding of Eretz Israel—*aliyah* and absorption, settlement, economic development, social construction, education and culture—in the political establishment.

The realization that Zionism is far from fulfilment must find its practical expression in the transfer of many of these tasks from the political establishment to the Zionist Movement in its capacity as a social-voluntaristic movement. To be sure, there are tasks that only the state can perform—the political and security tasks—and those in whose execution the state can assist: settlement, economic, social, educational. But the latter cannot be executed by the state alone, for they are essentially social tasks. The building of a society and the patterns of social responsibility, education, and cultural creation require the direct action of a social movement—or of a number of movements—both in Israel and in the Diaspora. And these movements must renew their appeal to the initiative of creative individuals, volunteers, for whom the fulfilment of Zionism is the stuff of their lives.

The concentration of these tasks in the State, and the materialism that has become so pervasive in Israel, have spurred the process
whereby the members of Israeli society cast off responsibility for anything that happens. This trend is the root of the crisis Israeli society has
been undergoing, a crisis that paralyzes it precisely when it faces a
grave external threat. People point to *mehdalim* ("bungles") which
they blame on the state leadership, and wait with growing disappointment for the leadership to come up with solutions, without showing
readiness to assume any responsibility themselves.

The nation must be educated to an awareness that "leadership"
and "government" are not one and the same thing, and that every
individual bears responsibility in his or her sphere of activity.

If we are to cope successfully with the dangers confronting us
and consummate the Zionist undertaking, Zionism must be crystallized anew as a movement with defined tasks and objectives, and the
Zionist Movement and the State of Israel must renew their call to
every individual Jew to be a personal, practical example of Zionist
implementation and realization.

Comments

YEHUDA BAUER

All discussion of Zionism in the late seventies of this century must start from the upheaval wrought by the Holocaust in the life of the Jews. After 1945, we face a situation in which, in all diasporas other than that of the United States, Jewish communities show a demographic decline and indeed face decimation, if not extinction. Even in the United States, the demographic survival of the Jewish community is far from being assured.[1] The most optimistic estimates of future developments indicate that the relative strength of the Jewish community in the States will decline. Loss to the Jewish community through intermarriage and the addition of non-Jewish spouses through conversion seem to have become a new reality. The birthrate of Jews is, in any case, too low to ensure group survival. Daniel Elazar sees a process of polarization taking place in American Jewry: Jews marginally concerned with their Jewishness will move away from the community, while religiously and otherwise committed Jews will strengthen their identification. One could well conclude from his analysis, that a much smaller number of "Jewish" Jews might compensate for the drifting away of a very large number of marginal Jews.[2] But it is difficult to explain how such very Jewish Jews could maintain their Jewishness without establishing a new and rather high wall around themselves in order to avoid being attracted to the larger American society. The same perplexing question could be posed—mutatis mutandis—for Soviet Jewry: if present trends continue, Jewish Jews would leave the Soviet Union, whereas others might well hasten their absorption into Soviet society.

1. The results of the National Population Study by Fred Masarik form the basis for various and conflicting estimates. However, most of these tend to be pessimistic. Cf. Elihu Bergman, "U.S. Jewry Dwindling," *Midstream*, October 1977, pp. 9–19.
2. Cf. Daniel Elazar, in *The Yom Kippur War and the Jewish People*, Moshe Davis, ed., New York, 1974, pp. 32–35.

The destruction of East-European Jewry removed from the scene those Jews who, according to Zionist thought, were ultimately to secure an established Jewish State by their immigration to it. The emergent Israeli state found a temporary substitute: the long-forgotten Jewry of Asia and Africa, the majority of whom immigrated to Israel as a result of the Zionist struggle for a Jewish State in the midst of a hostile Arab environment. These now form the majority of Israel's population. But no more Jews are left in the countries they came from.

Pre-State Zionism postulated the unity of the Jewish People and the necessity for recreating its polity in Palestine. It assumed the existence of a Jewish Diaspora that would provide the human material for such a polity. The Holocaust, developments in the U.S.S.R., and trends now apparent among American Jewry make this assumption doubtful. The first problem is, therefore: will there be a Jewish People, and if so, where?

The second problem is the reemergence of anti-Semitism. The Jew-hatred of the late 1970s is directed against Israel, the legitimate expression of the Jewish right to self-determination. One may be critical of Israel without necessarily being anti-Semitic. However, when one denies the right of Israel to be where it is, then one is denying the right of Jews to form a society of their own, and the right of that society to create a polity to its liking. It represents a denial of the Jews' right to national existence, just as in the past their right to a separate religion was denied.

A generation after the Holocaust, contemporary anti-Semitism has returned to the traditional picture of the Jew as devil, a picture rooted in Christian culture. The notorious Czarist forgery, the *Protocols of the Elders of Zion*, which emphasized the supposed Jewish lust for world power and the imaginary existence of a world Jewish government controlling world power, reappears both in its original form and—especially in Argentina—in newly adapted formulations.[3] People are tired of hearing about Jewish suffering. Ignorance about the Holocaust is a preliminary to denying the Holocaust.[4] Ignorance

3. Haim Avni, "Anti-Semitism in Latin America after the Yom Kippur War: A New Departure," in *World Jewry and the State of Israel*, Moshe Davis, ed., New York, 1977, pp. 71–72.
4. A classic example of how to present Hitler and his period without reference to either the Holocaust or the other mass murders committed by the Nazis is Joachim Fest's recent film about Hitler.

and denial of the Holocaust lead to the accusation that the Holocaust is an invention of the Jews, designed to extract reparations from the Germans.[5] The circle is then closed by relating reparations to the financing of world Jewish power.

Zionism was supposed to eliminate, or at least weaken, anti-Semitism by the establishment of a *normal* Jewish polity, and by that polity's capacity to fight for Jewish rights everywhere. This vision has been only partly realized. Indeed, Jews are no longer powerless, and Israel can and does defend Jewish rights. Jews can and do fight back, and that no doubt hampers anti-Semitism to a degree. However, the establishment of Israel has not eliminated anti-Semitism: on the contrary, Israel itself has become the target of an anti-Semitic campaign. Zionism postulated a Jewish People which would establish a political existence of its own in order to stand up to the nations of the world. Has it been successful? Are there alternatives to the Zionist premises in the fight for Jewish survival against Jew-hatred?

In trying to find our bearings in this quickly changing scene, we must start from a pedestrian, but essential differentiation: namely, the difference between Zionism as a concept and Zionism as an organized movement with all the trappings of political parties, congresses, and the like. The Zionist Movement has always been a minority movement within the Jewish People, and most often it was a small minority indeed. Its basic premise, on the other hand, was at times—and in recent decades, at most times—accepted by an overwhelming majority of Jews. The distinction drawn between those who saw (and still see) Israel as a haven for others and those who see themselves involved in the central position of Israel for the Jewish People, may in itself be valid enough. But it is largely an analytical distinction. In practice, most American Jews, for example, are somewhere in between: they certainly believe Israel should be a haven for those who need to go there, but they also believe that it is more than just a haven for others. In fact, most American Jews would, I think, see their support of Israel as a kind of insurance policy—you, or your children, might need it some day. Going beyond even that, most Western Jews do not see (or would like not to see) any contradiction between their two loyalties: to their country of residence and citizenship on the one hand, and to their Jewish peoplehood which encompasses the Jews of Israel

5. This is the tenor of contemporary Nazi literature; cf. Erich Kulka, *The Holocaust is Being Denied*, Tel Aviv, 1977.

together with Jews throughout the world, on the other. I would argue that Jews living within the parameter of such visions are Zionists, though they never join a Zionist group. Similarly, Israeli Jews have in the past poked fun at Zionism, its outmoded verbiage and its aged leadership; few Israelis have bothered about the Zionist congresses. Even the political leaders of Israeli parties have paid little more than lip service to the Zionist Movement, of which they were, so to speak, *ex officio* members. Yet the fact that Israelis represented the unity of the Jewish People in building the State, coupled with the overwhelming sense of post-Holocaust existence, made the average Israeli a Zionist in a very real sense.

Historically speaking, Zionism is a movement conditioned by the development of modern nationalism, of which it is a sub-species, on the one hand; and by very ancient and deep-seated religious-ethnic traditions of the Jewish People, on the other. But its appearance at the end of the nineteenth century may also be interpreted as a Jewish reaction to the near-absolute impotence of the Jews in a situation where power structures became necessary for the physical survival of national groups. One can easily be misled by the surprising success of Zionism. In 1917 the Balfour Declaration came to regard the Jews as a political factor of some importance. In effect, the Balfour Declaration was based on a misunderstanding and on a vast British overestimation of real Jewish influence in America and in Russia. This misunderstanding itself originated in the basically anti-Semitic concept of the *Protocols*, which maintained that the Jews were somehow a very powerful group. The British in 1917 interpreted that concept positively: if the Jews were so powerful, then it was best to be on their side. Very soon after World War I it became clear, however, that Jewish power was a mirage. As the 1930s progressed, Jewish powerlessness was realized by all, except by the Nazis. In this situation, Zionism may be seen as the embodiment of the Jewish desire to escape from a situation where political power was completely lacking. It was, of course, not the only such embodiment. In various ways, opponents of Zionism— Bundists, non-Zionist Orthodox movements, Jewish Communists advocating a state in Birobidjan, American non-Zionists and Territorialists—all tried to formulate an answer to this political problem. The Holocaust, on the one hand, and the Soviet campaign against the Jews between 1948 and 1952, on the other, resolved this question. The establishment of the State was undoubtedly an achievement of Zionism. Looked at in another way, Zionism was the last Jewish fortress that held out against the Holocaust and its aftermath. Looked at in still another way, Israel afforded an escape from powerlessness. The achievement of Zionism was, however, not only the rise of Israel. The emergence of American Jewry as a political force, dating from Abba Hillel Silver's leadership of American Zionism in 1943–44, was another manifestation of the escape from powerlessness. To view Israel as the main achievement of the Zionist Movement is not balanced; it would be more correct to say that in the wake of the Holocaust, which demonstrated the effects of Jewish powerlessness, Zionism revolutionized the whole approach of Jews themselves to the political sphere. The great achievement of Zionism, then, is the politization of the Jewish People, most clearly manifested in the emergence of the Israeli State and the parallel appearance of American Jewry as a political force. The power of American Jewry, while it does exist, is significant only because Jewry finds a ready response to many of its arguments among large parts of the general American population.

In this situation, it is clear that defense of the Jewish People against external attack cannot be effected by means different in principle from those developed by the Zionist Movement. In the present-day political world, relinquishing self-defense clearly leads to disaster. The tools developed over the last forty years by political Zionism, seemingly the best we have, could be used to better advantage, no doubt. While Zionism may, therefore, have failed to fulfil its messianic promise as an end to anti-Semitism which would coincide with the establishment of a Jewish State, it did furnish the only possible tools with which to fight the enemies of the Jewish People.

True, many Israelis do not believe in the continuation and development of the Diaspora; for them Zionism in effect means immigration of the Jewish remnant to Israel. But it is equally true that, for the sake of the existence of Israel as a prosperous entity, a viable American Jewish Diaspora is desirable. Other communities do not have any real prospect of mass survival. If American Jewry is to become heir to East-European Jewry in the sense that it is a large and viable Diaspora community, then Zionism, paradoxically, may have to accept the concept of partnership in a real sense. Historically speaking, this could be based on the idea of *Gegenwartsarbeit*, an old Zionist concept that justified the development of strong Jewish Diaspora institutions by committed Zionists, until the messianic promise might be fulfilled.

Realization that the American Diaspora and its development as a real partner is important for the future of Israel is growing in Israel. There is an obvious contradiction between that realization and the denial of the Diaspora mentioned above. Yet both these largely emotional reactions dwell side by side; both are legitimate Zionist conclusions. One is a messianic or pseudo-messianic attitude, which could easily lead to despair. The other is the only possible realistic attitude for Israeli Jews.

The problem, then, arises as follows: is the demographic and cultural rescue of U.S. Jewry possible, and if so, on what terms? Aside from the vague statement that, as yet, no demographic prediction has ever come true, the following possibilities seem to arise: neutralization of a large proportion of the intermarriage problem by conversions of non-Jewish partners and the education of children within the Jewish fold; recognition of the need for a higher Jewish birthrate; recognition of religious and cultural pluralism within Jewry. Alternatively, one may consider the possibility of a strictly closed, Orthodox Jewish community of lesser demographic strength and political power, with an overwhelming proportion of Jewry drifting away or disappearing in time. It would seem that the second alternative is increasingly preferred by some of the Orthodox elements, both in the U.S. and in Israel. This certainly seems to be the preference of neo-messianic Orthodox circles. An attempt to proceed to an examination of the other possibilities would, it is submitted here, be more in accordance with a Zionist attitude which is concerned with the entire Jewish People, and not only with one of its segments. Pragmatically speaking, it is doubtful whether the drift away of a large part of the non-Orthodox groups would not result in grave and imminent danger for the survival of Israel. Examined against the basic elements of Zionist ideology—recognition of the unity of a Jewish People scattered throughout the world with its political center in Israel—the problem of integrating the different religious and cultural approaches within Judaism is probably the most central conceptual problem the Jewish People now has to face.

It is perhaps doubtful whether there is need for any Zionist ideology other than what has been termed "elements of classical Zionist ideology." What is needed, it seems, is a rethinking of the Jewish position in the present-day world within the parameters of these very same elements.

ISRAEL KOLATT

Zionism has long been engaged in clarifying its ideology, but it runs the danger of becoming caught up in pedantic concepts and of becoming so enamored of its concepts that it loses its link with reality.

Zionism is a product of the era of ideology, though not only in the sense that its aspirations have been defined in accordance with values that are unrelated to empirical reality. Today it is generally agreed that the revolt against ideology which took place in the 1950s was not directed against every view that diverged from pragmatism, which is in itself ideology. Zionism was a product of the age of ideology in the narrower sense. It was not an ordering of reality in accordance with values considered as objective, but challenged as being personal and biased. It was to be an overall solution that claimed absolute validity for itself. Zionism includes a demand for total change and as such always contends with the danger of confusing its aspirations to be an exclusive solution with the reality of which it is only a part.

These aspirations have encompassed many realms: not only a concentration of population—a majority—and the establishment of a state, but also an end to the two-hundred-year-old controversy within Judaism that began with the undermining of the traditional worldview. Zionism believed it could resolve controversies between traditionalists and modernists, between Orthodoxy and Reform. However, the Jewish dialectic continued to operate with the Zionist Movement and within the Yishuv.

The Zionist Movement, from its beginnings in the last quarter of the nineteenth century, hoped to establish a Jewish center in Eretz Israel that would either continue tradition or change it, set Israel apart from the other nations or create a new integration between the Jews and the world, abandon universal movements or become part of them. All these dilemmas still confront us today.

The contentions of Zionism were drastically confirmed by the Holocaust, yet the movement came under attack for not effecting rescue operations. Zionism was confirmed by the creation of the State of Israel, yet the world scope of anti-Semitism did not diminish. Precisely because anti-Semitism has a pivotal role in the confrontation between liberal humanistic and totalitarian regimes, between humanistic and tyrannical societies, the Jewish question remained a world issue even after the State of Israel was established. On the other hand, the integration of Jews into the societies of their countries of residence and the flourishing of these communities also express the ongoing, universal character of Jewish existence.

If one examines the relationship between recent Zionist ideological clarification and Zionist reality, an interesting contradiction

becomes evident. In attempts at ideological definitions there is constant stress of the need for *aliyah* from the Diaspora, and the need to
make a sharp distinction between Zionists and those who are pro-
Israel. Yet in social and institutional reality the very opposite is taking
place—the Jewish Agency is incorporating elements whose attachment to Zionism in the pure sense is tenuous at best. The demand for
aliyah is becoming "ideology," the fact being that it is crucial for
Israel's existence. Here the Zionist Organization, and in its wake the
Zionist Movement, has given in to reality.

A situation has been created in Israel-Diaspora relations from
which the ideological discussion cannot be detached. As a preliminary
remark, it may be said that the dialogue between the Diaspora and
Israel is conducted essentially with United States Jewry, because of
the size and strength of the latter. Were it conducted, say, with the
Jewry of France, of South America, or even with that of Great Britain
and Canada, it would perhaps have taken a different direction.

It is the considered view of Diaspora Jews that the American
Jewish community draws its vitality in large part from Israel. Interest
in Israel draws people to community centers, to informal activities,
and, to a large extent, to religious movements. But it is precisely the
symbolic and sentimental attraction of Israel, and the function that
this attraction performs within Jewish life in the Diaspora, which
draws sharp criticism from Israeli Zionists. As a result, the same Israel
which plays such an enormous role for the Diaspora does not grant
that Diaspora the legitimation its leaders desire.

There is a paradox also on the Israeli side. Politically and mate-
rially, Israel benefits from the support of the Diaspora. The existence
of the State of Israel is virtually impossible without the Diaspora. Yet,
Zionist ideology retains its negative view of the *golah*.

To the many paradoxes in the relationship between Israel and
the Diaspora another may be added: the American immigrant, who
comes to Israel not because of persecution but because of his Judaism,
finds the Jewish nature of Israel wanting, whether because of Orthodoxy or what he calls "secularism."

Israel, for whom Ahad Ha-Am's "national spiritual center" is a
favorite term for its self-definition, finds itself confronted by a Diaspora claiming that it embodies the spiritual nature of Jewry more
than Israel does. In the spiritual self-identification of the Western Jew,
Israel is a "non-spiritual" center: Hebrew language, Hebrew education, and Jewish studies do not suffice to make Israel truly Jewish. This

definition links up naturally with the criticism within Israel of the shallowness of education and spiritual life, of the weakening of old loyalties attributed to the so-called secularism (a term borrowed from the Anglo-French and American context) which is not appropriate for Israel's intellectual heritage. Zionism without Judaism is presented as hollow for both Diaspora Jewry and for Israel. Here, at least, is a factor shared by both the Diaspora and Israel—even though it be a negative one. The pragmatic need becomes an ideology.

But practical, even intellectual, difficulties soon arise. The domination in Israel of Orthodox Judaism, which repels rather than attracts the majority of *golah* Jewry, undermines the basis laid by Zionism and the Jewish totality (*Kelal Israel*) for Jewish existence. Many Israelis will become alienated from Jewish traditions if they are established on defined religious foundations. Moreover, many Diaspora Jews do not define their Jewishness in religious terms.

Those who demand a religious identification for Israel adopt the absolutist claims that without divine sanction, society, culture, and art are left without a basis. This, it is maintained, has even greater validity in the Jewish field—Jews cannot continue to live on after the "death of God." Or, much is made of the shallowness of non-religious society and culture. Yet these assertions clearly have human and social referents. Societal existence and the depth and validity of culture are not divine but human attributes. The problem is not the acceptance of the trans-human symbol but the meaning and function accorded it in society and history.

Declarations about faith will not in themselves solve problems confronting the spiritual life of the Jewish People in Israel and the Diaspora. Intellectuals in recent times have done much to fuse the natural and metaphysical worlds or find ways of bridging them. Belief in an ultimate reality, in extreme human situations, in the existential experience and the concept of creation or the sense of world mystery and the infinite, has led to an attempt at bridging the abyss between belief and non-belief. The difference between the God-fearing and the secularists does not lie in ultimate belief; it lies rather in the demand that religious experience be cast in binding social patterns, in the contention that religious consciousness should be the product not of human experience but of a force from above.

In all these respects, the attempt to reestablish Judaism along the usual conventional distinctions will lead to rift and ossification. Judaism exists in a world marked by human experience, in which its history and tradition come under criticism, and decisions about belief and views are the exclusive domain of the individual. The problem before us is not that of a return to Orthodox belief and halakhah. The problem is to shape collective patterns for Jewish existence. That existence should not be made dependent on belief in God the Creator, who guides and commands. Yet it is no less difficult to incorporate a militant atheism into the new Jewish consensus. Jewish legislation, spiritual life and education, based as they are on upright and perfect belief in the Divine Presence, cannot accept the negation of Jewry's heritage. There can be no Jewish belief without the Psalms or Job. Whether these are divine writings which reveal man or human writings which reveal God, that will be left for each individual to decide. Law and social reforms in Israel will be decided within a universe that will include the whole range of views in Israel and the Diaspora.

In the continuing debate between Diaspora Jews and Israelis, the latter tend to present Israel's preferred status as an *a priori* attitude, on the basis of its being the only place with a Jewish majority and a Jewish sovereignty—even if the individual Jew in Israel has no advantage over the individual Jew in the Diaspora and there be no advantage in empirical Israeli life. However valid this assertion, there is a limited possible contradiction between norm and fact. If in policy and society Israel is in constant contradiction with the Jewish norm and relies only on its *a priori* status, this will lead eventually to a severance of the link between its postulate and reality. Its status will become like that of the Old *Yishuv* which, while enjoying the privilege of dwelling in the Holy Land, had no special status as a model, virtuous society, not even in a Torah sense.

The expansion of Zionism's perception beyond its own ideology to new concepts and a new reality requires a comprehensive view of the Jewish past—recent as well as historic. Much has been said of late about emphasizing instruction in the history of Zionism and the *Yishuv*. That is important. The 1880s, however, not only point to Rishon Le-Zion, Zichron Yaakov and the *Bilu*, but also to the large migration to the United States, the nascence of the revolutionary Jewish intelligentsia, the growth of Yiddish letters and the Yiddish press. The overall responsibility of Israel requires that it see in the past not only a series of options from which Zionism alone emerged as justified and victorious, but also the full range of Jewish life.

The creation of a joint social substructure for the sovereign Jewry of Israel and the voluntary Jewry of the Diaspora will not emerge from doctrines of one kind or another, but from a readiness to acknowledge a pluralistic Jewry that gives meaning to new experiences. The power of Israel will be in the strength of Jewish life; the Jewish test of the *golah* will be in the highest fulfilment of its Judaism, by *aliyah*. The creation of new Jewish social bodies which will unite Israeli Jews and Diaspora Jews and will have a common spiritual ground—whether religious or not—may provide a new base for Jewish existence.

DOV RAPPEL

Professor Schweid holds that Zionist ideology is an example of non-dogmatic ideology. It is difficult to agree with such a contention both in its general aspect—that there are non-dogmatic ideologies—and in its particular—that Zionist ideology is not dogmatic.

Every ideology is comprised of three parts: a description of facts, an assessment of those facts, and conclusions which follow from this assessment.

An example of ideology built on dogma is Professor Schweid's own assessment of overall Jewish reality when he speaks of "the tragic situation of the Jewish People in modern times." This is the cornerstone of Zionist ideology, for if the situation of the Jewish People were not tragic, there would be no need for drastic action to amend it.

A second unique feature of Zionist ideology, according to Professor Schweid, is that it is not fanatic. People, collectively or as individuals, may not be fanatic because of a syncretic outlook, or because of doubts concerning the absolute correctness of their ideology. For either of these reasons they are prepared to listen to an opposing view, and perhaps even adopt it. But how can an ideology as such be tolerant? Certainly not in the establishment of facts and not in the conclusions drawn from their assessment. Tolerance is only relevant to the assessment of facts. Yet how can an ideology include the assertion, "An assessment of reality opposed to ours is also correct"?

I am not ashamed to say that my ideology voids every other ideology. Only because of the injunction, ". . . thou shalt love thy neighbor as thyself" (Lev. 19:18), do I accept tolerance as a practical principle, but not as an ideological element.

I am prepared to accept Professor Schweid's view that the present situation of the Jewish People is tragic and must be amended. He maintains that the Jewish People is in danger and we must contend against that danger by means of education. The Zionist Movement must mobilize the Jewish People to build up Eretz Israel.

If Professor Schweid is referring to physical danger, the fear that the Jewish People will be physically annihilated, it would seem that the most effective escape from that danger is assimilation. Paradoxically, the horrors of 1940-45 proved that even the Nuremberg Laws (1935) gave way to assimilation: the descendants of Moses Mendelssohn lived unharmed in Germany during years of harsh persecution. On the other hand, even though less than a quarter of all Jews alive today live in the State of Israel, the number of those killed in the State of Israel because they were Jewish is several times greater than the number killed throughout the world for the same reason during the last thirty years. This would suggest, paradoxically, that physical security for Jews is not to be found in the State of Israel.

Professor Schweid may be alluding to the danger of spiritual annihilation by assimilation. Nevertheless, both of us would agree, it seems, that there is no cause for fear, even though we arrive at this sanguinity from quite different dogmatic paths. In my view, spiritual annihilation is unlikely. I believe in the word of God, "and yet for all that, when they are in the land of their enemies, I will not reject them, neither will I abhor them, to destroy them utterly, and to break My covenant with them" (Lev. 26:44). As a secular person, Professor Schweid establishes dogma as the fundamental ethical identity of all cultures. What is wrong, therefore, with assimilation? Even if we agree that in the secular Jewish approach there is nothing inherently wrong in abandoning Judaism for some other culture, we do not deny anyone the right to educate for Judaism.

"Education" suggests two things: efforts on the part of the educator and the positive results of these efforts. The apparently simple statement, "We must educate," suggests that there is a reasonable chance that the educational efforts will lead to desirable results. Since we feel it our duty to increase good, we must educate. It is thus necessary to examine whether secular-cultural Jewish education stands a reasonable chance of success.

To simplify the explication I will disregard several factors that might influence the outcome but are not related to ideology. I shall consider only content in education that is ideal. More precisely, I shall consider two pairs of educator-educatee. In one, both educator and educatee have accepted the *mitzvot* (commandments); the other pair is secular. In the first dyad the educator has no difficulty in explaining to the educatee why he should want to live in Eretz Israel. That is the Land God gave to our forefathers, the Land where the *Shekhinah* (Divine Presence) is. The *galut*, on the other hand, is an alien Land, dwelling there is both punishment and sin—punishment for the sins of our forefathers and the sin of having "scorned the desirable land" (Ps. 106:24). The savagery that our people encountered in the *galut* is no other than the fulfilment of the words of the Torah: "And among these nations you shall have no repose, and there shall be no rest for the sole of your foot" (Deut. 28:65). Such explanations seem reasonable. Consequently, the chances of educational success are reasonable.

Not so in the second, the secular, case. The educator acknowledges that he was born a Jew, but in his view that fact implies no obligation, there is nothing wrong in forsaking Judaism. And should the educator argue that education must remain faithful to the culture of our forefathers, the educatee will respond with two answers. First, in what way do you remain faithful to the culture of your forefathers? And second, since you hold that the details of Jewish culture, even those to which you adhere, have no binding validity, by what right do you demand that I adhere to them?

How will the educator explain the need to learn the difficult Hebrew language? Why study the Bible? For its religious content, which the educator does not acknowledge? Or to delight in the sublime ethical ideas and the lofty poesy? That can be achieved from translations.

Finally, we come to the main point at issue—Eretz Israel. When a Jew claims that his right to Eretz Israel was given to him because of his valor, he is not surprised that the opposing side refuses to accept his contention, and he is not dispirited. But when a secular Zionist bases his claim on the Bible and ancestral heritage, he himself does not believe what he says. How can he arouse belief among those whom he seeks to educate?

In short, if the educatees of the secular Zionist educator are intelligent and consistent, the chances of the latter's success are nil. And since there are no chances for success, the assertion "We must educate" has no validity.

What can be done?

The secular Zionist Ahad Ha-Am wrote that "more than the Jews preserved the Sabbath, the Sabbath preserved the Jews." It is imperative that we recognize the proper relation between the religious content of Judaism and the national existence of the Jewish People.

MUKI TZUR

I would like to clarify what Zionism means to me, the obligation it imposes on me, the perspective it gives my existence through the way it helps the Jewish People of whom I am a part. Such questioning is not new, but the situation has changed since the establishment of the State of Israel.

The rational, analytic nature of Zionism is manifested in the attempt to discover the sociology of the Jewish nation, entangled in the complexities of a changing world. Zionism focuses on the fluid experience of the present; it analyzes the past as history, as something which develops and changes. It does not stress that which was fundamentally eternal in the past. It lives on creation in process, and on a model for the future. The analytic and uncompromising nature of Zionism disturbs many who seek an anchor in more positive things. However much it deals with past history, or possible worlds of the future, its major form is the contemporary day-to-day experience of the Jewish community in Eretz Israel and Jewish existence in the *golah*.

The Zionist analysis has not changed in any fundamental way. It emphasized the nation's disintegration in the dispersion: on the one hand, Zionism contends that the nation is in danger of disappearing, while on the other, it claims that its position is so secure that assimilation is likely. This contradiction has generally been resolved by dividing the *golah* into two parts: the affluent *tefutzah* (dispersion), comfortable in the surrounding society and in danger of assimilation, and the *golah*, living under pressure and in danger of destruction. This division between *tefutzah* and *golah* has also found its expression in the dual nature of the State of Israel which, as a "night sanctuary" provides an answer to the *golah* and as *Zion* provides an answer to the *tefutzah*. This dual nature of the State of Israel is in constant tension. One pole represents the fight for survival by the Jews in its Eretz Israel form (which differs from the struggle for survival of the Jewish People in the *golah*), and the other is the moral-cultural expression of the society and individual in Israel (which also differs from the Jew's struggle for his identity in *golah*).

The fact that we use one term, "the assurance of Jewish existence," for both these struggles does not follow from the analysis, but results from a conception of the solution. There is no similarity between the struggle to remain alive and the desire to confirm one's moral-cultural experience. In pre-Emancipation Jewish history there are many instances in which the desire to stay alive clashed with the desire to affirm the tradition. Zionist thinkers have realized, however, that in the modern world these two struggles have become one, that assimilation cannot solve the problem of physical annihilation, that without Jewish security a normative system able to stem assimilation cannot emerge.

Zionism revolutionizes the analysis and converts it into a program for action when the distress of the "night sanctuary" awakens dormant powers which are capable of building up Zion, the most sublime aspiration of the Jewish People. Conversely, Zionism has also stressed that the Jew, contending with assimilation in order to discover his personal identity, is determined to establish a home that will not only express his strivings but will also offer protection.

The State of Israel, engaged in a struggle for physical survival, and at the same time building for itself a socio-moral foundation that will express its Jewishness and strivings, is still the scene of classic Zionist tension. But the almost mechanical conception of strength emerging from distress, and new construction from disintegration, is not on such sure ground. At times distress is followed by disintegration, hunger, and fatigue. This has been seen with every wave of settlement. The First *Aliyah* encountered an old disintegrated *Yishuv*, the Second encountered the sons of the First, whose youthful aspirations had come to naught, and so it continued. Even after the establishment of the State, it was clear that the tendencies of disintegration were still powerful. The *Yishuv*, with its fragile social fabric, its educating zeal, its demands on the individual, should have fallen apart. However, at the time the foundations for the Jewish State were being laid, other countries were closed to the Jews. Zionism provided the only solution, even though it failed to prevent the catastrophe both during World War II and afterwards. The establishment of the State of Israel, however, gave the status of the Jew too much stability. Fear of the Jews lessened; gradually they were considered a less dangerous element. It was only several years later that mass migration from the countries of the Third World began. Large clusters of the Jewish People could be absorbed by the State of Israel.

As a result of the establishment of the State, developed countries opened their gates to Jews, including Jews of Eretz Israel. The State of Israel, which had absorbed masses of Jews, made it possible for Israelis to be absorbed elsewhere. The illusion was created that the State of Israel was the least safe place for a Jew; the *tefutzah* was the safe refuge, the "night sanctuary." The struggle for survival in Eretz Israel was perceived as a direct continuation of the struggle for survival which was so much part of life in the golah. Now, however, it is precisely in Eretz Israel that the status of the golah is preserved. This conception is a dangerous illusion for the Jews of the world: should the Jewish State cease to exist there would be immediate danger for Jews throughout the world—without them having access to a state. If masses of Jews were uprooted in our time and there were no longer a Jewish State, we would witness a return to the reality of pogroms. But it is also a misconception of the status of the State of Israel. Apart from the traditional psychological conflict of the Jew with his surroundings, Israel has created a situation of genuine political conflict. Any attempt to restore to this conflict the dimensions of the struggle for survival of a Jewish community in the golah would be futile. However, in the Land of our Fathers, the Land of our choice, we are witness to a great Zionist achievement: Jews have acquired political status.

Yet, it could be thought, mistakenly, that this status frees Israel from social and psychological questions raised by Zionism. The truth is that since we are caught in the conflict, and the political answer in its completeness depends on the termination of the conflict, the Israeli is faced with the problems of identity and of society within the conflict situation. But even if the conflict is resolved and the State attains legitimation and security in the Middle East, questions relating to the individual's identity and the structure of the society will arise. Young people, free to enter advanced countries, will be confronted by the enigma of the meaning of existence.

There are those who maintain that the meaning of existence can be adequately explained only by traditional Judaism and that Zionism is merely one aspect which supplies traditional Judaism with a political and economic foundation: Zionism is no more than an instrument, a necessary tool. This seems to me a mistaken conception. Traditional Judaism, which does have something to say to our world, should be maintained. However, the Jew cannot go about his daily life, with all that it entails, and then live his Jewish life separately. It is necessary to maintain not only the synagogue but also the factory, not only the minyan but also the economic committee, not only the People of the Book but also the people of the field. In short, Zionism is not only an instrument, a way of analysis or a utopia that has been realized. It is a beginning.

Zionism, like the kibbutz, cannot return to trends of the past. Nor can it perpetuate its compromise with current reality, for it exists in a present which refuses to accept a rigid framework—it demands change in the individual's approach, in the shaping of society, in the preservation of sovereignty.

Any attempt to make Zionism merely a political movement, an individual search for a social utopia, is no more than an expression of the distress Zionism is seeking to resolve. It is inconceivable that distress be the main impetus for Zionism.

Broad vision and decisive action have guided Zionism successfully through many critical situations. But the Jewish People have paid dearly for their inability to confront the challenge of Zionism.

ALEX WEINGROD

In a recent study of ethnic integration in Israeli society, Inbar and Adler report a "surprising" result when Israelis of Moroccan and Rumanian origin were asked whether they had ever contemplated emigration; what they term "surprising" is the fact that few of the Moroccans answered affirmatively, whereas two-thirds of the Rumanians replied that they had thought of emigration. Hence the investigators concluded that the "Moroccan Israelis came to Israel for predominantly national and ideological reasons, with little or no economic expectations."[1]

The conclusion is certainly correct: Moroccan Jews, and for that matter, Jews from countries in the Middle East and North Africa, who flocked to Israel from 1948 on, were motivated by ideological factors. True, they also came to escape from persecutions and political uncertainties; yet there was also a deep, almost mystical sense of renewal, of *ahavat Zion*, and therefore, of Zionism. One cannot fail to be impressed by the messianic spirit of fulfilment which imbued tens of thousands in their move to Israel.

The astonishing thing, however, is that this aspect has prevailed. Now, thirty years later, the majority of those immigrants from the Middle East have become firmly attached to the Jewish State. Despite the myriad problems of adjustment and problems of the "social gap," they have become an authentic, well-rooted segment of the population. For the older, adult generation memories of the past thirty years evoke a

---

1. M. Inbar and C. Adler, *Ethnic Integration in Israel: A Comparative Case Study of Moroccan Brothers Who Settled in France and in Israel*, New Brunswick, 1977, p. 117.

smile; they are memories of difficulties encountered and surmounted. That same smile records the paradoxical appreciation of having come home. For the Israeli born in the Jewish State, Diaspora countries such as Iraq or Yemen have only a mythic implication; their reality is the "normal" one of being Jews in the Jewish State. Some Middle East immigrants have found it unduly difficult to adapt to a European-dominated culture. Nevertheless, there can be no doubt of their cultural authenticity: many have become thoroughly absorbed into the local scene. Moreover, they are Zionists.

There does not seem to be survey data summarizing the views on Zionism held by these Middle East settlers. Evidently it is not a salient topic for them. Can there be any doubt that Jews were meant to live in the Jewish State? The mystic element is prominent, the major thrust powerful and positive.

Professor Schweid analyzes the character of the Jewish State and the shape of future Israeli society. Zionism is not enough. I shall limit myself to criticizing a particular point: disappointment that more Diaspora Jews have not become immigrants; indeed, it has even been said that this has been a major failure. That is a legitimate complaint. Yet such criticism should not be interpreted as including Jews from the Middle East countries who have come in large numbers to Israel.

It is folly to suppose that any one group will bring about a moral regeneration. Cultural revitalization will be produced from the inner resources of our people, all our people. There is no one to save us but ourselves.

IV

Reformulations

Maintaining Zionism in an Age of Pro-Israelism

Arye L. Dulzin

We have entered a new era in which past attitudes are no longer valid. Clarifications are essential for the sake both of Zionists and of those Jews who, though they support Israel, choose not to be identified as Zionists.

Ben Gurion's maximalist demand that every Zionist come on *aliyah* or cease to call himself a Zionist is not our approach. There is, nevertheless, something deficient in a Zionism which does not ideologically confront the Diaspora as a *golah*, does not in principle regard the continued existence of the majority of the Jewish People there as abnormal, and does not look forward to the day—however distant—when every Zionist will find a way to live in Israel. Likewise, Zionism which does not attempt to influence the *Jewish* life of Jews remaining in the Diaspora, evades its responsibility.

Underlying the differentiation between a Zionist and a "supporter of Israel" is ideology. A Zionist is called on to subscribe to the Jerusalem Program adopted at the 1968 Zionist Congress. The final wording of the program reads:

> The aims of Zionism are: the unity of the Jewish People and the centrality of Israel in Jewish life; the ingathering of the Jewish People in its historic homeland Eretz Israel through *aliyah* from all countries; the strengthening of the State of Israel which is based on the prophetic vision of justice and peace; the preservation of the identity of the Jewish People through the fostering of Jewish and Hebrew education and of Jewish spiritual and cultural values; the protection of Jewish rights everywhere.

The first two points, in particular, were the subject of far-reaching discussions and compromises. The second point was hard-fought because the delegates from overseas resisted the inclusion of the personal *mitzvah* of *aliyah*. But most troublesome was the principle stated in the first point, that the aims of the Jerusalem Program are "the unity of the Jewish People and the centrality of Israel in its life."

Concerning the "unity of the Jewish People" there was no argument. But there is still some quarrel in Jewish circles today over the centrality of Israel. There are residual holdouts at both ends of the spectrum (among the ultra-Orthodox and the extreme New Left) and even in more tolerant religious circles. The great majority of the Jewish People are united behind the State of Israel. They recognize that resolutions against Israel by a hostile majority in the U.N. are often acts of anti-Semitism, aimed at every Jew, regardless of his land of domicile.

Zionists have to distinguish between what *is* and what *ought to be*. It must be faced that eighty percent of the Jewish People remain outside Israel. Many of these Jews cling to their exilic existence, while maintaining their undying attachment and longing for the only true (meaning spiritual) Homeland. But the reality of exile must not be elevated to the status of an ideal. As an ideological movement dissatisfied with the present condition of the Jewish People, Zionism cannot settle for the existing situation. The Movement must find ways of involving *galut* Zionists themselves in articulating the programs that will bring about the diminution, if not the dissolution, of the *golah*. This may appear an almost impossible goal, but it is nonetheless a crucial one.

The basis for a new ideological stance *vis-à-vis* the *golah* was suggested years ago by a leading Zionist thinker, the late Hayim Greenberg: "Wherever Jews live as a minority, where they are not politically or socially independent, where they rely on the good graces of the non-Jewish majority and are subject to the everyday pressures of its civilization and mode of life, such a place is *galut*." By this criterion, no Zionist can claim superior—or even equal—status for Diaspora Zionism. One cannot claim that Jews are entirely unlike the Poles, Italians and Irish, who as a national entity also share an American Diaspora. Neither are the Jews comparable to the Protestants, Catholics or Moslems; nor are they like the English-speaking people. Peoplehood is defined by Mordecai M. Kaplan as "a family of families, with its own life-style."

Hayei Sha'ah and Hayei Olam

How then shall we determine who is a Zionist rather than a supporter, or even a devotee, of Israel? Why is this question crucial? Is it because we must know upon whom we can count for mobilization in a variety of emergency situations? Should a genuine peace situation develop in the Middle East, and should Israel no longer suffer critical world public opinion, then many Jews identified as staunch supporters of Israel, but who are not Zionists, might quickly feel free to "doff their uniforms" and retire from the frontlines.

It is my view that the difference between a Zionist and a supporter of Israel may be best summed up by our ancestors' rubric, *hayei sha'ah* versus *hayei olam*. By *hayei sha'ah* (literally "the life of the here-and-now"), I refer to concentration on the pressing, urgent needs of today. By *hayei olam* (literally "everlasting life"), I think of those far-reaching visionaries who believe in the future solutions to problems that appear insoluble today. I do not want to suggest that the former are any less idealistic or devoted, but only that their horizon is circumscribed or limited. They may have a global vista but their perspective of space is not complemented by the perspective of time. And it is the perspective of time which characterizes the approach of *hayei olam*. Indeed, *hayei olam* is fully aware of *hayei sha'ah*, but transcends it.

A hallmark of modern Jewish history has been the ability of Jewish communities to organize themselves to face emergencies. Beginning with the Damascus Blood Libel of 1840, continuing through the pogroms and anti-Semitism of the last decades of Czarist Russia, and reaching its highest point in the aid extended by Jewish communities to the survivors of the Holocaust, Jews the world over have risen above themselves in fraternity and philanthropy, empathy and involvement. This is still where most Jews excel.

Wherein do Zionists differ? They are no less merciful, crisis-oriented or concerned with the suffering of the Jews. True, there was a classic Zionist argument as to whether the aim of Zionism was to save the Jews or to save Judaism. There were supporters of the Herzlian line who placed a priority on saving Jews; there were those who sought to save Judaism.

Herzl's towering stature and his position in Zionist history are firmly enough established so that one may allow oneself the determination that even he, the great visionary, sometimes lapsed into *hayei sha'ah*. There is no way of explaining the Uganda controversy without assuming that Herzl was so distressed over the miserable lot of East-European Jewry that he sought an immediate "night shelter" in East Africa. Yet the root causes for the Uganda conflict sprang from the underlying tensions between the Herzlian and the Ahad Ha-Amist orientations. Herzl, as the father of political Zionism, was understandably exercised by the questions of the hour. Ahad Ha-Am was more concerned with *hayei olam*.

There were two relevant ideological conflicts at the first all-Russian Zionist Conferences at the beginning of the century. In 1902, the first of these—held in my home town of Minsk—debated the spiritual and cultural directions of the Movement (known in Zionist circles as *Kultura*). Ahad Ha-Am pointed out what he considered to be the harmful consequences of regarding Hebrew as a Holy Tongue (the attitude of the Orthodox) or as a "classical" language (the viewpoint of the supporters of the Enlightenment). Ahad Ha-Am viewed Hebrew as an organic expression of national identity. (Ironically, he gave his speech in Russian; few delegates could have followed him in Hebrew, while it would have been unthinkable to speak the language of the other "enemy"—Yiddish.) There is a lesson in this. The argument over language and the role of Hebrew no longer applies in quite the same way. But there are many new elements in the current situation of the Jewish People for which an Ahad Ha-Amist approach, stressing the *hayei olam* aspect, is highly pertinent.

The second all-Russian Zionist Conference was involved in a debate over *Gegenwartsarbeit*, literally, "work in the present." Even the most optimistic Zionists of those days did not fully believe that there would be an immediate and total transfer to Eretz Israel of all the Jews then living in Eastern Europe. Meanwhile, millions of Jews were living under intolerable conditions. The hotly debated question was whether the Zionist Movement should be concerned with Jewish welfare in their lands of domicile. Those who supported the exclusive concentration on work in Eretz Israel emphasized three points: (1) the creation of the Jewish National Fund, which was to finance the acquisition of lands in Eretz Israel; (2) the Jewish Colonial Trust, which was to serve as the financial instrument for political and economic activities; (3) the acquisition of a charter from the Turks for Jewish settlement in Eretz Israel. The common denominator for all three was that they were activity-oriented and ostensibly practical.

Their opponents felt that the Jewish People, both as a collective body and as individuals, was paramount, and that Eretz Israel was an instrument for achieving this aim. They favored, therefore, far-reaching cultural, economic and political activities in the Diaspora. This second group, who supported the concept of "work in the present" alongside and sometimes superseding "work for the future," took the motto: "Work with Jews where they are at." There were many exemplary Zionists—Ahad Ha-Am, Martin Buber, Chaim Weizmann, Ze'ev Jabotinsky and Leo Motzkin—who held this view.

A Zionist Agenda

The two historic conflicts I have outlined provide us with direction in the current debate. The Zionist Movement has been involved in overseas work aimed at rescue operations of Jews in lands of extreme distress. Should it also be involved in political action in the Diaspora? Should it try to achieve greater security and perhaps even large measures of cultural self-sufficiency for Jews in countries which merely extend toleration to the Jews? For instance, how can Zionism seriously propose a program geared to acquiring Jewish cultural self-sufficiency in South America? The very fabric of those countries and the cultural infrastructure on which their regimes are based call for monolithic exclusiveness. Yet, were Czarist Russia or pre-World War Poland really tolerant pluralistic societies? The problems involved are not dictated by the nature of the regimes but by the needs of Jews—and Zionism ought to concern itself with the total needs of the Diaspora, not only the exigencies of the situation in Israel.

There are three areas whose very interrelatedness could make for a comprehensive Zionist agenda: an immense and intensive renewal of the movement for *aliyah*; a significant breakthrough in Jewish education accompanied by no less constant activity; and the enhancement of the quality of Jewish life in Israel and in the Diaspora. True, the conditions of battle differ from place to place. We must plan our deeds carefully in order not to win on one front, only to lose on another. At this stage of Zionism we are renewing our work. There is a three-way bond between the striving for *aliyah*, Jewish education and the quality of Jewish life. All three mutually influence each other, both in Israel and in the Diaspora.

Everybody understands the need for *aliyah* in the strengthening of Zionist achievements in Israel, but too few have given their attention to the far-reaching Zionist and Jewish influence that *aliyah* can have precisely on those Jewish communities in the Diaspora from which immigrants will come.

The two-pronged approach applies also in the area of Jewish education. Shortcomings in Jewish education are not a Diaspora monopoly. We have argued a great deal in Israel about *who* is a Jew, and not spoken at all about *what* it is to be a Jew. Just as many in the Diaspora do not know anything about Jewish life in Israel, so many of the young people growing up in Israel do not know the reality of Jewish life in the Diaspora today.

The very same phenomena may be observed when we come to the question of the quality of Jewish life. As great as was the Zionist vision of a perfectible society, so is the magnitude of the task which lies ahead of us. There will not be a great *aliyah* as long as the advance towards making Israel a society that will be an example to all peoples is held back. A socially backward Israel does not serve to attract an idealistic *aliyah*.

In truth, the Zionist Movement from its inception mobilized its efforts for long-range goals. At times, the effort to save Judaism rather than Jews, or emphasis on work in the Diaspora, put the Zionist Movement in direct conflict with apparently immediate Jewish needs. Chaim Weizmann, and later Louis Pincus, exhibited their grasp of the need to create a common program, a clearing house, if not an outright partnership, between the adherents of *hayei sha'ah* and *hayei olam*. Each in his day created an enlarged and broadened Jewish Agency. The partners of the Zionist representatives were as convinced in Weizmann's day as today, that the concept of partnership required them to support Jewish needs in Eretz Israel even when they might not agree with the ultimate aim of Zionism. They lent their support because the need was all too evident. But should an unforeseen Jewish need materialize elsewhere as well, they might be in an honest quandary. They would have to decide where to place their main commitment: to alleviate current Jewish suffering, or to concentrate almost exclusively on the future, in other words, to give ideology priority over emergency.

When Zionists place settlement in Israel above all other options offered to Soviet Jewish dropouts in Vienna, they oppose the squandering of world Jewish efforts and resources on individuals—even if they are Jews—who seek primarily personal comfort and gain. The commitment of the Zionist leadership on behalf of the entire Jewish People stems from a conviction that Zionism is concerned with long-range solutions to the needs of the Jewish People. At stake is the ability in the name of collective goals to withstand appeals for individual needs. *Hayei olam* makes demands on Zionists to assume a stewardship for the long-range solution of the Jewish People. Zionists want to know if those Russian Jews who choose between the United States and Israel will actively participate in the life of their respective Jewish communities. Will those who emigrate to the United States give their children an intensive Jewish education; will they direct them towards involvement in Jewish communal life? Zionist ideology emphatically insists that the creative survival of the Jews may best be achieved through communal cohesion rather than in the pursuit of a dubious individual *laissez-faire* for Jews.

The New Jewish Sociology

One of the many arguments that shook the Zionist Movement in its early days was not the diagnosis and therapy but the prognosis of the ailment that Zionism was intended to cure. One may wonder at the Zionists' endorsement of the British Government's offer of Uganda as a refuge for persecuted Jews. Did they really think that there would be a mass exodus by East-European Jews? Were they confident that the endless fears of the Diaspora would soon be terminated? In other words, the internal conflict was, in no small measure, a result of the estimation as to how immediate, all encompassing, and inexorable was the catastrophe that was expected to spell the doom of Jewish life everywhere. Indeed, an entire school of Zionist thought, which embraced a variety of political and cultural positions, was called "Zionism of catastrophe." One of its leading advocates was Jacob Klatzkin who, with considerable polemical ability, argued that the *golah* simply could not persist. It had but one prospect— disappearance, as a result of assimilation, persecution or both.

Klatzkin's theories have been both vindicated and confounded. The high degree of cultural assimilation and the accelerating intermarriage rate (he did not even dream of the new Jewish illness of zero population growth) are his vindication. His theories have been confounded by a resurgence of interest in Jewish study programs, a proud and assertive Jewish polity, and other developments in lands of opportunity and affluence for Jews. There is an overwhelming tendency among young Israeli adults to accept a simplistic condensation of his approach. They "know" that the *golah* cannot persist, even when they are confronted with the fact that the *golah* is alive and doing quite well in Hampstead and Scarsdale. This is often accompanied by frustration and anger for it seems to place in question the entire theoretical infrastructure of Zionism. A new Zionist ideology must, if it is to take itself at all seriously, examine what has changed as well as what has

remained constant in Jewish life. Today I believe that there is no longer any point in speaking about a Zionism of catastrophe. Schematically, I would divide the present situation of world Jewry into four categories: (a) Jews in distress; (b) tolerated Jewry; (c) emancipated Jewry;
(d) auto-emancipated Jewry.

Jews in Distress: There are still places in the world in which Jews are
in physical danger. Unfortunately, Iranian Jewry has recently been
hurled from the category of tolerated Jewry to that of Jewry in acute
distress. But this category of distress, applied to communities facing
physical danger, also must include Soviet Jewry, whose immediate
plight is spiritual and cultural rather than physical.

What is so perplexing about Zionist ideology is that it is predicated on the analysis of the Jewish condition and this changes unex-
pectedly. A Klatzkinite analysis, for instance, should have foretold the
sudden deterioration in the fortunes of the Iranian Jewish community.
Yet, until recently, had anyone insisted on such a reading of possible
developments, he would have been accused of alarmism. And more
astounding is the opposite development in the fortunes of Soviet
Jewry. Who at the time of the so-called "Moscow Doctors' Plot" would
have predicted the resurgence of a publicly articulated interest in
things Jewish by young Jews, or the Soviet regime's toleration of such
manifestations, or the granting of exit visas to Israel? The Zionist view
has found itself vindicated again and again. It is within Zionism alone
that one may find a conceptual framework by means of which the
caprices of events can be understood.

Another criterion for characterizing communities "in distress"
is their inability to sustain an independent Jewish cultural life. There
are such Jewish communities in Yugoslavia, Greece and Turkey, as
well as minute ones in Central America and the Caribbean, for example. The element of distress here is a function of size more than anything else. These communities are totally dependent on the ability of
Israel to sustain their educational and religious requirements. They
may yet disappear, but would have done so much earlier were it not
for the Jewish State.

Tolerated Jewry: This category includes the larger Latin American
Jewish communities. There is widespread realization that they are sit-
ting on a powder keg. Yet, many of them believe that conditions will
still improve. "Meanwhile, we are allowed to conduct Jewish cultural

life here," they say. "And if we wish, they allow us to leave." In fact, although the degree of tolerance may be sometimes greater, sometimes less, it is nevertheless still merely *tolerance.* The sudden shifts in the status of communities and the movement from one category to another, concerning communities in distress, apply here as well.

Emancipated Jewry: In countries of the free world, such as the United States, France, and Great Britain, Jews enjoy equality of rights. Formally, there is full equality, yet in a sense it is not completely full. Admittedly, whoever wants to live a proud Jewish life there is allowed to do so. The remaining limitations to total political, economic and even social integration with the non-Jewish population are fast disappearing. However, it is precisely because of the openness of these Western societies that a new and serious problem has emerged. Jews face oblivion. They may disappear by becoming indistinguishable from the general population.

Both the tolerated and emancipated Jewries maintain a measure of self-generated Jewish creativity. Apart from the United States, they cannot mobilize sufficient resources among their indigenous Jewish population, even where they number—as in the case of France, Britain and Argentina—several hundred thousand. They still require the assistance of Israel in training rabbis, youth leaders and teachers. They also require partial or complete direction from Israel in evolving curricula for their Jewish schools, programming ideas for their Zionist and general Jewish organizations, and even look to Israel for directives on matters of world Jewish policy.

Only the United States is a self-sustaining Jewish community. True, because of its sophistication and magnitude, it knows better than the smaller Jewish communities how to exploit the ancillary services which Israel can provide. Yet, in theory it could stand on its own. It has facilities for training rabbis, communal workers and teachers. It has a highly articulated sense of itself and its mission. It has evolved an indigenous leadership, native organizational forms and an enormous fund-raising mechanism. But has not much of this come to pass precisely because of the rebirth and existence of the State of Israel?

Auto-Emancipated Jewry: The fourth group is that segment of Jewry which lives in Israel—the Jewry that I call auto-emancipated—the only Jewry in the world which determines its own fate. Not every Jew who lives in Israel is consciously Zionist. Moreover, many of them find it hard to make a semantic distinction between their Israeli and their Jewish self. It is our duty to educate the young generation in Israel to a Zionist and an overt Jewish consciousness. In this effort, one thing is quite clear: all Jews in Israel live in a completely Jewish ambience, which is reflected in every aspect of the country. I say this in full realization that we face a very serious responsibility to maintain the Jewish and Zionist character of the Jewish State.

In my opinion, the classic Zionist analysis of the Diaspora has withstood the test of time. The Jewish stichic process—"the iron law of history"—has undergone modification but it is still an incontrovertible process. We have now transformed our battle from the struggle against the *distress of Jews* to a struggle against the *distress of the Jewish People*. This requires profound and revolutionary answers as to what it means to be Jewish in the contemporary world.

In its formative years, Zionism regarded itself as a revolution in Jewish life. This revolution was more far-reaching than the geographic transfer of the demographic center of Jewish life from Eastern Europe to the Middle East. Its aim was no less than the total restructuring of Jewish life everywhere. The achievement has been only partial and its completion is the challenge that faces us today.

Renewing the Zionist Vision

Daniel J. Elazar

The fundamentals of Zionism were established at the Movement's very founding and remain imbedded within it, shaping its subsequent development. Although the modes of expression of those fundamentals may be changing for the second or third time, the principles and relationships which comprise them remain firm.

Both biblical and Greek writings attest to the importance of foundings in human history; the history of Zionism is merely another confirmation of this historical truth. None escapes the patterns established at the founding. There can be new beginnings under certain conditions that may somewhat alter those patterns and their consequences, but those are rare enough.

The Persistence of Fundamentals

Zionism was an effort at refounding the Jewish People. As such it had to develop in relation to earlier refoundings and a much earlier founding. This in itself has dictated many of the parameters and paradoxes of the Zionist Movement and much of the dynamic which has animated it.

At the core of Zionism are the relationships between:

1. a Zionism which basically negates the Diaspora and a Zionism which basically views Israel as a haven for those who seek to escape from the Diaspora;

2. those who require an ideological basis for their Zionism and those who approach Zionism and Israel non-ideologically;

3. the major trends within the Zionist Movement, principally the socialist, liberal and religious camps.

Each of these relationships has been present from the founding, and the patterns of interaction which have animated them have given life to the Zionist enterprise.

Israel and the Diaspora

Despite the fact that the first issue has been minimized since the mid-1950s, an unclouded view of the situation leads to the conclusion that most Israeli Zionist thinkers still believe in the negation of the Diaspora; this is so even if they are prepared to recognize the reality of Diaspora existence and have consequently lowered their expectations regarding the fulfilment of their hopes for the ingathering of the exiles. Moreover, those who have developed a positive program to assist Diaspora Jewry in maintaining its Jewishness have made it clear that their reasons for promoting such a program are concerned with Israel's security and *aliyah*. They do not imply a recognition of either the legitimacy or the permanence of the Diaspora. Perhaps the major shift in their view is the expectation that the Diaspora is more likely to disappear through assimilation than through *aliyah*. Thus they seek to retard the former while doing their best to maximize the latter.

On the other hand, the Jews of the Diaspora (even such oppressed diasporas as the Soviet Union) essentially continue to look upon Israel as a place of refuge, although they now have growing doubts as to whether it is the safest or best refuge for Jews. They have become more sophisticated in their views, seeing Israel not only as a refuge from physical persecution but also as a place of refuge from assimilation. This means that Israel is evaluated primarily as to how well it is fulfilling its function as a haven (just as the Diaspora is evaluated by Israelis from the equivalent perspective of how close it is linked to Israeli ideas and policies).

A review of the program content of UJA missions, which represent popular expression of Zionism in the Diaspora, will indicate how much emphasis is still placed on Israel as a place of refuge, although in more sophisticated terms. The new sophistication involves utilizing Israel as a place to refresh one's Jewishness. I would submit that this is not a departure from the main theme, but an extension of it. I believe it is fair to suggest that the Diaspora criticism of Israel which has developed in recent years emerged principally when it became apparent that many Russian Jews were either leaving Israel or refusing to go there in the first place. It was from this point of departure that other criticisms about the quality of life in Israel were posed.

A Zionist Ideology?

The relationship between the ideological and non-ideological approaches to Zionism arose naturally from these differences in viewpoint. Obviously it is easier for those who are non-ideological to see Israel primarily as a haven. On the other hand, since the negation of the Diaspora is in itself an ideological position, it is, not surprisingly, related to other manifestations of ideological thinking. Here, too, basic thrusts remains unchanged, although concrete ones have changed drastically.

For most of those concerned with Zionist ideology there is no longer firm belief in the particular ideologies that existed until the establishment of the State. These ideologies have lost their ability to compel. The resurgence of interest in Zionism that has been marked in recent years has stirred a renewed concern with questions of Zionist ideology. Since this renewed concern is primarily manifested in Israel, even when it also influences Jews in the Diaspora, it is not surprising that the call for renewal is often the call for a renewed ideology.[1] Israel is, after all, the heir of European Zionism and, as such, concerned Israelis are likely to seek a proper ideological framework within which to express their concern. They are echoed in this by the Zionists of Latin America, the Soviet Union, and perhaps the rest of Europe, or the spokesman for approximately one half of world Jewry. If today there is a search for new ideological strengthening on the part of many Israelis, the search is in itself a reaffirmation of the importance of ideology to them.

On the other hand, the other half of world Jewry, the Jews of English-speaking countries and principally those of North America, whatever their concern for a Zionist renewal, do not seek such a renewal in the symmetries of ideological reconstruction. It may well be that what separates Zionists and non-Zionists today is precisely this division into those seeking an ideological basis for their concern about Israel, and those who are quite unconcerned. What do we do to revitalize our thinking about those questions for which Zionism came into being, when half of the Jews in the world believe in the importance of ideology and half do not?[2]

In the 1950s and 1960s, the "end of ideology" decades, the non-ideological types clearly had the upper hand within both the Zionist

1. Ideology as used here refers to a coherent, systematic and complete body of ideas designed to shape the thinking of large publics by providing them with explicit guidelines of the kind formerly provided in implicit ways by tradition.
2. It may well be that more than half do not. While the *spokesmen* for Israeli Jewry may be ideologically oriented, many Israelis, especially those of non-European backgrounds, may not be so, though they are slowly being absorbed into a system oriented towards ideological expression.

Movement and the State of Israel. Today they are being challenged again, though in a modest way, since the proponents of the ideological reinvigoration do not have an ideology to propound. Moreover, those who seek ideological invigoration are limited in their ability to present an acceptable ideology: any such ideology would probably have to include some sense of the negation of the Diaspora, and this would have immediate practical repercussions to the detriment of the unity of the Jewish People.

At the same time, those responsible for conducting the day-to-day business of maintaining the Jewish State are not likely to be particularly interested in, or concerned with developing a new ideology. Coming out of ideologically oriented traditions, they pay lip service to the need for ideology, mainly for aesthetic reasons; it gives them confidence when there is an ideological base underneath their essentially pragmatic response to daily problems. Thus they are often willing to fund ideological conferences and publications, but, in fact, the relevance of those conferences and publications to their own endeavors is very slight. From my perspective and most of those with an American background, the likelihood of the development of a new ideology is very slight. Yet it is possible to recognize the need that exists for some clarification of Zionist thought.

The Israeli Branch of Judaism

It is not far-fetched to suggest that, de facto, Zionism has become another branch of Judaism, parallel in its own way to Orthodoxy, Conservatism, Reform or Reconstructionism in the Diaspora. Like Communism, it is a secular rather than a theistic religion in its fundamentals. This does not mean that religious Zionists are not Zionists, but their Zionism plays a different role for them, representing as it were, an extension of a larger set of religious beliefs. Zionism serves as the basis for the Jewish self-definition of a majority of the Jewish population of Israel just as Conservative Judaism serves a majority of the Jewish population in the United States.

As a branch, or expression, of Judaism, Zionism has its own rituals and symbols, which have become part of the civil religion of Israel. Like other religious movements, Zionism in its first stages was messianic; its proponents expected it would achieve a rapid success which would in turn bring about the full achievement of its goals, namely, the redemption of the Jewish People in its own Land through political means. In fact, Zionism did capture a major share of the

Jewish People as its adherents and established a central place for itself among modern Jewish institutions. It did succeed in creating a Jewish State and transforming the Jewish People in the process, but, as in the case of every other religious movement, its messianic expectations were not realized.

Humanity, including the Jewish segment, is not yet redeemed, nor, apparently, is it ready for redemption. Zionism has entered the next stage in the development of religious movements, in which its proponents argue that the achievement of its immediate goals is only a prelude to the achievement of its ultimate messianic goals; further, that the movement is needed in both its ideological and institutional forms to pursue those ultimate goals eventually. Every great religion or equivalent movement has gone through the same process and has ultimately made the same claims. This does not invalidate the claims of Zionism by any means, but it does put the argument of contemporary Zionist theorists in proper perspective.

Zionism and Jewish Thought

Once we understand Zionism as another branch of Judaism, rather than as an all-encompassing revolutionary movement or a strictly organizational phenomenon, its present condition and needs can be clarified.

The revival of Zionist concern in the past decade has given rise to a new generation of Zionist thinkers and ideologists whose work is now beginning to capture the attention of the Jewish People. Such ideologists, probably without exception Israelis, have taken it upon themselves to grapple with these problems. The flowering of Jewish thought in the Diaspora, particularly in the United States, while clearly influenced fundamentally by the existence of Israel and concerned with coming to grips with that existence, cannot be considered part of the Zionist enterprise in any proper sense of the term.

Thinkers and thought do not spring out of a vacuum but are somehow related to larger human movements. Zionism as a significant movement does not exist in the Diaspora, despite the existence of Zionist organizations and the full panoply of Zionist politics. There are in the United States and Canada few Jews whose identification is purely Zionist. Thus Zionism cannot produce thinkers in those climes. That remains the province of Israel, where Zionism is the largest branch of Judaism.

The North American Diaspora will probably go down in history as an extremely creative one despite all its problems. By and large, North American Jewish thinkers start from theological rather than from political premises. The reverse is true in the case of Zionist thought. Yet just as Zionist thought moves from politics to the concerns of theology—if not to theology itself—so, too, does contemporary non-Zionist thought move from theology to politics. That is because of the particular character of the Jewish People as a theological-political phenomenon.

In my study of the American Jewish response to the Yom Kippur War, I suggested that the present generation of Jews has reversed the dictum of Y.L. Gordon, and become Jews in the street at a time when they have virtually ceased to be Jews in their homes.[3] In other words, for contemporary Jews who are concerned about their Jewish existence but who are too assimilated to have maintained a Jewish rhythm in their daily lives, their Jewish expression increasingly takes a political form. This is a response to the changed circumstances generated by the reestablishment of an independent Jewish commonwealth in the Land of Israel. It is the open and overt restoration of the political dimension of Jewish life precisely when religious and *halakhic* dimensions are on the decline.

Classic Divisions

In essence, the rebirth of Jewish political independence has brought with it a rebirth of the classic partisan division within the Jewish People, associated with Jewish statehood. That division found its classic expression in the Hasmonean state in the existence of Sadducees, Pharisees and Essenes; but in fact it can be traced back to the division that appeared in the First Commonwealth, with the rise of the Davidic monarchy, between supporters of the Davidic House, supporters of the prophetic tradition of Elijah, and Kenites or Rechabites.[4] Today the religious camp carries on the Pharisaic tradition, which for some eighteen hundred years emphasized the *halakhic* dimensions in Jewish life, and, through the *halakhah* had dominant if not exclusive

3. "The United States," in *The Yom Kippur War: Israel and the Jewish People*, Moshe Davis, ed. (New York, 1974), p. 286. Since this essay represents my cumulative thinking on the subject, I have taken the liberty of citing other articles of mine which treat aspects of it in greater depth.

4. For an elaboration of this thesis, see my "Community and State in Israel," prepared for the 1976 Summer Seminar of the Institute for Judaism and Contemporary Thought.

control over the Jewish People. The other two camps together represent a revival of the Sadducean approach to Jewish life, one which emphasized the political dimension as the basis for Jewish unity. To enlarge the picture, we can see in the kibbutz movement a current expression of the old Jewish instinct for messianic expression, through communal living, expressed in the past by the Kenites and the Essenes.

From our present perspective Zionism may be seen as the first step toward the revival of a Sadducean dimension in Jewish life. One reason for its great success was that such a dimension was exactly what was needed at the time, given the breakdown of Jewish religious belief and observance on the one hand, and the problem of Jewish physical survival on the other. While those Jews, including many Zionists, who seek a monistic Judaism or a Jewish People committed to a single ideology may be appalled by the existence of the three parties, in many respects it represents the true normalization of the Jewish People; not in the way that certain Zionist theorists sought Jewish normalization, namely, to make the Jews "like all the nations," but in the sense that a diversity of approaches to Jewish existence has been normal to Judaism in every period of full Jewish national existence. How then do we use that normalization to foster a proper Jewish existence in the Zionist spirit?

Towards a Renewed Zionist Vision

In understanding the reemergence of Sadducees (and, to a lesser extent, Essenes), and the way in which the normalcy they create differs from the normalization sought by Zionist theory, we can understand what must be done if Zionism is to meet the challenges of contemporary Jewish life in Israel and the Diaspora. Zionism as it is presently constituted—as a branch of Judaism particularly suitable for Israelis who have ceased to be Pharisees—has little to say directly to the Jews of the Diaspora.

We have already commented on the great difference that exists between Israel and the English-speaking diaspora with regard to the quest for ideologies. If anything, the Israeli man in the street has also become unideological, or is becoming so. While this may make it easier for him to communicate with his Diaspora Jewish counterpart on an inter-personal basis, it certainly does not make it easier for ideological Zionism to reach out to the Diaspora.

Finally, and perhaps most important because it is so fundamental, the underlying sense of negation of the Diaspora, which is basic to Israeli Zionism, clashes with the underlying sense of Israel as a haven, which is the basis of the Diaspora pro-Israel view. Much as these two approaches may be hidden on both sides in trying to accomplish day-to-day tasks and strengthening the unity of the Jewish People, they remain very real indeed. Fortunately, Jews, despite their tendency to fragmentation on matters of opinion, particularly regarding messianic elements, are notably good at federating with one another to accomplish perceived common goals.

Zionism can be restored as a positive factor in Jewish life only through the development of a new basic theory that will clearly link it with Judaism, not only de facto as at present, but de jure as well.

The Problematics of Zionist Theory

With a few exceptions, classical Zionist theory suffers from some very real deficiencies, stemming from the fact that it arose in the late nineteenth century out of a particular milieu of that period. It suffers additionally from the fact that it was primarily a polemic against assimilation, designed to restore political awareness to Jews; but it had little to say about political life once a Jewish political self-consciousness existed. Both of these deficiencies make it difficult today to build upon classical Zionist theory. We need a true political theory, not a nationalistic polemic, and it must be a theory that accords with Jewish tradition in the broadest meaning of the term.

Classical Zionist theory is permeated with late nineteenth-century romantic nationalism, based upon biological analogies, utopian expectations, and socialist slogans derived from the then current applications of Darwin, Marx, and other revolutionary theorists. Both the premises of those theories and the expectations they generated have become dissipated in the course of the twentieth century. However, it is important to recall that the same reasons which have since made those theories obsolete were those which made them so effective as political polemics at the time.

In the era of Emancipation, Jews had lost even that sense of the political character of the Jewish People which had been preserved within the framework of halakhic Judaism until the modern era. As a result, a major dimension of Jewish life had been abandoned, and the Jewish People itself was threatened with disintegration in the face of one attractive universalism or another. The first task of Zionist theory was to convince doubting Jews that there was a political dimension to Jewish life in the first place, and to stimulate them to desire the creation of Jewish polity. For that reason alone, it would have been incumbent upon Zionist theorists to speak in the political language current then. In fact, they were products of their environment and, as such, believed in the validity of the theories they espoused.

Now that we have a Jewish State and have reawakened a sense of the political dimension of Jewish life, even among Jews of the Diaspora, Zionist theory must address itself to questions relating to the character of Jewish polity and the power relationships within it. Since its primary purpose is no longer polemical, its primary product need not be, and indeed should not be, ideological. At the same time, it must contribute to the development of a new, or renewed, Jewish vision.

Both those seeking ideology and those rejecting it agree that there is today a crisis of Jewish vision, of which the crisis in Zionism is only one part. It is worth recalling that vision (*hazon*) is an older concept than ideology and more characteristically Jewish. It is significant that there is still no Hebrew word for ideology other than *idiologia*. From biblical times Jews have recognized the importance of having a proper vision. At the same time, traditional Jews have tended to reject ideology and other ideational systems that offer themselves as complete formulas for arranging thought, perhaps because they smack of idolatry, of seeking to place something other than *yir'at shamayim* (fear of Heaven, piety) at the center of human concern.

A proper Jewish vision requires a consensus built around shared questions and commitments rather than shared doctrines. Jews always have been better at wrestling with common questions than in finding common answers, but it is the fact of wrestling that has created Jewish solidarity. I would dare to suggest some of the central dimensions of the questions and commitments around which we must build this consensus and this vision.

Kinship and Consent

The Jewish People is a product of both kinship and consent.[5] The Torah tells us that we are both *am* and *edah*. As I understand the

---

5. See "Kinship and Consent in the Jewish Community: Patterns of Continuity in Jewish Communal Life," *Tradition*, vol. 14, no. 4 (Fall, 1974).

technical meaning of those two terms, *am* (people) implies a relation-ship established by kinship; *edah* literally refers to the political rela-tionship which is established as a result of consenting to the Covenant. Between the exodus from Egypt and receiving the Covenant at Sinai, the Bible tells us, a family of tribes was transformed into both an *am* and an *edah*. The combination of *am ve'edah* persisted unbroken down the years until the modern era, when, under the impact of emancipation, the Jews first ceased to be a coherent *edah*, and shortly thereafter began to lose their sense of kinship.

The Zionist revolution restored the sense of kinship to a very substantial segment of the Jewish People. Today there is a widespread sense of kinship upon which can be built a new sense of political consent. Consent, too, is a much older concept. One is reminded by Leo Strauss's distinction between ancient and modern liberalism that a similar distinction exists between ancient and modern consent. Ancient consent involved *consentio*, like thinking within a tradition. Modern consent involves agreeing to think alike, to think together. Nevertheless, the continuity of consent is at least as important as the continuity of tradition. To gain that continuity, it is necessary to restore the links between Zionism and Judaism.

Here we are faced with a problem that goes back to the roots of Zionism itself. As a revolutionary movement, Zionism had to break away from the continuity of Jewish history to a certain extent. The Jewish People, whose history had been dominated for so many centu-ries by the Pharisaic tradition, was faced with a major crisis as tradi-tion broke down in the wake of emancipation. Without some other galvanizing force of revolutionary dimensions, the Jewish People faced continued assimilation and erosion. Yet, in order to create such a new force, the existing tradition had to be vigorously assaulted.

At the same time, with the exception of a few extremists, the Zionist Movement did not seek to abandon its Jewish past but tried to transform the Jewish future radically. For example, it devoted consid-erable effort to absorbing certain Jewish traditions by reinterpreting them. We now know the end result of these efforts in cultural and moral terms: two generations of Jews have grown up in the Land of Israel, many cut off from knowledge of 3,000 years of Jewish tradition. They possess in its place a kind of Zionist-Israeli civil religion which focuses on a reinterpreted Jewish calendar and makes use of many traditional symbols; but this has led to a growing separation of large numbers of Israelis from their Jewish roots. As a result we have what

Dan Segre refers to as the Israeli colonial mentality, namely, the continued effort to imitate the perceived ways of the West, without having the Jewish authenticity which can provide a solid foundation for the development of an indigenous culture.[6]

It is ironic that the faith of the Fathers still may be the only vehicle through which non-religious Israelis will be able to develop that authenticity, but Zionism as it exists today is suffering from the problem of discontinuity. The original Zionists were Jewishly authentic because most of them came out of Jewishly authentic environments. Thus their revolution against those environments, no matter how extreme, could not damage their own Jewish authenticity. But although the generations they produced may be far less hostile to the same Jewish traditions against which their fathers revolted, they lack their fathers' authenticity. Thus Israel as a Zionist polity can only become authentic in its own right if it becomes Jewishly authentic first. It is a hopeful sign that many of the sons and grandsons of the fathers are desperately searching for that authenticity today.

An Operative Vision

The Pharisaic tradition offers one way of reaching out for Jewish authenticity. It is not yet clear whether this also applies to the Sadducean or Essenian traditions. One thing is clear, however: neither the Sadducean nor Essenian traditions of the past were secular in the way that the mainstream of the Zionist revolution sought to be secular. All three streams had as their starting point *yir'at shamayim.* Any Jewish commitment that does not account for the religious dimension would be less than adequate.

I should like to suggest some lines of departure, or paths to be followed if a new Jewish vision is to be forged. First, there must be a renewed sense of the Jewish Covenant (*brith*). For Jews this Covenant lies at the basis of our very existence. It sets forth the dimensions of the consent which originally transformed the family of the tribes into a people. Further, it continually transforms simple kinship into pursuit

6. In common parlance this is referred to as Levantinism. Jews from the Western Diaspora who have become reasonably well-rooted in their own Diaspora environments, notice this Israeli problem very quickly. While they, too, are often cut off from their roots, they have adapted to cultures which are rooted because they live as a minority within those cultures. Israelis, on the other hand, seek to borrow from another culture without having any model close at hand to determine what is for them authentic and what is not.

of a commonly agreed vision.[7] In Jewish tradition the Covenant has many dimensions. It informs every aspect of Jewish existence, creating the special psychology of Jews, who see themselves inevitably as *bnai brith*, equal partners in relation to one another, and with Heaven, in confronting the task of redemption. Because of this psychology Jews only act within a framework of agreeable consent.

In another dimension, the Covenant reaffirms the sense of Jewish uniqueness which Jews constantly encounter and which is already a major premise of the Bible. The Zionist revolution, along with its other goals, sought to eliminate Jewish uniqueness and to normalize the Jewish People. In the wake of events since 1967, there are few who have not come to recognize that normalization continues to be denied us. New Zionist theory must be developed to account for this uniqueness even in our own State. Jewish uniqueness includes a certain sociological uniqueness, too, something which social scientists ignore in their search for general laws of human behavior. Accounting for that uniqueness is as important for understanding the true condition of humanity as many scholars have thought explaining away Jewish uniqueness is for normalizing the Jews.

Leading out from the concept of *brith* is a second path, *hesed*, or the loving sense of obligation which true partners must share with one another and which is created by covenantal ties. *Hesed* involves the loving obligation of Jews toward one another and toward the Jewish People as a whole. In the Bible, we are taught that *hesed* is the dynamic dimension of *brith*, the relationship which flows from the covenantal partnership by which all Jews become *hasidim* toward one another. All Jews must relate to one another as *hasidim* or their *brith* is reduced to a narrow legalism. *Hesed* in the Zionist dimension of the Jewish vision is concerned with the survival and unity of the Jewish People, a survival and unity that is always in doubt, but at the same time is never doubted.

The loving obligation of Jews to one another as *hasidim* is linked with their obligation to Heaven. Thus a third path is their constant necessity, as Jews, to wrestle with God. The biblical origins of the word *Yisrael* in the story of Jacob refer precisely to that task. Thus the religious dimension of life for Jews is not a matter of finding some

7. I have elaborated on this in my paper, "Covenant as the Basis of the Jewish Political Tradition," prepared for the conference on "The Jewish Political Tradition and its Contemporary Uses," sponsored by the Institute for Judaism and Contemporary Thought in July 1975.

orthodoxy but of wrestling with God in the proper way. In an age of secularism and doubt, all Jews may not agree on the outcome of the struggle, but all must engage in it.

It is in considering Israel as engaged in a process, as well as pursuing survival as an entity, that *brith* and *hesed* attain full meaning. The daring Jewish notion embodied in the biblical *brith*, which presents God as limiting Himself by binding Himself in partnership with human beings, stands at the basis of all human freedom, not simply of Jewish existence. The Covenant raises humanity to the level of partnership with Heaven; even if humans are junior partners, they still have the freedom, as partners, to choose and consent. Any system of Jewish thought must wrestle with this responsibility.

The responsibility of freedom leads to the fourth and fifth paths, *tzedek u-mishpat* (justice and law), which oblige all Jews to strive for the creation of a just society. The task of creating *mishtar shel tzedek u-mishpat* (a regime of justice and law) in the Land of Israel and in every Jewish community is a continuing one. It is the way of Judaism that the fulfilment of this task can only take place within the framework of society, or more correctly, within a polity. This is where Zionism should add much to a new Jewish vision.

The creation of a fully just society, the Jewish vision suggests, is possible only in the messianic age. The Zionist vision, in common with all modern visions, held that the messianic age could be attained by human effort alone. Traditional Judaism has always seen human effort as a prerequisite for the coming of the Messiah, but the final attainment of the messianic age necessitates the intervention of the Almighty in response to that effort. Here, too, the covenantal dimension is apparent. As partners in the enterprise, the first steps in the task have been entrusted to humans, but since God is a partner, He, too, must participate, and at the appropriate time. The experiences of the twentieth century have taught us to be properly skeptical of human efforts to "bring the end" unaided. Zionist thought must be revised accordingly.

The Jewish vision demands fulfilment in a total political and social setting which, in our times, only a state can provide. Thus the successful management of a Jewish state is the major test of the validity of Judaism today. That is why Zionism has become the triumphant renewed vision for the Jewish People in our time. Stated in its most negative formulation, Israel is the only State we have or are likely to have. Therefore it is the focus of our vision. As in the case of any other experiment based upon a vision, it is not at all certain that the Jewish State will succeed, but without trying to make it succeed, we are not complete as Jews.

The perception of Israel's place in the Jewish vision does not rule out other important expressions of Jewish life in our time, such as the attempt to create a Jewish life, combining *brith*, *hesed Yisrael*, *tzedek* and *mishpat* on a voluntary basis, within the framework of a more universally oriented society. This is manifest in the effort to build a Jewish life in the United States and other free societies. In my opinion, only in messianic times will the question of Israel and Diaspora be finally settled. In the interim, in a world constantly growing more interdependent, both experiments are important to the Jewish People, even if the first should give us far more latitude to be authentically Jewish. Hence we confront two noble experiments from which consenting contemporary Jews choose more or less freely today. Yet with all differences between ancient and modern consent, the preferred answer for contemporary Jews must ultimately be the same as it was for traditional Jews.

Jewish Political Tradition

Zionism can function as the basis for the operative vision of the Jewish People only if its limits, as well as its possibilities, are appreciated. Since its focus is primarily on the political dimension of Jewish life, Zionism should seek to shape all branches of Judaism without attempting to be a substitute for the religious dimension. In that connection, Zionists today have a special obligation to work to recover the Jewish political tradition. I refer explicitly to a political *tradition*, not an *ideology*.

The Jewish national revival of our times led first to the restoration of Jewish political consciousness, then to the reestablishment of the Jewish polity. The next step in the process is the rediscovery of the Jewish political tradition. I would suggest that there is indeed such a tradition with all that it implies in the way of a continuing dialogue regarding practical or acceptable modes of political behavior, institutional forms and cultural norms. To suggest that there is a Jewish political tradition is not to suggest that there is a single uniform monolithic "Jewish way of politics." A tradition by its very nature is multi-faceted, even dialectic in character. Like a river, it has currents within it that are united because they are within the same banks, and in the long run flow in the same direction. A tradition is a continuing dialogue based upon a shared set of fundamental questions. For Jews, this dialogue began with the emergence of the Jewish People as a body politic. It has continued ever since.

In many respects Jewish political tradition has been most enduringly influenced by the Bible. While all of Jewish tradition has been filtered through the Talmud, the efforts of the rabbis after the Bar Kochba revolt to diminish the political tradition in the wake of the disastrous Roman wars (itself a political act of the first magnitude), meant that the Talmud was less informed by the political dimension. Indeed, with the revival of explicit political inquiry in the Middle Ages, Jewish thinkers and leaders, who otherwise relied on the Talmud, reverted to biblical sources for ideas regarding proper political behavior and institution-building. Centuries later, we find a much fainter echo of that process in the way that Zionists sought to base their quest for Jewish statehood in the Land of Israel on biblical sources. While Jews have been unconcerned with their political tradition as such since the Pharisees triumphed over the Sadducees, it is a tradition that continues to live in the way Jews behave politically—even in the way the State of Israel is shaped politically—even when Jews are unaware that they are living by, and within, that tradition.

Zionism and the American Experience

Needless to say, such a Zionism is Israel-centered by its very nature. What, then, of the Diaspora's role in this endeavor? For American Jews, at least, there is a role to be played.

If we can agree that the Jewish vision needs redevelopment today and that, at a time when we have a Jewish State again, its successful governance requires that it be linked to the Jewish political tradition, it may be that the American experience can offer much to help in this redevelopment. A certain curiosity, not to say irony, may be noted here. American thought (not necessarily American Jewish thought) is in many respects closer to biblical thought in its character than is the nineteenth century European thought out of which the ideologies of the Zionist Movement emerged and grew. That is because the founders of the United States drew much of their inspiration from Jewish sources (primarily, but not exclusively, biblical).[8] Many of the Puritans studied Talmud, Midrash and Kabbalah at a

8. See my article, "American Political Theory and Political Notions of American Jews: Convergences and Contradictions," *Jewish Journal of Sociology*, vol. IX, no. 1 (June 1967).

time when "progressive" Jews were abandoning those sources to find inspiration in what they perceived to be more relevant currents of modern secular thought. That is one of the reasons why Americans have never sought to express their vision through ideologies, but rather have emphasized the existence of an "American political tradition" and "American way of life." It is no accident that Abraham Lincoln referred to the Americans as "the almost-chosen people."

In some respects, American Jews have been as unaware of this biblical dimension of the American vision as Jews elsewhere, but more and more of them are discovering it now. This is one way in which American Jews may be able to make a signal contribution to the development of new Zionist thought.

An Approach to a New Emphasis

Israel Finestein

If the object of Zionism was the achievement of Jewish statehood, it has gained its purpose and is now at an end. This definition is by no means a caricature of a certain familiar outlook on Zionism. It lies behind many a policy and a slogan. The implications tend to inhibit argument. After all, it cannot be denied that the State was the product of the Zionist Movement. The creation of the Jewish State was the primary requisite of the Program enunciated in 1897 at the First Zionist Congress.

This definition of the purpose of Zionism, taken at face value, may all too easily be productive of tabloid thinking. It carries with it logical consequences that are hardly consistent with a reexamination, still less a reformulation, of Zionist objectives. These objectives attained, the rest is post-history. This is, however, an excessively simplistic approach to so ancient a concept as Zionism. The State is machinery, an indispensable device, a medium. The Jewish People denotes more than the State. The latter has its own imperative requirements as a sovereign entity, but does not imply the Jewish People as a whole.

The above definition of the aim of Zionism also involves the danger that the required degree of cultural mutuality between the State of Israel and the Jewish People may be obscured. That mutuality is a continuous process. The definition under review does not even merit the description of being anachronistic, since it was never the sole impelling force behind the ideology of Zionism. One can readily appreciate how, on given occasions and at critical periods, it could well have been deemed an impelling force for immediate ends. But Zionism is deeper than a reaction to crisis and tragedy.

The creation of a justly established, publicly recognized, and secure Jewish National Home was a vital ingredient of Zionism. This object required, in theory and in practice, that the national home should take the form of a Jewish State. Further, as a sovereign state, Israel has an inherent self-justifying claim upon the loyalty of her citizens. Israel is a democracy, where due process of law obtains, and it possesses vigorous and effective representative institutions. Israel has a developing life of its own. Its extraordinary amalgam of peoples and their problems reinforces the natural desire to let its inner life develop in its own way.

But the State of Israel is no ordinary state. It was too long in the making—a millenium and more—for it to be so; or for it to aspire to become so, quickly. Zionism involves a consideration of the relationship between the State of Israel and the Jewish People. It is a process for ensuring, as far as practicable, the recognizable and distinctive survival of Jews in the Diaspora, as well as for ensuring the distinctiveness of Jews in the State. Zionism is concerned with the relationship of the State to recognizably Jewish values. In essence, Zionism is concerned with Jewish self-consciousness. It goes beyond politics: it is related to identity, survival, and purpose.

To equate Zionism with *aliyah* narrows Zionism. This is by no means intended to derogate from the standing either of *aliyah* or its motivation. Not all Diaspora communities have regarded themselves as exilic in the original sense of that term. In numbers, Jewish achievement, the will to survive Jewishly, and deep-rootedness, they represent legitimate forms of Jewish life which are as much part of the Jewish People as the State itself. Their local allegiances and attachments are not superficial, nor is their concern for their Jewish future. Whatever may be said about their Jewish survival capacity in the modern world, there has occurred an historic upsurge of Jewish interest, study, and commitment among Diaspora communities. Many factors have proved conducive to this phenomenon, including the rebirth of the State of Israel. A formulation of Zionism which fails to take account of it, with its accompanying schemes and hopes for widening and intensifying Jewish consciousness, would amount to a grave misreading of the age.

The aims of Zionism are older than Herzl: the necessary reformulation is, in a sense, a return to premises and aspirations which preceded him. Herzl's brand of Zionism was political; his vision was Hebraic in a peculiarly limited sense. He propounded a political solution to a political problem, which he designated a national question. True, it was a national question in a special sense. He applied his mind to interactions between majorities and minorities. He saw the

Jews as everywhere an unassimilable minority, open to abuse; and when their numbers reached a particular proportion, he devised his radical solution for their homelessness. However, the national question, in terms of the inner life and the Hebraic tradition of the Jewish People, was, and is, an issue of a different kind.

Preeminent in Herzl's school of Zionism was the painful question of *wohin?* (whither?) when the majority declared "enough," or "keep out," or "go." His was a basic kind of auto-emancipation. Whatever else may be said for it—and much can be said—it barely touched on issues relating to the inner Jewish life, which, even by Herzl's time, had long been thrust upon the Jews.

One can detect an ideological affinity between Herzl's Zionism and that of Arthur Koestler, strange as it may appear. Both see in Zionism a means for presenting the Jews with stark alternatives: go to the Zionist State or allow yourselves in due course to perish Jewishly, for the fates are against survival anywhere else. There are, of course, sharp differences between Herzl and Koestler. The former may in his early days have advocated mass baptism as a radical method of relieving the Jews and Europe of the Jewish problem. But no such notions clouded his mind in maturity. Mr. Koestler sees no purpose in Jewish survival, except within the State, now that it is a reality; and even then, in little more than a political sense. He virtually proposes a cult of disappearance. Yet a comparison, however uncongenial, could possibly be made between these two figures. An ideological affinity springs from their dissociation, for whatever reasons, from the springs of Jewish life. Each was driven to see the politics, framework, technicalities, as the kernel of a solution. They have little to say about the heritage from which Zionism itself arose. Each in his own way repudiates the Diaspora in the interests of a formula which ideologically runs the risk of causing the Jewish People to cease being Jewish. Such are the pitfalls of political formulations.

At the heart of Pinsker's doctrine of auto-emancipation was the need to preserve distinctive Jewishness. The debate on the meaning of that word is interminable: it is linked with the Jewish past. It is related to the quality of the Jewish contribution to human life and thought; it belongs to that which gives Jews dignity, self-esteem, and the power to withstand. Pinsker's message was that the Jew is entitled, indeed obliged, to attempt to preserve his individual and group identity. Moreover, identity was bound up with the history of his people. According to Pinsker's postulation, a Jewish state would not and could not be an end in itself. Its wider purpose would be to increase and sustain the self-awareness of the Jews—culturally, intellectually, and morally.

A new and more profound implication must now be attached to auto-emancipation. That is to say, it is essential to perceive the importance of cultivating Jewish distinctiveness other than in political terms. The phrase "political terms" includes fund raising for Israel causes, political lobbying for Israel's policies, and engaging in the somewhat curious activity of Israel-modelled Zionist party politics in the Diaspora. Ironically, the very success of the Zionist Movement would jeopardize Jewish effort if it were to be channelled mainly into such causes.

With Jewish emancipation in the nineteenth century, there was a danger that Jews as Jews would gradually disappear within their respective environments. A great deal of Jewish history in that epoch deals with attempts to create bulwarks against such erosion. Excessive politization of Jewish life could now threaten Jews with a different kind of erosion—erosion of the consciousness and attachment to those very factors of Jewish experience which supplied and nourished the matrix from which Zionism itself grew.

Jews, given the opportunity to enter the Western world as emancipated citizens, were immediately faced with questions which were both ideological and practical. How were they to ward off the engulfing tide of assimilation? Was it obligatory, or desirable, to do so? If indeed it was, on what grounds? What was the role of Judaism in answering these questions? Without Judaism, what was the rationale for individual and collective Jewish survival?

Overshadowing such questions, or it might be more apposite to say underlying them, was the unperceived relationship between all these topics and the messianic and restorationist elements in Jewish tradition. Emancipation raised issues and prospects hardly envisaged in the long Jewish experience. These issues have not been stilled by the establishment of the State of Israel. Indeed, it has brought them into sharp focus, and, to a certain extent, enhanced their urgency.

To treat Jewish life everywhere outside Israel as a kind of temporary phase, however extended, before certain dissolution, or as some sort of expatriate anomaly, or as an outhouse species of Israeli culture, would be to fly in the face of history contrary to present actuality. Zionism must take into account that there are long-established communities in the Diaspora which expect to remain, and which regard themselves as destined to remain, in whatever numbers, as Jewish collectivities bound up with their Gentile environments.

The Program enunciated in Jerusalem in 1968 at the 27th Zionist Congress did well to acknowledge the continuing need to preserve and strengthen Jewish identity the world over. In this recognition, the Congress was in the mainstream of Zionist thinking. There have been positive signs that it is being followed up. But not even that affirmation caught the heightened nuance of present requirements. Statehood and its internal and external realities are one thing. The needs of the day go beyond any incidental attribute of Zionism and, in the modern world, are at the core of the movement. Zionism has to come to terms with Diaspora realities. That is the extent of the change, and it must be stated explicitly.

Obviously these themes cannot be detached from our philosophy of Jewish history. If we contemplate the future on the premise that all the streams of Jewish history have been and are in a state of confluence towards a center, that view at once controls and conditions the approach to any prospective reformulation of Zionism. That theory will not be analyzed here in any detail. Suffice it to say that it may equally well be the case that a central and creative feature of Jewish history has been the state of tension—a continuing process of action and reaction—between the fact of an inward-looking *klal Yisrael* (Jewish community as a whole) on the one hand and the fact and idea of dispersion on the other.

Jewish life demands high ideals, even though these may impose a heavy burden. The world has ill requited the Jewish performance. But at the end of all discussion, the fact of outstanding pressures is not adequate reason, intellectually or even emotionally for retaining and developing Jewish distinctiveness. There must be more wholesome, rational and consistent groundwork for so universal a Jewish phenomenon. We have become what Jewish history has made us. We have become invested with a high self-consciousness of Jewish identity and Jewish achievement. In the maintenance thereof, the centrality and potential of the State of Israel are acknowledged by the whole world. But in the nature of things there must be reciprocity. The Jewish People in all its diversity of culture and aspiration is an independent entity.

The appeal of Zionism was a moral and highly cultivated one, and remains so, as long as it is true to itself. The movement was nurtured in Jewish tradition and was not ashamed to declare its roots in ancient prophecy. We may perhaps understand why Ahad Ha-Am's misunderstood idea of a spiritual center was all too readily regarded as capable of detracting from the practical work of state-building. But there is nothing in Ahad Ha-Am which decries the importance of that work. His concern was that such work be pursued, but in a context that was wider than political.

The center, even if it were to be in the form of an independent sovereign state, would still have its wider purposes to serve. And Ahad Ha-Am defined those purposes in terms of the regeneration of the disparate elements of the Diaspora. Any reformulation of Zionism must have direct relevance to the present age.

Zionism in the International Arena

Annie Kriegel

In this paper, I wish to dwell on two sets of considerations: those which, in my opinion, have already become established, and those which still deserve careful elaboration. Let me deal first with those that are no longer the subject of controversy or conflicting views, but are established facts to be transmitted to the younger generation deliberately, as befit established facts in the realm of historical knowledge. Such facts should not only be transmitted to the younger generation but should serve as a basis for analysis.

The Zionist Project

Two groups of facts, it seems to me, were established unequivocally. The first group should be considered not as ideology or culture (vague and dubious terms), but as *logic*, for instance, the Zionist project which has prevailed, and will prevail in the foreseeable future, over all previous projects and logics conceived and tested by Jews since the eighteenth century. The traditional society of the Western world adopted a modern outlook after the Age of Enlightenment and the French Revolution. The Jewish People, established as a minority in Europe, was preoccupied by disturbances taking place in Europe from the seventeenth century through the nineteenth. During the latter century the Jews sought to develop several emancipation projects, generating a competition which led to a process of natural selection. Ultimately the Jewish People chose a single course, thus recording in history and reality its will to survive.

The fact that Zionism finally triumphed after a hundred and fifty years of theoretical polemics and zealous activity does not mean that it was necessarily intrinsically the most just, but rather that the forces it set in motion, and existing circumstances, proved to be the most favorable and propitious. Neither does this mean that Zionism, once triumphant, eliminated all other competitive projects. On the contrary, it absorbed many elements of other projects. In this context I should like to stress the universal aspect of the process. Jews followed the modernist trend because such a process inspires and serves as the basis of solidarity between Jews and all other human groups, who, like the Jews, defied attempts to exclude them from the mainstream of history. I refer to the proletariat—women, youth, Blacks, Arabs, colonized and oppressed people, and other minorities.

The four main characteristics of the Zionist project, or logic, that prevailed over all the others (such as traditionalism, liberal or socialist assimilationism, cultural autonomy) are the following:

1. The *scene* for the survival of a modern group does not lie in the spiritual, cultural, or religious domain, or in the economic or social field. It must be anchored in the political domain, where creative and protective attributes are the signs of modernism. Zionism is a polity, as are practically all other new logics which inspired the great achievements of the last two centuries.

2. The *level* at which the survival possibilities of a modern human group lie is not that of the individual, but of the group or community. Liberal emancipation on the individual level constitutes a prerequisite for the emergence of leaders open to modernism, science, and democracy. Total emancipation, however, cannot be attained except on group level.

3. Today, the *institutional form* which the emancipated community prefers is that of the nation-state. The state offers the group maximum chances of survival. With its institutions, the state guarantees the tools for survival: territorial possessions, a language, a society structured upon its offices and institutions. Yet the state *is* law, which is the rationale of the state. Thus it is easy to understand that a people created and nurtured by law would be so readily inclined to accept the institutions of a state—an organized society governed by law. As soon as the national state was adopted by the Jews, therefore, it ceased to represent the narrow sector of Jews in Western Europe and America; it became the institutional emblem of modernism throughout the world.

4. The *tool* with which one can create the foundations of such a national state is a movement, which is the product of an encounter between logic and popular expectation, triggering off action and energy. This movement must have established institutions and responsible bodies which presage the forthcoming state. Its first assignment is to

achieve the difficult task of "the European exodus," the shift of populations, the uprooting and resettling in a new environment, where everything must be created afresh. I refer to *aliyah*. The first group, in which it is possible to recognize old disputes, old differences, old paradoxes and divisions mingled together includes:

Individual emancipation	Collective emancipation
faith	law
eschatology	history
politics	culture
ideology	practice

The Jewish Code

Now I come to the second group of facts: the centrality of Israel in the system represented by Zionism on the international scene. This centrality is, in fact, a direct corollary of the success of the Zionist project, the project to establish a national state. Of the many ways to define this centrality, I consider the most apt to be that Israel is not only the most stable and endowed with the highest degree of historical initiative, but above all that it provides the *code* on which Judaism and Jews throughout the world base their identity.

The formula is simple: henceforth Jews will "recognize" themselves in Israel. In the sense that Hegel gave to the term "recognition," Israel is the necessary mirror which enables the Jewish People to exist as one People and every Jew to look upon himself as a Jew. Consequently, the distinction between anti-Semitism and anti-Zionism is becoming more and more obsolete. True, anti-Semitism seems to belong more to the past, and to the Right, whereas anti-Zionism belongs more to the contemporary scene and to the Left; but there are transitory attributes of analysis that exist because of a rather belated awareness of the present situation of Judaism.

Let us consider the Jewish community of France as an example. The phenomenal success of the "Rassemblement" ("12 hours for Israel" rally) at the Porte de Versailles, which attracted one hundred thousand persons, did not come about because it was a festival and that people love festivals, nor was it due to the fact that it is easier to identify with Israel for twelve hours than for twelve years. To the astonishment of Jews and non-Jews alike, the meeting was a success for two reasons: on the one hand, it showed that the Jewish community, despite its historic, cultural, social, and geographical divergencies, was exceptionally *unified*. In France, where one Jewish group within the community passionately argues with the other, especially over the twofold criterion of the duration of settlement in France and the purity of the French language, the Jewish community suddenly found itself united as never before. This unity is so remarkable that today one may expect, not a "Jewish vote," in the American sense (such a vote does not conform to the traditions and forms of French political life, where neither side offers any absolute guarantees—a prerequisite for any collective commitment by a community), but it is possible to define, on the political level, those preoccupations common to all the Jews of France. Thus, should an important event occur in French politics, legitimate political passions that might shake the French electorate would not endanger the unity of the Jewish community.

The other aspect of the "Rassemblement" stresses that we could expect complete unity among the Jews of France in the affirmation of their Jewishness on the simple basis of Israel. This is all the more surprising in a country where political Jacobinism tends to give preference to the individual over the sub-national group or community, where liberal emancipation has gained such a preeminent place: one hundred thousand individuals took the trouble to gather and affirm their Jewishness. The Jewish community of France is united because it is coherent, and its coherence stems from Israel. This phenomenon is not uniquely French; it is also in evidence in Italy. A remarkable thesis was recently presented at the Sorbonne by a young German sociologist on the Jewish community of Florence. Its conclusions were quite clear: Israel has substituted for religious practice, as the factor of identification, unity, and coherence, of the ancient Florentine Jewish community.

The New Situation

Herzl distinguished himself from all other Zionists by suggesting that the uniqueness of the Jewish People could best be safeguarded if it were endowed with the type of institution which was becoming the most universal and common at the time, namely the national state. On the international stage there are national states, joint international institutions, regional systems, and—very pertinent in our case—trans-national forms, pertaining to populations not necessarily of the same territory, but rather in the ethnic, spiritual, or religious sense. In this category we may include the Catholic Church, the Arab League, world Communism, and Zionism. Its importance lies in the fact that in this way, Zionism is linked to the general and the universal without being severed from Judaism. This would expose the false claims made against us by young supporters of universal projects in the Diaspora. It is the irony of history that projects that aggressively start out as universal become narrowly sectarian and particularistic at a later stage, whereas a project like Zionism, which never claimed to be other than distinctive and particular, has become universal and world-wide.

This attitude to the universal explains how, in comparing the issues which dominated the recent conference of European Communist parties in East Berlin, Vatican II in Rome, or the Arab League meetings at Rabat and elsewhere, one can rediscover interests on the external and internal levels, common to trans-national players, interests similar to ours. This category of players is characterized by the fact that they are composed of two elements: a national and a non-national element; in the case of Zionism, Israel and the Diaspora. In actual fact—and to offset our tendency to self-pity—it should be stated that Zionism has two advantages over other actors in this category: on the one hand, the state level is unique, and must remain so. Zionism is not faced with the difficulty that makes management of the Communist parties or the Arab League so complicated, namely, tensions among the various states that constitute these bodies. Moreover, in Zionism the center and periphery are clearly distinguishable, whereas in all other movements, there is disagreement as to the need for a center.

Second, once Zionism is defined as belonging to the trans-national category, it becomes obvious that the outstanding problems are similar to others in the same category. To begin with, a *modus operandi* must be established between the national and non-national elements. This working relation may be analyzed as the relation between the center and the periphery. In our case the need of a center and its character are not under discussion—the State of Israel is the center.

On the other hand, discussion may, and should, arise over three points:

1. the durable and non-durable nature of coexistence between

the national and the non-national elements, in other words, the continuation of the present situation in which Zionism is based on the
State of Israel and on the Diaspora;

    2. mutual relations between the State of Israel and the Diaspo-
ra, thus ensuring a two-way exchange of resources;

    3. finally, unilateral exchanges between the two components,
Israel and the Diaspora, from the periphery toward the center.

    Discussion of the above three points seems to me indispensable
if we are to define terms of reference.

    The working relation between the components of contempo-
rary Zionism may also be analyzed from the viewpoint of relations
between an element which is inherently national and one which is
not. In this connection, I should like to indicate one aspect: the Diaspora, as the non-national element, can play an important—perhaps
even indispensable—role in mitigating severe hardships which, in the
life of a state, are the price of efficiency. Every state is in some way
oppressive, bureaucratic, parochial, hostile to any heterodoxy. Such
faults are even more pronounced when a state has heavy defense bur-
dens. Thus, in the case of Zionism, the Diaspora may protect Israeli
society vis-à-vis the State.

Aliyah Potential

Finally, the working relations between the two components of Zionism may be analyzed from the viewpoint of *aliyah* and its place in
Israeli life. Added to its traditional task of increasing the population of
Israel (populating the State was a corollary and a consequence of the
Zionist project of founding a state), *aliyah* may have another task. The
traditional objective of augmenting the population is not urgent, since
this may be effected by natural growth. The new objective of *aliyah*
could set in motion a dynamic and original process through which
Israel is accepted as part of the world, through which Israel and the
nations are in a state of mutual recognition. *Aliyah* would offer Israel a
solution to the problem facing every state: the way in which it can
adapt itself to the rest of the world.

    One must also consider *aliyah* from the viewpoint of the Dias-
pora. Israel continues to serve its traditional purpose of providing a
sanctuary for persecuted Jews, as in the case of Soviet Jews, who
believe they cannot live a Jewish life in the Soviet Union. *Aliyah*
offers Diaspora Jews the inalienable right to decision, which arises

from national sovereignty. Certain decisions may be taken after mutual deliberations and consultations between the two components of the Zionist Movement—the State and the Diaspora. But some of the most important decisions for the survival of the Jewish People are, obviously, only within the competence of the citizens of Israel. Those who wish to share in the totality of decision-making pertaining to the destiny of the Jewish People, cannot remain outside the State.

I would like to express here my negative attitude to a formula which has been frequently used. I object to the formula, "Israel, the Jew of nations," first of all because it implicitly denies the Zionist achievement. In the light of this formula, Zionism has attained nothing else but to transfer Jewish oppression from the individual to group level. That is not true. I further object to this formula because it is biased and encourages a tendency among young Jews in the Diaspora—a fascination with oppression. Jewish youths who have known persecution from hearsay alone, dream of achieving, through this persecution, solidarity with all the other persecuted groups. But the Jew is no longer the Wandering Jew. It is wrong to hanker after oppression, because today it may be overcome. Jews know what it is to be oppressed. Jewish youth, desirous of inventing something new, must direct their thoughts toward attaining liberty and dignity.

Prospects for Post-Holocaust Zionism

David Polish

When the Jewish State was restored, it achieved, *de facto*, the political objectives of Zionism, as defined by the Basle Program: "a publicly and legally assured home in Palestine." Thus theoretically, Zionism as a relevant political idea became problematic. Conversely, while the claim to Jewish statehood had been ratified by the United Nations, that claim continues to be challenged in many places. But since the challenge is now resisted by the entire Jewish People, the need for a Zionist movement becomes equally problematic. Before the reestablishment of Jewish statehood, the distinction between Zionism, non-Zionism, and anti-Zionism could be easily defined. Zionists wanted a Jewish State, anti-Zionists opposed it, and non-Zionists (as well as some anti-Zionists) were willing to help support depoliticized Jewish settlement in Palestine. Today most Jews are committed to Jewish statehood. The "non-Zionist" may support statehood, but will not come on *aliyah*. According to one definition, nearly all Jews living outside Israel are Zionists, but if *aliyah* is the criterion, then Jews who reject *aliyah* for themselves are not Zionists. In the first case, either Zionism has indeed "captured the communities," or the term "Zionism" has been reduced to irrelevance through universal adoption. In the second case, the term has become illegitimate, as Ben Gurion argued.

I am not suggesting the dissolution of Zionism, but on the contrary, the need for a reformulation of Zionist ideology and goals in the light of historical events. Only in this way can it survive. Zionist Orthodoxy could render the movement archaic. Renovated Zionism would be in the tradition of all political movements which undergo change once their initial objectives are fulfilled, once they discover that there is no such achievement as final fulfilment, that unexpected contingencies and dangers are born out of consummation. The American, French, and Russian revolutions remind us of both the inner and external struggles that had to be waged for survival.

This principle applies equally to the development of Zionism, especially since the Holocaust. Classical political Zionism contemplated the withering away of the Diaspora, either through the inner dynamics of assimilation, or through categorically denying the Diaspora's validity. In either case, the objective of statehood was the elimination of the anomalous Diaspora. It would give survivalist Jews the opportunity to live authentically in their own Land, and assimilationists in the Diaspora the opportunity to disappear as Jews. As will be shown, contemporary Zionism is no longer irrevocably committed to that idea. European history invalidated the thesis of Israel as a sustaining cultural center for the Diaspora. A spiritual center cannot nourish its dependents indefinitely. It is a form of colonialism which requires either that the colonists go home some day or else impels them to "go native" and break away from the homeland. There is no escape, even in spiritual Zionism, from the eventual alternative of returning, or assimilating.

Was Ahad Ha-Am contemplating an indefinite center-diaspora relationship, or was he thinking, more realistically, of replenishing the Diaspora so that it would qualify for eventual transference to the homeland? I believe that the latter makes more sense, both in terms of Ahad Ha-Am's own position and in terms of the impossibility of a continuing relationship between an elite minority and an inferior majority. Spiritual Zionism is untenable because, above everything else, it is predicated on the absence of a relationship of equals; hence it is colonialism. Obversely, it is equally colonialist from the perspective of the rich and powerful majority confronting the weak minority which is constantly in need of help. In terms of history, spiritual Zionism has even less validity in a post-Holocaust world where we lament the Jewish People's failure to provide a haven for countless victims, whether they were spiritually ready or not for *aliyah*. Pre-Holocaust spiritual Zionism was based on a modicum of trust (misplaced even then) in European Jewry's host nations. Clearly, for our time, even more than for pre-Holocaust Jewry, spiritual Zionism alone is untenable.

On the basis of differing premises, political Zionism did not and spiritual-colonial Zionism could not have supported too sanguine a hope for the viability of the Diaspora. These contrasting premises require an approach toward a renewal of Zionism. We begin with the assumption that if it can be convincingly demonstrated that the Diaspora has no future, then Zionism has no future, and the priorities of the Diaspora should be reordered. We should then devote ourselves to transferring to Israel in planned fashion those of our resources that we can feasibly confer upon it. This we are not prepared to do.

Diaspora (read American) Jewry faces the paradoxical condition of being devoted to Israel and at the same time insisting on its own survival capability. Such a paradox could not have been supported under classical political Zionism. But the American, if he is a Zionist, is beset by concern that he is living in the *galut*. The non-Zionist entertains no such doubts. The Zionist is torn by the conflict between his conviction that the American experience is historically different and his apprehensions, bolstered periodically by grim fact, that the unprecedented defenses against the *galut* may prove to be all too vulnerable. A Zionist, whatever his motives for not emigrating to Israel—confidence in the future, guilt, belief that he aids Israel best from Chicago or New York—is at times, haunted by apprehension of the *galut*. There has always been a hierarchy of *galuyot*, from the most degrading to the most sublime, as there is today from the Soviet Union to the United States.

The American Zionist believes in the strength and life-expectancy of the *galut*, but there is no guarantee that he can beat the actuarial tables. This is what was communicated with difficulty, but with some success, to Israelis during the Twenty-Ninth Zionist Congress (1978) where Americans and Israelis debated whether the Diaspora should be acknowledged as viable. Most Israelis believed that American Zionists were waging a battle for their claim to vitality and durability. I consider that as long as American Jewry is viable, it should not be undermined by fruitless prophecies of doom. It serves no purpose to falsify the nature of the struggle, at the center of which is massive assimilation, a kind of internal, silent Holocaust. But it likewise serves no purpose to obliterate many signs of Jewish renewal, much of which is derivative from Israel's own renewal. At this time, a gratuitous negative verdict could be disastrous to American Jewry and to Israel. Both urgently need one another.

The issue of *shelilat ha-golah* (negation of the Diaspora) is not merely an academic exercise but a mischievous one. If spiritual Zionism did not reckon with the Holocaust, neither did classical political Zionism, which regarded the end of the Diaspora with enthusiasm. But Israel, standing alone in this post-Holocaust age, would not be a liberated but an isolated state, reduced to what its adversaries, in their ultimate strategy, have long envisioned. Yet, at the Congress, it was clear that a substantial number of Israelis are still locked into the *she-lilat ha-golah* syndrome. It is therefore all the more significant that with surprisingly little debate, the Congress endorsed the following statement at its first business session: "The continuity of Jewish life in the Diaspora is a reality and Zionism seeks to strengthen Jewish life and self-realization. Dynamic Jewish communities in the Diaspora, committed to Zionist ideals and emotionally tied to Eretz Israel, help to insure the survival of Israel and of the Jewish People . . . Zionism aims at a democratic, egalitarian and pluralistic society in which all of its citizens will enjoy equal rights. Zionism expects that every Jewish community throughout the world will give expression to Jewish heritage, values, and ideals." This marks a radical departure from previous Zionist thought. In fact, it marks an end to the heresy that the Diaspora deserves to live. It puts an official quietus on *shelilat ha-golah*. That statement could contain the nucleus of a reformulated Zionist perspective. It acknowledges that there is a strong Diaspora and it acknowledges that it has a right to exist. I believe that the Congress dealt with this resolution out of the same pragmatic considerations which prompt American Zionists to insist on the viability of American Jewry—that to do otherwise would be to invite adversity. To reject viability is to prophesy and to hasten disintegration, which for Israel as well as American Jewry must be opposed as vigorously as possible.

There are derivatives of this position, more far-reaching than may be contemplated or presently conceded. One is that the *galut* plays a critical role in the survival of the People and the State. Another is that the People, not the State, is the ultimate goal of Statehood. The order of words in the first statement of the Jerusalem Program is not fortuitous: "The unity of the Jewish People and the centrality of Israel in Jewish life . . ."

The third derivative is that an alternative to mutual dependency as presently obtains, or to colonialism as implicit in spiritual Zionism, is authentic collaboration for as long as collaboration can be sustained. This is far more demanding on the State than the term suggests. It does not mean assistance alone, but assistance as the product of consultation. That projection brings us to examination of another heresy: the Diaspora should have a voice in Israel's internal affairs. This heresy has been fought on the grounds that Jews outside of Israel lack the qualifications to have such a voice, that they may only give support and intercede on behalf of Israel. The first argument against this new heresy is that there are indeed limited non-political areas, such as fiscal, economic, and educational matters where Diaspora Jews do have the opportunity of consulting with Israelis. The reconstituted Jewish Agency is an example of common decision-making in these areas. The second argument is that Israel is a sovereign state and non-Israelis would be intruding in its internal political affairs and infringing on its sovereignty. Third, Israel alone must assume the obligation and consequences for its decisions, just as Israel's people incur the physical jeopardy of their decisions.

Responses to such arguments are based largely on radical changes in the Jewish world and in world affairs in general. The first contention can be dealt with most easily. The reconstituted Jewish Agency reflects some adaptation on the part of Israel to the concept that, unlike other sovereign powers, it lives in a special relation to its Diaspora Jews and does accord them certain prerogatives. What other national body in the world enters into such an intensive and continuing discourse with its own adherents in distant places on matters of fiscal policy, development, and education? This relationship is limited, however, and at times flawed by two factors. The first is that for its own reasons Israel has restricted the activity and role of its Diaspora constituents to non-political areas. From the opposite direction, professional fund raisers from the Diaspora often regard Israeli operations with disdain. Under such conditions, the best illustration we have of limited consultative relationship, however noteworthy, has reflected competition as much as collaboration. Besides, American Jewish bodies have generally served more as effective interpreters of Israeli positions than formulators of their own position. Perhaps this is as it should be, but then the best they can claim is that they are collaborative, not consultative.

Another contention concerning infringement on sovereignty does not adequately consider the unique condition of Israeli sovereignty which could become a paradigm in a changing world order. Sovereignty in principle and in reality, no longer is, if it ever was, an absolute. Without suggesting an analogy within Jewish life, we have seen examples, not of consultation alone but even of incursion upon the sovereignty of nations which has been accepted by a large segment of world opinion. This has applied whenever a rescue operation is involved, or in the outstanding example of Entebbe, and others.

Beyond this example, however, national entities are increasingly involved in sharing their sovereignty, though not surrendering it, to be sure. Even though the sharing is conditional, its existence is in itself significant. The NATO relationship comes to mind.

The Diaspora-Israel relationship cannot require equal sharing. This is presently true, yet not necessarily true for all time. Two arguments can be offered against this position which has had great merit until now. First, there is no doubt that American Jewry has enjoyed a privileged sanctuary since the founding of Israel, and in full awareness of this, has been reluctant to press its views on Israel. Yet it is becoming increasingly evident that Israel's struggle for security and the retention of its sovereignty will significantly affect the position and the condition of American Jewry. The Yom Kippur War, the racist resolution by the United Nations, and the period of tension between Israel and the United States, have shattered the serenity and immunity of American Jewry. The recrudescence of anti-Semitism in the United States is not only the undertow of events in the Middle East but is part of the effectively designed campaign for the American mind against Israel and its ally, American Jewry. Whatever the unpredictable future may hold, it is clear that the age of invulnerability for American Jews is over. Malignant anti-Semitism aside, the political strength of American Jewry has been successfully challenged (not only in Washington but in the Jewish abandonment of America's cities), and the implications of this fact are far-reaching. Thus its intimate bonds with Israel are imposing a growing price on American Jewry, and it does not exactly occupy a position of immunity.

The second rebuttal against the contention that American Jewry makes no real sacrifices on behalf of Israel flows from the new condition confronting Jews in the United States. While the rebuttal is largely speculative, it is rooted in prior conditions which legitimately point to the future. It will be remembered that in 1967 and in 1973 large numbers of American Jews volunteered for a wide range of civil service in Israel, including labor in kibbutzim and medical aid for military casualties. Admittedly, this did not constitute military duty, but it does point toward an aspect of Diaspora relationship to Israel that has not been adequately pursued, namely, periods of intensive "peace corps" activity in Israel by American Jews. Without reducing the urgent primacy of *aliyah*, the supplementary necessity of a growing peace corps, even should *aliyah* significantly increase, would not only respond to Israel's needs but would give living evidence of the physical as well as existential relationship of Diaspora Jews to Israel. As Kurt Lewin indicated, we are a People by virtue of a common fate and destiny. In addition, we are a People linked not only by intangible spiritual and ancestral bonds, but in the twentieth century we are linked by a global connection which gives our relationship to Israel a configuration never contemplated by classical Zionism. As Daniel Elazar has demonstrated, we are a world polity possessing those characteristics which normally define national bodies. It might be added that this, too, could become a paradigm for the emergence of other kinds of global polities which would not replace, but would coexist with, sovereign national entities.

The Jewish polity is a living, immutable demonstration that the State of Israel came into being through the efforts of *both* the *Yishuv* and the Jewish People. In large measure the State exists for the sake of the People as well as for its own sake. While there may not be another entity or relationship quite like that of Jewish People-State of Israel, it is a reality and its validity should be recognized structurally as well as conceptually. Since this entire entity, People-State, is engaged in a common struggle for survival, it would be an error to insist on total compartmentalization. I stress the word *total* because it must be recognized that there are areas where this principle cannot be applied— decisions of war, defense, and international relationships.

The proposal for a consultative relationship could be construed by some as an advocacy of dual loyalties. Aside from the fact that this charge already is advanced without benefit of consultative status, it should be met not by denial but by suggesting that dual loyalties are not to be equated with conflicting loyalties. The growing complexity of global relationship could see increasing signs of more pluralistic relationships. While nationalism becomes more intense on one level, it becomes more interconnected, often in apparently paradoxical configurations, on another level.

It is not within the province of this paper to outline the structure and methodology of the consultative process. It would, admittedly, be difficult, but within Jewish and Zionist history, this consideration should not in itself invalidate the attempt to outline such a process. What should be considered is that this proposal is being presented with growing conviction on the American scene and has adherents in Israel as well. The Task Force on Israel-American Jewish relations, initiated by the American Jewish Committee, has developed this concept in considerable detail. The platform of the American Reform Zionist Association, ARZA, has expressed similar advocacy.

Are the factors here presented sufficient to assure an identifiable Zionist presence on the Jewish scene, especially when bodies such as the non-Zionist American Jewish Committee advocate the principle of consultation? There is no way of knowing. Perhaps, except for structure, Zionism, even in its renewal, is destined to be absorbed by a Jewish community, bent on appropriating the Zionist idea. In that case, there still remains the Zionist principle that *galut* is *galut*.

Zionism as Ideology and Historical Force: A Current Evaluation

Nathan Rotenstreich

In many historical, social, and political movements, two components may be distinguished. First, there is the substantive component, constituted by the movement's *ideology*, which may embrace various ideas, trends, attachments to cultural legacies, utopian visions, and the like. Then we find what may be termed the *energizing component*. This consists of those socio-historical forces which absorb the ideological elements and give them a particular realization in a particular historical context.

This schematic distinction is helpful when we seek to evaluate the present meaning and role of Zionism. In what follows, we shall first sketch how Zionism originated as an ideology and became an historical force. Then we shall examine the extent to which it still embraces those two components today, in both the Diaspora and in Israel.

Sources of Zionist Ideology

Zionist ideology may be characterized in terms of the renascence of the Jewish People and culture, which manifested itself in the modern national Jewish movement, in the trend towards normalization of Jewish existence, in the shift from Messianism to modern historical aspirations, and so on. We must sift these general trends for the essentials which, in their combination or integration, created the *Gestalt* or profile of Zionism in its substantive aspects.

As a point of departure, let us indicate some features of traditional Jewish culture that pertain to the understanding of Zionism. In the first place, traditional Jewish culture involved a certain combination or synthesis between its *Weltanschauung* (articles of belief, codes

323

of behavior) and the subject or carrier of the latter (i.e., the Jewish People itself), since a view of the position of the Jewish People in the world was part and parcel of that *Weltanschauung*. Thus conceived, its position served to some extent as a barrier between Judaism and those universalist religions which regarded themselves as continuations of Judaism and negated the position of the Jewish People as the basic subject and carrier of the religion. Although an inherent paradox characterized the Judaic tradition, as a religion referring to the universe and its creator, and yet implying the special status of the Jewish People as a particular people, that paradox gave additional momentum to the particular relationship between the Jewish People and the Jewish religion philosophically and theologically.

It is significant that when Zionism arose, it too offered a certain fusion between a *Weltanschauung* and the Jewish People as the subject of that *Weltanschauung*. For this meant that the Jews could view a national awareness of a modern kind as a reinterpretation of the basic or primary position of the Jewish People in the Judaic context. Moreover, in the traditional Jewish outlook, the position of the people was not unconditionally related to factors operating in the present, such as continuity in space, a legal or linguistic framework, etc. Instead, its position was anchored in the religious obligations put before the whole people (not only before individuals). Zionism presented itself as a series of new obligations addressed to that same people. Thus, Zionism emerged against the background of Jewish tradition as a reformulation of trends and notions inherent in the tradition, and at the same time as an adjustment to the modern world and its conceptual texture and ideological aspirations, without misgivings about the validity of that adjustment as constituting in a sense—like every adjustment—a shift from one realm to another. On the contrary, Zionism could present itself as a synthesis between themes inherent in the Jewish tradition and emerging trends of the modern world.

Of the latter trends, the most important were the two aspects of the rise of national movements in Europe. Such movements either aimed at the political unification of divided peoples—like the Italians and Germans—or advocated independence for ethnic groups and peoples which formed parts of empires, such as the Austro-Hungarian. Zionism had to take both of these aspects a step further. The aspect of unification—let us recall Moses Hess' reference to that trend and achievement in Italy—was found to involve, if applied to the Jewish People, the unification of geographically scattered groups and not only an integration of adjoining cities and duchies. The aspect of independence, first applied to groups living within empires, was extended to become the notion of independence of a people scattered among other peoples or numerous political entities

The first substantive feature of Zionism may thus be seen as a certain continuity from the traditional position of the Jewish People in the Jewish religion to an interpretation of peoplehood in terms of modern nationalism. The second, complementary feature is a rather paradoxical continuity in terms of Jewish Messianism. On the one hand, Zionism is a continuation of Jewish efforts towards redemption through the ingathering of the Jewish People in the Land of Israel; on the other hand, Zionism *neutralizes* that redemptive aspect by shifting the endeavor from future eschatological expectations to present historical and empirical acts. By their very nature, these lack the eschatological dimension and lead to involvement and entanglement in the historical process.

In a sense, this shift from messianic eschatology to historical activity was more dramatic than the previously discussed shift from peoplehood as an addressee of revelation to peoplehood understood in national terms. The shift from Messianism to participation in history required a fundamental change in the traditional Judaic conception of time. This conception distinguished between the present age, which possessed merely interim status (although it had already lasted many centuries), and the age of the Messiah, when the Jewish People would at last return to playing an active role in history. By contrast, Zionism claimed that the opportunity for the Jews to reenter history was at hand, and that the time called for a new responsiveness.

The change required in the conception of time may also be formulated in other terms. Previously, only isolated historical events outside the Jewish realm had to be taken into account, for example, the willingness of a prince or duke, for various reasons, to offer the Jews asylum, or legislation based on what was known in the Middle Ages as "privileges." Zionism demanded that the Jews take into account not merely particular *events*, but also historical *processes*. Now time appeared as an historical context which has—or may have—characteristic features of its own and can set patterns for Jewish behavior, including Jewish independence in the national and political sense. This is so once the trend towards independence is conceived as historically, humanly, and universally valid, and as something demanding a corresponding manifestation in the Jewish People.

Consequently, while the line of continuity from peoplehood in the religious sense to peoplehood in the modern national sense is a question of emphasis, the line of continuity from messianic expectations to involvement in history is more than a shift in emphasis. It is a shift in orientation, even when those involved in it consider themselves as continuing the previous line. In both respects, i.e., in the reformulation of the position of the Jewish People as well as in the reformulation of redemption as independent existence in history, Zionism appears as a modern phenomenon with traditional roots.

Other Jewish Responses to Modernity

There were other Jewish responses to modernity. One of these was assimilation, in the sense that it was an attempt to bring about conformity between Jewish existence and the surrounding world in terms of citizenship, culture, loyalty, language, etc. Assimilation was an acknowledgment of the value of the surrounding modern world, as providing a factual or even an *a priori* legitimate replacement for the traditional Jewish environment.

Whatever assimilation's historical outcome (especially in Germany), we should try to understand its ideology. It was an attempt to maintain a separate Jewish existence on the basis of one of the traditional facets of that existence, namely religion, the significance of which was stressed on philosophical or theological grounds. Moreover, there was a correlation between the isolation of the religious factor from the total context of Jewish existence and the emphasis placed on its value. Such emphasis was motivated both by the sense of the substantive significance of Jewish religion and by a sociological reading of the situation, namely, that without adherence to Jewish religion, assimilation would bring about a total dissolution of Jewish existence. Assimilation as a modern trend must be seen, structurally speaking as an attempt to maintain a *separate element* of Jewish existence within the context of a constantly increasing *integration* of Jews into the surrounding culture.

A similar structural logic may be discerned in at least two other modern attempts to rebuild Jewish national existence. One of these was based upon the predominance of the Yiddish vernacular as a factor which reinforced Jewish collectivity. The other sought to establish territorial autonomy, to be achieved within the framework of existing states and safeguarded by state legislation and by an inner Jewish cohesiveness expressed in language, cultural activity, education, etc.

There is no need to go into detailed analysis of these attempts and the social movements which they created. From a structural point of view, their significance lies simply in their parallelism with assimilation in general, despite the fact that their objective cannot be defined as assimilation. Indeed, they were attempts to preserve Jewish collective existence in a visible form which would be *different* from Jewish beliefs and the congregational embodiment of those beliefs. But all these attempts, despite their substantive differences, were similar in the sense that they isolated from the totality or complexity of Jewish collective existence *one element* or mode of that existence. By isolating religion, language or cultural activity, they may be viewed as attempts to find a "last refuge" for Jewish collective existence.

In contrast to these attempts at isolating a single element, Zionism must be seen as an attempt to recreate a *collective* Jewish existence, composed of a variety of factors. Collective existence could not rely on a single factor. The geographical (or geometrical) manifestation of that collective existence would be a separation in space from existing states or societies, to be achieved through the establishment of a Jewish state or society. By definition, the latter would necessarily involve more than one factor: a territorial basis, a societal context, and the institutional framework of statehood and government.

Incidentally, it should be noted that Zionism could aspire only to what we might term an *integrated* collective life as opposed to an *harmonious* collective life, let alone an harmonious synthesis of the different components constituting collective existence. This is because Zionism did not merely involve the absorption of previously existing elements, but forced changes upon them. If Jewish religion, and even tradition (*halakhah*) was to become integrated in a broader context of collective life, the very shift from singularity to compositeness was bound to change the face of *halakhah*, or at least its locus. The same applies to the territorial aspect: the Land of Israel had been the Holy Land, bound up with historical associations, but it was now to be brought into everyday life and thus to alter its meaning by changing its function within the totality of the factors making up Jewish existence. So, too, the language, Hebrew, changed its character through the shift from written to spoken tongue, from a medium for only certain kinds of ideas, arguments and deliberations, to a medium of expression in the broadest sense of the term.

The lack of static equilibrium between the various elements combined in Zionism required a dynamic attempt at their integration. *Different* attempts to establish an equilibrium were what stimulated (again, structurally speaking) the development of different ideologies *within* Zionism.

The Energizing Component

At the beginning of our exploration, we distinguished between the substantive aspect of Zionism and its energizing force. Schematically, we may say that the energizing force lies within socio-historical circumstances which evoke certain reactions and responses. In Zionism the energizing component lay in a heightened awareness that Diaspora existence was not an ineradicable curse, a fate to which one had to submit, but rather a socio-historical condition which had been and might be altered by human actions. To be sure, the emphasis on human deeds endowed this reaction with modern meanings and thus enhanced the modern face of Zionism. Moreover, once the Diaspora was grasped as a socio-historical condition which admitted, or even called for, a socio-historical analysis, such an analysis was bound to be concrete. Its frame of reference was the concrete situation of the nineteenth and twentieth centuries.

This analysis led Zionists to understand the Diaspora as an inherently discriminatory situation or—in even sharper terms—as continually creating anti-Semitism, even if they granted that the sources of anti-Semitism lie in religious attitudes which predate the modern era. It followed that anti-Semitic discrimination could not possibly be overcome in a state which, like Czarist Russia, was not built on the rule of law (was not a *Rechtsstaat*); even in a state like Germany during its liberal period, which was built on the rule of law and granted legal rights to the Jews, those rights lacked a basis in the true feelings and attitudes of the non-Jewish majority. To use the famous distinction suggested by Marx in a different context, political emancipation, although it involved legal emancipation as well in this case, was not "human" emancipation. As long as a distinction was perceived between the Jews and the outside world, even a distinction diminished by the impact of the outside world on the Jews and preserved largely because of the Jews' own efforts to maintain their separateness, integration in the surrounding world was impossible. Thus Diaspora conditions would prevail, discrimination would endure, and no legal or political system could cover the real human condition pertaining to the Jewish situation. Insofar as the East-European Jews —obviously, this is again a schematic description—were concerned, the emerging factor lay in their refusal to believe that emancipation would come, whereas with Western Jews, i.e., in Austria and Germany, the characteristic impelling attitude was one not of disbelief but of disappointment.

The energizing factor in its two regional forms was a negative force. When allied with the new conceptions about the profile of Jewish existence (discussed earlier in this essay), it brought about modern Zionism and gave it its momentum as a major influence in the Jewish history of the last hundred years.

In rather different ways, the energizing factor may be seen in the work of two of the founders of Zionism: Herzl and Ahad Ha-Am. Herzl emphasized the clash between the Jews and the surrounding world. In his view, Jews had sought to strike roots in the world, but were being rejected by it. Against this view, Ahad Ha-Am emphasized that their environment was having a cultural and social impact on the Jews whether or not they sought it. The very presence of the Jews in the world, together with the shift from religious traditions to modern culture, had produced an impact of that world on the Jews, the corollary of which was a contraction of the Jewish substance or of what Ahad Ha-Am called the "national ego." Hence, attempted withdrawal from the surrounding world and efforts to preserve Jewish uniqueness were deliberate reactions on the part of the Jews.

We find a negative symmetry between Herzl and Ahad Ha-Am. What one saw as an objective factor, imposed by the surrounding world, the other saw in terms of a Jewish decision, and vice-versa. Where Herzl saw an objective factor of rejection, Ahad Ha-Am saw a Jewish factor of decision for autonomy. Where Herzl saw a factor of Jewish decision, namely, the attraction towards the world, Ahad Ha-Am saw a factor of objective impact, since the world at large sweeps the Jews along with it, whether they like it or not.

There were clashes between the trends represented by Herzl and Ahad Ha-Am; their views were regarded as conflicting. They were, as we may put it, two different interpretations of the energizing force of Zionism: that of rejection and that of contraction. Rejection served as a direct energizing force, impinging on the Jews as such, while contraction was an energizing force only within the context of adherence to Judaism. Historically and typologically the two views differed in basic emphasis, but retrospectively it may be said that they could coincide or coexist, and even reinforce each other. The impact of the modern world on the Jews persisted even when the modern world did not provide room for them, legally or politically, and discrimination against them was ever present. It may be apt to apply the statement of a great philosopher in referring to different philosophical systems and the polemics among them: they were right in their affirmations and wrong in their negations. Both rejection and contraction, either as separate forces or in combination, served as energizing factors for Zionism.

The Current Situation

The changes in the Jewish situation since World War II are so visible that there is no point in enlarging on them, although the full consequences of those changes are not as visible and even subject to controversy. For our analysis, the most notable change is in the energizing component of Zionism. For part of European Jewry, auto-emancipation offered a substitute or replacement for the political emancipation they could not hope to achieve. For the rest of European Jewry, auto-emancipation served as either a safeguard in case emancipation should fail, or as a realization of human and Jewish aspirations which converged in the notion of independence in a Jewish commonwealth, where the impact of Jewish culture would be promoted by escape from the duality vividly described by Buber in his *Drei Reden über das Judentum.*

The current Jewish situation in many parts of the world, especially in the United States, lacks a negative energizing force for Zionism. American Jews owe their legal, political, economic and cultural emancipation to the structure of the system to which they objectively belong. They may still have to struggle against defamation, but they do not have to struggle for emancipation. The constitution and dynamic processes of American society have provided the Jews with such a measure of equality, that to strive for equality does not have to become a focus of Jewish effort. In the other main Western countries the process was more complicated, but there, too, the situation of the Jews today approximates that of American Jewry.

Emancipation provides a framework for the dual existence of Jews who adhere to the surrounding culture, yet remain both objectively and in their own self-awareness, custodians of the vestiges of Jewish life. Already during the nineteenth century, Western Jewry did not really conceive of this duality as a predicament or dilemma to be resolved, or endangering Jewish culture, or increasingly transforming the living adherence to the Jewish tradition into a merely symbolic adherence. Duality was conceived as a challenge only to the extent that Western Zionists, mainly in Germany, absorbed Ahad Ha-Am's influence more than Herzl's. By contrast, American Jewry developed what can perhaps be described as a static and tacit acceptance of duality. This very acceptance and adjustment has removed the ground for the energizing impact which is a possible response to duality.

Even if American Jewry does not affirm the Diaspora explicitly, it does do so implicitly, and obviously, affirmation of any kind is not a source for energizing forces and their correlation with negative attitudes.

Instead, two attitudes at once distinct and overlapping have emerged in American Jewry, with the rest of Western Jewry, deliberately or not, following along the same path. One attitude is a sense of belonging to the Jewish People "at large," that is, to the Jewish People beyond the boundaries of any particular country. In this form ethnic awareness, while connoting a sort of distinctiveness, also implies a universalization of Jewish loyalty, an adherence to the Jewish People which, by definition, oversteps political boundaries. The second attitude is devotion to the State of Israel, financial and political support for the State, and concern for its fate. However, such belonging and devotion have not been transformed into energizing forces for substantial emigration to Israel, since they do not imply any doubt about Western Jewry's ability to survive.

In its classical period, Zionism attracted only certain groups within the Jewish People. It never became a focal point for all Jewish efforts, never made them converge into one major stream. Today, in a sense, it indeed is a general focus of Jewish energies, in view of the correlation which now exists between the feeling of belonging to the Jewish People and devotion to the State of Israel. Here, however, Zionism plays a role only in terms of its embodiment and fulfilment in the State of Israel. Thus the achievements of Zionism, as distinct from its ideology, have become a common denominator for the expression of Jewish sentiments. Moreover, this process has brought about the neutralization of both ideological analysis and ideological adherence and affirmation. We witness a de-ideologization of Jewish life, paralleled by a sentimentalization of Jewish belonging. At the same time, hesitations regarding support of Israel are often expressed by precisely those Western Jews who still have an ideological commitment of some sort.

At this juncture, an interesting contrast may be pointed out between the condition of Western Jewry and that of Soviet Jewry. Western Jewry does not perceive any existential clash in maintaining the duality mentioned above: its preservation of vestiges of Jewish life despite its adherence to the surrounding culture. Soviet Jewry, to the extent that it has become actively Jewish, does experience that duality as a clash, for two major reasons. In the first place, the Soviet system is explicitly ideologically loaded, while the system of the West may be presented and experienced as ideologically neutral, even when it has obvious philosophical groundings in the notions of freedom and equality. To experience such a cultural duality might be viewed in the West as part and parcel of the modern condition, whereas in the Eastern block experience of duality is part and parcel of a price one pays for the very citizenship one enjoys. In the second place, the West does not prosecute Jews for expressing loyalty to the Jewish People, whereas the Bolshevist East, being ideologically rigid and politically secluded, sees the universalization of Jewish loyalty as treason to the State and its ideology.

The character of the State of Israel being basically Western in its structure and orientation, reinforces Soviet suspicion of Jewish loyalty. Furthermore, the revival of Russian nationalism within the Soviet Union in recent decades has become an additional factor in the syndrome of the withdrawal of Soviet Jews from the surrounding world, in contrast to acceptance of duality characteristic of Western Jewry. Accordingly, while Western Jewry does not currently experience pressures which might stimulate changes, including emigration to Israel, Soviet Jewry is still affected, at least partially, by energizing factors of that kind.

Israel and Zionism Today

There are few cases in which the special causes of an historical or social phenomenon have provided the *raison d'être* and, therefore, the continuing profile of that phenomenon. One such case is the State of Israel and its meaning within the context of contemporary Zionism, which is very much related to the circumstances in which it was born.

The State of Israel came into existence, insofar as the internal Jewish context is concerned, through the aspirations (and eventually the decision] of the *Yishuv* in Mandatory Palestine for independence.

To this extent, it resembled the various other new states emerging after World War II. But the *Yishuv* viewed itself not merely as a national entity confined to its own boundaries, but also as the protagonist or pioneer of the Jewish People outside the prospective Jewish State. Conversely, the support which the *Yishuv* received from Jews everywhere was due particularly to the impact of the Holocaust and to Jewish—even Western Jewish—awareness, implicit or explicit, of the basic differences between a post-factum collective existence, a sort of congregational mode, and a political entity imbued with the attributes of territory, society and sovereignty.

The dynamics of the internal Jewish context were also matched by the response of the non-Jewish world after the Holocaust, in the sense that the non-Jewish world became more sympathetic to Jewish aspirations for the preservation of the Jewish entity through a collective mode of existence. On the borderline between the Jewish context and the non-Jewish response was a further significant feature, to some extent unique for utopian aspirations, namely, the realism characteristic of Zionism as a movement, the ability of its leaders to take advantage of opportunities which opened up in changing historical situations. It was this realism which led to their acceptance of partition: Jewish independence was to be territorially established in only part of the Land of Israel, while simultaneously Arab nationalism in its Palestinian manifestation would coexist alongside the Jewish independent entity.

Herzl had conceived of the Jewish State as the consummation of a rapid process of Jewish immigration. He saw statehood as epitomizing the end of the process, and certainly not as an instrument for promoting the very process itself. What eventually happened, however, was that the State of Israel came about in a situation where it immediately became a major instrument in attracting immigration and fostering it. Hence the notion of the Jewish State as an instrument, and not as an end, became not only a notion related to a scale of values, or what is called the continuum of means and ends, but took concrete shape within the context of Jewry after World War II. Besides becoming the focus for the sense of Jewish belonging and the embodiment of Jewish collectivity, the State also became the major tool in promoting the increase of its own Jewish population, in creating a Jewish society and concurrently manifesting its existence. The State of Israel became an objective for Jews elsewhere and a solidifying factor for Jews within its boundaries. The framework constituted by its institutions had to create a social basis for the society already existing within it, rather than the other way around.

This duality of instrument and symbol has also manifested itself in Israeli society's ambivalent self-consciousness in regard to Jewish history. Theoretically, a case can be made for regarding the State of Israel and Israeli society as a link in the chain of Jewish generations, all the more so because generations of Jews invested so much of their hopes and aspirations in the concept of the ingathering of the Jews in the Land of Israel. For Jews in the contemporary world, the State of Israel, both prior to and since its emergence, has been a continuation and embodiment of traditional Jewish aspirations. In practice, however, the very fact that the State of Israel is a sovereign and comprehensive Jewish entity—after so many centuries without there being one—accentuates the complementary aspect of its existence, namely, that it is not only a continuation of other forms of Jewish existence, but very much a new beginning.

Objectively speaking, Israeli society thus finds itself caught in the dilemma between continuity and innovation. It cannot easily resolve its problems by simply opting either for preserving continuity or for making a leap. The Zionist dimension of the State of Israel is bound to guide it in both directions. But the sense of a new beginning is less in need of guidance than the sense of continuity and affinity, since the new beginning as such is a momentum within the life horizon of the participants in Israeli society. Awareness of continuity, on the other hand, means seeking to interpret non-present factors in such a way as to make them present. Within the boundaries of Israeli society, therefore, the Zionist commitment should emphasize continuity. The sense of a new beginning largely takes care of itself by its very momentum.

This reflection leads us to a reformulation in terms of a third duality or dilemma, namely, between normality and uniqueness. The task of contemporary Zionism and the State of Israel is also to establish a new dynamic between these two components. In a way, it was easier to be a unique people whose life was shaped by Jewish religion and Jewish imperatives, when Jews lived on the margins of world history. The abnormality of their factual existence was reinforced by the character of the Jewish tradition, which not only entailed minute observance and detailed life-style, but was also a sublimation of the Jewish People's separate existence. The problem which Jewish culture now faces, given the State of Israel as a beginning, is how to be a unique people against a non-unique background, namely, against a background consisting of attributes of collective existence common to many other peoples, such as territorial basis, societal infrastructure, and government.

The problem can also be defined as maintaining a unique culture despite involvement in the general trends of historical life. For instance, the clash between the State of Israel and Arab nationalism is a clash within the modern historical process; it has little to do with the Jews' ancient past, but relates to their attempt to be an entity within the present, looking forward to the future and striving for their share in it. The vestiges of religious attitudes may reinforce that clash—and they actually do so—but somehow the relationship of cause to effect has changed: the present absorbs traces of the past, including religious tensions, but the past does not simply create the factors operating in the present.

Moreover, no historical entity may be viewed as one whose collective existence is safeguarded. The Jewish collective entity in particular, cannot be viewed as safeguarded though having entered into a relationship with historical factors which operate in the present, socially, culturally, politically or nationally. To be a partner in the historical process is to risk an encounter with dangerous historical forces, since it is a continual attempt to take advantage of those forces and direct them in accordance with the objectives of the particular historical entity.

There is more than historical irony and tragedy in the fact that Zionism today cannot appeal to Jews struggling for emancipation or to those who feel disappointed by it, that it lacks the negative energizing forces described earlier in our analysis. In the present situation, Zionism can be reformulated and reconstituted in only one way: that the attraction of a comprehensive Jewish collective existence become a positive energizing force operating on Jews outside the Jewish State, leading them beyond the realm of the emancipation which they enjoy and which they do not see as endangering their existence as Jews.

For European Jewry at the turn of the century, auto-emancipation served as emancipation attainable only through adding the "auto." For Western Jewry in the contemporary world, auto-emancipation cannot be plausibly presented as replacing the striving for emancipation, but only as a new stage of existence, *going beyond* emancipation and not just running parallel with it. Such a move from emancipation to auto-emancipation is by its very nature a process which lacks negative energizing forces. Instead, there are forces which may negate it. Therefore, the sentimental attachment of the Jews to the State of Israel in all its manifestations is not a helpful factor in this respect, since sentimental devotion and its practical expressions seem to Jews a legitimate substitute for that move from emancipation to auto-emancipation.

Can Zionism exist today outside broad and vague loyalty to the State of Israel? More specifically, can the attempt to maintain and enhance the State of Israel, as the only comprehensive mode of Jewish collective existence, become itself an energizing force for a renewed ingathering? There may be no historical parallels for positive energizing forces, but precisely here the unique situation of the Jewish People needs to manifest itself again. This is not to affirm that such a change must be possible; it is simply to locate the area in which it would have to occur.

Crisis and Challenge in Zionism

Avraham Schenker

It has been said that the Zionist idea has won out in Jewish life, but that the Zionist Organization is dead. Whether or not we carry the description of the current crisis in Zionism to such extreme formulation, it is clear that we are involved in a crisis of definition as well as of condition. Zionists—those affiliated with some part of the World Zionist Organization, or at least those who describe themselves as Zionists—are uncertain about the definition of that label. The Israeli finds something paradoxical, if not hypocritical, in anyone who calls himself a Zionist but does not come on *aliyah*, or does not consider *aliyah* as the essential option of Jewish life. The activist Jew in the Diaspora, wholly involved with Israel in various ways, cannot understand the difference between a member of the Zionist Organization who does not go on *aliyah*, or even consider *aliyah*, and himself, who is openly and positively supportive of Israel in every way. This is not only an ideological problem, which leads to debate, polemics, or reformulation. It is an existential problem which stems from the changing realities of Jewish life in today's world.

"Instant" Zionism

Let us take as our starting point the Six Day War and the Yom Kippur War. In seemingly contradictory fashion, both simultaneously revealed and concealed two central facts. On the one hand, the centrality of Israel in organized Jewish life came sharply to the fore, both in the euphoria following the victory of the Six Day War and in the profound concern following the victory-stalemate of the Yom Kippur War. What was called "instant" Zionism, involvement with the concerns of Israel by all organizational factors of Jewish life, is part of the phenomenon of the Jewish relationship to Israel in our time; so much so, that the president of a large non-Zionist organization declared emotionally that "we are all Zionists now." This relationship even led the Chairman of the World Zionist Organization to state that all Jews are Zionists today, except that some were ready to proclaim it and some, even though they were carrying out the duties of Zionism, were not ready to state it openly.

On the other hand, we should also recognize that these expressions of concern, sympathy, and involvement with Israel hide a growing sense of isolation, and the consequent unease of Jewish communities regarding their "vulnerability" within the society in which they live. The "Zionism-equals-racism" resolution adopted at the United Nations Assembly in November 1975 highlighted both the centrality of Israel and the sense of isolation of Jews and Jewish communities. The fact that anti-Zionism and anti-Semitism were increasingly identified in Jewish minds as having the same roots and reflecting an inseparable link, served to underline a process which had begun in the first decade after the establishment of the State of Israel and reached overt expression with the 1967 and 1973 wars.

The assumption that Zionism sought an answer to the problems of Jewish existence through the establishment of a state was clearly valid as an ideological-political conception. It was hoped that in their own state, the Jews would be the masters of their fate. Zionist ideologists assumed that the political state was the essential answer to the needs of the Jewish People; such a state would enable the Jewish People, collectively or individually, to "use" it as an instrument for solving the anomalies of Jewish existence in the Diaspora, whether of political, economic, social, or even psychological origin. They did not take into consideration the State itself and the dynamics stemming from its needs as a political entity, and in relationship with the Diaspora communities. The World Zionist Organization, Theodor Herzl's great contribution to the fulfilment of the Zionist idea, viewed the State as an instrument for Zionists to utilize or even "manipulate" in order to continue the process of dealing with the essential problems of the Jewish present and the Jewish future. Even the Zionist leaders who had settled in Israel long before the State was a reality and devoted themselves primarily to creating the structure and the infrastructure of the State-to-be, still viewed it as an instrument of the Jewish People dispersed in the Diaspora, not as the instrument of a sovereign state.

Israel-Diaspora Bond

When we come to the essential ambivalence of the Israeli-Diaspora relationship, which is at the root of the Zionist ideology, we are confronted with a contradiction, or a conflict of interests, between the needs of the State and the needs of the Jewish communities in the Diaspora. The State, particularly in its infancy, needed and demanded full support—political, financial, and emotional—in order to assure its survival and development. Jews throughout the world accepted this need willingly, and almost instinctively shifted the focus of their concerns to firmly establishing the State-community in terms which reflected the actions of any organized Jewish community within a hostile, or different, surrounding society. Those same Jewish communities which established schools, synagogues, hospitals, cemeteries, or welfare institutions as the instruments of community existence and self-definition, shifted their concerns to establishing settlements, universities, yeshivot, and hospitals in Israel.

In the major centers of the Western world, Jewish communites saw themselves as stronger and more secure than the infant State, surrounded by its enemies. But, just as the Six Day War and the Yom Kippur War simultaneously revealed and hid basic phenomena, so did the growing focus on Israel in the agenda of Jewish life reveal and hide basic problems which are the essence of the Zionist ideological crisis.

The key problem of Jewish life in our time, according to some, is Jewish identity. In an increasingly open and mobile world grappling with a weakening framework in which the accepted anchors of religion, community, and culture in their traditional forms are under constant attack, the problem of Jewish identity cannot fail to present a serious challenge to the Zionist Movement. Jewish tradition has always placed a high priority on education as the instrument of identity and continuity. But the failure of Jewish education in our time to prevent intermarriage, assimilation and gradual withdrawal from the community, puts the traditional approach in question. The problem which every member of the Zionist youth movement discussed in his small circle—"Are the Jews a nation, or a religion or a culture?"—remains applicable in our time as it was in the early part of the century. Then the Zionist Movement gave an unequivocal answer: "Jews are a nation, with all the consequences that follow from this axiom."

No less persistent is another question, which confronted those who were trying to break out of the contradictions of Jewish life in the early days of the Zionist Movement: should Jews adopt universalism or particularism, or, to put it in another form, the individual or collective solution or "escape" from, or within, the surrounding society? Here again the Zionist Movement was in no doubt: universalism is a dead end. While individuals may withdraw from the group, the collective entity cannot and will not be permitted to integrate into the larger society. For the universalists, the ultimate blow would come with the Holocaust.

Yet, we again become confronted with a contradiction. Just when Jewish faith, the Jewish community, even the Jewish family, were being weakened in the general process of social and political change, the State of Israel came into existence: it provided the substitute to anchor Jewish identity. In this sense Zionism takes on the aspects of a secular religion, a framework for the community, even a substitute for the family as the basis of self-identity. This is all too apparent when we consider the role of the Zionist youth movements and the women's organizations, as well as the focal place of fundraising agencies in the organized scheme of Jewish life.

Thus the centrality of Israel supplied a very real need of Diaspora Jewry by providing the anchor for Jewish identity. In this sense, the notion of a spiritual center for the Jewish People as projected by the Ahad Ha-Amist school was proven correct, even if in a rather distorted fashion. Ahad Ha-Am projected a spiritual and cultural center in Israel which would fructify and radiate on the entire Jewish world; instead, the growing centrality of Israel has become an enduring symbol of ambivalent Jewish identity (despite the debate on "Who is a Jew?").

A Changing World

The anomalies of Jewish life in the Diaspora are quite different from those that, at one time, were part of Jewish life in Eastern and Central Europe and generated the Zionist Movement. Then, we saw a Jewish mass, living under difficult economic and restrictive conditions. Today, particularly since World War II, we see Jewish communities almost everywhere enjoying rising economic wealth and status. In the old days, the Jew who broke out from narrow confines to acquire a university education was the exception rather than the rule.

Today, the exception is one who does not have a higher education. Formerly, we saw compact communities with centralized institutions. Today, we are confronted with a renewed dispersion even within the seeming concentration of Jews in urban centers. In the past, Jewish communities needed to establish and maintain Jewish institutions to serve their community needs. Today, these needs are increasingly met by governments at various levels.

Most decisive of all, perhaps, is the fact that in the early days of the Zionist idea, Jews were alienated from the mainstream. Today, Jews are more often among those who seek to preserve the *status quo* in a changing world which may threaten their new status. The shift to the Right in the socio-political spectrum, manifest in Jewish life during recent decades, is evidence of this change in the self-image of the Jew in society. True, social instability, political crisis or economic inflation affects the entire society without changing the essential marginality of Jewish life in almost all communities of the world. But the factors that brought about the formulation of Zionist ideology and the organization of the instrument for its implementation, are changed beyond recognition. These are the elements the Zionist Movement must consider if it is to remain a valid basis for the Jewish People in its relationship to the State of Israel and in the self-awareness of the Jewish State in its relationship to the Diaspora.

There can be no escape from defining the issue in its sharpest terms. Does the State of Israel, as it tries to meet its own essential needs, seek to organize the Jews as friends of Israel for the sake of their political, economic, and even psychological support; or, does the State recognize the needs of the Jewish People as expressed by the Zionist Movement and is it prepared to wage the ideological battle which is the essential basis for meeting those needs? In other words, is there a contradiction between the needs of Israel and the needs of the Jewish People? Are the needs of the Jewish People, in terms of its self-identity and collective continuity, met by organizing them to meet the needs of Israel? On the surface, the answer would seem to be affirmative. The broad sympathy and support for Israel, expressed in philanthropic terms, and to a lesser degree, through political action, is a real factor in maintaining a meaningful, organized Jewish community life in the Diaspora. Yet, we have been witness to persistent concern regarding certain processes in Diaspora communities. Immediately following the Yom Kippur War, an important research project, carried out in Jewish communities on the attitudes of Jews to Israel, revealed a growing polarization. Those who were already involved and committed became more involved and committed. Those who were apathetic moved further away from the organized Jewish community. The growth of assimilatory phenomena, such as intermarriage and non-affiliation with an organized Jewish group, or even the static and diminishing population statistics in the main Jewish centers as a result of a lower Jewish birthrate, are all evidences of deep crisis and the failure to meet the underlying needs of the Jewish People, the very basis of Zionist ideology.

Are we then in the midst of a profound contradiction which links Israel and the Diaspora so inextricably and, at the same time, prevents either from confronting its essential problems? The problem of the Diaspora is assimilation, while that of Israel is *aliyah*. These problems cannot be resolved unless we revert to a classical reformulation of Zionism in terms of the contemporary Jewish condition. By "classical," we mean an approach that is pessimistic about the long-term possibilities of collective Jewish national existence and creativity in the Diaspora. The pejorative "negation of the *golah*" distorted the historical situation. The establishment of the State of Israel in itself strengthened the Jewish consciousness of the Diaspora communities. As Israel increasingly became a component of Jewish self-definition in the Diaspora, it was possible to view the Jewish situation in more optimistic terms. But the fundamental processes of community breakdown, acculturation, assimilation, and technological macro-organization all operate against collective Jewish continuity. It is therefore likely that we are in a race between the short-term optimistic impact, stemming from the influence of the State of Israel, and the long-term pessimistic outlook which is the result of socio-political and economic developments.

Both elements are necessary to a modern reformulation of Zionist ideology. However, we must not make the mistake of balancing both elements equally: they are not comparable in substantive terms, to borrow Prof. Rotenstreich's definition in another context. Israel is still on the offensive in dealing with the problem of Jewish existence, whereas the Diaspora communities are on the defensive in dealing with their local problems. The vaunted interrelationship between Israel and the Diaspora is not a balanced one. The Diaspora is important and even necessary to Israel's self-definition. Israel is central and essential in the Diaspora's self-awareness.

The Israel Reality

Yet it would be a mistake to equate Israel and Zionism. The crisis of Zionism is a reflection of the crisis in Israeli society. There has been a diminution of the sense of national purpose. The Yom Kippur War succeeded in shattering the myth of Jewish superiority. The sense of collective national endeavor has been lessened by individualistic materialism. The creative momentum which brought about the unique achievements of the Zionist Movement—Zionist youth activities, land settlement, the Histadrut, Youth Aliyah—has slowed down very significantly.

The crisis of *aliyah* is reflected in the problem of those Jewish communities in distress which seek havens, but not in Israel. On the other hand, the slow, rather weak stream of *olim* from affluent Western countries to Israel cannot be separated from the impact of Israeli emigrés on Israeli society and on Jewish communities abroad. It would be wrong to see a cause and effect relationship between *yeridah* (emigration) and *aliyah*, but the ideological consequences of these phenomena cannot be ignored. While Zionism always had roots in a catastrophic view of society (anti-Semitism, political upheaval, economic marginality), its implementation was inseparable from idealistic vision.

The social struggle within Israel, the search for a quality of life which is less exploitative and more egalitarian, the key role of Jewish-Arab relations in determining the nature of Israeli society not only in the political sphere, but in the socio-economic relationship, the profound ambivalence of Israeli cultural creativity in search of a balance between the universal and the particular, between the Jewish past and the Jewish future—these are all part of Israeli reality. They are no less part of the Zionist vision. But are they indeed part of the Zionist reality?

There is also a crisis of Zionist organization manifest in the ambivalent attitude of the governments of Israel, past and present, regarding the form and structure of their relationship with the Diaspora. The state apparatus, functioning through its ministries and embassies, has not satisfactorily implemented the Charter (*Amanah*) which the Knesset gave the World Zionist Organization. When David Ben Gurion likened the Zionist Organization to a scaffolding, to be removed once the building (the State) is erected, he also meant that the

State would become the organizing instrument of Jewish national liberation, or Jewish self-emancipation, or even Diaspora Jewish continuity. While Israel's leadership has not followed Ben Gurion's approach, it has remained ambivalent in its attitude to the World Zionist Organization and to the Expanded Jewish Agency. The ambivalence also leads to a crisis of ideology.

Is Israel a Zionist State? The question is not rhetorical. In its relations with the Jews of the Diaspora, the State has clearly given priority to an approach which is pro-Israel rather than Zionist in its essence and practice. Representatives of Israel at the highest level have covered the face of the globe for Israel fund-raising campaigns and the sale of Israel Bonds rather than for the purpose of encouraging *aliyah* and Zionist affiliation. Is it any wonder, then, that the Jew of the Diaspora is confused about the meaning of Zionism?

The anti-Zionism resolution of the United Nations Assembly in November 1975 beclouded the issue, and even distorted it. Arab states sought to shift the conflict from the political to the ideological arena. By equating Zionism with racism the issue was shifted from the search for a political solution (whether imposed by force of through negotiation) to questioning the very basis for Israel's existence. Here the response of Jews throughout the world was instinctive and instructive. By wearing a badge which proclaimed "I am a Zionist," they expressed Jewish support for the survival of Israel. It was a great demonstration of the central position of the Zionist idea in modern Jewish history.

It also demonstrated, however, that the State of Israel was in danger and had to be protected and strengthened. It was not the Jewish continuity in the Diaspora, but the State of Israel which was put in question. Organized Jewish communities felt more identified and involved with Israel. In many cases, their sense of isolation was identified with Israel's blatant isolation in the community of nations. But the focus of their Zionism had shifted, subtly to be sure, from the survival and continuity of the Jewish People to the survival and continuity of Israel; or rather, the basic shift of Zionist ideology which came about with the establishment of the State of Israel was affirmed.

It is perhaps not accidental that the post-Yom Kippur War period has seen a revival of a neo-Bundist or "new Babylon" conception, especially among American Jews, and somewhat less within French Jewry.

Fundamentally, the situation of Diaspora Jewry in relation to the surrounding society and to itself has not changed: it has remained on the defensive. Yet its relationship to the centrality of Israel in terms of self-identity or self-awareness has not been lessened. Both approaches are essential components of Zionist ideology in our time.

The role of the State of Israel cannot be fulfilled in this fashion, however. It is the old-new ingredient in Zionist ideology. Pre-State, it was an aspiration, a vision, a hope—the longed-for instrument of national liberation and social change. Post-State, it is an evolving reality which must be measured against that aspiration, not for itself, but in terms of the Jewish People and its situation. This requires the patience of an historical outlook grounded in the Jewish reality. The Zionist Movement and the State of Israel cannot expect to achieve territorial concentration of the Jewish People through preachment or resolution. Yet it must determine its priorities in terms of the race between the optimistic present and the pessimistic future facing the Jewish Diaspora. The reformulation of Zionist ideology in classical terms means combining the need for Jewish identity in its modern implication with the goal of establishing a special society, seeking to express the universal need for social change in terms of the particular expression of the Jewish People.

Survival, Normalcy, Modernity

Isadore Twersky

Following William James who began his work *Varieties of Religious Experience* (chap. II), with a "circumscription of the topic," I may more modestly note at the outset that the following is a highly compressed personal statement, almost a soliloquy, touching upon three broad themes or central motifs which invariably are associated with discussions concerning Zionism: (1) crisis and survival; (2) history and normalcy; (3) tradition and modernity. The format, imposing inevitable constraints, necessitates a measure of selectivity as well as simplification, i.c., of direct statement unencumbered by scholarly documentation or digression. The subject in any event is so vital and so comprehensive, so suggestive and so resonant, that it would not be possible to cover everything even allusively. This is a genuine excuse for fragmentariness or choppiness.

Survival

Survival is the core and catalyst, the underlying conception and overriding objective of contemporary Judaism. Its closest competitor for this position of centrality is *crisis* and often the two are coupled. Historians and sociologists, pundits and prophets (self-styled), political leaders and fund raisers, all talk eloquently and alarmingly about crisis and survival, about the proliferating crisis which casts gloom over the prospects for survival. In this context, I should declare unequivocally, without any intention of being paradoxical or perverse, that while I am deeply conscious of crisis I am not really apprehensive about survival. Jewish survival *per se* is not a source of anxiety and perplexity for me. The reason for this apparent serenity is not insensitivity or indifference, not withdrawal or wistfulness, but unshakable conviction, unwavering faith, and a special historical consciousness nurtured by the record and realities of the Jewish past. Let Rabbi

347

Moses Maimonides, whose own life was punctuated by crisis and disintegration, subversion and suffering, speak to this issue *(Epistle to
Yemen)*:

> The divine assurance was given to Jacob our father that his descen-
> dants would survive the people who degraded and discomfited them as
> it is written: "And your seed shall be like the dust of the earth" (Gen.
> 28:14). That is to say, although his offspring will be abased like dust that
> is trodden under foot, they will ultimately emerge triumphant and vic-
> torious, and as the simile implies, just as the dust settles finally upon him
> who tramples upon it and remains after him, so shall Israel outlive its
> persecutors.
>
> The prophet Isaiah has long ago predicted that various peoples
> will succeed in vanquishing Israel and lording over them for some time.
> But that ultimately God will come to Israel's assistance and will put a
> stop to their woes and affliction as is suggested in the following verse:
> "A grievous vision is declared to me; the treacherous one will deal
> treacherously and the spoiler will spoil; Go up O Elam, besiege O
> Media! but ultimately the sighing thereof I shall make to cease" (Is. 21:2).
>
> We are in possession of the divine assurance that Israel is indes-
> tructible and imperishable, and will always continue to be a preeminent
> community. As it is impossible for God to cease to exist, so is Israel's
> destruction and disappearance from the world unthinkable, as we read,
> "For I the Lord change not, and you, O sons of Jacob, will not be
> consumed" (Mal. 3:6).[1]

Should you think for a moment that the Rambam is a prejudiced and therefore unreliable witness, should you look upon him as a
great, influential thinker who has been "brainwashed" by religious
ideas and is consequently incapable of calm reflection and realistic
dispassionate appraisal, let us briefly introduce another witness—a
total outsider who is the antithesis of Rambam in every sense. I refer
to Nicholas Berdyaev, the Russian religious philosopher who died in

---

1. Note the similar emphasis in a purely *halakic* context (Mishneh Torah, *'Issure Biah,*
xiv,4):

> They should say to him (the prospective convert) further, "Be it known to you
> that the world to come is treasured up solely for the righteous, who are Israel. As
> for what you see that Israel is in distress in this world, it is in reality a boon which
> is laid up for them, because it is not granted them to receive the abundance of
> good things in this world like other peoples, lest their hearts should wax haughty
> and they should go astray and squander the reward of the world to come, as it is
> said, 'But Jeshurun waxed fat and kicked' (Deut. 32:15)."
>
> "Nevertheless, the Holy One, blessed be He, does not bring upon them too
> many calamities, lest they should altogether perish. Rather, all the heathen shall
> cease to exist, while they shall endure."

exile from Soviet Russia in 1948 and in many respects may be viewed as a forerunner of the contemporary dissident movement; his little book *The Meaning of History* has been acclaimed as "the book for which modern Christian apologists have been waiting." Let him also speak to this issue:

> Their destiny is too imbued with the "metaphysical" to be explained either in material or positive-historical terms. Moreover, it presents no sign of that antithesis between the metaphysical and the historical, which I regard as an obstacle to the apprehension of the inner significance of history. I remember how the materialist interpretation of history, when I attempted in my youth to verify it by applying it to the destinies of peoples, broke down in the case of the Jews, where destiny seemed absolutely inexplicable from the materialistic standpoint. And, indeed, according to the materialistic and positivist criterion, this people ought long ago to have perished. Its survival is a mysterious and wonderful phenomenon demonstrating that the life of this people is governed by a special predetermination, transcending the processes of adaptation expounded by the materialistic interpretation of history. The survival of the Jews, their resistance to destruction, their endurance under absolutely peculiar conditions, and the fateful role played by them in history; all these point to the particular and mysterious foundations of their destiny.

The fact is, of course, that there is no need to adopt a metaphysical or mystical posture, a romanticizing or lyricizing mood, or, if one's commitment and *Anschauung* predispose him to it, there is not even need to operate with traditional covenantal premises, promises and predictions. One may operate with a hardheaded pragmatism and thoroughgoing empiricism, and still unreservedly endorse these judgments inasmuch as the turbulent and majestic saga of Jewish history authenticates the promises and validates the conclusions. The tenacity, resilience and creativity of the Jewish community through the ages, through all transmutations and convolutions, in the face of incessant trials and tragedies, are existential propositions—simple, incontrovertible facts. Demographic dispersion, political disintegration, economic dislocation, social alienation, psychological oppression, subtle as well as crude discrimination, theological indictment, and brute physical annihilation—all must be assessed from a special historical perspective variously described as purposive, providential, or messianic. No heroic adjectives and certainly not hackneyed epithets can capture the uniqueness and quintessence of this truly unparalleled record.

What is it, then, that generates so much anxiety and produces so much rhetoric, sometimes bordering on the neurotic, about the uncertainty of the future? Why is it that beneath the surface of our achievement and confidence there lurks a stubborn disquiet and a persistent, gnawing restlessness? If the answer to the question "Will Judaism survive?" is unequivocally affirmative—the pure empiricism provides a strong presumption for continuity while the divine promise is a firm guarantee—there still remains a worrisome, even awesome, question: "*mi yiḥyeh?*" who will survive? Will our children and grandchildren, our friends and neighbors, our cousins in all corners of the world— will we *all* survive as Jews, committed, concerned, creative? Herzl remarked: "Whole branches of Jewry may wither and fall away. The tree lives on." Who will be part of the eternal tree, the tree of life, and who, *ḥas ve-shalom* (God forbid!) will be the transient, decaying branch? Will we survive as a large, flourishing nation or a minute, fragile entity?

Here the answer is very equivocal and uncertain and therefore so terribly unsettling. Far from being escapist or complacent,[2] the confident awareness which was our premise, or point of departure, accentuates the apprehensiveness inasmuch as we dare not write off large segments of the Jewish People. I recognize ideological pluralism and social heterogeneity as facts of life, not necessarily as intrinsic values. Every individual is of concern to us; no effort should be spared to enlarge the group of survivors. Our destinies are somehow interwoven. *She'erit ha-peletah* (the surviving remnant) is a consolatory concept but it is not an ideology which one consciously and resignedly embraces *ab initio*. "The Torah is very solicitous for the lives of Israelites" (Rambam, Mishneh Torah, *Roseah u-Shemirat Nefesh*, xiii, 14) and this certainly means spiritual as well as biological. Everyone potentially should be included in that special group referred to as "among the remnant are those whom the Lord shall call" (Joel 3:5). The massive dimensions of assimilation and desertion, of religious and biological erosion, coming in the wake of the attempted Nazi

2. I am clearly not advocating quietism, passivity, misplaced Utopianism; as a matter of fact I take issue with the view that our religious tradition prescribes passivity while proscribing activism. This widespread assumption should be investigated dispassionately. Moreover, involvement with and concern for the totality of the people of Israel is a religious-historical mandate. "Kol yisrael 'arevim" (All Jews are responsible for each other) (*Sanhedrin*, 39b; see Maimonides, *Hilkot Mamrim* II, 4 and commentaries) is a firm directive for activism and harmony, for responsible action. It is only in relatively recent times that the passage in *Ketubot*, iiia (*shalosh shevuot*) has become an ideological crux.

genocide, are simply appalling. The various guises and expressions of anti-Semitism should not be glossed over or misconstrued. They must become catalysts for systematic reflection and introspection which make us move with zeal and determination on all fronts and respond vigorously to ever-changing stimuli. Crisis is enervating, conviction is energizing; the two must therefore interact and the latter must prevail.

In this context, obviously, the State of Israel has a unique role not only as the embodiment of the Zionist dream, as the incipient fulfilment of a fervent hope patiently nurtured through the ages, but as a unique symbol and source of solidarity, ideological identification and historical awareness, of renewed confidence and inspiration. The impact of Israel has already been immense and its centrality in Jewish life is virtually a *consensus omnium*. There is little *Jewish* opposition to Israel today; philanthropic identification, political admiration, religious motivation, nearly universal emotional and intellectual commitment—and above all the steady trickle of *aliyah*—are concurrently expressions and buoys of this centrality. Israel has both a visionary and a pragmatic thrust. However, the future of Israel is itself part of this very problematic because I do not believe that political sovereignty or normalcy is *eo ipso* the absolute condition for historic continuity, creativity and survival. Statehood is a precious boon; its Jewish character must be patiently fought for and its historic potential realized. This is the background against which Zionist reformulation or, more appropriately, Jewish revitalization, should be discussed.

History and Normalcy

Is Zionism in need of doctrinal-programmatic reformulation and revitalization and if so, what should be its nature and direction? These questions are linked quite logically to a cognate prior consideration: have the goals of Zionism been completely fulfilled, or has its program been only partially realized? Clarification of this issue hinges on an indispensable differentiation between two definitions or conceptions of Zionism: a bare-bones, essential, even monolithic one which concentrates on a political objective, and a many-tiered, hyphenated one which includes social, cultural, spiritual, ethical, and religious aspirations. This differentiation, far from being merely a matter of semantics, also provides a sharp focus for viewing and assessing various corollaries and repercussions.

It may be said that the essential goal of Zionism, the common denominator of the various ideological tendencies associated with it and its very nerve center, was political regeneration: proclamation of the rights of the dispersed-despised-depressed Jews to national self-determination and restoration of sovereignty in the Land of Israel as the basis of free collective existence. Its single overriding aim, unadorned and unobstructed, was to restore a missing dimension—territorialism and political normalcy—to the Jewish historical existence. In terms of the inner processes of Jewish history, Zionism emerged in a time of crisis as a critical-constructive reaction to the problems and failures of various attempts to integrate Jews coming out of the ghetto into modern society regardless of the price to be paid in effacement of identity or distortion of essence. It broadcast an ideological innovation which should supersede emancipation, assimilation, conversion and related phenomena: national normalcy and independence as the solution to the problems of the Jews. From this vantage point, the State of Israel, despite its territorial fragmentization and special status in terms of global diplomacy and geo-politics as well as the fact that the Diaspora has not been liquidated, is unquestionably the glorious, perhaps miraculous, fulfilment of the Zionist dream.

It follows, therefore, that Zionism is not in need of reformulation, for its goal of political normalcy, however hedged, has been achieved. Zionism may continue to maximize its aims by insisting on the negation of the *galut*, by unnerving Diaspora Jews religiously, nationally and existentially. It should not, however, weaken foundations of Jewish existence anywhere because of *a priori* assumptions. To assert this, however, is not necessarily to ensconce nationalism or normalcy as the ultimate consummation, to view it as a self-sufficient achievement, as a desirable transmutation of Jewish history and a replacement for all other values. If Zionism is seen as restorative, then it means rectifying the imbalance or reestablishing the equilibrium between the religious-spiritual spheres and national-territorial bases of Judaism and Jewish history. It means re-creating the full dialectic, the fructifying tension between these forces which is the individuating feature of Jewish history and Jewish peoplehood. During its long exilic period, Judaism had been deprived of one of its major components; an abnormal condition, sometimes described as "emancipation from state and territory," developed and persisted for such a long time that most ceased to apprehend its nature, to resist it, or react to its repercussions.

Removal of the abnormality, often depicted in clinical-pathological metaphors (e.g., by Leo Pinsker), should not mean introducing political sovereignty and normalcy as a self-sustaining ersatz; it should be seen as injecting a vital, energizing force which would avoid overspiritualization while simultaneously guarding against spiritual atrophy by restoring all of the special richness and resonance of the Jewish dialectic.

A new form of imbalance, radical political normalcy, is not the goal. Just as the passive, resigned Diaspora Jew had—and still has—to be aroused and made cognizant of a serious political deficiency, so the serene Israeli who may be inclined to carry the marked modern Jewish preference for the national over the religious component to its extreme and embrace normalcy *per se* will have to be aroused and made aware of a serious spiritual deficiency. From a Zionist perspective, Jewish history bears the indelible stigma of national abnormality and consequently everything about it is seen as negative and aberrant; institutionalized religion is obviously the greatest villain, for it was the mainstay of this ignoble past. Hence the tendency, conscious and unconscious, to obliterate or liberate oneself from this legacy. Needless to argue, this warped and quite prevalent perspective needs to be corrected.

It is relevant to remember that most of the vociferous, often virulent criticism and denunciation of Zionism from disparate quarters, from Orthodox and Reform, from Left and from Right, even from assorted non-Jews, nucleated around one major issue variously formulated: Zionism would destroy the uniqueness of Judaism, would obliterate its special spirituality, aristocracy, universality, its extraordinary *élan* and virtuosity. The religious criticism is well known. We may note, for example, that Franz Rosenzweig was emotionally and intellectually ill at ease with Zionism on the grounds that it would transpose Judaism from glorious eternity into dull temporality. "In order to keep unharmed the vision of the ultimate community it must deny itself the satisfaction the peoples of the world constantly enjoy in the functioning of their state." The Norwegian playwright Henrik Ibsen asked: "Who needs a Jewish state? For 2,000 years the world had at least one noble people, a people of aristocrats who did not descend to the level of having its own police, army, prisons, wars, intrigues and all the corruption that comes with political power." In short, there was a rather widespread feeling and suspicion that political normalcy was irreconcilable with spiritual adventure, religious virtuosity, intellectual creativity, and aristocratic (i.e., passional, suffering) existence.[3] Obviously it was the task of Zionism to dispel this suspicion and to demonstrate that unfragmented Jewish existence was possible, that one part need not be sacrificed for the other. We did not struggle to substitute one abnormality for another.

Simple, one-dimensional national normalcy not as a vital means but as an absolute value—a seductive but specious concept—is an historical aberration. The historical process is an amalgam of continuities and discontinuities; the above is such a radical disjunction that it makes itself irrelevant and illegitimate. (We should not confuse this with the question of whether or not the messianic era will be the fulfilment or destruction of history, whether it will consummate or consume the past; I, for one, do not find "secular messianism" a particularly enlightening explanatory category.) Moreover, it cannot endure; all indications are that it will move from fragility to futility. From both points of view, empirically and axiologically, it is unattractive and unstable and cannot provide spiritual-ideological sustenance for the State of Israel or for world Jewry.

The normalcy which should be espoused is that underscored, for example, by the Maharal of Prague who eloquently and forcefully noted that the very delineation of the Jews as *am kadosh* (a holy nation) necessitates political normalcy and clear national identity. Without it, the component of *am* is missing; before we will be in a position to realize the noble goal of *kadosh* we must establish the *am* firmly. Aristotle taught, and many Jewish thinkers repeated, that a definition must have genus and species, must start with an inclusive, common category and move to an exclusive, particularistic feature: for example, man is a rational animal. In our case, the genus is *am*-nation and the species is *kadosh*-holy. To expunge the species and dwell exclusively on the genus is as lopsided or ludicrous as deleting rational from the definition of man and leaving only the genus of animal.[4]

3. I would suggest rereading the powerful little book *Zionism Reconsidered*, Michael Selzer, ed., New York, 1970, sometimes superficial, occasionally disingenuous, but interesting and provocative.

4. It is only after Israel has certain common national characteristics and accoutrements—land, language, sovereignty—that its unique feature, *kedushah* (sanctification) can be appreciated; indeed this must be silhouetted against the background of the accepted political insignia, because only after the general characteristics of something are recognized is it possible to underline its distinct and distinctive features. The latter must reside in a political-physical reality.

Allow me to mention my favorite—and probably the clearest—expression of this relationship of complementarity and reciprocity: the relationship of *Pesach* and *Shevuot* as formulated very succinctly in the *Moreh Nebukim* by Maimonides and more expansively by the author of the *Sefer ha-Hinnuk* (*mitzvah* 306). The political *ge'ulah* (redemption) of Pesach which bestowed normalcy upon the Israelites or initiated the process of political normalcy was incomplete without the crowning spiritual achievements of *Shevuot*. That (and not agricultural or other considerations) is the underlying rationale of the counting of the *omer*: the act of counting concretizes and dramatizes the great passionate yearning for Torah.[5] In literary terms, one might describe this as enjambement. To proclaim political normalcy as a self-sufficient goal is to deny that *Shevuot* is the indispensable complement to and culmination of Pesach. Hence any such proclamation should be repudiated, because it is incongruous, and could only impoverish Israel and befuddle its Jewish character. The above, clearly axiomatic in my opinion, need not have been belabored were it not for the fact that there are vocal, aggressive, respected protagonists of the flat, one-dimensional normalcy.

Maharal, of course, expressed this in his medieval scholastic terminology, utilizing the concept of matter and form: "Every nation has two aspects: one as a people and this aspect stands in the relation of matter, and one as a particular people, and this stands in the relation of form." Form molds and fashions the amorphous matter, endowing it with unique traits.

5. Here is the formulation of the *Sefer ha-Hinnuk* as translated by G. Appel, *A Philosophy of Mizvot*, New York, 1974, p. 40:

> The reason for this commandment may be explained as follows: The Torah is of the very essence of Israel. Indeed, it is for the sake of the Torah that heaven and earth were created; as it is written, "If my covenant be not with day and night, if I have not appointed the ordinances of heaven and earth" (Jeremiah 33:25). The main object and purpose of their deliverance from Egypt was in order for them to receive the Torah at Sinai and to keep it, even as God said to Moses, "And this shall be the token unto thee that I have sent thee; when thou hast brought forth the people out of Egypt, ye shall serve God on this mountain" (Exodus 3:12): that is to say, Israel will receive the Torah which is the essential thing and for which they were delivered. This constitutes their ultimate good, and it is of greater import for them than their liberation from bondage. Therefore, God set their liberation from bondage as a token for receiving the Torah, since that which is of relatively secondary importance is set as a token for that which is of primary importance. Hence, since the receiving of the Torah is the essential reason for Israel's existence, and for its sake they were redeemed and were elevated to the high position which they reached, we were therefore commanded to count the days from the morrow of the festival of Passover until the day the Torah was given. We are bidden to do so in order to demonstrate our great and heartfelt yearning for that notable and longed-for day.

It is noteworthy that a perceptive theoretician, Thorstein Veblen, who praised the "intellectual. preeminence of Jews in Europe" even though a prerequisite for this preeminence was the "loss of allegiance,'" becoming "renegade Jews," etc., understood that Zionism *should* bring in its wake an intensification of historical concerns and traditional preoccupations, *should* use normalcy as a springboard, *should* release energies which would turn the returning Jews inward.

> As bearing on the Zionist's enterprise in isolation and nationality, this fable appears to teach a two-fold moral: If the adventure is carried to that consummate outcome which seems to be aimed at, it should apparently be due to be crowned with a large national complacency and, possibly, a profound and self-sufficient content on the part of the Chosen People domiciled once more in the Chosen Land; and when and insofar as the Jewish people in this way turn inward on themselves, their prospective contribution to the world's intellectual output should, in the light of the historical evidence, fairly be expected to take on the complexion of Talmudic lore, rather than that character of free-swung skeptical initiative which their renegades have habitually infused into the pursuit of the modern sciences abroad among the nations. Doubtless, even so the supply of Jewish renegades would not altogether cease, though it should presumably fall off to a relatively inconsiderable residue.

He then concludes rather wistfully:

> There should be some loss to Christendom at large, and there might be some gain to the repatriated Children of Israel. It is a sufficiently difficult choice between a life of complacent futility at home and a

---

Actually, the full dialectic of Jewish national-spiritual existence is already unfolded in this remarkable passage of the *Sefer ha-Hinnuk*. In keeping with his unequivocal explanation, the author answers the following question: if the political redemption from slavery in Egypt was only instrumental why do we not start counting on the very first night of Passover? This would certainly be much more dramatic, fully expressive and repercussive. His answer is that political *ge'ulah*, although instrumental, is a laudable and memorable phenomenon, an indispensable achievement, which should not be eclipsed. By giving it "its day," its importance, even though not absolute, was recognized.

Note also how Maimonides (throughout *Hilkot Melakim*) has added a spiritual dimension to political existence. The king is portrayed not only as a temporal sovereign, endowed with vast powers and prerogatives, but also as a spiritual leader, charged with the duty to study Torah relentlessly, and generally committed to an exacting scale of values and ideals.

thankless quest of unprofitable knowledge abroad. It is, after all, a matter of the drift of circumstance; and behind that lies a question of taste,
about which there is no disputing.

We need not here critically appraise Veblen's sophisticated,
cosmopolitan, but hollow call to assimilation which equated Jewish
contributions to civilization with renegade status and, while exalting
this, pejoratively dismissed Jewish concerns as parochial or irrelevant;
the foibles and fallacies as well as factual inaccuracies of his contention are easily spotlighted. Nor need we indicate our outrage at his
condescending characterization of the Zionist dream as "a life of complacent futility at home." It is obvious, however, that what is lament-
able for him should be laudable for us (particularly if we demonstrate
that authentic Jews also contribute to the advancement of science and
scholarship). A Jewish contribution colored by "Talmudic lore" would
indeed be exciting and unique—and something to be undertaken
without defensiveness or self-consciousness.

So much for the political definition of Zionism and the thesis of
normalcy, the latter appropriately seen as a prerequisite and complement, as a vital component of healthy, dynamic Jewish existence.

We must return to the second conception of Zionism, the many-
tiered, hyphenated one. If Zionism is a utopian adventure and an
experiment in social engineering, the road to fulfilment is still a long
one. If Zionism is a secular revolution and negation of *all* exilic history, it has not achieved its goal and its dream remains—I would inter-
ject, happily—unfulfilled. If Zionism is a romantic revolution against
the petrified, institutionalized *halakah* and an attempted liberation of
all modern Jews from the stultification of normative religion, it was
aborted. If, in short, Zionism has metapolitical aspirations and preten-
sions, its saga can only be described as a fusion of frustration and
fulfilment, failure and triumph. Protagonists of these various ideologies therefore contend that Zionism is in need of reformulation and
revitalization.

However, at this point, it should be noted that Zionism as a
spiritual program or cultural ideology or historical-philosophical conception sometimes seems slightly imperious or imperialistic in its confrontation with the Jewish past generally and the modern Jewish experience in particular. In other words, there is here a case of "misplaced concreteness," to use A.N. Whitehead's phrase. Zionism in this
broad metapolitical sense is often equated with modern Judaism, and

their destinies are linked, whereas proper historical perspective requires that it be viewed and assessed as one of many competing ideologies and programs. Zionists were not the only ones to grapple with the problems of the modern age. Moreover, Zionism in this sense, unlike the political one, did not develop new teachings *ex nihilo*. A good example is the poignant, resonant statement of Martin Buber, characteristically elegant and rhetorical, in *Die jüdische Bewegung*:

> To create! The Zionist who feels the whole holiness of this word and lives up to it seems to me [in contrast to other types of Zionists, from whom he differentiates himself] to be of the highest rank. To create new works from out of the depth of one's primeval unique individuality, out of that uniquely individual, incomparable strength of one's blood that has been for so fearfully long cast in the irons of unproductivi- ty . . . that is an ideal for the Jewish people. To create the monuments of one's essence! To let one's way burst forth into a new intuitive view of life! To set forth a new form, a new configuration of possibilities before the eyes of infinity! To let a new beauty glow, to let a new star ascend in the enchanted night sky of eternities! First, however, to penetrate to one's self, with bloody hands and undaunted heart to struggle through to one's essence itself, from which all these wonders will rise to the sur- face. To discover oneself! To find oneself! To gain oneself by struggle![6]

In this case much of what is presented as Zionist ideology is actually a continuation of tendencies, attitudes and criticisms begun by the Enlightenment and sustained throughout the nineteenth century. This moving response to crisis and its resounding call for renewal should be seen as a variety of modernity. Buber's anti-Talmudism (and the same may be said for Gershom Scholem), the call to shatter the "irons of unproductivity," is a Haskalah stereotype and I see no reason to romanticize it, rehearse it unreflectively, record it as the most promis- ing prescription, or recognize it as the highest form of Zionism. The notion that there is no creativity, no challenge, no dynamism, no romance, no opportunity for self-expresion and self-renewal in tradi- tional Judaism of the modern age is neither novel nor correct. I am not easily persuaded, for example, that the anarchic nonnormative reli- giosity of X is a more authentic, creative experience than the crystal- lized, normative religiosity of Y, or that it is more conducive to self- discovery and self-knowledge. Jews committed to *halakah* usually

---

6. I take this quotation from Gershom Scholem's critical analysis of "Martin Buber's Conception of Judaism" (*On Jews and Judaism in Crisis*, New York, 1976, p. 132); Scho- lem's essay, and its underlying attitudes, is very relevant *per se*.

quested for spirituality and religious adventure; they sought to coordinate medium and mood, external observance with inner meaning. Sometimes, to be sure, the spiritualizing speculative or pietistic quest is overshadowed and an uninspired and uninspiring routinization of religious behavior emerges. Such atrophied patterns of behavior, however, are aberrations. To set up a Spinozist-Mendelssohnian definition of Judaism as all deed and no creed or experience and then to condemn this as inadequate and unattractive is hardly proper procedure. In sum, autobiography, usually interesting, need not become rigid ideology, nor does it necessarily yield profound philosophy.

In any event, I mean to suggest that the medley of contemporary spiritual-historical-cultural problems is best defined as the general concern of Judaism rather than the exclusive concern of Zionism. A revitalization of Zionism will be a part of a rejuvenation of Judaism— *biklal matayim manah* (the greater includes the lesser). It follows that the problems of Diaspora Jewry and those of Israeli Jewry, the crucial political difference notwithstanding, have much in common. They should not be separated but be analyzed together. Moreover, those engaged in the process of analysis and reflection, of prescription and decision, need not—I would say, should not—confine themselves to the works of the "founding fathers" of Zionism. This issue is frequently raised and heatedly debated in the context of the reformulations of the Zionist program. Clearly we must turn to pre-modern and pre-Zionist sources as well as to non-Zionist writings in our quest for renewed vision, strengthened dedication, and unswerving commitment—a quest for *kelal Yisrael* in Israel and elsewhere.

This leads to our final reflection on tradition and modernity or what I am wont to designate as "Judaism in modern times" *vis-à-vis* "modern Judaism."

Tradition and Modernity

Obviously, only a fallacy compounded of reductionism and precursorism could equate Judaism in modern times with modern Judaism. Yet this confusion between a historical-chronological concept ("modern" as an aspect of periodization) and an axiological concept ("modern" as an ideal, an aspiration, a consummation) has been dominant. Should one constitutive or organizing principle (an apparently dominant ethos or *Zeitgeist*) completely eclipse or subordinate other principles, sometimes complementary, sometimes antagonistic, sometimes independent? In studying and teaching the modern period most have consciously or unconsciously allowed this assumption to be operative. As a result, our conception of and approach to modern Jewish history has been seriously skewed. Writers have concentrated on what is new rather than on the new emerging organically from the old, being forced into it, or coexisting with it. Much has been written and constructed in terms of ideology (Zionism and Israel) or hindsight (the destruction of European Jewry), and neither is a completely appropriate category. In large measure, the modernity of the social-political transformations of the Jewish community—where the process variously referred to as naturalization, reform, civic amelioration or emancipation was clearly novel and unprecedented—carried over to the intellectual-cultural realm in which enlightenment, the historical twin of emancipation, although of great significance, was by no means exclusive or exhaustive.

Now for reasons of scholarly integrity and intellectual honesty, as well as educational value and ideological edification, in studying Jewish intellectual and cultural history of the modern period, in studying philosophy, mysticism, *mussar* (ethics), in studying Hebrew and Yiddish literature, in studying Zionism and anti-Zionism, in studying the recrudescence of anti-Semitism or its new motives and expressions as well as various Jewish reactions, in studying the total Jewish historical experience and its manifold expressions, our net must be cast more widely. We must identify multiple foci and analyze the multi-faceted repertoire of concepts and values, ideas and ideals, instead of a monolithic scheme or a linear development, in order to be cognizant not only of discontinuities and ambiguities but also continuities and commitments. The lodestar should be comprehensiveness rather than modernity. Only by separating modernity as a chronological designation or a socio-political concept with attendant ideological aspirations and cultural implications from the destiny and struggle, triumphs and setbacks of Judaism as a whole in modern times will we be able to place the issue of Zionist reformulations in the proper perspective.

For example, the story of modern Jewish philosophy is almost exclusively a tale of the speculations, experiences, and lucubrations of German-Jewish writers starting with Moses Mendelssohn. The third part of Julius Guttmann's classic *Philosophies of Judaism* consists of Formstecher, Hirsch, Krochmal, Steinheim, Moritz Lazarus, Hermann Cohen and Franz Rosenzweig. We may note parenthetically the special emphasis even of this partial presentation: whereas the bulk of Guttmann's great oeuvre is devoted to *Jewish Religious Philosophy in the Middle Ages*, the modern section is prudently and suggestively entitled "Jewish Philosophy of Religion".[7]

Obviously this should not stand as a full, balanced presentation of Jewish thought in modern times. Where is the *Mesillat Yesharim* of R. Moses Hayyim Luzzatto, the *Nefesh ha-Hayyim* of R. Hayyim of Volohzin, the *Sefer ha-Tanya* of R. Shneur Zalman of Ladi, *Iggeret Mussar* of R. Israel Lipkin-Salanter in which there is so much that is new and fresh? These works, which continue traditional Jewish thought with all its tension and complexity—faith and reason, intellectualism and voluntarism, spontaneity and conformity, ritual and ethics, objective norm versus subjective experience, debate concerning the hierarchy of religious values (intellectual-cognitive *vis-à-vis* emotive-ecstatic)—have received some monographic treatment but have not been integrated into the full-orbed history of this genre known as modern Jewish thought.[8]

Note also that if struggle and self-identification are the key elements or stimulating factors, the partisanship remains striking and the need for a panoramic view remains pressing. We may mention Michael Meyer's first-rate book *The Origins of the Modern Jew*, an attempt to probe how "the period testifies to the modern Jew's persistent desire to explain continued Jewish identification in terms of the cultural values dominant in his generation." The result is a learned, insightful, urbane analysis from Mendelssohn through David Friedlander to Leopold Zunz. However, such a presentation tells me that we need a companion volume; we need to consider alongside of this

---

7. To be sure, Jewish philosophy of religion rather than Jewish religious philosophy is itself a hallmark of modernity, a major intellectual change (which may perhaps be traced back to Judah Abarbanel or del Medigo). Mendelssohn already emphasized that his two philosophic works, *Phaedon* on the immortality of the soul and *Morning Hours* on the belief in the existence of God, are not to be assessed as contributions to Jewish doctrine but rather to general doctrines of rational religion. Guttmann (p. 291) curtly notes: "As a philosopher of religion, too, he cannot be considered a philosopher of Judaism." This accentuates the problematic nature of such historical scholarship.

8. Professor N. Rotenstreich is more expansive and more creative. In his book (*Jewish Philosophy in Modern Times*), he takes note of a Luzzatto, not Moses H. Luzzatto mentioned above but Samuel D. Luzzatto, and concludes with a chapter on Rav Kook called "Harmony and Return" and one on A. D. Gordon called "Between Man and Nature." No sooner is the literary framework enlarged and room is made for such important writers representing a more colorful spectrum of positions and programs, than the question of selectivity becomes more acute and more lacunae are quickly underscored.

"persistent desire" the equally persistent desire to explain Jewish identification and sustain Jewish creativity in terms of cultural or religious values *inherent* in the Jewish tradition and not merely in terms of extraneous shifting values dominant in one generation and dormant in the next. We need a study of the varieties of traditional experience and expression in the modern age. Sartre has put it well: "One must write for one's age, but that does not mean that one has to lock oneself up in it. To write for one's age is not to reflect it passively; it is to want to maintain it or change it, thus to go beyond it toward the future." We may interpolate that the best route to the future is often via the past. The tyranny of the present—a stultifying solipsism—is potentially worse than the tyranny of the past. Franz Rosenzweig spoke of bringing the periphery into the center. I might add that lest you think that the traditionalist camp is bland or homogeneous, merely consider the intellectual skirmishes between various creative individuals who belong to this group, the great variety of religious postures, social positions and cultural attitudes.

Equally telling is the study of Hebrew literature in the modern era. This has been artificially confined to what is known as modern Hebrew literature, i.e., belles-lettres, occasionally and *inconsistently* peppered with some essayists or scholars (Krochmal, Ahad Ha-Am, or S. Rappaport) and very recently sporadic literary attention is being devoted to some Hasidic works (notably the *Shivḥe ha-Besht* and *Likkute Moharan*, the extraordinary tales of R. Nahman of Bratzlav), but it is not the total study of Hebrew literature in the modern era which should include the continuation of pre-modern forms, values, and visions (see the eloquent and erudite essay by Prof. Dov Sedan, *'Al Sifrutenu* [Concerning Our Literature].

A piquant illustration is the disputed role of R. Moses H. Luzzatto. Some list him as the father of modern Hebrew literature because he wrote dramas and poetry which may show influence of Italian pastorals and Rousseau-like "return to nature" themes while others omit him. The point is that even those who include him in a place of honor do so by fragmentizing his personality and achievement, by writing in the light of what is to become quantitatively important later or what one thinks (à la Hegel) is philosophically-teleologically important. Precursorism always produces an extra measure of straitened scholarly interests or narrow exegetical pursuits. It is anemic. It colors and constricts the scope of inquiry and perception of the past.

The following is noteworthy. The 1965 issues of *Moznayim* contain articles relating to the heated debate which came in the wake of a proposal for a revised high school curriculum for the study of modern Hebrew literature. Many agitated readers—writers, teachers and concerned laymen—felt that this carefully prepared proposal mercilessly dismembered the corpus of Hebrew literature. The Haskalah writers were dropped; works of Gordon, Peretz, and Shimoni were expunged; Berdichevsky, Brenner, Gnessin and Steinberg were to be assigned to a new *genizah*. Proponents argued that there was need to base the literature curriculum on purely literary-esthetic criteria; opponents rejected the sharp bifurcation between works with formal-literary value and works which embody and include national-historic values. This was, in their opinion, a serious disjunction which was simultaneously undesirable and untenable. The outrage was sustained by interesting, revealing idioms and metaphors quarried from traditional sources and saturated with traditional associations: *perikat 'ol Torah* (casting off the yoke of Torah); a generation that has a father but no grandfather; literature without historic continuity is inconceivable; neglect of Haskalah literature is like cutting off a limb from a living being (*'ever min ha-ḥay*); and similar exclamations of anger and indignation. Obviously, it is possible to appreciate the cultural-ideological issue and its repercussions without taking a stand on the academic issue of the appropriate definition of "literature." Reviewing these articles led me to exclaim "Ribbono shel 'olam!" If such a curricular "reform" touching only the modern period releases such a massive flow of adrenalin and wrath, how should we react to the radical surgery performed on other areas and eras of Hebrew literature and Jewish thought?

Undoubtedly the most serious casualty of the modernist reductionism has been the investigation and appreciation of rabbinic literature. Talmudic scholars have on the whole been ignored—one might say that benign neglect, lack of enthusiasm and animosity alternate one with another—or else are lumped together and treated as parts of a completely uniform phenomenon: a blanket of bland homogeneity is spread over the creative figures of rabbinic literature. The background for this is bi-dimensional. The Talmud was attacked or dismissed, by Jews and non-Jews, as dry and irrelevant on practical-religious grounds or from the point of view of religious phenomenology: law is uninspiring. It was also attacked on intellectual grounds: as a subject of study it was dry and technical, lacking sophisticated methods of analysis and interpretation (see e.g., M.L. Lilienblum). The scholarly faults of this conception are transparent; its educational shortcomings are regrettable—and most relevant to our practical problems.

Modernity is not synonymous with experiences and adventures of Judaism in modern times.

Reformulation

In arguing that the various expressions of modernity, their seminal importance notwithstanding, should not be allowed to preempt all our energies and attention, I am frankly concerned not only with the scholarly shortcomings but with the adverse education-al-existential effects as well. If there is consensus concerning the fact that this generation needs rejuvenation, needs, in the most colloquial sense, to find roots, and this need is universal (in Israel as well as the Diaspora), we dare not constrict the field of its vision or the parameters of what is relevant and possibly stimulating. Viewing our problem as a comprehensive spiritual-historical one has two corollaries: 1) it underscores that we face a common challenge; 2) it prevents us from limiting our conceptualization and analysis and introspection to Herzl and Pinsker, Nordau and Ahad Ha-Am. When I suggested this, I was not being atavistic or anachronistic; I merely thought that it was important to recognize the timeliness of timeless insights. Our youth must be free to choose—yes, to choose traditional forms and values, which, if properly presented, are quite attractive and persuasive. "Self-affirmation," so frequently discussed and held aloft as a modern ideal, need not be exclusively in secular or anti-traditional terms. The question of influence and relevance needs to be reviewed carefully. Moses Hess and Moses Hirsch, R. Israel Ba'al Shem Tov and R. Israel Salanter—who is the more influential and relevant? Why should our youth become acquainted only with Judah Leib Gordon and not with R. Eliezer Gordon of Telz; or with Perez Smolenskin and not with R. Naftali Zvi Yehudah Berlin? We may go further and ask: why should "Revolutionary Jews from Marx to Trotsky" (title of a recent study) be given such prominence? Revolutionary Jews from the Ba'al Shem Tov to Rabbi Kook deserve, at the very least, equal time and enthusiasm.

We need to recognize that the modern postures frequently glorified—romanticism, antinomism, etc.—are not the only options and we need particularly to acknowledge that secularism is not irreversible. Again I should say that there is both proof and promise for this.

The phenomenon of *teshuvah* in different forms and on different levels is widespread and impressive; the list of *baale teshuvah* tells an important, enthralling story. Moreover, while assimilation and erosion of tradition is usually by default, *teshuvah* is by deep, consuming commitment. In addition, there is a divine promise: *sofam shel yisrael la'asot teshuvah* (in the end all Jews will repent). There is no intrinsic, ineluctable clash between tradition and the modern age; this has been conclusively proven. It is a matter of choice, of identification, of hierarchy of values and commitments, determined in large measure by education, by sociological facts, by models and alternatives. Hence when I submit that a *halakic* regimen is the best guarantee for continuity and survival of *kelal yisrael* as a great, creative, committed community, I am not saying that we substitute hypothetical imperatives for categorical imperatives, that we act out of expediency, that we sacrifice conviction and sincerity in the interests of continuity. It is sometimes said—it was said to me in debate—that there is no way at this stage of modernity to return to tradition with integrity and sincerity. I believe that the abiding truth of our tradition may be espoused with verve and conviction by many "modern" Jews if we only give them a chance, if we alter our educational assumptions and aspirations, values and objectives, procedures and premises. People change their political persuasion because of altered perceptions of contemporary events; the same may be true for spiritual persuasions and intellectual convictions. The fact is that scientists and humanists alike have been doing this. Otherwise, the scenario is one of self-fulfilling prophecy; we perpetuate a certain kind of education predicated on certain values, we transmit a certain kind of ideology which prescribes certain attitudes, and wonder why the results are generally monolithic as well as predictable.

    As far as the traditionally committed Jew, guided by the Torah, is concerned, he should set an example which literally commands respect, irresistibly attracts and fascinates and ultimately leads to emulation and identification. Ethical impeccability—consistent, ennobling, moral behavior—is a key determinant here; that trait which the *halakah* prescribes as necessary for *kiddush ha-shem* (see Maimonides, "Yesode ha-Torah," v. 11) and as the basis for projecting an attractive profile in the eyes of non-Jews (see *Sefer Mizvot Gadol*, positive commandment, 74) is also the indispensable prerequisite for convincing fellow-Jews of the viability and superiority of our tradition. Moreover, he should concentrate upon a few guiding principles

in the initial stages of expounding the religious tradition and bringing
people close to it. Again, this is not a concession, a compromise, or an
act of expediency. It is a fully-sanctioned prudential-pedagogic ploy.
(See, e.g., *Sukkah*, 46B; R. Joseph Albo, *'Ikkarim*, III, 290.) For us,
Torah is an indivisible entity but it cannot be transmitted all at once.
Gradualism is the necessary approach.

Finally, while emphasizing that our spiritual-cultural problems
are universal and that therefore to speak only of Zionist reformulation
is to miss the real point, it is obvious that there is a crucial difference
between Israel and the Diaspora. Present indications are that spiritual
survival in the Diaspora will indeed be a matter of *she'erit ha-peletah*,
whereas in Israel there is a *chance* for it to encompass the majority of
the people. The chance must be converted into a probability and then
into a reality. This is where the political normalcy makes all the difference. It does not automatically guarantee such survival, but creates
conditions for large-scale survival, conditions which require imagina-
tive, sensitive molding. These conditions are unique to Israel. This is
how the Zionist reality is to be perceived and ultimately how the centrality of Israel may be fully appraised and praised.

Zionism: The Moral Challenge

Ephraim E. Urbach

In the Jewish world today there is more than a measure of confusion and vagueness concerning the current meaning and importance of Zionism. Did the establishment of the State in fact spell its
demise? If not, what are its tasks today? What is its place within the
context of Jewish world views? To dispel this confusion—which, it
seems to me, stems in part from attempts to establish as legitimate
Zionism what clearly is not Zionism—it has been suggested that we
engage in a reformulation of Zionist ideology. In this vein, Nathan
Rotenstreich, basing himself on the Italian philosopher Benedetto
Croce, posed the question: What is dead and what is alive in classical
traditional Zionist ideology?

It is my belief that we might do better by speaking of a crisis in
the realization by Zionists of the Zionist ideal and ask forthrightly
whether, in fact, we are still Zionists. Moreover, the Zionist Movement
did not produce a system of thought comparable in rigor and exacti-
tude to the original subject of Croce's query, Hegelian philosophy. I,
for one, would be at a loss if I were expected to present a formulation
of classical-traditional Zionist ideology. What is attributed to Zionism—the renascence of the Jewish People and its culture, the trend
towards normalization of Jewish existence, the replacement of Messianism by modern historical aspirations—may easily be discerned in
modern non-Zionist, and even anti-Zionist movements. The Haskalah
(Enlightenment), Western Jewish liberalism and Reform, Orthodoxy
of the Hirsch stamp, Autonomism, and the Bund, all in some measure
presented themselves as a primary synthesis between inherent trends
in Jewish tradition and emerging trends in the modern world. They
claim to be modern phenomena.

The question of what was innovative in Zionism was posed
more than four decades ago by Nahum Sokolow, a man closely associated with the Zionist Movement from its inception. His answer was

unequivocal. Zionism—the Zionism of Herzl and of the movement he founded—contained nothing which had not been said earlier. However, it was unique in that it contained and created a framework for bringing a program to realization. Moreover, it transposed the ideal from the ghetto enclosure to the wide arena of world affairs.

This Zionism became the central issue of the Jewish People, arousing fierce opposition from extreme Orthodoxy and extreme assimilationism, but at the same time rallying round it vast segments of the people. Indeed, Herzl saw his major achievement in the fact that he succeeded in uniting under one banner Jews of diverse views from many different countries. This was not ideology but the bridging of ideologies.

Ahad Ha-Am, who was an ideologist, said of the First Zionist Congress that it was neither realistic in its essence nor Jewish in its spirit. Later he changed his view; his early assessment, as well as that of other Jewish thinkers of the time, missed the point. Ever since the First Congress, Zionism has been a catalyzing agent, using this-worldy means to channel Jewish longings for the recreation of a Jewish State in Eretz Israel. That was its concern. Later disputes and polemics within the Zionist world left untouched this core of the Zionist idea. Many of these polemics could have been engaged in before the formulation of Zionism at the First Zionist Congress, and in fact were. To a certain extent, the debate between Ahad Ha-Am and Berditchevsky was unrelated to Zionism: the former, presenting his views on the spiritual center, spoke of a spiritual ego, the latter called for a Nietzschean transformation of Jewish values.

There were Jewish socialists who became Zionists because they believed that their socialism could be realized only within the framework of a Jewish State. Similarly, there were religious Jews who expected that Zionism would revitalize Jewish religion. Still others saw in Zionism a means of replacing the onerous burden of traditional religion by secular Judaism. Diverse groups attached diametrically opposed ideological hopes to the Zionist idea, yet none realized its own specific goal. Instead, a common denominator was created, namely, the Zionist idea of establishing a Jewish State, the forging of a will to see such a state. Fully devoted to this aim, religious Jews and Jewish socialists alike made concessions in regard to some of their ideals. Those who did not evince such a readiness for compromise, and who granted supremacy to other allegiances, left their groups. The Zionists who remained were well aware that their Jewish religious, or liberal, or socialist ideals were far from being achieved. Instead, their Zionism meant regaining our country, reuniting our people and reestablishing our state—to use the formulation of an exceptional but forgotten pre-Herzlian Zionist, Dr. Isaac Ruelf, whose book (in German) bearing the Hebrew title *Aruchas Bas Ami (The Healing of My People)* appeared in 1883.

This Zionism was less a vision of the end of days than a necessary means for achieving often contrary goals defined from contrasting perspectives. In this sense, the structure of Zionism reflected the structure of the traditional messianic idea. The Ingathering of the Exiles, the Redemption of the Land, even the advent of the King-Messiah, were themselves not the end of days. Within the religious context, eschatological aspirations were left for the time when the world would be set right under the Kingdom of the Almighty, and all creatures form one band to do His will wholeheartedly. The Ingathering, the Redemption of the Land, the Messiah, were all instruments. Similarly, the Zionist Movement was a means for realizing the various lofty ideals its adherents attached to it.

Level-headed Zionists such as Ahad Ha-Am, who preached a cautious realism rather than an illusory messianism, were no less drawn to the messianic element than such enthusiastic Zionists as Rabbi Kook for example. We now know that the establishment of a spiritual center, a kind of nursery for morality, as called for by Ahad Ha-Am, is perhaps more illusory a messianism than those features of Zionism he criticized.

A careful examination of the various historical manifestations of Zionism, even when there was a radical alienation from the Jewish past, reveals that in none was the world to be abandoned—a world and future transcending the achievement of Zionism's immediate goals.

That being the case, the establishment of the State does not constitute a turning point in Zionist ideology; it certainly does not spell its demise. However, because of the centrality of the State, the readiness to sacrifice other values for it, the fact that for many it is the only great reality in Jewish life, it has been suggested that the State may become an object of idolatry. I do not think that danger is imminent; not if we look at all that the state has achieved. There are changes, positive and negative, never before dreamt of, events belying the cause and effect theories of historians.

Let me dwell for a moment on the subject of the Ingathering of the Exiles. The large-scale Magic Carpet operation which in 1949 brought almost the entire Jewish community of Yemen to Israel, the mass *aliyot* from Iraq, Libya and elsewhere in North Africa, Iran, Kurdistan, and recently the non-Ashkenazi Jews of the Soviet Union, were an outcome of the existing State, but that was not the only moving force. And even if we consider that all these communities retained a strong messianic attachment to Israel, the events are not fully explained. Recently a Soviet official was asked by an Iraqi minister why the Russians permit an emigration that reinforces Zionist strength in the State of Israel. His reply was that they were doing on a lesser scale what Iraq did in the 1950s.

Some may see in these events the hand of Providence; others may prefer to call it the subtlety of historical reason. Whatever the case, the fact remains that this *aliyah*, so different from the remnants of European Jewry who arrived during the War of Independence, brought with it many unforeseen problems. The social structure of the *Yishuv* was completely altered, and established institutions made many mistakes, resulting in problems and social tensions which to this day are endangering the quality of life and morality in the country.

Problems, however, call for action, and in the State of Israel no one can evade the responsibility for maintaining the quality of life. The State creates the genuine framework for contending with problems, for living them. Here, in Israel, we are responsible for everything. If there is discrimination, social inequality, violence, bloodshed, it is we who bear the responsibility for eliminating such evils. This, not idolatry, is what the State provides. We must also face other problems, such as that of a majority and its relations to a minority. Life in Israel means a greater commitment, a readiness to assume responsibility, to make sacrifices in all walks of life.

Historically, Jewish uniqueness was in part not only the result of minute religious observances which defined a style of life; it was also the result of a singular attitude and attachment to national freedom, a special stance in the face of wicked or tyrannical powers (identified as the Kingdom of Edom, or another such kingdom), as well as lofty ideas concerning the messianic future. There was a striving to realize these, if not fully, at least partially, in this world.

The State created a framework within which ideological differences and controversies invariably connected with that longed-for future can be confronted squarely, not as vestiges of a past maintained for existential or nostalgic considerations. We live with problems of the meaning and possibility of a secular Judaism, of saving religious Judaism from becoming merely external.

If this is not enough to preserve us from the danger of idolatry, and it is said that "we cannot inherit the land because there is no man who does not sin; the attribute of Justice will immediately act against him," then let it also be said that "God is full of mercy, and atonement comes from Him, may He be blessed." I believe that living in Israel will lead us see that atonement will come from Him.

Zionism means the will to join actively in the Israel experiment. A Jew involved in activities for Israel becomes a Zionist when life in the sovereign Jewish State takes precedence for him over all other material and even spiritual values. This is not intended, of course, to minimize the importance of the spiritual, moral and social problems of Jewish existence. But it does help us pinpoint the source of real danger to Zionism. The danger does not come from Jewish ideological rivals, such as the remnants of that Orthodoxy which believed human endeavors are not needed to bring about the messianic age; nor is it found in those who espouse humanist, socialist, or revolutionary ideologies which, in the view of their adherents, do not require a separate Jewish national existence, but greater assimilation and integration of Jews into their cultural and social milieus. The real danger lies in the non-fulfilment by so-called Zionists, of their personal duty to come on *aliyah.*

I mentioned above the mass *aliyah* of Oriental Jewry. It contrasts sharply with the lack of substantial *aliyah* from the West; it applies also to the affluent Jews of Algeria and Morocco—and at present from Iran—who, when forced to emigrate, chose to go, not to Israel, but to France or the Americas. Today we are also witness to the large drop-out rate among those Ashkenazi Jews who are allowed to emigrate from the U.S.S.R. to Israel. Nor should we forget the *yordim* (emigrés from Israel). It would seem, then, that among large sectors of the Jewish People, including a significant proportion of those who have lived, or are living, in Israel, values other than life in the sovereign Jewish State have assumed supremacy.

One such value—and here, perhaps, we may observe genuine idolatry—is the worship of the Golden Calf: the desire to lead a life of ease, to become rich with minimal effort. True, the love of wealth is deeply rooted in human nature; we have reinforced that trait by associating esteem, not with Torah, wisdom, devotion and pioneering, but rather with conspicuous consumption, luxury, and wastefulness.

Philosophers, psychologists, sociologists and modern sophists bend their energies and talents to justify the unrestrained satisfaction of all impulses and urges. Even if advocates of permissiveness do not necessarily advocate personal pleasure as the sole criterion for judging individual actions, they do create an atmosphere which fosters moral abandon.

History teaches that sensualism and the abandonment of restraints by large sectors of the population have destroyed cultures and societies, large and small. Western society, too, cannot long withstand the pernicious influences of its consumptionism, permissiveness, and violence. In the final analysis, Zionism and the State of Israel, which have their roots and being in the Western world, would suffer a similar fate.

Zionism is a brave and daring struggle against the debasement of man. Zionists must mobilize to improve our society by uprooting the adoration of wealth. Only if we succeed in reviving the moral consciousness of our society, will we be able to send to the golah teachers and emissaries worthy of the name to encourage aliyah, unconditional aliyah.

The challenge of Zionism is great. Its success and impact on human civilization (I choose that term advisedly) in these muddled and dangerous times depends on nothing less than the number of Jews who are ready to fulfil their moral obligations to Zionism. Fulfilment means involvement and responsibility. In the golah it means preparation for aliyah, followed by personal aliyah. It means encouraging the desire among Jews, if they are unable immediately to make the decisive step, to see themselves as candidates for aliyah. That, more than ideological reformulation, is what is needed. For we shall get out of Zionism no more than we put into it.

Contributors

MICHEL ABITBOL.
Lecturer, Division of Asian-African Jewish Communities, Institute of Contemporary Jewry, The Hebrew University of Jerusalem

MARCOS AGUINIS.
Physician and writer, Buenos Aires

MARCUS ARKIN.
Director General, South African Zionist Federation; former Professor of Economic History, Rhodes University, Grahamstown, South Africa

HAIM AVNI.
Director, Division of Latin American Jewry, Institute of Contemporary Jewry, The Hebrew University of Jerusalem

YEHUDA BAUER.
Head, Institute of Contemporary Jewry; Professor of Holocaust Studies, The Hebrew University of Jerusalem

DORIS BENSIMON.
Professor of Sociology, University of Caen, France

HAYYIM J. COHEN.
Associate Professor, Department of Near Eastern Language and Literature, New York University

MOSHE DAVIS.
Founding Head, Institute of Contemporary Jewry; Professor of American Jewish History and Institutions, The Hebrew University of Jerusalem

SERGIO DELLAPERGOLA.
Lecturer, Division of Jewish Demography and Statistics, Institute of Contemporary Jewry, The Hebrew University of Jerusalem

ARYE L. DULZIN.
Chairman, World Zionist Organization and the Jewish Agency, Jerusalem

DANIEL J. ELAZAR.
Professor of Political Science, Bar Ilan University, Ramat Gan, and Temple University, Philadelphia, Pennsylvania

ISRAEL EVEN-SHOSHAN.
Director, Institute for Leaders from Abroad, Jerusalem

NACHMAN FALBEL.
Head, Brazilian Center for Jewish Studies; Professor of History, University of São Paulo, Brazil

ISRAEL FINESTEIN.
Judge, Circuit Court, London

JOEL S. FISHMAN.
Coordinator for Educational Projects, School for Overseas Students, The Hebrew University of Jerusalem

ALFRED GOTTSCHALK.
President, Hebrew Union College—Jewish Institute of Religion; Professor of Bible and Jewish Religious Thought, Cincinnati, Ohio

BEN HALPERN.
Professor of Near Eastern Studies, Brandeis University, Waltham, Massachusetts

FRITZ HOLLANDER.
President, Swedish Jewish Community, Stockholm

JOSÉ A. ITZIGSOHN.
Psychiatrist, Jerusalem; former Professor of Psychology, University of Buenos Aires

CHARLOTTE JACOBSON.
Chairman, World Zionist Organization—American Section, New York

ZEV KATZ.
Department of Russian Studies and School for Overseas Students, The Hebrew University of Jerusalem

EPHRAIM KATZIR.
Fourth President of The State of Israel

ISRAEL KOLATT.
Associate Professor, Division of History of Zionism and the Yishuv, Institute of Contemporary Jewry, The Hebrew University of Jerusalem

ANNIE KRIEGEL.
Professor, Department of Social Sciences, University of Nanterre, France

DAVID LAZAR.
Cultural Attaché, Israel Embassy, Paris

SCHNEIER LEVENBERG.
Representative of the Jewish Agency in London; Honorary Vice-President, Zionist Federation of Great Britain and Ireland

NATAN LERNER.
Executive Director, World Jewish Congress, Jerusalem

PETER Y. MEDDING.
Associate Professor, Institute of Contemporary Jewry and Department of Political Science, The Hebrew University of Jerusalem

SHULAMIT NARDI.
Assistant to the President of The State of Israel

AMNON NETZER.
Head, Department of Indo-Iranian and Armenian Studies; Senior Lecturer, Persian Language and Literature, The Hebrew University of Jerusalem

YEHUDA NINI.
Head, Center for Study of Eretz Israel and the Yishuv; Senior Lecturer, Department of Jewish History, Tel Aviv University

DAVID POLISH.
Rabbi, Beth Emet–The Free Synagogue, Evanston. Illinois

EMANUEL RACKMAN.
President, Bar Ilan University, Ramat Gan

DOV RAPPEL.
Senior Lecturer, School of Education, Bar Ilan University, Ramat Gan; member, Kvutzat Yavneh

AVRAHAM SCHENKER.
Head, Department of Development and Services, World Zionist Organization, Jerusalem

ELIEZER SCHWEID.
Associate Professor of Jewish Philosophy, Institute of Jewish Studies, The Hebrew University of Jerusalem

GIDEON SHIMONI.
Lecturer, Division of History of Zionism and the Yishuv, Institute of Contemporary Jewry, The Hebrew University of Jerusalem

ISADORE TWERSKY.
Director, Center for Jewish Studies; Professor of Hebrew Literature and Philosophy, Harvard University, Cambridge, Massachusetts

MUKI TZUR.
Member, Kibbutz Ein Gev

EPHRAIM E. URBACH.
Professor of Talmud, The Hebrew University of Jerusalem

HAROLD M. WALLER.
Associate Professor, U. S. Politics and Methodology, Department of Political Science, McGill University, Montreal, Canada

MICHAEL WALZER.
   Professor of Government, Harvard University, Cambridge, Massachusetts

MORDECAI WAXMAN.
   Vice-President, World Council of Synagogues

ALEX WEINGROD.
   Professor of Studies in Social Integration, University of the Negev, Beersheba

GEOFFREY WIGODER.
   International Coordinator, Seminars on Zionist Thought in Contemporary Jewry, World Zionist Organization, Jerusalem

MICHAEL ZAND.
   Professor of Persian Language and Literature, The Hebrew University of Jerusalem

EDITORIAL ASSOCIATES
   Dora Camrass
   Francine Schnitzer

EDITORIAL COORDINATOR
   Lottie K. Davis

Abbreviations of Names of Institutions

ADEI	Associazione Donne Ebrai d'Italie
ARZA	American Reform Zionist Organization
CJC	Canadian Jewish Congress
CRIF	Conseil Representatif des Institutions Juives de France
CZA	Central Zionist Archives
CZF	Canadian Zionist Federation
ECAJ	Executive Council of Australian Jewry
FAZ	Federation of American Zionists
FGEI	Federazione Giovanile Ebraica d'Italie
FSJU	Fonds Social Juif Unifié
IUA	Israel United Appeal
JIA	Joint Israel Appeal
ORT	Organization for Rehabilitation through Training
OSE	Oeuvre de Secours aux Enfants Israélites
SAZF	South African Zionist Federation
SJA	Student Jewish Associations (South Africa)
UCII	Unione delle Comunità Israelitiche Italiane
UDAI	Unione Democratica Amici di Israele
UJA	United Jewish Appeal
VKK	Vsesoyuzny Koordinatsionny Komitet
WIZO	Women's International Zionist Organization
WZO	World Zionist Organization
ZFP	Zionist Federation in Persia
ZOA	Zionist Organization of America